Modern Data Processing

MODERN DATA PROCESSING

Third Edition

Robert R. Arnold
Dean of Instruction, Occupational Education
San Diego Mesa College

Harold C. Hill
Professor of Data Processing
San Diego City College

Aylmer V. Nichols
Director, Electronic Data Processing Services
County of San Diego

John Wiley & Sons
Santa Barbara   New York   Chichester   Brisbane   Toronto
A Wiley/Hamilton Publication

Library of Congress Cataloging in Publication Data:

Arnold, Robert R
    Modern data processing.

    "A Wiley/Hamilton publication."
    Includes index.
    1. Electronic data processing.   2. Computers.
I. Hill, Harold, C., joint author.   II. Nichols,
Aylmer V., joint author.   III. Title.
QA76.A68   1978   001.6   77-14941
ISBN 0-471-03361-8

Printed in the United States of America

10 9 8 7 6 5 4 3 2 1

The Authors

Robert R. Arnold has been Dean of Instruction, Occupational Education, at San Diego Mesa College since 1966. He previously served for eight years on the business faculty and as Coordinator of Data Processing at San Diego City College. His educational career also includes three years as Coordinator of Business Education for the San Diego Community Colleges which included the coordination of data processing programs and courses in three colleges. Before entering the educational field, Mr. Arnold served in office management and administrative positions in business and government agencies for over ten years.

Harold C. Hill has been on the faculty of San Diego City College since 1962, serving as professor of data processing and past chairman of the Data Processing Department. He was previously engaged for twenty-five years in administrative, managerial, and data processing positions in military, industrial, and financial organizations. While serving in the United States Navy Mr. Hill participated in the design, installation, and supervision of a number of major data processing facilities. This included major responsibility for the design and installation of a worldwide communications network and data processing system for personnel accounting and distribution. He has also designed and supervised data processing systems for several large industrial and financial organizations.

Aylmer V. Nichols has been employed in the data processing field for more than thirty years. He is Director of Electronic Data Processing Services for the County of San Diego, a position that he has occupied since 1965. Prior to that time he was engaged in the design of data processing systems and the supervision of data processing installations. He has also served as consultant to state and county government administrators in the justification and selection of electronic data processing equipment and the analysis of data processing systems. He is a pioneer in the field of data processing education, having designed and taught the first data processing course for San Diego City College in 1956. Mr. Nichols has been awarded the Certificate in Data Processing by the Data Processing Management Association.

Preface

Although the text of this edition of *Modern Data Processing* has been re-organized, revised, and augmented, the primary objectives remain unchanged. They are:

1. To provide a comprehensive view of the many data processing techniques and applications for those desiring a general knowledge of this important and dynamic field
2. To provide a good foundation for those planning advanced study in data processing.

The book is designed for use in basic data processing courses or for independent study. No background in data processing or other subjects is required for comprehension.

Although the book still covers the full range of data processing methods and devices, the emphasis given to different topics has changed significantly from previous editions. A single chapter on manual and mechanical data processing has been retained as a result of our continuing belief that the reader should be aware of all commonly used data processing methods. However, punched card data processing is no longer covered in the main text. Punched card machines have ceased to be a major means of processing data, although the punched card itself continues to be an important document in electronic data processing systems. In recognition of the fact that some punched card machines are still in use as auxiliary card-handling devices, a condensed description of the basic punched card machines appears in the Appendix.

The emphasis on computers has been increased by the addition of two new chapters covering minicomputers and microcomputers and the social and economic effects of computers.

Other revisions in the third edition of the text are:

1. Updating of all chapters to reflect the latest technological developments
2. A revised and expanded chapter on recording data for computer processing
3. Reorganization of electronic data processing chapters to facilitate understanding
4. Relocation of the data communications chapter immediately following the electronic data processing chapters
5. Relocation of the systems chapters so that they follow the discussion

of data processing methods, devices, and operations

6. The addition of a preview outline at the beginning of each chapter
7. The addition of important words and phrases at the end of each chapter
8. An expanded glossary.

The text is organized as follows: Chapter 1 presents an overview of data processing that serves as a general introduction and frame of reference to assist in comprehending and relating the topics in succeeding chapters. Chapter 2 outlines the history of data processing from ancient recording and computing techniques to modern mechanical and electronic devices. Chapter 3 presents a survey of data processing applications in various fields, with emphasis on business. This chapter also includes a brief description of basic business operations to aid in understanding the main sources of data and common data processing applications. Chapter 4 surveys manual and mechanical data processing methods and devices— some conventional and others newly developed.

Chapter 5 describes the most commonly used codes, media, and devices used to record data for computer processing. Chapters 6 to 10 are concerned with electronic data processing, including a survey of computer characteristics, physical elements and functions of a computer system, and numbering systems. Data communications is discussed in Chapter 11. Chapters 12 to 16 cover electronic data processing program development, programming systems, the BASIC programming system, problem-oriented programming languages, and electronic data processing operations.

Chapters 17 and 18 are devoted to systems study and design. Systems study aids are described in Chapter 17, and principles of systems study and design are covered in Chapter 18. The uses of computers in industrial automation are outlined in Chapter 19. Chapter 20 surveys the social and economic effects of computers.

End-of-chapter review questions and lists of important data processing words and phrases are furnished as a guide in reviewing important text material and as a basis for discussion. The glossary contains definitions of terms that appear in this book, or that the reader is likely to encounter in supplementary reading. A discussion of basic punched card machines appears in the Appendix. A workbook containing lists of terms, review questions, and exercises is available to reinforce the text.

We express appreciation to the many individuals and companies who provided information and illustrations for this book, or who otherwise assisted in its preparation. Specific credit is included with illustrations wherever appropriate.

Robert R. Arnold
Harold H. Hill
Aylmer V. Nichols

Contents

6   ELECTRONIC DATA PROCESSING: INTRODUCTION   115

7   EDP CENTRAL PROCESSING UNIT   130

13 PROGRAMMING SYSTEMS 250

14 BASIC PROGRAMMING SYSTEM 264

Modern Data Processing

FUNDAMENTALS OF DATA PROCESSING

Although the term "data processing" is of relatively recent origin, the activity itself is not new. On the contrary, there is evidence that the need to process data originated as far back as the beginning of recorded history, when people's activities first exceeded their ability to remember the details of their actions. Throughout history, commercial and governmental activities have created the need to process data of one kind or another.

In its broadest sense, data processing refers to the recording and handling of data that are necessary to convert it into a more refined or useful form. In the past these tasks were referred to as record keeping or paperwork. They were accepted as a routine clerical activity. Recently, with the advent of more sophisticated electromechanical and electronic business machines, the terms "paperwork" and "record keeping" have been replaced by the phrase "data processing." In addition, the volume of data has grown to such proportions that data processing has become a major activity attracting a great deal of interest. This interest is justifiable, but it should not lead to the conclusion that data processing is an end in itself. It is rather a means of achieving objectives that are almost as varied as the nature of data.

DEFINITION OF DATA

Because of the widespread application of new data processing techniques to banking operations, billing, and other financial situations, there is a tendency to assume that the term "data" refers primarily to accounting or other business functions. Actually, data can include any facts, figures, letters, words, charts, or symbols that represent an idea, object, condition, or situation. Thus, data can include such diverse things as completed election ballots, inventory figures, gas meter readings, school attendance records, medical statistics, engineering performance reports, and production figures. In fact, this list could continue for pages because examples of data can be found in every field of activity.

There are, of course, differences in the types of data handled in various fields. In science, for example, chemists, physicists, and mathematicians find it necessary to perform vast calculations on relatively limited amounts of data. This is also true of the many fields of engineering, where extremely complex design and performance calculations must be made.

In business and government operations the situation is usually quite different. Here the data is voluminous and repetitive, but processing requirements, although varied, are generally less complex. In this book attention will be focused mainly on this type of data processing, although the techniques to be discussed will be found to some extent in virtually every field.

DATA VERSUS INFORMATION

There is a significant difference between data and information that can be described by one word: *usefulness*. No compilation of data, regardless of how vast, can be called information unless it has been organized in a meaningful way and is useful to someone. In other words, data becomes information when it achieves relevance.

Thus, data is the raw material used to produce information. Information consists of *selected data*—data selected and organized with respect to user, problem, time, place, and function. The conversion of data to information is a primary function of data processing (Figure 1–1).

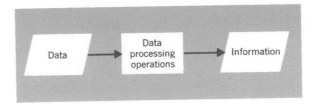

Figure 1-1.

THE NEED FOR DATA PROCESSING

Although the needs for gathering and processing data have many specific origins, in general they may be classified as *external* or *internal*. In business organizations external requirements may be regarded as mandatory since they are imposed by various government agencies, unions, or stockholders. The federal government, for example, requires quarterly reports on the income taxes and social security taxes withheld from the pay of employees, and state and local agencies require reports of sales taxes collected.

In addition to the financial and statistical data required by governmental agencies, business enterprises must furnish annual reports to stockholders, and various data to customers, creditors, and the general public. Some external data needs have their counterparts within the organization. Payroll records, for example, provide necessary internal data and also form the basis for financial and personnel reports to the government and to unions.

Internal needs fall broadly into two classes: *operations* and *control*. First, a tremendous amount and variety of routine operating documents are necessary as evidence of (1) primary transactions with customers and vendors; and (2) subsequent activities involving production, personnel, materials, equipment, and accounting. For example, the issuance of a purchase requisition indicating a departmental need for materials may start a chain of events requiring the completion of many additional forms and records. These might include a request for quotation, purchase order, receiving record, inspection report, inventory record, and voucher check in addition to necessary accounting entries.

The second internal need is for data to be compiled in informative reports for use in analyzing progress, determining policy, solving problems, and planning actions of the future. The much-discussed "information revolution" of recent years has created a whole new dimension in data processing. The objectives of data processing now extend far beyond the routine handling of transaction documents and records of other types. Providing management with timely information to facilitate greater control and improved decisions has become increasingly important.

The demands and opportunities of the new information technology are tremendous. There is a growing awareness that information is a vital resource of any organization and that improved data processing is a means of providing the needed information. Thus, as never before, central management is now in touch with its entire organization; as never before it is conscious of the effects of various influences on its goals; and as never before it is in a position to take prompt and appropriate action in time to produce desired results.

THE NEED FOR IMPROVED DATA PROCESSING TECHNIQUES

Throughout the centuries the changing nature and volume of data, combined with technological progress, resulted in a gradual evolution in data processing methods. In this century, especially in the last two decades, the evolution has been accelerated by the urgent need for better ways of handling data. Let us consider some of the factors that created the need for more efficient data processing techniques.

Volume of Data

Business organizations have grown in size and complexity during the past century, particularly since World War II. This growth has resulted in an enormous amount of paperwork generated, among other contributing factors, by a large volume of transactions. For example, one large insurance company with approximately three million accounts sends out over ten million premium notices each year and processes an equal number of payments. It is apparent that if this mass of data had to be processed manually, the results would be chaotic. The number of people who would have to participate in such a clerical operation would cause confusion, delay, and an excessive amount of errors.

The growth of business has, of course, been matched by an increase in government agencies that make ever-growing demands for reports of all kinds. The resulting mass of data received by government agencies requires processing of such magnitude that it simply cannot be handled by clerical personnel using traditional methods.

Clerical Costs

The rapid increase in the number of clerical workers is a clear indication of the mounting paperwork burden. In 1910, only one in twenty employed persons was engaged in clerical work. By 1940, the proportion of clerical workers had risen to one in ten. Today, about one in seven employed persons is in a clerical occupation. This influx of clerical employees has been accompanied by rising wage rates and fringe benefits, which have greatly increased clerical costs.

The awareness of rising personnel costs in business and government has stimulated interest in the use of mechanical and electronic devices as a more efficient and economical means of processing data. Although more and more mechanical and electronic equipment is being used to replace human effort, new clerical jobs created by the growth of business and government continue to outnumber the jobs eliminated by automation.

In large organizations, clerical jobs are usually specialized to facilitate the orderly division of work. As a result, clerical work is likely to consist of the routine and repetitive handling of large quantities of similar data. Human beings tend to become bored with repetitious work, and boredom leads to carelessness, which, in turn, increases the chance of error. In this respect, machines have a distinct advantage over humans. A human cannot be depended upon to react in exactly the same way time after time to a given set of conditions. Neither can two humans be depended on to react in the same way to the same set of conditions. Machines, on the other hand, are not subject to boredom, are consistent in their reactions, and are more accurate than humans. Thus, the search for improved techniques has been spurred by the realization that the more the human element can be eliminated from the processing of data, the more accurate the results will be.

The Need for More
Timely Information

The fast pace of modern business activity places new demands on management for accurate and rapid responses to changing conditions. The effective control of large organizations requires that executives make daily or even hourly decisions about many matters. An executive who is deprived of up-to-the-minute information by inefficient processing methods is therefore seriously handicapped.

Success in business today is based not only on a good product. A company's competitive survival may depend on the way it manages information—on its ability to maintain control over costs, and on the speed and flexibility with which it responds to new market conditions, actions of competitors, and technological advancements. The development of information systems capable of providing the complete and prompt information needed for today's management decision-making requires improved data processing techniques.

THE DATA PROCESSING CYCLE

Aside from the sheer volume of data, we might ask what there is about processing data that consumes so much time and effort and creates such a need for mechanical and electronic devices. Actually, from the time of origin to the time of arrival in a final, more useful form, data may go through a number of operational steps referred to as the *data processing cycle*. This cycle may be roughly divided into the following steps: origination of data, data recording, data manipulation, report or document preparation, data communication, and data storage. These steps are illustrated in Figure 1–2.

Origination of Data

The raw material for data processing originates on various business forms, often referred to as *source documents*. This original data might be handwritten, typewritten, or prepared in a variety of other ways. For

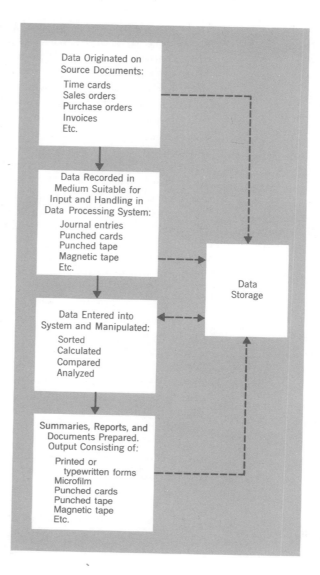

Figure 1-2. *Steps in the data processing cycle.*

example, payroll time data might be handwritten by the worker or a timekeeper, stamped in numerals by a time clock, or punched into a card. Other examples of source documents include sales orders, purchase orders, invoices, and material requisitions. These original documents are especially important for two reasons: (1) they provide verification of all transactions, and (2) they are the basis for all further actions.

Recording Data

The basic function of this step is recording data in some form that allows it to be handled conveniently in whatever system is being used. This might involve making a manual entry in a journal or register of some type,

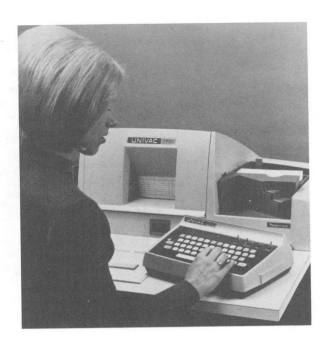

Figure 1-3. *Recording data from source documents on punched cards.*
(Courtesy Sperry UNIVAC, A Division of Sperry Rand Corporation.)

punching holes in a card, punching holes in paper tape, recording magnetized spots on magnetic tape, writing or printing data in magnetic ink, or using some other medium acceptable to the system as a means of entering and later transferring the data from one step to another (Figure 1–3).

In some cases recording may be combined with the preparation of original documents through a technique called *source data automation.* For example, by using a typewriter equipped with a magnetic tape recording device, it is possible to prepare simultaneously a typewritten document, such as a sales invoice, and a magnetic tape containing the same or selected data. Thus, the original data is automatically recorded in machine language for entry into a computer system.

Data may also be recorded and transmitted directly into a data processing system without the need for document preparation. For example, the time reporting discussed in the preceding section could be accomplished by inserting the worker's coded badge or identification card into a data collection device capable of reading and transmitting directly to a remote computer the data about the employee and his time of arrival or departure (Figure 1–4). In some computer systems data is entered directly into the computer through a typewriter-like console keyboard.

The following steps can also be important parts of the data recording function.

Editing. This is the process of selecting significant data and eliminating data that does not need to be recorded for further processing.

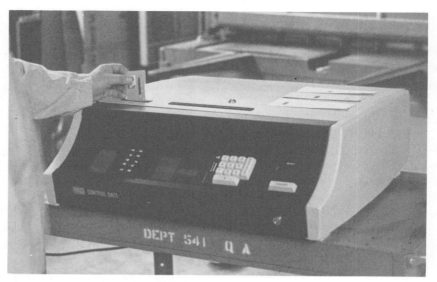

Figure 1-4. *Source data terminal used to collect computer data from industrial production departments.* (Courtesy Control Data Corporation.)

Coding. As a means of further reducing the amount of data to be recorded and processed, abbreviated codes are often used to condense the data. The technique of converting data to symbolic form has been used in many fields as a means of saving time, effort, and space, and as a convenient device for identifying and distinguishing data. The most familiar types of codes used to express words or ideas are the *alphabetic,* which consists of letters; the *numeric,* in which numbers are used; and the *alphanumeric,* which uses both numbers and alphabetic characters. The designation of units in a large organization as departments A, B, C, etc., is an example of the use of alphabetic code. Examples of the use of numerical codes include credit cards, bank accounts, and social security numbers.

Classifying. Classifying is the process of identifying one or more common characteristics to be used as a means of systematically grouping data into classes. Categories might include type of product, location, department, price range, etc. Classifying may occur as a separate step. However, since the need is usually anticipated at the time data is recorded, classifications are generally determined and entered as part of the recording process.

As defined here, classification is an initial step that precedes the actual sorting of data. For example, classifications such as department number, age group, sex, etc., may be entered on personnel records even though the records are to be filed alphabetically. The presence of such classification data makes it easy to rearrange records at any time for statistical or other purposes.

Codes are used extensively as a means of identifying different classes of data. Numbers or letters of the alphabet, or a combination of both, can be assigned to previously planned classifications to provide quick recognition and ease in writing. For example, the names of the states are frequently designated by code numbers such as 01 = Alabama, 02 = Alaska, etc.

Conversion.   Conversion is a means of transforming data from one recorded form to another. For example, data recorded in punched cards may be converted to magnetic tape, or vice versa, by the use of special equipment designed for this purpose. Such conversion changes the recorded form of data but not the nature of the data. Conversion, as well as re-recording in the same form, may occur at various times during the processing cycle.

Copying and Duplicating.   These are processes by which facsimiles of data can be prepared for distribution to more than one user or for use in different steps in the processing cycle.

Verifying.   This essential function assures that all parts of the recording process have been accomplished without error, and that accurate data is entered into the processing system.

Manipulation of Data

If the original form of data were suitable for all purposes, less processing would be necessary. Seldom, however, can the real objective of a transaction or situation be attained without converting data into a more useful form. This conversion is accomplished by means of one or more of the following procedures.

Sorting.   Sorting is the process of arranging or selecting data according to (1) order or rank or (2) common characteristic. Sorting according to order or rank, known as sorting in *sequence,* takes place when data is arranged in numeric or alphabetic sequence. Sales invoice data, for example, might be arranged according to sequence of invoice numbers or customers' names. Sorting according to common characteristic, known as sorting by *classification,* takes place when data is arranged in similar groups. For example, customers could be classified by geographic area, by salesman, or by type of business. Like other steps in the processing cycle, sorting is simplified by expressing data in codes.

Comparing and Analyzing.   By these processes we determine such factors as the nature, proportion, relationship, order, similarity, or relative value of data.

Calculating.   Calculating refers to the arithmetical processes of multiplication, division, addition, or subtraction, which are necessary to convert data into a more significant form. For example, an employee's weekly hours of work and his hourly rate of pay become much more significant when they are multiplied together to determine his weekly earnings.

Summarizing and	**Summarizing.** Summarizing is the process of condensing data so that
Report Preparation	the main points are emphasized. Summarizing generally involves listing

or tabulating data and totaling each list. The running of a list on an adding machine is one form of summarization.

Summarizing is related to sorting since the arrangement of data into
categories is usually part of the summary process. The sorting operation in itself may be meaningless, however, unless the results of the separation are known. Summarizing carries the process one step further
by providing totals to indicate the individual or comparative values of
various classes of data. As an illustration, the daily sales of a store may
be listed by departments. This operation achieves a distribution of sales
data. However, the relative performance of each department cannot be
ascertained at the end of a weekly or monthly period until the data is
summarized by totaling each list. Thus, the detailed lists are condensed
into totals that provide management with useful information.

Report Preparation.   The processed information that results from the
data processing cycle is known as *output*. This could include documents
such as payroll checks or statements of account; or finished reports such
as a sales analysis, expense distribution, inventory, or weekly payroll.
The means by which the processed information is finally recorded is
known as the *output medium*. Depending on the type of processing system
being used, output media could consist of typewritten documents or
reports, printed forms, punched cards, punched paper tape, magnetic
tape, or other special forms.

Data Communications   Communication is the process of transferring data from one point to
another during the processing cycle or of delivering the final results to
the user. Many methods may be used, ranging from the very simple to
the highly complex. Data in written, punched card, or other form may
be transported internally by hand or by a conveyor mechanism of some
type. Externally, data is often transported by mail.

Almost any process of transmitting information may be considered
a form of data communications. However, in this period of advanced
technology the term "data communications" generally refers to the electrical transmission of data that has been transformed into a special code.
It is now possible to transmit data between a wide variety of devices,
internally or externally, by direct connection or by means of telephone
circuits, telegraph circuits, or microwave. Teletypewriter service is probably the most familiar example of wire communication. This method
enables data in typewritten, punched tape, or magnetic tape form to
be transmitted between units in the same building or city, or thousands
of miles apart (Figure 1–5).

Data Storage   Upon completion of the processing cycle, or possibly at a point of intermediate results during the cycle, data must be stored so that it is readily

Figure 1-5. *Teleprinter communication terminal designed for transmitting and receiving data over the telephone exchange network.* *(Courtesy Western Union Data Services Company.)*

retrievable. The storage of data is a matter of monumental proportions in some organizations. This is especially true of certain governmental agencies and business firms that have a large number of documented transactions. It is of utmost importance in such organizations to design a storage system that will facilitate the retrieval of data needed for current operations and safeguard data that may be needed for reference in the future. Storage techniques depend, of course, on the type and volume of data involved.

In conclusion, let us emphasize that the steps of the data processing cycle outlined above are the basic elements into which all data processing problems subdivide. All or some of these functions have to be performed whether they are done manually, by mechanical means, or by electronic computer. In spite of the vast differences in these methods, however, the objective of data processing remains basically the same—the conversion of data to useful information.

METHODS OF PROCESSING DATA

Detailed discussions of the methods of processing data will appear in later chapters. However, to provide the reader with a frame of reference for use in relating these methods, the following summary is offered.

| *Manual and Mechanical* | Manual data processing techniques are used to a certain extent in every organization, and they are still the predominant method of processing data in countless small organizations. It is possible to complete by hand all the operations in the data processing cycle, from the preparation of original documents to final reports, by using the tools and materials that have been standard for hundreds of years: pens, pencils, journals, ledgers, worksheets, folders, trays, files, and various other manual devices. However, few organizations today can tolerate time-consuming methods. Consequently, organizations that still find a manual system to be the most practical employ at least some of the modern devices that have been developed to improve efficiency. |

Such devices as accounting boards, or pegboards, document control registers, and edge-notched card systems provide a means of eliminating the tedious recopying and resorting of data. These and other devices, which will be discussed in detail in Chapter 4, have done much to improve the speed and accuracy of manual data processing.

A wide variety of mechanical and electronic equipment is in use today not only in small offices but also as part of the most complex data processing systems. Included are typewriters, still the most commonly used office machine, calculating machines, and cash registers.

Although these devices generally require manual aid, recent advancements have made them much more automatic. In addition, their versatility has been increased by the attachment of mechanisms that enable them to simultaneously produce magnetic tape, punched paper tape, or punched cards while performing a primary function. These by-products then serve as input to computers. For example, sales transactions recorded on a cash register may be simultaneously recorded on magnetic tape or punched paper tape by means of a special attachment. The tape may then be used as a means of entering and processing the sales transactions in an electronic computer. It is also possible for data to be transmitted directly into a computer system while being recorded on an adapted mechanical or electronic device.

Punched Card Machines

Although the origin of punched card data processing dates back to 1887, the use of punched card equipment developed very slowly until the 1940s. After that time the phenomenal growth of this method assured that punched card machines would become a very important part of data processing history.

Punched card equipment eliminates much of the human effort required in the processing of data by performing six data processing operations automatically: recording, sorting, comparing, calculating, summarizing, and reporting. Punched card machines do have certain limitations, however. Since they are predominantly mechanical, the speed of processing is limited by the movement of mechanical parts and devices. Moreover, since each machine in the system performs a special function, the processing steps are not continuous. Cards must be transferred manually from one machine to another for the performance of various operations.

As a result of these limitations and the development of faster, more compact, and less costly computers, punched card machines are rapidly becoming extinct as a means of processing data. The only punched card machines widely employed today are the *card punch,* which is used to record source data in punched cards; the *verifier,* which checks the accuracy of the card punch operation; and the *sorter,* which arranges punched cards in alphabetical or numerical sequence or by classification. It is now more economical to use computer systems to complete the processing functions previously performed by the other punched card machines: the *collator, reproducer, calculator,* and *accounting machine* (see Appendix for descriptions).

Electronic Data Processing

The most significant development in data processing is the electronic computer, which has a vastly superior capacity to perform computations and other functions at incredible speeds (Figure 1–6). This results from the fact that processing in a computer is accomplished by the movement of electrical impulses through the computer's circuitry rather than by the movement of mechanical parts. Through instructions programmed into the computer by means of magnetic tapes, punched paper tapes, or punched cards, thousands of complex operations can be completed in a second.

Figure 1-6. *Electronic data processing system.*
(Courtesy International Business Machines Corporation.)

Computers are generally able to perform all the manipulative steps in the data processing cycle automatically. However, in spite of the impressive speed with which computers operate, processing is not dramatic because there is no visible evidence of what is taking place: the manipulation of data occurs entirely within the computer. Computer operations are usually classified under three headings: input, processing, and output.

Input.   Before data from source documents can be entered into the system, the data must be converted to code symbols recorded in one of several ways: as punched holes in cards; as punched holes in paper tape; as minute magnetized spots on magnetic tape; or as actual characters, readable by humans as well as machines, printed by hand or by machine. Some source documents may be entered directly into the system. Included are prepunched bills, or checks on which information has been preprinted in magnetic ink. Data also may be read directly into a computer by means of optical character recognition equipment, which can interpret printed copy and handwritten numbers.

Processing.   After the data has been recorded in one of the forms mentioned, it is read by an input component of the computer system and transferred electronically to a storage unit within the computer. The *storage unit,* or *memory,* is the mechanism that retains information for recall or use in further processing.

All processing steps are performed automatically within the components of the system in accordance with a series of instructions called a *program,* which is stored in the computer. The computer is also able to make logical decisions according to the instructions it has been given. The completely automatic execution of these functions at fantastic speeds makes the electronic computer unique and gives it the greatest advantage over other systems.

Output.   The results of the processing that has taken place within the computer may be recorded on magnetic tape, magnetic disk, or punched cards; or may be recorded by direct connection between the processing unit and a printing device.

Electronic data processing has a number of advantages over other methods. The principal ones are as follows:

1. The speed of processing is many times faster than that attainable in other forms of data processing.
2. Once data is entered into the system, the processing is continuous.
3. More compact equipment and storage results in a saving of space.
4. Accuracy is generally greater than in other systems.
5. The superior speed, capacity, and versatility of the electronic computer make possible the completion of tasks that could never be at-

tempted with other systems because of the impossibility of completing them in time for the results to be useful.

CONCLUSION

Inevitably, the electronic computer dominates any discussion of data processing methods today. This is understandable because computers are the most versatile and spectacular performers in the field of data processing. They have not, however, eliminated all other methods, nor is it likely that they will do so in the foreseeable future. On the contrary, the use of other general office machines and data processing equipment is rising annually. However, this equipment is increasingly oriented to the requirements of new electronic data processing systems.

In all probability, because of differences in volume and nature of data, many organizations will continue to find it more efficient to use manual and mechanical methods to process data. It should also be pointed out that when electronic computers are used, they do not operate in isolation. Their performance is usually supplemented by other operations involving a variety of manual and mechanical methods. It is not uncommon to find manual, mechanical, and computer methods used side-by-side in organizations because each one is the most suitable for a certain type of operation.

For these reasons, in the succeeding chapters of this book, computers will be treated not only as the most significant method of processing data, but also as one of a number of methods currently in use. Attention will also be given to the other techniques that form the basis of manual and mechanical data processing systems and that perform auxiliary functions in electronic data processing systems.

We hope that this approach to data processing will develop an appreciation of the full range of data processing methods and devices now available, and of the importance of selecting the method that is most appropriate for the task to be accomplished.

IMPORTANT WORDS AND PHRASES

data	source document	output medium
information	source data automation	data communications
data processing cycle	output	

REVIEW QUESTIONS

1. Define data.
2. What is the basic difference in the processing requirements of business data and scientific or engineering data?
3. Distinguish between data and information.
4. Discuss the nature of external and internal needs for processing data.

5. What main factors have created the need for more efficient data processing techniques?
6. What are the steps in the data processing cycle?
7. What is the basic purpose of the data recording step?
8. Define coding, classifying, and converting.
9. Explain the ways in which data may be manipulated in order to change its form or arrangement.
10. What methods of processing data are commonly used today? Describe each.
11. What are the principal advantages of electronic data processing over other methods?

2

HISTORY OF
DATA PROCESSING

The history of data processing reflects the search for more efficient ways of gathering, recording, and handling data in order to keep pace with the increasing volume and complexity of governmental and commercial activity.

The techniques that appeared in response to changing needs throughout the centuries were often a clearer indication of the facilities then available than of the true need. Thus, the history of data processing also reflects the technological progress of civilization.

Technological advancements have been readily adapted for data processing purposes. The discovery of better ways of processing data has not always resulted in the abandonment of older methods, however. Instead, many of the older techniques have been adopted as part of later developments. In many cases the older methods continued to be used in their original or somewhat modified form. For this reason, the events to be related in this chapter will not be presented in a single chronological sequence. Instead, special techniques will be grouped so that the various steps in their evolution may be more easily related. The history of data processing will be considered under four headings: recording techniques, computing devices, punched card machines, and electronic computers.

HISTORY OF RECORDING TECHNIQUES

Today's data processing requirements and the incredibly technical devices that are used to fulfill them present a dramatic contrast to the earliest record-keeping activities. The greatest contrast, of course, is found in prerecorded history. In the day-by-day struggle for existence in the

Stone Age, the exchange of goods by force rather than by trade created no need for a record of transactions. However, as families joined to form tribal groups, and as the tribes grew into nations, trade became the means of exchange. Because business transactions date back further than recorded history, it is conceivable that situations arose in which there was a need for record keeping. As an aid to memory, the early businessperson probably used scratches on rocks, notches on trees, or marks on the mud wall of the house.

As trading activity grew, transactions increased in complexity, and a solution was found to the need for some kind of written record. The oldest surviving written records are in the form of pictographic writing on clay tablets made by the ancient Sumerians, the predecessors of the Babylonians, during the period 3700 to 3000 B.C. Other archeological findings dating from 3000 to 2600 B.C. include clay tablets with cuneiform characters in the Sumerian language. These tablets were prepared by marking wet clay with the cut end of a reed. Since this method produced wedge-shaped marks, such writing was called cuneiform, from the Latin *cuneus,* meaning "wedge." To make the records permanent, tablets were placed in the sun or baked in an oven.

Clay tablets were also used by later Near Eastern and Mediterranean cultures, including the Assyrian and the Babylonian (Figure 2–1). The first records of actual business transactions date from around 2600 B.C. in Babylon, which was a well-developed civilization and commercial center even before that time. The merchants of Babylon had scribes prepare records of receipts, disbursements, contracts of barter, sales, money-lending, and many other business transactions by scratching the necessary information on slabs of wet clay with a stylus. These scribes played an important role in the commercial and governmental affairs of the Babylonian Empire.

It is interesting to note that the later Babylonians seemed to anticipate

Figure 2-1. *Babylonian clay tablets.*
(Courtesy Yale University.)

our modern ledgers and filing cabinets by storing their tablets in jars and arranging them in approximately the same way that we now arrange card systems and loose-leaf books.

The clay tablets used by the Babylonians were cumbersome and difficult to handle. (One is tempted to speculate on the amount of excessive record keeping that might have been discouraged in more recent times by the continued use of this technique.) Therefore, the need for a more practical recording medium became apparent.

This need was met in Egypt by the use of papyrus and the calmus. The papyrus was a tall water plant formerly abundant on the delta and banks of the Nile. Its stems were used to make the writing material, also called papyrus, which was the predecessor of paper. This was accomplished by soaking, pressing together, and drying thin sheets of the bark laid crosswise to form a fairly substantial writing surface. The calmus was a sharp-pointed pen also made from the reed plant. The exact origin of these writing materials is not known, but it is placed in the third millennium B.C., possibly even before the clay tablets of the Babylonians.

Government bookkeeping grew to enormous proportions under the Pharaohs, who could be regarded as the leaders of a large business concern. In effect, the entire state was one establishment with thousands of employees. The Egyptian scribes kept exacting records of practically everything, including slaves; harvesting operations; accounts and lists of wages for day-workers; and receipts and payments of jewels, gold, grain, or livestock from warehouses that constituted the Egyptian treasury. The multitude of documents necessary to record the many transactions was maintained by a large staff of scribes and assistants who reported to the prime minister, who, in turn, reported regularly to the king on the status of the treasury.

It is not definitely known whether the Babylonians learned bookkeeping from the Egyptians or vice versa, or if their bookkeeping systems developed independently. In any event, the same kinds of primary entries, the same classification of accounts, and the same control methods are found on Egyptian papyrus rolls and on Babylonian clay tablets.

Papyrus, which originated with the Egyptians, was used later by the Greeks and Romans. In fact, it was the most widely used ancient writing material until it was gradually replaced during the third and fourth centuries A.D. by parchment made from the skins of animals. Single sheets of papyrus were usually about 2 feet long. For more lengthy documents, however, a number of sheets were stuck together to form rolls of 10 to 50 feet. It is interesting to note that after almost two thousand years the roll has reappeared in such forms as adding machine tapes and magnetic or paper tapes used as input or output media for computers.

Another recording device of ancient times was the tablet book consisting of two to ten sheets of wood coated with wax and tied together with thongs. Records were scratched on the waxed surfaces with a pointed bone or metal stylus. By obliterating the writing, the tablets could be used again and again. This device was used extensively by the Greeks and Romans for record keeping. In Cicero's time, around the second quarter of the last century B.C., it appears that most of the public and private accounts at Rome were written on waxed tablets. This is presumed to have been true of most of the Graeco-Roman world at that time.

These tablet books, or codices, had several disadvantages, however. They were clumsy; there were limitations on the size of leaves and the number of leaves that could be conveniently bound together; and the records were not permanent since the wax was soft and could be rubbed off. These disadvantages were overcome by some Romans by using a codex made up of leaves of parchment instead of wood. At first scribes used these for everyday purposes, making entries with split-reed pens. In the later part of the first century A.D. they were used occasionally for literature in place of the papyrus roll.

In spite of the fact that the parchment codex seemed to be a forward step, it did not develop greatly in the first two centuries A.D., and the use of wooden tablets remained much more common. This technique was still in use in England at the end of the fourteenth century A.D.

Orderly bookkeeping procedures were a characteristic of both the Greeks and Romans, although their techniques were far from reaching the double-entry stage of accounting. Their accounting consisted mainly of individual records of debts, receipts, expenditures, and miscellaneous inventories, rather than accounts in the modern sense with debit and credit entries. Nevertheless, they were aware of the importance of efficient record keeping. The Athenians were first to employ the technique of auditing records to get accurate unbiased facts, discover shortages, and prevent losses. They took inventories regularly and enacted laws requiring the publication of financial statements. The Romans designated officials known as *quaestors* to examine the accounts of provincial governors. Julius Caesar insisted on proper accounting of receipts and disbursements, and thus maintained the treasury of the Roman Empire at its highest level. The emperor Augustus is said to have established the first government budget in the year A.D. 5 in order to control spending in the Empire.

During the Dark Ages there were few record-keeping developments of any significance. The next interesting event in the story of business records was the development of wooden tallies in England. Although the notching or scoring of sticks as a means of recording numbers may be traced back to neolithic and even paleolithic times, this technique was probably used most widely in England after the invasion of William the Conqueror in 1066. During his reign a survey was made showing all the crown property and the tributes, or taxes, due on the property. The details of the survey were included in a record called the Doomsday Book, which was used to determine the revenue to be collected from each tax-payer.

The sheriff of each county had the responsibility of collecting for the king all the rents, taxes, fines and penalties, and other revenues. It was customary for the sheriff to travel to Westminster each year at Easter to pay into the Exchequer approximately one-half of the total amount for which his region was liable. For this he received a receipt in the form of a tally, a narrow shaft of wood, usually hazel wood, on which notches were cut to represent the total value. A notch as thick as a man's palm represented £1,000; the thickness of a thumb, £100; and of a little finger, £20. The thickness of a grain of barley corn was worth £1, and scratches took care of the shillings and pence.

After being cut and inscribed, the tally was split in two. One part was retained by the sheriff for a receipt, and the other was kept by the department of the Exchequer. Later in the year, at Michaelmas, when the time came for final settlement, the sheriff submitted his halves of the tallies as evidence of payments already made. If they matched the halves held by the Exchequer, he was given credit for them. However, if the sheriff's portion of any tally had been altered, he was subject to imprisonment.

In spite of the crudeness of tallies, they were used extensively, mainly because this carefully scored wooden object was a comprehensible record to the people of that era, most of whom were illiterate. Although tallies were used mainly for the settlement of government revenues, this system of recording transactions was later extended for commercial use. It continued in use even after better writing methods were available and the people were more literate. In fact, it was not until 1826 that the use of tallies was abolished by an act of parliament. In 1834 they were condemned to be destroyed by a statute of William IV and, consequently, were thrown into the heating stoves of the House of Commons. Apparently the stokers lacked restraint because the resulting blaze not only destroyed the tallies but also the parliament buildings, which were set on fire by the overheated stoves and burned to the ground.

Developments in commercial accounting that led to our modern methods were an outgrowth of Italian commerce during the thirteenth century. The initial departure from simple bookkeeping methods is credited to a Florentine banker who devised the first complete bookkeeping system in 1211. The earliest known system of complete double-entry bookkeeping is one that originated in Genoa in 1340. The first printed text on double-entry bookkeeping was written by Luca Pacioli, a monk of the order of St. Francis, at Venice in 1494. Pacioli's *Summa de Arithmetica, Geometria, Proporcioni et Proportionalita* includes a detailed description of the double-entry system then practiced, which extended the knowledge of double entry well beyond the boundaries of Italy. The name "Venetian method" or "Italian method" was given to the method he outlined, which formed the basis of double entry as we know it today.

During the four hundred years following Pacioli's treatise, there was a further refinement and development of bookkeeping systems. However, relatively little change occurred in the techniques of recording business transactions except for an improvement in writing materials. Of particular significance was the increased use of paper. Although paper can be traced back to the second century B.C. in China, it did not become available to the rest of the world until the eighth century A.D., when it was discovered by the Arabs. The manufacture of paper in Europe was originated by the Moors in Spain about the middle of the twelfth century. The first large-scale manufacture of paper in Italy occurred in 1276. Mills were subsequently set up in France, Germany, and England, and by the second half of the fourteenth century the use of paper had become well established in all of Western Europe.

The introduction of paper brought the quill pen into use. Metal pens were known to the Romans and were produced in small quantities in Europe in the eighteenth century. However, they did not come into common use until 1828, when large-scale production of pens with efficient slip-in points began in Birmingham, England. The first significant production of fountain pens occurred in the 1880s.

Another noteworthy development was the widespread use of graphite lead pencils. Earlier, the Egyptians used metallic lead to rule lines, as did medieval monks, but it was not until the sixteenth century that graphite became a standard writing material. In the beginning stages metal clips were used to hold the graphite rods, or the rods were held with twine that was unwound as the graphite wore down. About 1686 the lead pencil took on its present form when a method was found for casing the graphite in wood. Starting in the late eighteenth century, pulverized graphite was mixed with clay to bind it and to provide varying degrees of hardness—the more clay, the harder the pencil.

As the twentieth century approached, there was a most significant occurrence in the history of recording techniques: the development of the typewriter. Although many attempts were made to invent typewriters, starting as early as 1714, the first practical machine was patented in 1868 by Christopher Latham Sholes, Carlos Glidden, and Samuel W. Soulé of Milwaukee, Wisconsin. It was crude and lacked the keyboard arrangement that was adopted later. However, after many improvements, on March 1, 1873, E. Remington and Sons, the famous Mohawk Valley, New York, manufacturers, contracted to make the machine. The first commercial typewriter, the Remington No. 1 (Figure 2–2), was made in September 1873. The early Remington had many of the features of a modern typewriter except for the shift key, which was not invented and added until 1878.

This typewriter marked the beginning of a series of advancements that were to be of tremendous significance in the field of data processing. Many of the most important devices used today in data processing and related fields were made possible by the development of the electric typewriter by James Smathers in 1920. This led to the design of many special purpose machines, including composing machines to set up copy for offset printing; bookkeeping machines that combine a typewriter with a computing mechanism to facilitate the preparation of accounting records; Graphotype machines used to make impressions on printing plates for addressing machines; teletypewriters that activate distant units by means of telegraph or telephone lines; automatic typewriters that produce magnetic cards or tape that, in turn, can be used to activate the originating machine or others like it; and input or output devices for electronic computers. This list could be much more extensive, but these examples provide ample evidence of the value of the typewriter in addition to its basic usefulness for routine office work.

With the dawn of the twentieth century came the invention and perfection of many other business machines that were to relieve the manual drudgery that had been inherent in the handling of data for centuries. Most of these machines are classified as adding, calculating, or bookkeeping machines, which will be discussed in the following section.

EVOLUTION OF COMPUTING DEVICES

Throughout history people have experienced an ever-increasing need for numerical calculations and have continually sought ways to meet this need with a minimum of mental and manual effort.

Primitive people, like their successors, were blessed with an inherent means of counting in the form of fingers and toes. There were, of course,

Figure 2-2. *Remington No. 1 typewriter with footpedal carriage return, 1893.*

(*Courtesy Sperry Remington, A Division of Sperry Rand Corporation.*)

limitations on how far one person could go with these facilities. Eventually these limitations were overcome by the discovery that pebbles, grains of corn, and other small objects could be used for counting.

The problem of how to handle pebbles conveniently was solved in the Tigres-Euphrates Valley about five thousand years ago by the design of a clay board with a number of grooves into which the pebbles were placed. This device enabled the pebbles to be moved from one side of the board to the other to facilitate counting operations. This technique, which was the predecessor of the abacus, became known in Asia, where it was adopted and modified by the Chinese and Japanese. The *abacus* in its present form is believed to have been invented in China about 2600 B.C. The Japanese had a similar device called the *soroban.* The abacus apparently did not reach Europe until the beginning of the Christian era, because the *abax,* as it was called by the Romans, was first described by Greek authors about A.D. 300. It is of exactly the same design as the Chinese and Japanese devices.

The abacus consists of several rows of beads that slide on sticks or wires mounted in a rectangular frame. The frame is divided by a cross member so that each row of beads has a sector with one, or on some abacuses, two beads, and another sector with four or sometimes five beads. Figure 2–3 shows a typical abacus. Although simple in appearance, the abacus, in skilled hands, is an amazingly versatile and efficient computing device. It is still used extensively in some parts of the world.

After this first milestone, around four thousand years elapsed before the next significant developments in computational aids. One obstacle to the invention of mechanical computing devices was the use of Roman numerals throughout Europe. Roman numerals may add dignity to monuments, but the multiplication of MCMXIX by XVIII presents quite

Figure 2-3. *Abacus.*

(Courtesy International Business Machines Corporation.)

a challenge. The gradual acceptance of the Arabic numeral system, starting around A.D. 1200, provided a simpler means of calculating.

However, in spite of the improved numeral system, no mechanical aid to calculation of any merit appeared until the seventeenth century, the great century of mathematical progress. Then, in 1617, a Scot by the name of John Napier developed logarithms, a tabular system of numbers by which many arithmetical calculations are simplified. By using tables of logarithms the operations of multiplication and division may be more easily performed through addition and subtraction, respectively.

This development stimulated the invention of various devices that substituted the addition of logarithms for multiplication. Included was a device invented by John Napier in 1617 that later became known as "Napier's bones." It was a mechanical arrangement of strips of bone on which numbers were printed. When brought into combination, these strips could perform direct multiplication.

Another outgrowth of logarithms was the slide rule, conceived by William Oughtred in 1621. The slide rule, which was perhaps the first analog computer, performs multiplication and division by adding and subtracting. "Log tables," and their embodiment in slide rules, were immensely helpful in certain fields. The engineer, for example, needs to multiply more often than to add, and is often content with the degree of accuracy obtained from the highly portable slide rule, which is approximate rather than absolute. The businessperson, however, needs to add, and even a fractional error can be costly if applied to a large sum of money or if repeated in a large volume of transactions. To add figures exactly, measuring an analogy of the quantities as the slide rule does is of no use; it is necessary to count actual digits as the abacus does. Thus, the slide rule proved to be most useful in activities that required fast relational computations.

Success in the development of a digital counter was first achieved by Blaise Pascal. In 1642, at the age of 19, he invented a device to assist in adding long columns of figures at his father's tax office in Rouen, France. His gear-driven machine, the size of a shoe box, consisted of a row of wheels with teeth numbered from 0 to 9 (Figure 2–4). The first wheel represented units; the second, tens; and so on. On turning the first wheel five spaces, 5 would show in a window at the top of the machine. Turning it two more spaces produced a total of 7. The addition of seven more caused the indicator to proceed through 0 to 4. Meanwhile a lever on the units dial had moved the tens dial one-tenth of a revolution so that the machine had "carried one," showing a total of 14.

It was a simple device, more like a mileage gauge or revolution counter than a modern computer. However, it pointed out three principles that were utilized in later developments: that "carry over" should be automatic, that subtraction could be accomplished by turning dials in reverse, and that multiplication could be performed by repeated addition.

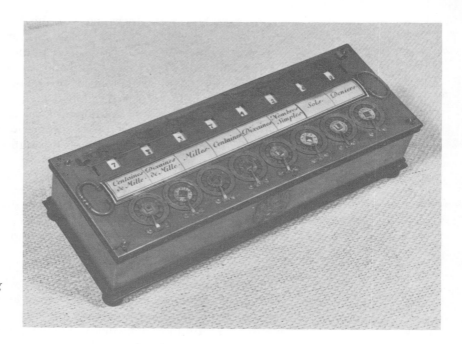

Figure 2-4. *Pascal's adding machine, invented in 1642.*
(Courtesy International Business Machines Corporation.)

The German philosopher and mathematician Gottfried Leibniz conceived a calculating machine in 1671 that employed the principle of multiplication by repeated addition. The most important component of this device, completed in 1674, was the stepped wheel, a cylindrical drum with nine teeth of increasing length along its surface. When the drum was rotated, a gear sliding on an axis parallel to that of the drum engaged some of the teeth, thus being rotated an equivalent number of steps. This feature of the Leibniz machine is still found in some present-day calculators.

Numerous attempts were made throughout the next century to produce a satisfactory machine. Unfortunately, although the ideas were good the results were not. The first commercially successful calculating machine was that of the Alsatian inventor, Charles Xavier Thomas, who in 1820 further improved on the Leibniz cylinder idea by adding a crank. This machine is often considered the predecessor of all present-day desk calculators because it was widely copied in Europe and was brought to the United States, where it led to further developments.

In 1887 Dorr Eugene Felt patented a key-driven adding machine known then as the "Macaroni Box," and now as the Comptometer. The machine has, of course, undergone considerable refinement since Felt's day. About the same time, William S. Burroughs, a bank clerk who was suffering from poor health, decided to invent a machine that would alleviate the drudgery of bookkeeping. In 1884 he succeeded in develop-

Figure 2-5. *The first practical adding-printing machine, designed by William S. Burroughs in 1884.*
(Courtesy Burroughs Corporation.)

Figure 2-6. *An early rotary calculator, about 1914.*
(Courtesy Monroe, A division of Litton Business Systems, Inc.)

ing a key-set adding-printing machine with a crank (Figure 2–5). The machine was patented by 1888 and was successfully marketed in 1891. This was a significant advance, for the machine had the ability to record and summarize as well as calculate.

The Monroe calculator, incorporating previous designs by Frank S. Baldwin, was introduced in 1911 by Jay R. Monroe and Baldwin (Figure 2–6). It was the first keyboard rotary machine to attain commercial success. This was the culmination of forty years of work for Baldwin, who invented his first calculator in 1872.

The first accounting machine, a teller machine for certifying pass-books, was developed for the National Cash Register Company in 1909 by Charles F. Kettering. However, the large-scale development of the accounting machine did not occur until after the close of World War I. By means of a tabulating carriage, this machine made it possible to sort data into a number of columns in addition to performing the functions of recording, calculating, and summarizing.

Another device that is now used for computing as well as for recording and controlling purposes is the cash register. The cash register was invented in 1879 by James Ritty of Dayton, Ohio (Figure 2–7). It was made commercially successful by John H. Patterson, who founded the National Cash Register Company in 1884. Since the advent of these machines, they have provided invaluable service in stores throughout the world.

Electromechanical machines came into general use about 1920. Electric activation provided greater speed and facility in the use of adding, calculating, and bookkeeping machines. However, all these machines, while quite efficient, were limited in two ways. First, they were manual rather than automatic, since they required some form of action by an operator, such as depressing a key, bar, or lever, to perform each processing step. Second, the machines functioned independently of other units of equipment, although each machine was capable of performing one or more of four processing steps: recording, summarizing, calculating, and, to a limited extent, sorting.

The limitation of machine independence was overcome by the use of

Figure 2-7. *Original cash register, invented in 1879.* *(Courtesy NCR Corporation.)*

punched tape, which made it possible for accounting machines, typewriters, adding machines, calculators, and other mechanical equipment to be used in combination with each other and with punched card or electronic computer equipment. Today magnetic tape generally provides the common medium that permits communication between the various types of equipment.

Both of the limitations mentioned above were overcome by the punched card system, which first introduced compatibility of machines. In addition, these machines provided a means of performing a greater number of operations automatically. For the first time, a series of machines was able to perform a variety of functions through the use of a single medium—the punched card.

HISTORY OF PUNCHED CARD MACHINES

Although the punched card medium was new to the field of data processing, it had been used earlier for other purposes. As far back as 1725, perforated paper was employed in the operation of a loom designed by Basile Bouchon. In 1728, M. Falcon, a French engineer, invented a loom that operated through the medium of perforated cards. This technique was later adopted for use in the first successful machine to operate from punched cards—a textile loom conceived in 1801 by another Frenchman named Joseph Marie Jacquard. In his automatic loom, which revolutionized the weaving industry, weaving was directed by a card in which punched holes supplied instructions that controlled the selection of threads and application of designs.

The first attempt to use the punched card principle in a mathematical application was made by the English mathematician Charles Babbage. In 1812 he began work on what harsh critics called his "folly." It was a "difference engine" designed to calculate and print mathematical tables. After almost a decade of work on the "difference engine," Babbage turned his attention to a more ambitious project, the "analytical engine," a device with many far-reaching innovations. Included was a memory unit that would store data in the form of holes punched in cards. In addition, the device had a mill or arithmetic unit where the mathematical computations would be made, and a control unit for directing operations. Unfortunately, Babbage's engine seemed to be capable of everything except of constructing a mechanism such as Babbage had in mind were not solved for a full century.

Surprisingly, Jacquard's success in the use of punched cards failed to inspire another successful application of this technique until 1887, when Dr. Herman Hollerith, a statistician with the Census Bureau, developed a mechanical system of recording, computing, and tabulating census data. Hollerith, who had been engaged by the Census Bureau in

1880, was motivated by the obvious need for a more practical method of handling census data. The 1880 census data was written on large cards that had to be hand sorted into desired classifications, such as age, sex, occupation, and location, and counted manually. They were resorted and counted again and again to provide all the required information.

The magnitude of the task made it apparent that the 1890 census, involving millions of additional people, might not be completed by the end of the decade. This would have prevented the reallocation of Congressional seats every ten years as required by the Constitution.

By 1887, when the 1880 census report was finally completed, Dr. Hollerith had finished his plans for a new system that utilized punched holes in a long strip of paper tape as a means of recording facts. However, this was found to be impractical, so the 1890 census data was placed on cards by means of holes cut with a hand-operated punch. The cards were individually positioned over mercury-filled cups. Rows of telescoping pins descending on the card's surface dropped through the holes into the mercury, thus completing electrical circuits and causing pointers on appropriate counting dials to move one position (Figure 2–8). By the use of this device, which could tabulate cards at the rate of 50 to 75 a minute, it was possible to complete the 1890 census of 62 million people in one-third the time needed for the 1880 census of 50 million.

Figure 2-8. *Hollerith tabulating machine, 1890.*
(Courtesy International Business Machines Corporation.)

In 1896 Dr. Hollerith organized the Tabulating Machine Company to promote the commercial use of his machines. Among the first users were railroads, insurance companies, department stores, and a steel company. Other early users of punched cards were the city of Baltimore, the Bureau of Vital Statistics of New Jersey, and the Board of Health of New York City.

Meanwhile, James Powers, a statistical engineer employed by the Census Bureau, was asked to develop improved methods for handling the 1910 census. In 1908, Powers patented his first punching machine, which contained several innovations. The success of this machine and related sorters and tabulators in the 1910 census encouraged Powers to start the Powers Accounting Machine Company in 1911. Through a series of mergers, the Powers line later became part of the Remington Rand Company and more recently the UNIVAC Division of Sperry Rand Corporation.

In the same year, 1911, the company that had been formed by Dr. Hollerith to develop his equipment merged with two other companies and became the Computing-Tabulating-Recording Company. In 1924 the C.T.R. Company's name was changed to International Business Machines Corporation.

The use of punched card machines developed gradually from 1900 to 1915, during which time about three hundred companies adopted the equipment, then with increasing speed in the 1920s. Several significant advancements occurred in the late 1920s and early 1930s. Punched cards with a greatly increased capacity of 80 and 90 columns of information were introduced. Machines were developed that could not only add and subtract figures but also multiply. This gave them the ability to perform full-scale record-keeping and accounting functions. The introduction of machines that could handle alphabetic information made it possible to use the punched card method for name-and-number jobs such as payrolls and inventories.

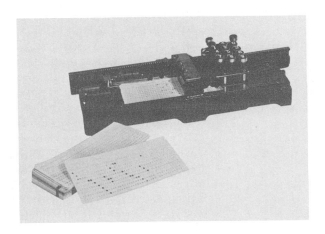

Figure 2-9. *Mechanical key punch, 1901.*

(Courtesy International Business Machines Corporation.)

Figure 2-10. *Punched card sorter, 1925.*

(Courtesy International Business Machines Corporation.)

These innovations and many others increased the speed, versatility, and usefulness of punched card machines. This resulted in the constantly increasing use of these devices for business data processing as well as for scientific computations and statistical studies. However, since standard punched card machines are electromechanical, they have several limitations. First, the speed of the machines is limited by their basic design and by the physical or mechanical manipulation of cards. Second, since each machine is designed to perform a special function, the transfer of cards from one piece of equipment to another for various operations not only takes time but also creates the possibility of error.

The first successful attempt to overcome these limitations by combining the various operations in a single device was made by Professor Howard Aiken of Harvard University, who worked from 1939 to 1944 in conjunction with engineers from International Business Machines Corporation. This joint effort resulted in the completion in 1944 of the Automatic Sequence Controlled Calculator, known as Mark I. This was an electromechanical machine, consisting mostly of parts from standard IBM equipment or modifications of them. It made use of relays and was controlled by punched paper tape. Thus, Babbage's dream of a hundred years earlier was fulfilled.

Several other large-scale digital machines using electromechanical techniques followed the one at Harvard. Aiken designed the so-called Mark II for the U.S. Naval Proving Ground at Dahlgren, Virginia, and several relay calculators were designed and built in the Bell Telephone Laboratories during the World War II period.

In spite of the fact that these computers were a great improvement over devices previously available, they failed to meet the vast data re-

Figure 2-11. *ENIAC, the first all-electronic digital computer, 1946.*
(Courtesy Sperry UNIVAC, A Division of Sperry Rand Corporation.)

quirements of science and engineering that developed swiftly during World War II. Since these machines were electromechanical devices employing electrical relays or counter wheels, their effectiveness was restricted by slowness and mechanical operating difficulties. These problems were overcome by the next major development in data processing history, the advent of the electronic computer.

DEVELOPMENT OF ELECTRONIC COMPUTERS

The first machine to use electronic tubes for calculating was the ENIAC, Electronic Numerical Integrator and Computer, developed between 1942 and 1946 at the University of Pennsylvania by Dr. John W. Mauchly, J. Presper Eckert, and their associates. ENIAC occupied the entire basement of the university's Moore School of Electrical Engineering (Figure 2–11). The computer weighed almost 30 tons, contained more than 18,000 vacuum tubes, and required more than 1,500 square feet of floor space.

It was designed mainly for solving problems in ballistics at the Aberdeen Proving Ground, but it contained advancements that were adopted for use in other computers designed for business applications. In this machine the switching and control functions, once performed by relays, were handled by vacuum tubes. Thus, the relatively slow movements of switches in electromechanical computers were replaced by the rapid motion of electrons. This innovation made it possible to perform computations one thousand times as fast as before. However, although ENIAC represented a great advancement and was adaptable to a variety of applications, its limited storage facilities and the difficulty of presenting instructions were serious restrictions.

In the early stages of computer development, machine instructions were programmed on interchangeable control panels, cards, or paper tapes. It was necessary to wire or read detailed instructions into the machine as work progressed. Since the computer processed data according to predetermined instructions, its operations were very inflexible.

To increase the computer's capacity to work problems without the assistance of an operator, it was necessary to have its program stored in a high-speed internal storage unit or memory. This would give the computer access to instructions as rapidly as they were needed. With an internal storage system, the computer could process a program in a manner similar to that in which it processed data. It could also modify its own instructions as required by progressive stages of work.

These characteristics were incorporated in the stored program digital computers that marked the next great milestone in the development of electronic computers. The first to be completed was the EDSAC (Electronic Delayed Storage Automatic Computer), which came from the laboratories of Cambridge University in England and was placed in operation in May 1949. This machine utilized mercury acoustic delay lines as storage. These devices consist of thin tubes of mercury with crystals at both ends. When an electrical impulse is entered on the input crystal, it causes the crystal to vibrate mechanically, thus sending an acoustic signal through the fluid to the output crystal. When this sound wave hits, it causes a mechanical vibration in the second crystal. This vibration becomes an electrical signal: the image of the one originally transmitted. The reformed and amplified electrical impulse is fed back to the input crystal and the process is repeated. Through this loop process data represented by a set of impulses spaced periodically can be kept circulating through the mercury until needed.

The EDVAC (Electronic Discrete Variable Automatic Computer), which was comparable to the EDSAC, was completed in the early 1950s. This machine was designed at the University of Pennsylvania for the United States Army. It also used the sonic delay properties of mercury for storage. The EDVAC was maintained at Aberdeen Proving Ground until March 1963, when it was discarded.

Another project for a high-speed electronic computer using delay line storage was started in 1945 and completed in 1950 at the National Physical Laboratory, London. This well-designed machine, called the ACE (Automatic Calculating Engine), was compact and highly reliable in operation. It used standard punched card equipment for input and output. Whereas both the EDVAC and the EDSAC required that instructions be placed in consecutive positions in storage, the ACE adopted the so-called two-address code whereby each instruction contains not only the location of the number to be acted upon, but also the location of the next instruction. This procedure reduced the waiting time inherent in delay line storage devices by allowing the use of better programming techniques.

Several other machines were constructed using the principle of acoustic delay line storage. Notable among these was SEAC (Standards Eastern Automatic Computer), developed by the Bureau of Standards in Washington, D.C., for government use. Another computer in this group was UNIVAC (Universal Automatic Computer), developed by Eckert and Mauchly, builders of ENIAC. The first UNIVAC was delivered to the Bureau of the Census in 1951. This computer was used almost continuously 24 hours a day, 7 days a week for over 12 years. In 1963 it was judged of sufficient historical interest to be placed on exhibition at the Smithsonian Institution after having been replaced at the Bureau of the Census by new computers.

UNIVAC was one of the first machines to use magnetic tape as an input-output medium. It featured speed, reliability, memory capacity, and the ability to handle both numbers and descriptive material equally well. These features made computers economically attractive for commercial use. As a result, the first UNIVAC computer was delivered to a business concern in 1954.

UNIVAC I was the first of a line of computers produced by Remington Rand, which in 1949 acquired the Eckert-Mauchly Computer Corporation, originally formed as a partnership in 1946. The Remington Rand organization later became the UNIVAC Division of Sperry Rand Corporation.

During the early 1950s many new computers were developed by universities, industrial laboratories, and machine manufacturers. A family of machines typical of this period employed an entirely different type of internal storage comprised of a cathode ray tube system. Many of these machines derived their logical inspiration from a series of now classical reports by Dr. John von Neumann, Dr. Herman Goldstine, and Dr. Arthur Burks dating back to 1946. The prototype for an extensive group of machines sponsored by the U.S. government was the computer built at the Institute for Advanced Study in Princeton by a group including von Neumann and Goldstine. This computer was completed in March 1952.

Dr. Jay W. Forrester at the Massachusetts Institute of Technology directed the production of Whirlwind I. This machine used a special cathode ray tube of a type devised by Forrester. Another type of cathode ray storage machine was developed at the University of Manchester in England.

An additional form of storage introduced in the early 1950s to enlarge the memory capacity of computers was the magnetic drum. The first fully electronic computer constructed with this type of storage was the prototype SEC (Simple Electronic Computer), developed at the Electronic Computation Laboratory of Birkbeck College, University of London. A very large class of machines using the magnetic drum as the principal form of memory was prevalent later in the 1950s. Particularly notable was the IBM 650, which was used extensively for business calculations as well as scientific purposes.

The mid-1950s constituted a period of transition in the history of computers. Many of the computers developed were designed expressly for business use. Although basically similar to previous computers in the way they processed data, the new business systems were adapted to handle the vast quantities of data typical of business operations. Instead of the punched cards or punched tape used for input of data in early computers, magnetic tape was used for externally storing data. The new technique increased input speed from 50 to 75 times that of cards and also improved output and storage.

As far as internal storage was concerned, the cathode ray tube was abandoned and the acoustic delay line diminished in use. The magnetic drum remained but was relegated to a secondary position in favor of magnetic cores, a more rapid technique that was destined to become the most widely used form of internal storage. Magnetic cores are small rings of ferromagnetic material. When strung on a complex of wires, these cores constitute a high-speed internal storage system in which items of information can be located and made available for processing in a few millionths of a second.

Technological advancements in electronics and solid-state physics resulted in the so-called second generation of computers in the mid-1950s. The first generation used vacuum tubes in their circuits. They were bulky, demanded considerable power, and produced heat, which created air conditioning problems. The second generation used solid-state devices, such as transistors, which generate less heat and are generally smaller and more reliable. As a result, the physical size of computer systems was reduced significantly.

Modular or "building block" concepts were applied to the design of internal circuitry and to the design of other major pieces of hardware in computer systems. This allowed the systems to be easily expanded instead of being replaced as users required more speed or more storage capacity. Improvements in peripheral devices, such as increasing the printing speed of output units, allowed them to be directly interconnected with the computer and used on-line, without unduly reducing the overall speed of the system. Other advancements included built-in error detection and correction devices and improved programming techniques, which reduced the need for operator intervention. Also, teleprocessing equipment was developed to expedite the flow of information to and from computers over long distances.

Along with these improvements came the development of disk storage, which provided a new means of storing information in a unit resembling a coin-operated record player. Before its development, in both electromechanical and electronic data processing systems, information was batched, or sorted into sequence before processing. With the introduction of disk storage, the processing of individual transactions in random sequence became practical, as it was possible to locate and update any one record in a stack of rotating disks in a fraction of a second.

The next major advancement occurred in 1964 with the introduction of what has been described as the third generation of computer equipment. This equipment features microminiaturized components such as integrated circuits and thin-film memory, and other significant innovations resulting from continued progress in electronic technology. Techniques include etching or printing instead of wiring circuits and the use of tiny crystal structures rather than tubes or relatively large transistors. These features made possible the development of computer systems that are smaller in size, greater in capacity, and faster, with operating speeds measured in billionths of a second. Another important characteristic of the newer equipment is greater compatibility of components, which affords flexibility in modifying or expanding computer systems without altering the basic systems. Of particular significance is the fact that most computers are now truly general purpose and thus can handle both business and scientific applications with equal facility.

Along with improvements in the basic design of computers, the following developments have occurred. Many data recording devices have been devised to capture data at the point and time of origin in a form the computer can process. Optical scanners and magnetic ink character recognition devices provide more effective methods of collecting data. Increased use of random access storage devices, such as magnetic disks, has facilitated the storage and rapid retrieval of greater amounts of data. Data communications equipment is increasingly being used to transmit data directly to computer storage, to connect computers with other computers, and to permit interrogation of a computer system from remote terminals. In addition to these advancements, the sophistication of programming techniques has increased tremendously.

Starting in 1970, new lines of computers featured large-scale integration of circuitry (LSI), which is the next link in the vacuum tube/transistor/integrated circuit chain of developments. The new circuits are many times more densely packed than those in preceding systems, and they produce greatly increased internal processing speeds (Figure 2–12).

Another development of the early 1970s was the *microprocessor*. A microprocessor results from putting the complete central processing unit of a computer into one or a small number of integrated circuit chips. Working systems assembled with microprocessors and other chips are called *microcomputers*. Three decades after the first electronic computer, the microcomputer now offers many advanced concepts and features that promise to have a dramatic effect on the future of computer use.

Figure 2-12. *Electronic data processing system.*
(Courtesy Sperry UNIVAC, A Division of Sperry Rand Corporation.)

Rather than speculate about future advancements in the computer industry, let it suffice to say that continuing changes are inevitable as designers strive to develop more versatile and useful computers that will perform at even faster speeds, store more information, require fewer instructions, need less power, occupy less space, and reduce the ratio of cost to performance.

IMPORTANT WORDS AND PHRASES

abacus	stored program computer
ENIAC	UNIVAC

REVIEW QUESTIONS

1. Describe the two oldest surviving records of actual business transactions.
2. What was the purpose of wooden tallies? What was the main reason for their extensive use?
3. Where and in what period did the double-entry system of accounting originate?
4. Where and by whom was the first successful digital counter developed?
5. Who was the inventor of the first punched card data processing system? Under what circumstances was the system developed?
6. When and where did the first electronic computer originate? What was its abbreviated name?
7. What principal characteristic distinguishes each of the three generations of electronic computers? What is the latest development in computer design?
8. What were the significant contributions of the following men to the development of data processing equipment? (a) Dorr Eugene Felt, (b) William S. Burroughs, (c) Jay Monroe and Frank Baldwin, (d) Charles Babbage, (e) Professor Howard Aiken, (f) John W. Mauchly and J. Presper Eckert.

3

DATA PROCESSING APPLICATIONS

This book is concerned primarily with methods of processing data regardless of its origin or nature. Nevertheless, it must be recognized that the majority of data processing takes place in a business environment. For this reason a knowledge of basic business operations is helpful in understanding the main sources of data and common data processing applications. These operations are reviewed in this chapter, but without detailed reference to a particular type of data processing since they can be performed by any of the methods available.

Also presented in the chapter are selected examples of major data processing applications designed to show how various users are taking advantage of modern technology. Included are computer applications in business, government, and other fields.

BUSINESS

Basic Business Operations and Sources of Data

In business and industrial firms, most data results from the need to record transactions as they occur. Thus, data reflects the routine day-by-day activities of the various operations. In a typical manufacturing organization, such as a producer of electrical appliances, there is a wide range of activities involving eight basic operations. These are (1) *purchasing* required goods and *receiving* the purchased items, (2) *storing* these items and maintaining *inventory control*, (3) *producing* goods for sale, (4) *selling* these products, (5) *delivering* the products sold, (6) *billing* customers, (7) maintaining *accounts receivable* and *collecting* payments from customers, and (8) *disbursing* for *accounts payable* and *payroll*.

Although these operations are based on a manufacturing organization, most of the operations, except production, are typical of other firms that distribute goods and render services. A wholesale distribution firm, for example, buys finished goods and sells them to its customers. Such a firm does not need a production operation. However, the other basic operations are the same as those found in a manufacturing company. This is also true of various retail organizations.

Service organizations such as insurance companies, banks, and other financial institutions are not involved in selling and delivering material goods. Nevertheless, they do purchase supplies and services from other companies, bill customers for services, collect from them, and so on.

Because the basic operations are interrelated, the communication of information throughout an organization is necessary. For example, the quantity of items ordered by a customer is required not only in filling the order and billing the customer but also for sales information and inventory control purposes. In many cases the output of one operation may be the input for another. Thus, in the interest of speed and efficiency, it is important that the data required in more than one operation be transferable without unnecessary duplication of business forms and without rewriting information. This is a major objective in planning operations and designing data processing systems.

The most common basic operations will be described briefly along with the principal types of records and reports that originate with each operation and the related data processing applications. This should provide a useful background for understanding not only the sources of data but also the nature of basic data processing applications to which references will be made later in this book.

Purchasing and Receiving. Purchasing involves the procurement of merchandise, materials, equipment, supplies, and services necessary to equip, maintain, and operate a business.

In small organizations each department may be responsible for its own purchases. A large organization ordinarily has a centralized purchasing department responsible for the procurement of all goods and services.

The procurement process in a large organization usually begins with the completion of a *purchase requisition.* This document is a request that the purchasing department secure certain goods or services. It may be prepared in the department where the goods or services are required or in the stockkeeping department. Purchase requisitions are usually made in two copies, one of which is retained by the originator.

Purchasing departments generally have available information about sources of supply, prices, specifications, terms, and shipping conditions. In the absence of such information, the purchasing department may send a *request for quotation* to prospective suppliers. This document requests prices for goods or services in the quantities specified.

PURCHASE ORDER

ESD ELECTRIC SUPPLIES DISTRIBUTING CO.
WHOLESALE DISTRIBUTORS

PURCHASE ORDER NO	DATE	PAGE
L 429 SD	01/22/76	1

INVOICING INST.

SHOW ABOVE ORDER NO. COMPLETE, INCLUDING ALL LETTERS
Mail all invoices in duplicate to:
P.O. Box 1310, San Diego, Calif. 92112
Invoice each Purchase Order separately. Invoices dated after the 25th of the month considered following month billing

SHIP TO

TO

BELL ELECTRIC CO.
C/O JOHN SHANNON MC GEE CO.
1443 E. 4TH ST.
LOS ANGELES, CA. 90033

ELECTRIC SUPPLIES DISTRIBUTING CO.
435 SECOND AVENUE
SAN DIEGO,CALIF. 92112
ALL SHIPMENTS MUST BE SHIPPED TRANSPORTATION PREPAID.
Any transportation charges not allowed to be billed with material.
Include Packing Slip with each shipment.

SHIPPING INST.

VENDOR CODE	RESALE NUMBER	FOR ESD USE ONLY	FRT. ALLOWED	SHIP VIA	WHEN
085	SYFH98-043433		☐ FULL ☐ NO		

ITEM NO.	ESD STOCK NO.		QUANTITY		DESCRIPTION	
1	415472		10		3203-2	BELL COVER
2	415537		6		32350	BELL POWER COVER
3	416002		9		3223-V	BELL COVER
4	416045		2		3223-2V	BELL COVER
5	416096		50		3224-V	BELL COVER
6	416169		5		3224-2V	BELL COVER
7	416355		1		3229-2V	BELL COVER
8	416606		150		3240-AL	BELL COVER
9	417327		2		3276-3	BELL BOX
10	417386		1		3276-4	BELL BOX
11	417440		1		3277-3	BELL BOX
12	417637		10		3373	BELL CLUSTER COVER
13	417939		1		3940	BELL EXTEN ADAPTER

Do Not Write in This Space

AUTHORIZED BUYER

STANDARD CONDITIONS APPLYING TO ALL TRANSACTIONS UNLESS OTHERWISE PROVIDED IN WRITING

This order is placed with the understanding that all items shall conform to all applicable U.S. Government regulations including their processing and/or manufacture. Unless otherwise stated this certifies that materials covered by this Purchase Order are for resale and billing to us is not subject to state sales tax.

Seller will protect and defend purchaser from all suits or actions incident to damages, defects and failures resulting from the use or performance of the sellers product. Evidence of product liability "Vendors Endorsement" to be furnished to purchaser.

Patent claims or royalty charges: It is understood that you guarantee to protect us against loss (including counsel fees) on account of patent claims or royalty charges in connection with any of the articles or materials covered by this order.

Where applicable, all material shipped on this order must bear underwriters approval. If otherwise, get permission from us before shipping.

This order is placed with the understanding that today's prices, or prices as shown, will not be exceeded. In the event of a price increase, notify us prior to shipment for our approval.

IMPORTANT - - - - All packages MUST show current catalog number of contents.
UNPACKAGED items must be similarly tagged or labeled for shelf identification.

IMPORTANT NOTICE - WIRE AND CABLE: Ship only in standard coil, spool or reel lengths. Odd length will not be acceptable unless first approved by us.

DEB-U BUSINESS FORMS PRINTING, INC. 0357

Figure 3-1. *Purchase order.*

When the source of supply has been determined, the next step is to issue a *purchase order* (Figure 3–1). This is the basic procurement document that authorizes the vendor to deliver specified goods or services at the prices indicated. The original and one copy are usually sent to the vendor with one copy to be returned as an acknowledgment. Additional copies may be distributed as follows:

1. To the purchasing department files
2. To the receiving department so that the shipment may be checked when received

3. To the accounting or accounts payable department
4. To the stockkeeping department
5. To the department originating the request

Additional responsibilities of the purchasing department may include (1) following up to assure delivery at the proper time, (2) checking and approving invoices for payment, and (3) securing adjustments for shortages, poor quality, and other problems.

The primary work of the receiving department consists of receiving, unloading, and unpacking materials. The goods are then inspected and compared to the description on the purchase order, and any discrepancies are noted. After checking has been completed, a *receiving report* is prepared. This is the basic document of the receiving department. It is designed to record in detail what materials were received and from whom. The report also may include an *inspection record.* Copies may be distributed to some or all of the following departments:

1. To the receiving department files
2. To the purchasing department so that the receipt of the goods may be audited
3. To the accounting or accounts payable department
4. To the stockkeeping department or other department originating the request
5. To the inspection department if it is separate from the receiving department
6. To the production department if raw materials were received

After the checking of goods and preparation of reports have been completed, the goods are delivered to the stockkeeping department or other department requesting them. The department that takes possession of the goods generally acknowledges receipt by signing a copy of the receiving report.

The end results of the purchasing operation can be of great value to a company by assuring the availability of adequate supplies of goods without maintaining excessive inventories. Much of the success of the purchasing function involves judgment in buying materials of the right quality from the right sources at the right price. However, an effective data processing system also plays an important role by insuring that information about procurement needs is rapidly and accurately handled throughout the process of completing a requisition, placing an order with a supplier, and following up to be sure the goods are received as ordered. The information output of these functions becomes a major source of input for the accounts payable and inventory control applications.

Stockkeeping and Inventory Control. The stockkeeping department is responsible for the storage and protection of all materials and supplies received by or made by a company that are not required for immediate use. The transfer of materials from an outside source to the stockkeeping department is documented by the *receiving report* discussed in the preceding section. The transfer of goods from the production department is documented by a *production order*.

In industrial organizations the storeroom serves as a source of materials that are issued whenever needed. Materials are issued in response to a *material requisition*. This form generally consists of at least four copies distributed as follows:

1. To the files of the requisitioning department
2. To the accounting or cost department
3. To stockkeeping (two copies, one of which is attached to the goods being transferred)

Goods that are being held for sale are released for delivery upon receipt of a *sales order* originating in the sales department.

An important responsibility of the stockkeeping department is the maintenance of *stock records*. A stock record is kept for each item of inventory and shows quantities received, quantities issued, and quantities on hand. Depending upon the methods of the particular business, the stock record may be a loose-leaf ledger, ledger card, visible card or record, punched card, or a form of computer storage.

Stockkeeping also encompasses the replenishment of supplies that reach a specified minimum level called an *order point*. When the quantity of any item reaches the order point, a *purchase requisition* for a new supply is sent to the purchasing department.

Stock on hand is called *inventory*. Whether an inventory is one of raw materials, manufactured parts, or finished products for resale, control of the inventory is a major data processing application.

There are two main objectives of an *inventory control system:*

1. To keep stocks of merchandise sufficient to meet the needs of the business and its customers
2. To maintain these stocks at levels that are adequate but at the same time keep the investment in inventory as low as possible

Whether manual or computer methods are used to process inventory data, the system should:

1. Provide complete and accurate information so that control decisions can be made promptly in response to changing business conditions
2. Provide timely answers to such questions as: What needs to be purchased or produced? How much is needed? How much time can be allowed to secure the additional stock?

Input documents of the inventory control application are those described above—receiving reports, production orders, stock requisitions,

MANUFACTURER HS SERIAL	DESCRIPTION		COUNT	UNIT COST	VALUE
ZENITH REC TUBES					
70 6366 010783	12BR7	Z REC TUBE	10	1.15 EA	11.50
70 6367 010784	12BT3	Z REC TUBE	6	1.25 EA	7.50
70 13862 010785	12BV7 ZENITH REC TUBE		3	1.32 EA	3.96
70 6368 010786	12BV11	Z REC TUBE	4	2.26 EA	9.04
70 6369 010787	12BW4	Z REC TUBE	3	1.16 EA	3.48
70 6370 010788	12BY7A/12BV7/12DQ7	Z REC TUBE	30	1.32 EA	39.60
70 6371 010789	12BZ7	Z REC TUBE	3	1.31 EA	3.93
70 6380 010790	12C5/12CU5	Z REC TUBE	4	1.72 EA	6.88
70 6373 010791	12CA5	Z REC TUBE	2	1.58 EA	3.16
70 6375 010792	12CL3	Z REC TUBE	1	1.41 EA	1.41
70 13861 010793	12CN5 ZENITH REC TUBE		2	.00 EA	
70 6376 010794	12CR6	Z REC TUBE	1	.93 EA	.93
70 6378 010795	12CT8	Z REC TUBE	2	2.63 EA	5.26
70 13860 010796	12CX6 ZENITH REC TUBE		1	.00 EA	
70 6393 010797	12D4	Z REC TUBE	4	1.18 EA	4.72
70 6381 010798	12DB5	Z REC TUBE		1.02 EA	
70 6387 010799	12DQ6B/12GW6	Z REC TUBE	10	2.05 EA	20.50
70 6388 010800	12DS7	Z REC TUBE	5	1.88 EA	9.40
70 6389 010801	12DT5	Z REC TUBE	3	1.07 EA	3.21
70 6390 010802	12DT8	Z REC TUBE	5	1.44 EA	7.20
70 6391 010803	12DW4A	Z REC TUBE		2.05 EA	
70 6392 010804	12DW7	Z REC TUBE	1	1.28 EA	1.28
70 13859 010805	12048 ZENITH REC TUBE		1	.00 EA	
70 13858 010806	12EC8 ZENITH REC TUBE		1	.00 EA	
70 13857 010807	12ED5 ZENITH REC TUBE		2	.00 EA	
70 6394 010808	12EG6	Z REC TUBE	2	1.32 EA	2.64
70 6395 010809	12EK6/12DZ6/12EA6	Z REC TUBE	1	1.24 EA	1.24
70 6398 010810	12F8	Z REC TUBE	3	1.14 EA	3.42
70 6396 010811	12FQ7	Z REC TUBE	4	1.33 EA	5.32
70 13856 010812	12FQ8 ZENITH REC TUBE		1	.00 EA	
70 6397 010813	12FX5	Z REC TUBE	10	1.31 EA	13.10
70 13855 010814	12FX8A ZENITH REC TUBE		7	.00 EA	
70 13854 010815	12GB3 ZENITH REC TUBE		2	.00 EA	
70 6399 010816	12GC6	Z REC TUBE	10	1.84 EA	18.40

Figure 3-2. *Physical inventory value report.*

sales or shipping invoices. Output documents include purchase requisitions and management reports of inventory status, age, turnover, etc., needed for control purposes and management decisions (Figure 3–2).

Sales and Sales Analysis. Sales transactions in wholesale and manufacturing firms are recorded on a *sales order.* The sales order is originated by a salesman or by the order department as the result of a mail order, telephone call, or personal contact with the customer. Copies may be distributed as follows:

1. To the files of the sales or order department
2. To the customer to acknowledge the order
3. To the stockkeeping department
4. To the production department if manufacturing is involved
5. To the shipping department
6. To the salesman
7. To the billing department for preparation of a sales invoice, or to the accounting department if the sales order also serves as a sales invoice

The selling process may require the preparation of other forms and reports including *contracts, estimates* and *bids, order confirmations, back orders,* and *change orders.*

COMMODITY	CURRENT QUARTER SALES					FISCAL YEAR-TO-DATE SALES				
	NO. TRANS.	SALES	G.P.	G.P.%	% OF G.P.	NO. TRANS.	SALES	G.P.	G.P.%	% OF G.P.
ADJUSTMENTS	22	78	111	142.3	.4	56	348	276	79.9	.3
GALV COND -INCL CPLGS & ELLS	235	11612	2473	21.3	7.9	790	32202	6821	21.2	7.5
OTHER COND -INCL CPLGS & ELLS		0	0	.0	.0	12	2414	590	24.4	.6
ALUM COND -INCL CPLGS & ELLS	4	873	233	26.7	.7	12	2414	590	24.4	.6
EMT - INCL ELLS	190	3428	563	16.4	1.8	613	15053	2599	17.3	2.9
REGULAR FLEX	57	696	259	37.2	.8	204	2998	1131	37.7	1.2
OTHER FLEX	36	642	138	21.5	.4	119	1808	491	27.2	.5
FIBRE -INCL ELLS, ETC		0	0	.0	.0	11	266	106	39.8	.1
TRANS/KORDUCT -INCL ELLS, ETC	35	772	316	40.9	1.0	90	1481	525	35.4	.6
PLAS COND -INCL ELLS,FTGS,ETC	134	2694	770	28.6	2.4	310	5145	1536	29.9	1.7
BUILDING WIRE -COPPER	416	19388	4089	21.1	13.0	1118	51288	11992	23.4	13.2
BUILDING WIRE -ALUMINUM	6	4379	247	5.6	.8	23	21729	1503	6.9	1.7
ROMEX, BX & CABLE -COPPER	101	4883	1564	32.0	5.0	281	13507	3624	26.8	4.0
ROMEX, BX & CABLE -ALUMINUM	1	10	7	70.0	.0	1	10	7	70.0	.0
BARE & WEATHERPROOF -COPPER	16	1434	255	17.8	.8	50	3059	534	17.5	.6
BARE & WEATHERPROOF -ALUMINUM	30	13151	781	5.9	2.5	69	34543	2143	6.2	2.4
OTHER WIRE -COPPER & ALUMINUM	32	445	157	35.3	.5	144	4028	968	24.0	1.1
CORD -COPPER & ALUMINUM	46	1516	516	34.0	1.6	128	3408	1365	40.1	1.5
BOXES -INCL BOX MATERIAL	549	3832	1113	29.0	3.5	1717	11979	3594	30.0	4.0
FITTINGS & OTHER CONDULETS	1434	10742	2016	18.8	6.4	4330	32149	6150	19.1	6.8
CONDULETS -CROUSE HINDS ONLY	501	4072	735	18.1	2.3	1391	11118	2026	18.2	2.2
WIREMOLD	101	1018	195	19.2	.6	272	1930	409	21.2	.5
DISTRIBUTION EQUIPMENT	687	17533	3028	17.3	9.6	1884	41322	6814	16.5	7.5
GUTTER, ETC -ALL MFRS	161	1473	202	13.7	.6	540	5198	763	14.7	.8
MOTOR CONTROL	351	5988	1043	17.4	3.3	855	15894	2422	15.2	2.7
METERS, MOTORS, XMFRS, ETC	5	255	25	9.8	.1	16	1336	203	15.2	.2
SCHEDULE MATERIAL	899	9622	1976	20.5	6.3	2618	23713	5214	22.0	5.7
FUSES	492	4197	556	13.2	1.8	1262	7695	1164	15.1	1.3
TIME SWITCHES	40	1558	364	23.4	1.2	108	4107	736	17.9	.8
TOOLS	594	5390	1375	25.5	4.4	1804	16680	4720	28.3	5.2
TAPES, COMPOUNDS, SOLDER, ETC	244	3323	696	20.9	2.2	712	11309	2586	22.9	2.8
LUGS & CONNECTORS	247	2154	430	20.0	1.4	694	10223	1918	18.8	2.1
STRUCTURAL MATERIAL	148	1792	351	19.6	1.1	499	5989	1424	23.8	1.6
POLELINE HARDWARE -INCL PORC	64	7916	1199	15.1	3.8	166	26548	3930	14.8	4.3
SCREWS, NUTS & BOLTS	170	537	377	70.2	1.2	544	1821	1268	69.6	1.4
SIGNALING DEVICES & EQUIPMENT	22	383	75	19.6	.2	104	1501	282	18.8	.3
HEATERS, FANS & APPLIANCES	9	192	39	20.3	.1	28	696	158	22.7	.2
FIXTURES, STREET & FLOOD LGHTS	145	9950	1860	18.7	5.9	473	22573	4559	20.2	5.0
BALLASTS	42	2156	468	21.7	1.5	137	3109	719	23.1	.8
LAMPS -LARGE	399	7868	861	10.9	2.7	1353	22806	3511	15.4	3.9
LAMPS -PHOTO & PROJECTOR		0	0	.0	.0		0	0	.0	.0
LAMPS -AUTO, MINIATURE & OTHER	2	4	1	25.0	.0		42	4	9.5	.0
ZENITH -ALL PRODUCTS		0	0	.0	.0		0	0	.0	.0
TOTAL WAREHOUSE SALES	8667	167956	31464	18.7		25533	473025	90787	19.2	
TOTAL DIRECT SALES	242	194410	13921	7.2		680	527768	35691	6.8	
TOTAL SALES	8909	362366	45385	12.5		26213	1000793	126478	12.6	

Figure 3-3. *Sales analysis report.*

Sales analysis reports are a major data processing application and output of the sales operation (Figure 3–3). The purpose of sales analysis is to provide management with answers to such questions as:

1. How much of each type of product or service was sold during a specified period?
2. In what territories were the sales made and by which salespeople?
3. What items need to be promoted or dropped from the line?
4. What trends are apparent in sales over several periods of time?

An efficient data processing system can provide management with timely answers to these and other questions for use in making effective decisions.

Billing.   The purposes of the billing operation are to prepare customers' *invoices* and to provide the accounting department with a record of charges to be made against customers' accounts (Figure 3–4). Invoices are the basis on which the seller claims payment for goods furnished or

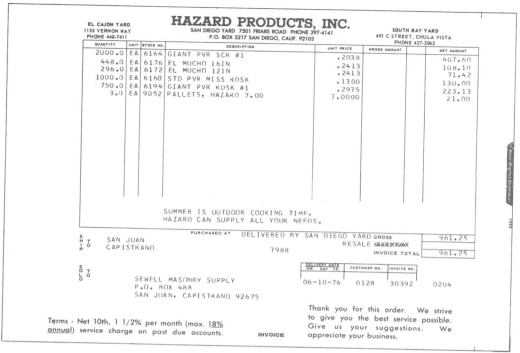

Figure 3-4. *Sales invoice.*

services rendered. Billing may be done manually, by a combination of manual and machine methods, or by electronic computer equipment.

Regardless of the method employed, the billing procedure generally involves the following steps:

1. Coding descriptions for classification purposes and to reduce them to more concise form
2. Inserting unit prices from catalogs or price lists
3. Making extensions by multiplying the quantity of each item by the unit price
4. Totaling extended prices
5. Adding taxes, shipping costs, or other charges and entering the total amount of the invoice
6. Writing or typing invoices in the required number of copies

One copy of the sales invoice is sent to the customer. Other copies are usually distributed to the department responsible for posting accounts receivable, to the salesperson or sales department, and to the files of the billing department.

The choice of a billing system is dependent largely on the volume and nature of transactions, but regardless of the system used, a high degree of accuracy and speed is essential. Undercharges result in a loss of profit, and overcharges create poor customer relations. Speed in issuing invoices to customers is important for a number of reasons; mainly it enables both parties to record transaction data promptly, and it expedites payment for the goods.

Accounts Receivable. An accounts receivable system consists of a running record of the amounts charged to customers, the amounts credited to them as a result of payments or allowances, and, finally, the balances owed by them.

Input documents for the accounts receivable application include sales invoices, cash receipts records, and credit memorandums, all of which are posted to customers' ledger accounts.

The basic output document in this operation is the *statement of account* (Figure 3–5). It is customary to provide customers with statements at regular intervals to inform them of the status of their accounts. The usual time for mailing statements is at the end of each month. However,

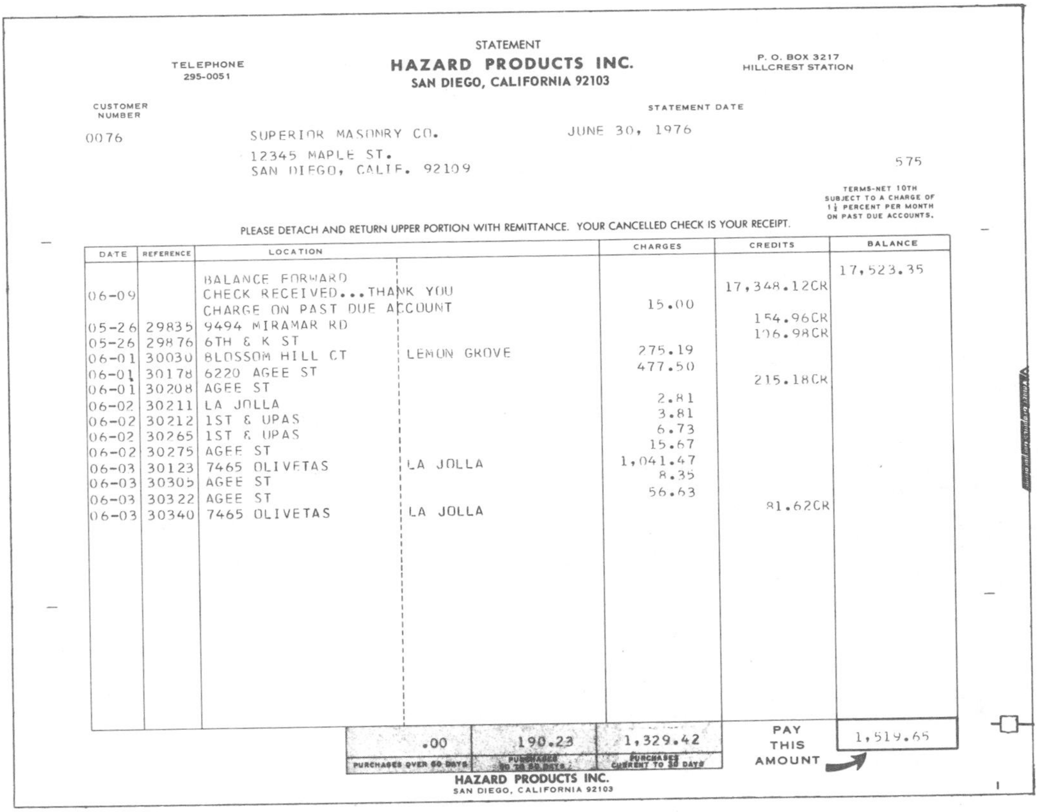

STATEMENT
HAZARD PRODUCTS INC.
SAN DIEGO, CALIFORNIA 92103

TELEPHONE 295-0051

P. O. BOX 3217
HILLCREST STATION

CUSTOMER NUMBER: 0076

SUPERIOR MASONRY CO.
12345 MAPLE ST.
SAN DIEGO, CALIF. 92109

STATEMENT DATE: JUNE 30, 1976

575

TERMS-NET 10TH SUBJECT TO A CHARGE OF 1½ PERCENT PER MONTH ON PAST DUE ACCOUNTS.

PLEASE DETACH AND RETURN UPPER PORTION WITH REMITTANCE. YOUR CANCELLED CHECK IS YOUR RECEIPT.

DATE	REFERENCE	LOCATION		CHARGES	CREDITS	BALANCE
		BALANCE FORWARD				17,523.35
06-09		CHECK RECEIVED...THANK YOU			17,348.12CR	
		CHARGE ON PAST DUE ACCOUNT		15.00		
05-26	29835	9494 MIRAMAR RD			154.96CR	
05-26	29876	6TH & K ST			106.98CR	
06-01	30030	BLOSSOM HILL CT	LEMON GROVE	275.19		
06-01	30178	6220 AGEE ST		477.50		
06-01	30208	AGEE ST			215.18CR	
06-02	30211	LA JOLLA		2.81		
06-02	30212	1ST & UPAS		3.81		
06-02	30265	1ST & UPAS		6.73		
06-02	30275	AGEE ST		15.67		
06-03	30123	7465 OLIVETAS	LA JOLLA	1,041.47		
06-03	30305	AGEE ST		8.35		
06-03	30322	AGEE ST		56.63		
06-03	30340	7465 OLIVETAS	LA JOLLA		81.62CR	

PURCHASES OVER 60 DAYS	PURCHASES 30 TO 60 DAYS	PURCHASES CURRENT TO 30 DAYS	PAY THIS AMOUNT
.00	190.23	1,329.42	1,519.65

HAZARD PRODUCTS INC.
SAN DIEGO, CALIFORNIA 92103

Figure 3-5. *Statement of account.*

when the volume of accounts is very large, a *cycle billing* plan may be used as a means of spreading the work load over the entire month. Cycle billing is accomplished by dividing customers into groups and mailing predetermined batches of statements daily, weekly, or at other convenient intervals.

Statements may be prepared (1) by copying data from the customer's ledger account, (2) by posting to the statement and to the customer's ledger account simultaneously during the month, or (3) by using a combination statement-ledger form whereby a copy of the statement is used as the ledger.

Accounts receivable reports are another form of output that provides valuable information to management. The principal type of report is the *aged trial balance,* which shows the condition of each account, identifies delinquent accounts requiring attention, and provides an overall summary of the accounts receivable situation (Figure 3–6).

Accounts receivable reports, along with the individual accounts receivable records for each customer, provide the information needed for credit management and collection activities. An effective accounts receivable system affords a means of monitoring orders to assure that customers do not exceed established credit limits. The system should also facilitate collection activities that insure rapid cash receipts and minimize bad debt losses.

Disbursing: Payroll and Accounts Payable. There are two major types of disbursements: (1) payroll, which represents payments for the services of personnel; and (2) accounts payable, which represents payments to other companies for purchases of materials, supplies, equipment, and outside services.

R. E. HAZARD CONTRACTING CO.

ACCOUNTS RECEIVABLE TRIAL BALANCE — COMMERCIAL — APRIL 30, 1976

CUSTOMER NAME / JOB NO. JOB LOCATION	TOTAL OWED	TOTAL OWED CURRENTLY	0-30 APRIL	30-60 MARCH	60-90 FEBRUARY	OVER 90 DAYS	RETENTION OWED	REMARKS
ARMER ELECTRIC CONT CO 5039								
76000 REHCC VARIOUS JOB VARIOUS LOC	11434	11434	11434					
BALESTRERI FISH MARKET 5053								
75118 FOOT OF MARKET ST	293697						293697	
D A BERRY BUILDERS 5058								
76000 REHCC VARIOUS JOB VARIOUS LOC	33590	33590	33590					
THE DAMIAN APTS 5062								
76011 MISSION BAY NORTH	124408						124408	
76032 MIRA MESA 29	2285150	2056625			2056625		228525	
HAYNES DEVELOPMENT CO 5066								
76042 6431 GRACE COURT	492273	616500	616500				75773	
C E HOFF PLUMBING CO 5067								
75090 E STREET CHULA VISTA	1063225	934345	934345				128880	
K M HOWLETT MORTUARY 5099								
76052 MORTUARY 4759 IDAHO ST	133800	133800	133800					
HUILLET CO 5115								
76028 LA JOLLA TOWNHOUSE	148485	47160			47160		101325	
WILLIAM R LEDGER CO 5194								
76000 REHCC VARIOUS JOB VARIOUS LOC	278524	278524	278524					
NICHOLS CORPORATION 5210								
75072 POWAY IND PARK	1908658	48095			48095		1860563	
RANDAL AND ROUTE 5221								
76036 BARRETT JCT SHOPPING CENTER	218326	72795				72795	145531	
GROUP TOTAL	7191770	4232868	2008193	95255	2056625	72795	2958902	
FINAL TOTAL	7191770	4232868	2008193	95255	2056625	72795	2958902	

Figure 3-6. *Accounts receivable trial balance.*

The payroll function involves the preparation of many types of forms and reports. *Time cards* originating in production or other departments generally provide the data from which payrolls are prepared. A time card is ordinarily made out for each employee showing the time worked during a pay period. Time cards also may be used for making labor distribution charges to expense accounts.

The *payroll* generally consists of a list of employees, hours worked, rates of pay, gross earnings, deductions, and net pay (Figure 3–7). *Payroll checks* and *earnings statements* are prepared from the payroll (Figure 3–8). The earnings statement is a statement showing the computation of gross earnings, various deductions, and net earnings. The payroll check and the payroll may be prepared simultaneously using methods that will be discussed in later chapters.

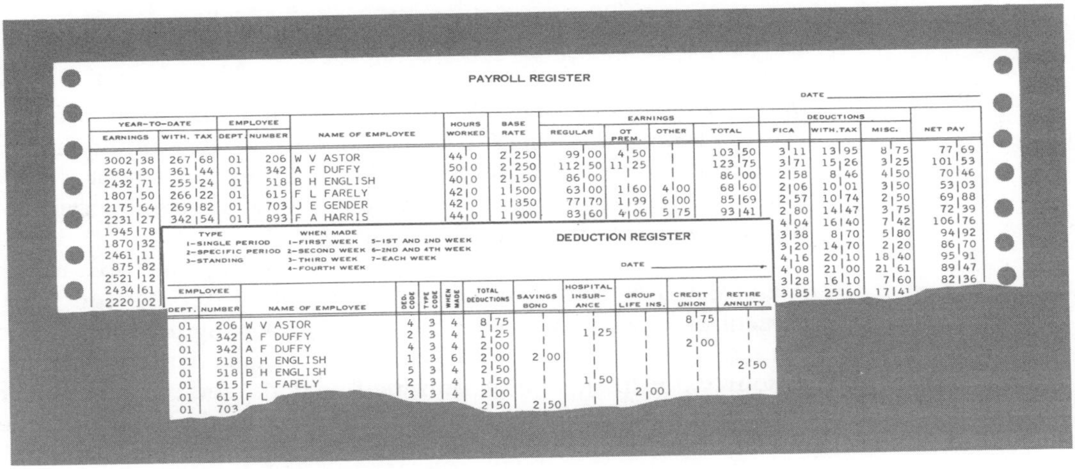

PAYROLL REGISTER

DATE ____________

YEAR-TO-DATE EARNINGS	YEAR-TO-DATE WITH. TAX	EMPLOYEE DEPT.	EMPLOYEE NUMBER	NAME OF EMPLOYEE	HOURS WORKED	BASE RATE	EARNINGS REGULAR	EARNINGS OT PREM.	EARNINGS OTHER	EARNINGS TOTAL	DEDUCTIONS FICA	DEDUCTIONS WITH. TAX	DEDUCTIONS MISC.	NET PAY
3002 38	267 68	01	206	W V ASTOR	44 0	2 250	99 00	4 50		103 50	3 11	13 95	8 75	77 69
2684 30	361 44	01	342	A F DUFFY	50 0	2 250	112 50	11 25		123 75	3 71	15 26	3 25	101 53
2432 71	255 24	01	518	B H ENGLISH	40 0	2 150	86 00			86 00	2 58	8 46	4 50	70 46
1807 50	266 22	01	615	F L FARELY	42 0	1 500	63 00	1 60	4 00	68 60	2 06	10 01	3 50	53 03
2175 64	269 82	01	703	J E GENDER	42 0	1 850	77 70	1 99	6 00	85 69	2 57	10 74	2 50	69 88
2231 27	342 54	01	893	F A HARRIS	44 0	1 900	83 60	4 06	5 75	93 41	2 80	14 47	3 75	72 39
1945 78											4 04	16 40	7 42	106 76
1870 32											3 38	8 70	5 80	94 92
2461 11											3 20	14 70	2 20	86 70
875 82											4 16	20 10	18 40	95 91
2521 12											4 08	21 00	21 61	89 47
2434 61											3 28	16 10	7 60	82 36
2220 02											3 85	25 60	17 41	

DEDUCTION REGISTER

TYPE: 1–SINGLE PERIOD, 2–SPECIFIC PERIOD, 3–STANDING

WHEN MADE: 1–FIRST WEEK, 2–SECOND WEEK, 3–THIRD WEEK, 4–FOURTH WEEK, 5–1ST AND 2ND WEEK, 6–2ND AND 4TH WEEK, 7–EACH WEEK

DATE ____________

EMPLOYEE DEPT.	EMPLOYEE NUMBER	NAME OF EMPLOYEE	DED. CODE	TYPE CODE	WHEN MADE	TOTAL DEDUCTIONS	SAVINGS BOND	HOSPITAL INSURANCE	GROUP LIFE INS.	CREDIT UNION	RETIRE ANNUITY
01	206	W V ASTOR	4	3	4	8 75				8 75	
01	342	A F DUFFY	2	3	4	1 25		1 25			
01	342	A F DUFFY	4	3	4	2 00				2 00	
01	518	B H ENGLISH	1	3	6	2 00	2 00				
01	518	B H ENGLISH	5	3	4	2 50					2 50
01	615	F L FAPELY	2	3	4	1 50		1 50			
01	615	F L	3	3	4	2 00			2 00		
01	703					2 50	2 50				

Figure 3-7. *Payroll and deduction registers.*
(Courtesy International Business Machines Corporation.)

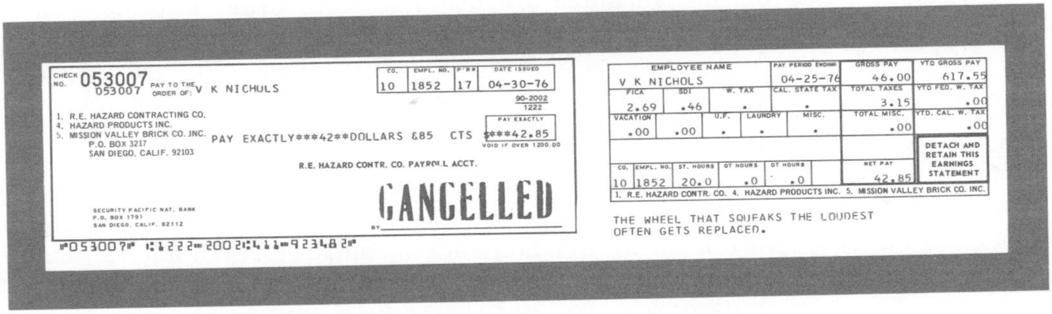

CHECK NO. 053007
053007 PAY TO THE ORDER OF: V K NICHULS

CO.	EMPL. NO.	P/RR	DATE ISSUED
10	1852	17	04-30-76

90-2002
1222

1. R.E. HAZARD CONTRACTING CO.
4. HAZARD PRODUCTS INC.
5. MISSION VALLEY BRICK CO. INC.
P.O. BOX 3217
SAN DIEGO, CALIF. 92103

PAY EXACTLY***42**DOLLARS &85 CTS — PAY EXACTLY $***42.85 — VOID IF OVER 1200.00

R.E. HAZARD CONTR. CO. PAYROLL ACCT.

CANCELLED

BY ____________

SECURITY PACIFIC NAT. BANK
P.O. BOX 1791
SAN DIEGO, CALIF. 92112

⑈053007⑈ ⑆1222⑉2002⑆411⑉92348 2⑈

EMPLOYEE NAME			PAY PERIOD ENDING	GROSS PAY	YTD GROSS PAY
V K NICHOLS			04-25-76	46.00	617.55
FICA	SDI	W. TAX	CAL. STATE TAX	TOTAL TAXES	YTD FED. W. TAX
2.69	.46	.	.	3.15	.00
VACATION		U.F.	LAUNDRY / MISC.	TOTAL MISC.	YTD. CAL. W. TAX
.00	.00	.	. / .	.00	.00
CO. / EMPL. NO.	ST. HOURS	OT HOURS	OT HOURS	NET PAY	DETACH AND RETAIN THIS EARNINGS STATEMENT
10 / 1852	20.0	.0	.0	42.85	

1. R.E. HAZARD CONTR. CO. 4. HAZARD PRODUCTS INC. 5. MISSION VALLEY BRICK CO. INC.

THE WHEEL THAT SQUEAKS THE LOUDEST
OFTEN GETS REPLACED.

Figure 3-8. *Payroll check and earnings statement.*

The *earnings record* is a permanent document showing the cumulative earnings and deductions for each employee. This record provides a basis for preparing reports of social security, unemployment insurance, and income tax withheld. It also serves to indicate when the employee has reached the maximum earnings subject to social security or unemployment insurance.

Accounts payable disbursement procedures include checking invoices and verifying liability by means of purchase orders and receiving reports. Upon receiving approval for payment, the disbursing office issues an ordinary *check* or a *voucher-check*. A voucher-check is a check with an attached voucher containing spaces for date, description, gross amount, discount, and net payment. Copies of the voucher are usually distributed to the payee, to the accounting department for accounts payable posting, and to the files of the disbursing office.

Summary of Basic Operations. The preceding discussion was designed to provide an awareness of the importance of data processing in completing some of the common applications originating with basic business operations. As indicated earlier, not all of these operations are found in every business, and there are variations in the magnitude and nature of the procedures in different companies. Nevertheless, it is apparent that a central data processing department might provide service to each of the operations found in a company.

In conclusion, it should be noted that the designated operations have been treated as primary activities. This implies that other functions such as data processing and accounting are supporting activities. Thus, the operating records, many of which are handled by data processing, serve as source documents for accounting functions, and the combined operating and accounting records form the basis of the reports needed by management to control operations and make profitable decisions.

Major Business Applications

Certain types of businesses stand out as having been most aggressive in adopting automated data processing systems to solve their paperwork problems. Included are manufacturing firms, insurance companies, banking and other financial institutions, public utilities, and airlines.

A high volume of essential data handling and need for control are major characteristics of these organizations. For example, manufacturing concerns use electronic data processing equipment for such activities as sales forecasting, material requirements determination, inventory management, production scheduling and control, and many other functions. In addition, they process vast amounts of accounting and payroll data, often involving thousands of employees. Computers, usually highly specialized, are also used to position machine tools and to control other manufacturing processes. These functions are part of industrial automation, which is discussed in Chapter 19.

In large insurance operations, computers may be used to prepare notices of premiums due, compute dividends, calculate agents' commissions, make the millions of computations used in actuarial departments, and prepare statistical tables.

Most banks throughout the country have converted to electronic data processing as a means of handling the estimated 28 billion checks that are written in the United States each year. In 1956 the American Bankers Association adopted magnetic ink character recognition (MICR), which permits characters printed in magnetic ink on checks and deposit slips to be read directly by both people and machines. After the essential data has been printed on documents in magnetic ink, the documents can be entered into an electronic system and processed automatically.

Electric, gas, and telephone companies find high-speed computers useful in preparing monthly bills for thousands of customers. Data obtained by reading meters is entered into the system by punched cards or possibly magnetic tape. Adjustments are then made automatically on customers' records, and the computer completes the task of printing names and addresses on bills, listing consumption figures, calculating costs, adding taxes, and totaling bills.

Most airlines now use computer reservation systems that store and display information for all flights. A typical system enables an agent to ascertain instantly, by depressing keys on a terminal device, whether a seat is available on a particular flight or a flight near the requested departure time. As soon as the desired information is displayed and the passenger indicates acceptance, the agent enters a confirmation message reserving a seat in the passenger's name.

In organizations of all types, computers are being used extensively for personnel record keeping, billing, payroll, and other accounting. Sales analysis and inventory control are other areas where these techniques have been applied with very satisfactory results.

Management Information Systems

The applications above emphasize the use of computers in solving accounting or other paperwork problems. Because of their great capacity and speed, computers have been extremely effective in processing massive quantities of accounting transactions and producing essential documents and reports. However, in recent years increasing attention has been focused on computer applications providing information for management control purposes. The emphasis here is not on traditional record keeping but on responding to information requests and providing reports for management use.

At the mid-management level, computers can provide timely and accurate information to aid in controlling various operations. Included are purchasing, inventory control, production scheduling, and sales analysis. There is, however, the possibility that managers may be swamped with too much data. The solution to this problem is a concept known as *management by exception*. This is a means of cutting down the amount of detail usually brought to the attention of managers by selecting only those items requiring action. For example, in an inventory control situation minimum and maximum quantities can be established for each item. As inventory balances are reviewed automatically, only those items that are overstocked or understocked are called to management's attention. The items that meet satisfactory standards are passed over.

The extension of this principle to many facets of business control and planning relieves management of much tedious analysis of data, promptly focuses attention on matters requiring decision, and allows management to concentrate on more productive tasks.

At the general mangement or executive level, computer-based information systems are being used increasingly for planning and policy-making. Here the problems of concern are long range and broader in scope, perhaps involving the entire enterprise.

With proper programming, the computer can be used to *simulate* complex events to assist management in making decisions concerning production, marketing, finance, facilities, and other strategic questions. This technique, also known as *management by projection,* depends on the development of a mathematical model of the process or situation to be simulated. Systems and objects are represented by numbers, which can be stored and manipulated by the computer.

A situation to be simulated must be well defined. Its actual characteristics are recorded in as much detail as possible. Variables are then introduced and altered to bring about varied results. Thus, by representing a company in a numerical model and by manipulating the model, it is possible to see what would happen to the real company if certain changes were made. As an example, a firm considering the opening of a new branch may use the simulation technique to test many different locations as a means of choosing the one most likely to be successful.

Simulation provides management with a rapid form of trial and error, allowing many solutions to a problem to be tested without tampering with the actual system. Although this approach may require consideration of anticipated rather than actual conditions, it provides management with a more scientific method of planning actions than would otherwise be possible. Thus, effective use of the computer can eliminate much of the uncertainty from business decision-making.

Data Processing in the Organizational Structure

Data processing is generally regarded as a service function for other operations in the organization. This is especially true in organizations that have electronic computers.

When computers first began to appear in large organizations, they were almost always placed in the controller's department. This was a natural decision since many of the clerical functions of that department could be performed by the computer. However, the range of computer applications soon extended far beyond accounting operations. Computer services to the entire organization increased, and the computer was recognized as a vast source of management information.

In some companies separate computer departments have been established in the controller's organization. This has often led to the creation of a key position near the top of the financial organization structure. In other cases, data processing has been established as a separate staff function outside the controller's organization. This means that the department can make a more direct contribution to management planning and control, and can serve all functional departments since it is not subordinate to any one department (Figure 3–9). The data processing department may be headed by a top-ranking staff executive with a title such as "Vice-President, Management Services," or "Vice-President, Management Information."

The top computer executive generally works with noncomputer executives in determining what the computer is to do for them. Another part of his or her job is working with the chief executive officer in planning the overall use of the computer in current as well as future operations. This includes use of the computer in functional areas other than finance

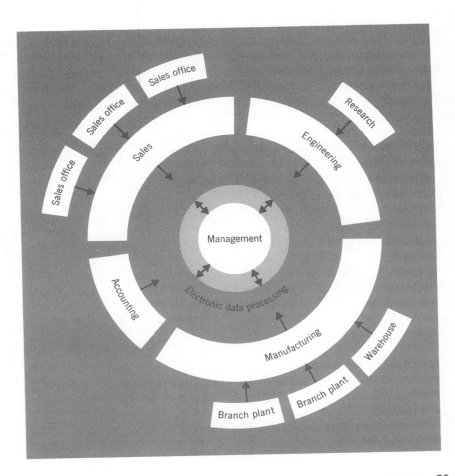

Figure 3-9. *Chart depicting electronic data processing as a separate staff function.*

and administration, such as marketing, manufacturing, distribution, research, development and engineering, and management planning.

It should be noted that the prominent status and central position of data processing within the organizational structure occurs primarily when a large computer system is involved. This centralized approach is being altered in some companies, however, by a new concept in data processing systems called *distributed processing*. This approach originated as a result of the influx of low-cost minicomputers with impressive capabilities. In distributed processing systems minicomputers may replace or augment the central computer. In either case various tasks are assigned to minicomputers on a departmental basis or by type of task. In organizations utilizing manual and mechanical methods, the processing of data within the various departments has always been the standard procedure.

GOVERNMENT

Although government agencies exist for different reasons than business organizations, they process comparable types of data. In fact, a large quantity of the data handled by some government agencies originates in business offices. Examples of such data are income tax reports, reports of unemployment insurance and social security withheld, and sales taxes collected.

An analysis of the basic operations of business reveals that most of these operations also exist in government, the exceptions being production, selling, and delivery for profit. There are, however, additional types of data that are unique to federal, state, and local governmental agencies. Examples include census data; election results; records pertaining to veterans' benefits, unemployment benefits, and social security; motor vehicle registration; law enforcement data; and licensing activities. Government agencies also handle tremendous amounts of statistical data of all kinds, often compiled into elaborate reports. In the final analysis, however, government and business data differ more in volume than in nature.

Because of population increase, the data processing work load at all levels of government has grown tremendously. Consequently, electronic data processing systems are being used today in virtually every area of government. Applications cover a very wide range from standard accounting to extremely complex systems for the processing of special kinds of data. For example, the Internal Revenue Service, faced with the probability of having to process 126 million yearly tax returns of all classes by the late 1970s, has established a vast automatic data processing system. The pinnacle of the system is the National Computer Center in Martinsburg, West Viriginia, now the largest data processing operation in the world.

In operation 24 hours a day, 7 days a week, the National Computer Center updates, maintains, and analyzes a centralized master file of more than 100 million accounts for every business and individual taxpayer in the country. The major data processing equipment utilized in this vast undertaking consists of five large-scale computer systems, one medium-sized computer system, and two magnetic-tape-to-microfilm converter systems. This equipment and its operation are supported by a permanent staff of approximately 300 employees and a magnetic tape library of over 60,000 reels of tape.

Taxpayers file their returns with the ten Regional Service Centers, where the information is transcribed from the returns and documents to magnetic tape. Magnetic tape output files from the service centers are used as input data to the National Computer Center, where the information is applied against the master file to update taxpayer accounts. From this operation, tape files are generated, converted to microfilm, and distributed to the service centers for use as research material; refund data on tape is sent to Treasury Disbursing Offices, where refund checks are printed and mailed to taxpayers; and tape files of bills, notices, and mailing labels are forwarded to service centers to be printed and sent to taxpayers.

The Veterans Administration has converted 4.5 million compensation and pension accounts to electronic data processing. Under the current system, the Department of Veterans Benefits processes claims for payments and provides check-payment data on magnetic tape to the Treasury Department for the automatic preparation of checks, and for the sorting of checks by destination code to facilitate delivery by the Postal Service.

Electronic data processing equipment is also used at the Social Security Administration in Baltimore to maintain the records for 172 million accounts. Every quarter the agency receives over 70 million reports from 4.5 million employers. It also pays monthly retirement benefits to 22 million persons. The challenge of processing this amount of data would be staggering without the aid of computers and other mechanical and electronic data processing equipment.

Because of the large volume of data it must handle, the Bureau of the Census has necessarily pioneered the use of new data processing techniques. A summary of the methods employed by the Bureau of the Census during the past century provides a clear indication of the degree of progress that has been made in data processing. In the first century of census taking, the pencil was the principal tool used. With it, a clerk could record about 2 items a minute. The first punched card tabulator used in the 1890 census could tabulate 200 items a minute. By 1950 the speed of punched card tabulation had been increased to 6,800 items a minute. The UNIVAC I computer, installed in 1951, raised the tabulating speed to 30,000 items a minute. In 1963 the UNIVAC I was replaced by a new UNIVAC computer capable of handling about 3 million items a minute. Most of the processing for the 1970 census was handled by a complex of four UNIVAC computers—two 1107's and two 1108's. These computers provided about five times the capacity of the equipment used to process the 1960 census. Another indication of progress is that each 1108 computer can do the work of about nine UNIVAC I's.

Included among the many tasks for which the Bureau of the Census uses electronic computers are sorting and rearranging hundreds of millions of items of statistical data; tabulating and summarizing statistical material; inspecting statistical reports for completeness and consistency; computing averages, rates, and percentages; and preparing the printed tables of census results.

Applications of the magnitude of these examples are a good indication of why the federal government has become the largest single user of electronic computers with over 8,700 installations. Computers are also being used extensively in states, counties, and cities for such diverse applications as social services, pollution monitoring, and law enforcement in addition to a wide range of administrative operations.

OTHER APPLICATIONS

In addition to the business and government applications mentioned above, modern data processing techniques play a vital role in many other fields. Computers have been used in the areas of science and engineering for applications of tremendous variety. For example, problem-solvers can "converse" with computers such as the IBM System/3, shown in Figure 3–10. By entering data directly from the typewriter keyboard in the easy-to-use BASIC language, which will be described in Chapter 14, mathematicians, scientists, and engineers can solve just about any problem that can be expressed in mathematical terms.

In medicine, computers are being used increasingly to process data obtained from patients' case histories, to abstract information for use in diagnosis, and to summarize and analyze research information. In hundreds of hospitals across the country computers are handling the increased paperwork load created by Medicare as well as standard business operations such as accounting, billing, and inventory control. Other applications range from scheduling linen distribution and menu planning to computer analysis of electrocardiograms.

In high schools, community colleges, and universities, educators are bringing the computer into the classroom while applying it to complex administrative tasks. Among the most frequent administrative applications are scheduling rooms and courses, registration, handling scholastic records, payroll, budgeting, and accounting. Academically, the computer is being used increasingly for problem-solving and other student projects, especially in disciplines such as mathematics, business, science, and engineering, which involve extensive computational work.

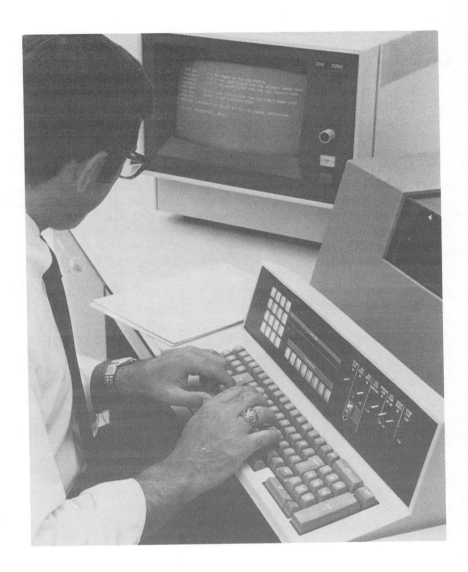

Figure 3-10. *Use of computer for problem solving.* (*Courtesy International Business Machines Corporation.*)

To provide students with this experience, many schools utilize computer time-sharing services, which will be described in later chapters.

Computer-aided instruction has received a great deal of attention, but its full potential has not been realized because of the lag between technology and the development and implementation of effective instructional programs. However, continued interest and progress in this area is inevitable.

Examples of specific applications in the preceding fields as well as other fields will appear throughout this book.

purchase requisition   sales order   voucher-check
purchase order   sales analysis report   management by exception
receiving report   invoice   simulation
material requisition   statement of account   management by projection
inventory   aged trial balance   distributed processing
inventory control system

REVIEW QUESTIONS

1. Describe briefly the following basic operations of business: (a) purchasing and receiving, (b) stockkeeping, (c) sales, (d) billing, (e) accounts receivable, (f) disbursing.
2. Describe the purpose and origin of the following basic documents: (a) purchase order, (b) receiving report, (c) material requisition, (d) sales order, (e) shipping order, (f) invoice, (g) statement of account, (h) voucher-check.
3. What are the two main objectives of an inventory control system?
4. Sales analysis reports are designed to provide management with what types of information?
5. What are the two major characteristics of organizations that have been most aggressive in adopting automated data processing systems?
6. Define "management by exception" and "management by projection."
7. Discuss the role of the data processing department in a large organization.

4

MANUAL AND MECHANICAL DATA PROCESSING

CHAPTER PREVIEW

In addition to the modern developments in electronic data processing, a number of techniques and devices have also been developed to simplify the processing of data by traditional manual methods. Likewise, a great many new and improved devices have been developed to increase the efficiency of mechanical data processing.

At times the standard mechanical business machines have been all but written off in favor of the more sophisticated electronic data processing systems. Mechanical devices have not become obsolete, however. Instead, machine manufacturers have been stimulated to make advancements in traditional equipment, to develop new manual, electrical, and electronic units with added features, and to produce new types of equipment and devices that speed individual operations and make them more automatic and accurate.

As a result, improved mechanical and electronic devices are filling a constantly growing demand for easy-to-use equipment that is practical for organizations with moderate data processing requirements. Such equipment also plays an important role in organizations with computers. It may be used independently to perform special functions in any part of an organization, or it may be used in a decentralized location—branch office, warehouse, etc.—as an adjunct to a centralized computer system. Many machines become an integral part of more sophisticated systems by preparing original documents and simultaneously producing by-products such as punched cards or tapes for processing by electronic computers.

Technological advances in data processing equipment and related office machines are now progressing with amazing speed. For this reason, it would be futile to try to discuss specific features and models of equipment. A detailed discussion would soon be outdated by rapid developments. Instead, this chapter will present a survey of the general characteristics of the major manual and mechanical data processing techniques and equipment. To the extent possible, equipment will be grouped according to steps in the data processing cycle.

RECORDING TECHNIQUES

The traditional method of completing accounting and other record-keeping procedures is by means of pen-and-ink entries in standard journals, ledgers, and other record books. This manual approach to record keeping generally involves rewriting the same data several times, which consumes much time and creates a chance of error.

Thus, as the volume of record-keeping activities increases, the need for more rapid and economical methods becomes evident. As a result, transaction documents and, in the case of accounting, subsequent entries in journals, subsidiary ledgers, and general ledgers are not always prepared in the conventional step-by-step manner. Instead, more than one document or record may be prepared simultaneously by means of special forms and devices. Original data also may be recorded in such a way that it may be used repeatedly without having to be rewritten.

There are various ways of eliminating the need to rewrite data. Later chapters will include such methods as recording data on punched cards, magnetic disks, or magnetic tapes. In manual data processing this objective may be achieved by the use of carbon paper in handwritten or typewritten documents. Variations of this technique and some of the other methods that can be used to decrease manual effort are outlined in the following sections.

Special Forms

Most manual and mechanical recording operations are greatly facilitated by the use of special forms. Printed forms serve a number of important purposes including the following:

1. They identify the specific data that must be recorded for various uses.
2. They standardize the arrangement of data on source documents. This makes it easy to locate specific items of data and to process the documents.
3. They make records easy to recognize and to file.

4. They eliminate the need for recopying repetitive data that must appear on all transactions of a similar type.
5. They facilitate the use of multiple copies.

The last purpose is important in any type of operation. The use of multicopy forms is especially valuable in a manual operation, however, since it greatly reduces clerical costs by eliminating the need to recopy data. In addition, specially prepared sets of forms can eliminate many handling steps such as aligning separate forms and inserting and removing carbons.

Multicopy forms are generally constructed in two ways. *Unit sets* are groups of forms containing an original and a number of copies assembled as a unit. Each unit is self-contained, instead of being part of a large pad, and may be completed by hand or by typewriter. *Continuous forms* are similar to unit sets in basic construction except that individual sets are joined in a continuous arrangement of accordion-pleated folds (Figure 4–1). The folds are perforated to facilitate separation of individual sets. Continuous forms may be processed on a variety of equipment including typewriters and computer printers.

The carbon handling problem is often solved by the use of one-time carbon paper. In this method, sheets of inexpensive carbon paper are interleaved between the various pages of multicopy forms. After a form has been completed, the carbon paper is separated and discarded.

Figure 4-1. *Continuous forms with disposable carbon.* *(Courtesy Moore Business Forms, Inc.)*

Carbon handling can be eliminated entirely by the use of *carbonless papers,* which are chemically treated or coated so that when pressure is applied images are automatically formed or deposited on copies.

It is possible to record the various steps of a transaction simultaneously by using an *accounting board* (Figure 4–2), also known as a *pegboard, poster,* or *posting board.* This device consists of a flat writing surface generally equipped with pegs along the edge of the board. The pegs are used to hold in place different forms that are especially designed with corresponding holes along the edges. Forms are planned so that moving a form one step in either direction changes its position one writing line in relation to the other forms on the board.

When a series of related forms is aligned with carbons between forms, it is possible to record data on all of the forms at once by writing with pencil or ball-point pen. This method requires that the various forms be designed so that identical data appears in the same location on each form. Thus, data written on the top form also appears by means of carbons in appropriate spaces on the forms beneath. For example, in a payroll application a check can be prepared and the necessary entries can be made on the employee's earnings record and on the payroll journal all in one writing. A payroll journal page is first placed on the board, where it remains. Next, a pay check and the proper employee's earnings record are positioned on the board. They are arranged so that as the check is completed and as the detailed earnings data is entered on a stub

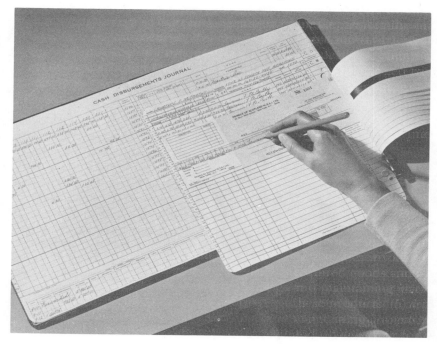

Figure 4-2. *Accounting board with payroll setup.* (*Courtesy Shaw-Walker Company.*)

attached to the check, the entries are simultaneously recorded on the next vacant line of the employee's earnings record and on the payroll journal (Figure 4–2). This procedure is repeated until all pay checks are written. Thus, as pay checks are prepared manually, two additional records are prepared automatically.

This principle is useful for other accounting work such as recording accounts receivable. In this case, a customer's statement and entries to the customer's ledger account and the sales journal can be completed at the same time. Additional applications include simultaneous preparation of checks and check registers, and checks and accounts payable records. These devices are also used extensively in medical and dental offices for recording charges to patients' accounts and payments received.

Accounting boards are an effective and yet relatively inexpensive method of handling accounting data. They eliminate a great deal of recopying that would otherwise be necessary in a manual system, and provide an efficient means of recording and summarizing data.

Document Control Register

Another method of handling accounting forms is the *document control register* (Figure 4–3). This is a metal box designed to hold and feed continuous multicopy forms. By means of a hand crank or electric drive, forms are automatically fed and positioned on a writing surface so that all copies can be completed simultaneously by hand. Carbon copies result from the insertion of roll carbon between the various copies. Forms feed across sheets of roll carbon that are held in a fixed position from within the register. Carbonless forms may also be used.

Registers are manufactured in various models including manual and electric desk units and portable units used by outside salespeople. Some models contain a cash drawer that opens only when a form is issued or a key is used. As completed forms are ejected from the desk units or cash-drawer models, one of the copies is automatically retained in the register with the remaining supply of blank prenumbered forms. Thus,

Figure 4-3. *Carbomatic autographic register.*
(Courtesy Standard Register Company.)

control is maintained over both forms and documents since the contents of the locked register are accessible only to authorized persons with keys.

These devices can be used to record on the same type of form such transactions as cash sales, charge sales, cash received on account, credits and allowances on charge sales, and cash paid out. Document control registers improve manual operations by (1) reducing the time spent on paperwork, (2) increasing the accuracy of accounting work, and (3) facilitating the control of documents.

Typewriters

Although standard manual and electric typewriters are the most widely used methods of recording business data, automatic typewriters are of greater significance to data processing. Automatic typewriters can type complete letters, contracts, and documents of many types without human intervention. These machines may be operated singly or as a battery of machines automatically controlled from one source with an operator changing paper and inserting variable data as required.

Automatic typewriters are important to data processing not only because they can be activated by tapes or other media but also because of their ability to produce by-products such as magnetic tape. These by-products serve as input to computers and other machines.

Applications involving the use of automatic typewriters are generally referred to as *word processing*. Because the technology employed is comparable to a certain extent, automatic typewriters are thought of as typewriters that process words the way that computers process numbers. Thus, the key factor that differentiates office equipment as "word processing" or "data processing" is the extent to which processing involves words rather than numbers.

Most automatic typewriters employ one of the following storage and control media:

1. Punched Tape. Correspondence or data of any type may be punched into tape by the tape punch on the typewriter. When this master copy is fed through the typewriter's reader unit, the tape, in turn, mechanically activates the keys and controls the other machine operations necessary to type a document or letter. The tape even stops the typewriter at predetermined places for the manual insertion of variable data such as names and addresses, prices, quantities, or parts specifications. Tapes can be filed for future use.

2. Magnetic Tape. In this method, typed information is recorded and stored on tape mounted on a changeable cartridge, cassette, or open reel. Text can be corrected or revised by backspacing or repositioning the tape and typing over unwanted information. The new information is automatically stored in place of the old.

Completed tapes can be used for the automatic production of documents at speeds generally over 150 words a minute. As in the case of punched tape, magnetic tape can be coded to instruct the machine to stop typing at certain points so that variable information may be inserted manually. The machine will then continue to type the stored sections of the document, automatically adjusting word spacing and line endings to the manual insertions.

3. Magnetic Cards.   Magnetic card systems use an oxide coated mylar film identical in size to the familiar punched cards in use today. These cards normally have a capacity of a full typewritten page, but some systems can store more than one page on each card. When completed, the magnetic card may be stored for later use or may be reused immediately.

To illustrate the capabilities of magnetic card equipment, the typewriter shown in Figure 4–4 features an electronic memory that holds up to 8,000 characters or about 2½ average-length pages of typewritten information. Material can be entered into electronic memory via the machine's familiar "Selectric" typewriter keyboard. After entry into memory, major revisions to a document can be made without time-consuming retyping of good material. For example, as an additional word or phrase is typed, the ensuing text is moved over in memory. If a deletion is made, the text following it closes up in sequence. The system then elec-

Figure 4-4. *Mag Card II typewriter.*
(Courtesy International Business Machines Corporation.)

tronically scans the newly revised text, rearranging line endings and page endings to a specified length. Information in memory may be used to produce a completed document automatically or may be recorded on a magnetic card at 200 characters a second. At a later time, recorded cards may be electronically read back into memory at the same speed for use in reproducing or revising documents.

During the past decade the most widespread use of automatic typewriters has been in organizations having a large volume of paperwork. Government agencies and firms such as banks, insurance companies, and law offices regard paperwork costs in the same manner that a manufacturing organization regards production costs. A major step that aided in the reduction of paperwork costs was the development of automatic typewriters.

The most common office application for automatic typewriters continues to be correspondence and lengthy documents requiring text revision and repetitive use. However, many companies are finding this type of automation useful in high-volume applications containing a great deal of repetitive data that can be typed automatically. For example, sales orders can be handled automatically by preparing the following input material:

1. A master tape or card for each customer, containing name, address, code, delivery instructions, and terms
2. A master tape or card for each product sold by the firm, including description and code

Using these master inputs, an operator can easily prepare a sales order as follows:

1. The master input for the customer placing the order is first selected.
2. Inputs for each item being sold are then assembled.
3. These inputs are fed into the machine, which automatically types the standard data on a sales order form and automatically stops at predetermined places for the manual insertion of variable data.
4. The operator manually types the variable data such as date, quantities, prices, totals, and discount. (Some automatic typewriters can be coupled with computing devices that automatically extend prices and compute totals.)
5. While typing the sales order, the machine can make a master input to be used in preparing production orders, bills of lading, and invoices.

Purchase orders can be handled in a similar manner by preparing a master tape or card containing the product number and description of each stock item. In fact, any procedure that involves the repetitive typing of standard data may be performed efficiently on an automatic typing system at speeds ranging from 100 to 350 words a minute.

By using continuous forms or stationery combined with a special platen and automatic forms-feeding device, it is possible for an automatic typewriter to type a series of documents or form letters without the help of an operator.

Reproducing Processes

Organizations often require more copies of a document than can be provided by the use of carbon paper. In other cases it may be discovered sometime after the initial preparation of a document that additional copies are needed but are not available. A wide variety of duplicating and copying machines is produced today to meet both of these requirements.

Duplicating. *Duplicating* is a high-volume process that generally ir.volves the preparation of master copies such as stencils and plates. These are used to reproduce copies by means of ink or the transfer of dye. Included in this category are the well-known stencil, spirit, and offset processes.

In the *stencil* or *mimeographing* process, ink is forced from a saturated pad through a stencil as it is rotated on the drum of the duplicating machine.

The *spirit* process, often referred to as the *hectograph* process, employs special carbon paper containing aniline dye to produce a master from which an image is transferred to papers moistened with a special liquid.

Offset duplicating is a versatile method producing a high quality of work. Offset is the process used most often in data processing for the reproduction of documents, reports, and other materials where quantity and appearance are important factors. Continuous-form offset masters can be used with computer print out devices and other business machines to prepare data for reproduction.

In the offset process, the inked image is transferred from a master on one rotating cyclinder to another cylinder wrapped with a rubber blanket. In turn, the blanket transfers the image to copy paper that is fed into the machine and pressed against the blanket by an impression cylinder.

Copying. *Copying* is a process of making reproductions directly from the original by chemical reaction or photography. Because of the relative slowness and greater expense of the copying process, it has been used mainly for single-copy or low-volume reproduction of 12 to 15 copies. However, copying machines can also be used as a basis for high-volume duplication since most machines are capable of making masters for at least one of the duplicating processes. Consequently, by means of a two-step process: (1) a copying machine may be used to prepare a duplicating master from an original document, and (2) that master can then be used to produce multiple copies. This could occur immediately after the preparation of the original document or at some later time when the need arises.

The functions of copying and duplicating have been associated even more closely by the introduction of copier-duplicators. These are devices that combine the functions of copying and duplicating in a single system operating in an automatic cycle. Examples of such systems include electrostatic copying combined with offset, and heat-transfer copying combined with spirit duplicating. Depending upon the methods employed, high-speed copier-duplicators are able to produce up to 5,000 copies an hour.

There are many different kinds of machines and methods that can be used to produce exact copies of documents. However, the most prevalent today is *electrostatic* copying. This is an electrical dry process that uses fused powder or charged microstatic particles instead of ink to produce a permanent print. This is also referred to as the *xerographic* process. Two methods are used: transfer and direct. Transfer employs ordinary bond paper, and the direct process requires specially coated paper.

Although the office copier field has rapidly grown into a major industry, the regular use of copiers for data processing applications has been fairly limited. However, it appears that the need to copy continuous-form computer print out, already a copier application, will bring about a significant increase in the use of this technique for data processing

Figure 4-5. *Microfilm reader-printer.*
(Courtesy 3-M Company.)

purposes. Computer systems that print at the rate of over 2,000 lines a minute will produce only one copy. Consequently, as these systems become more prevalent, copiers will have to be used to reproduce additional copies.

Microfilming is generally regarded as a technique for storing and retrieving data rather than as a copying method. However, paper copies of original documents can now be prepared conveniently by the use of microfilm. This was made possible by the development of reader-printers that not only project a filmed image on a screen but also produce a full-sized paper print of the projected document when a button is pressed (Figure 4–5). Microfilm equipment can also be used to prepare offset and spirit masters from microfilm negatives for multiple reproduction of documents.

MANIPULATION OF DATA

One of the most common sorting operations in data processing is the arrangement of numerically coded data into proper sequence. In some cases it may be necessary to sort the same documents several times according to different classifications. For example, sales documents might be arranged by codes representing products, salespeople, or customers for various reporting or recording purposes. The following methods may be used to sort numerically.

Sorting

Reverse-Digit Sorting.   A fast method of sorting a large volume of data is the *reverse-digit method.* In this method, the digits are sorted from right to left. The arrangement of a group of coded documents into numeric sequence would proceed as indicated in Figure 4–6. It should be noted that in the second and succeeding sorts the order of sorting must be from the bottom of the right-hand stack to the top of the left-hand stack. This is necessary to keep the digits in proper sequence. One of the main advantages of this method of numerical sorting is that data is never sorted into more than ten groups at one time regardless of the number of documents or number of digits.

Block Sorting.   When the volume of documents is so great that it is inconvenient to complete all sorting in one operation, the documents may be separated into smaller groups by means of *block sorting.* To accomplish this the left-hand digits of the codes are sorted first. Sorting operations can then be performed on individual groups using the reverse-digit method. For example, in the preceding illustration of reverse-digit sorting, the codes beginning with "0" would be sorted first. This method allows the documents in the first group to be released for other processing while the remainder of the sorting is being completed.

Similar techniques can be used to facilitate the handling of alphabetic data. In this case, the first step might be to sort the documents into

Original Random Sequence

725	071	251	945	326	061
984	086	527	246	282	566
381	367	742	552	354	272
374	962	577	047	056	

First Sort

(0)	(1)	(2)	(3)	(4)	(5)	(6)	(7)	(8)	(9)
		272				566			
	061	282				056	047		
	251	552		354		326	577		
	071	742		374	945	246	527		
	381	962		984	725	086	367		

Second Sort

(0)	(1)	(2)	(3)	(4)	(5)	(6)	(7)	(8)	(9)
				742	251	061	071	381	
		725		945	552	962	272	282	
		326		246	354	566	374	984	
		527		047	056	367	577	086	

Third Sort

(0)	(1)	(2)	(3)	(4)	(5)	(6)	(7)	(8)	(9)
047			326						
056		246	354		527				
061		251	367		552				945
071		272	374		566		725		962
086		282	381		577		742		984

Figure 4-6. *Reverse-digit sorting.*

groups such as A–D, E–H, I–M, N–S, and T–Z. Each of these groups may then be sorted into single alphabetic units. The first group, for example, would be sorted into separate stacks for A, B, C, and D. Finally, papers in each alphabetic stack may be sorted into proper order. The first two steps of this procedure are known as *rough sorting,* and the last step is known as *fine sorting.*

Edge-Notched Cards. This sorting system involves the use of specially designed cards with holes prepunched around the four edges. Cards are available in various sizes and shapes. Data can be transferred to these cards from other documents or entered directly by means of typewriter or handwriting. Thus, the cards can be used both as recording documents and as a sorting system.

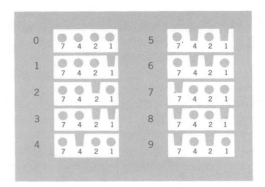

Figure 4-7. *Coding system used to express digits on edge-notched cards.*

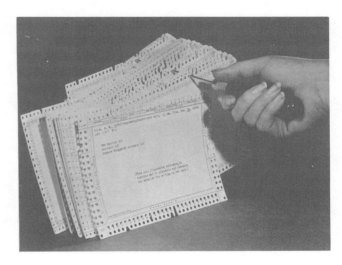

Figure 4-8. *Sorting edge-notched cards with a needle.*
(Courtesy McBee Systems, A Division of Litton Industries.)

The holes spaced along the edges of the card are used to code data. Numerical coding is accomplished by using a group of four holes for each digit in the code. These holes are assigned values of 7, 4, 2, and 1. Data is coded by notching appropriate holes with a hand notcher or electric key-operated notcher so that the holes become slots. By notching one hole or a combination of two holes in each group, it is possible to record all numbers from 1 to 9. Zeros are not notched. Figure 4–7 shows the pattern of notched holes used to represent each digit.

Sorting of edge-notched cards is accomplished by running a needle through one of the holes in a group of cards. When the needle is lifted, the cards with the holes notched out fall free and the cards without notched holes remain on the needle (figure 4–8). In this way the un-notched cards are easily sorted into a separate group. Figure 4–9 shows how a group of cards can be arranged in sequence according to a single digit in four sorts.

The process shown in Figure 4–9 is repeated for each digit in a code number. For example, to place code numbers ranging from 1 to 999 in

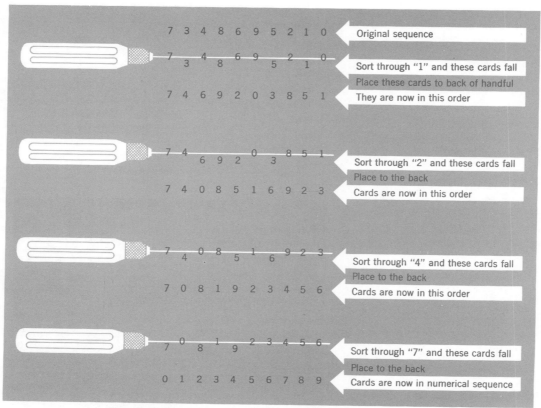

Figure 4-9. *Sequence sorting in an edge-notched card system.*

sequence, the operation illustrated would be performed three times. The cards would be sorted through the four positions of the units field, the four positions of the tens field, and finally through the four positions of the hundreds field. When the quantity of cards to be sorted is relatively small, the sorting is done from units to hundreds. However, when the quantity is large, the cards may be block sorted into hundreds first in order to produce manageable batches. Sorting would then continue through the units and tens positions.

Another coding method is direct coding, in which a certain condition or identification can be expressed by notching a special hole designated for this purpose. For example, data such as months, designated years, model numbers, etc., might be assigned specific locations on the card and coded with a single notch.

The edge-notched card system has been found useful for a number of applications including sales analysis, payroll, expense distribution, property records, inventory, billing operations, and bibliographic data. The system can be used by small, medium-sized, or large organizations. The basic units necessary to use the system are a hand punch, a sorting needle, and an alignment block. However, other equipment is available for larger operations.

Calculating and
Summarizing

Next to the typewriter, machines that perform arithmetic operations are probably the most widely used in business. These machines have been employed for decades to assist in compiling statistics, figuring payrolls, preparing statements, and performing hundreds of other business operations involving arithmetical functions. Included in this category of equipment today are various types of electronic calculators that are commonly used for many operations. These devices have the advantage of being faster, more versatile, and more economical than the electromechanical adding machines, key-driven calculators, and rotary calculators that preceded them.

Also prevalent today are electronic accounting machines and special purpose machines used for more sophisticated record-keeping and billing operations. These machines also represent a major advancement over electromechanical models.

Even with the increase of more powerful electronic computers, these machines are likely to remain in use. One reason for this is that in large automated systems it is often more practical to perform tasks of limited volume and complexity on standard machines. Also, there will continue to be many offices that cannot justify the use of more expensive electronic computer systems.

Although the machines in the following discussion function electronically, they are included here because of the extensive amount of manual activity involved in their operation.

Electronic Calculators. Many changes have occurred in the size, capabilities, and price of electronic calculators since their introduction approximately fifteen years ago. Components are now being mass produced in smaller sizes at a fraction of their former cost. Features that were considered innovative a few years ago have become standard today. Since the range of calculators in the market is vast, this discussion will be limited to the general characteristics, main classifications, and functions of this type of equipment.

Electronic calculators have a number of advantages. Since they have no moving parts, they operate silently at speeds measured in milliseconds. As control keys are released, answers appear almost instantly above the keyboard in an illuminated display window. A main feature of this type of calculator is the automatic storage of intermediate answers so that they can be used as a basis for further calculations. In addition, constant figures such as divisors or multipliers may be stored. This enables the operator to retrieve constant or repeat factors for use in current computations by pressing a "recall" key, thus eliminating manual re-entry.

Buffered keyboards allow operators to enter new problems while the machine solves a previous problem. This feature enables users to enter calculations faster than ever before. Another feature contributing to speed is the chain calculation capability that nearly all machines have. This feature enables the operator to perform a series of add, subtract, multiply, or divide operations without having to depress the equals key after each operation.

Most electronic machines have automatic or "floating" decimal placement, and some have a key to select the number of decimal places desired and another to control rounding off or straight elimination of extra digits. Some models can be programmed to carry out the same mathematical routine repetitively upon manual insertion of the necessary figures for each new problem.

Electronic calculators may be classified as hand-held, display, and printing desktop. The now-familiar *hand-held, portable calculators* are ideal for home use or for the traveling businessperson. They are also useful for taking inventory in a stockroom or warehouse or for field applications such as preparing sales orders at a customer's place of business or completing calculations at a construction site. Hand-held calculators usually display their results, but a number of companies are now marketing hand-helds with print out capabilities.

Desktop display calculators use electronic display as their only means of output. They come in a wide range of capabilities, shapes, and sizes. This group generally begins in size where the hand-held calculator stops. Functional capacities range from simple machines that perform the four basic arithmetic operations to extremely complex calculators with extensive programming capabilities.

Desktop printing calculators are also available in a wide range of models. A number of these printing models also have electronic displays. Some offer the flexibility of using either print output or display, or both (Figure 4–10). Since these machines can be used to record or list a series of figures, they also qualify as summarizing devices.

Figure 4-10. *Model 1450 Electronic Printing/Display Calculator.*

(*Courtesy Monroe, The Calculator Company.*)

Electronic calculators can also be classified into three functional groups. These groups are general purpose, preprogrammed, and user programmable.

General purpose calculators command the largest portion of the calculator market, as they are designed for the countless organizations and individuals whose need is for a machine capable of performing the four basic arithmetic functions.

Preprogrammed calculators, on the other hand, are designed for organizations that need to perform large numbers of complex calculations unique to a particular application. Specialized calculators are available for such applications as banking and finance, insurance, securities, real estate, wholesaling, retailing, science, statistics, and engineering.

User programmable calculators are the most sophisticated calculator equipment available today (Figure 4–11). In fact, these calculators resemble minicomputers in many respects. They are programmable, have input-output devices, store data and programs, and have internal memory. Programs consist of detailed instructions that are stored in memory. When activated, these instructions direct the machine to perform the calculations required to solve a given problem as the user keys in the variables. Programs cover such areas as loan amortizations, interest calculations, payroll, invoicing, sales analysis, discounts, and many others. Programmable calculators are likely to become more prevalent, as they are easier to use and less expensive than minicomputers. Users may also find them to be economical alternatives to computer time-sharing or service bureaus for certain applications.

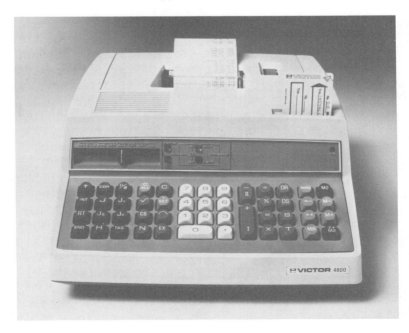

Figure 4-11. *Model 4800 Electronic Programmable Printing Calculator.*

(Courtesy Victor Comptometer Corporation.)

The characteristics of speed, silence, ease of operation, versatility, and economy are certain to result in the further development and widespread use of all types of electronic calculators.

Electronic Accounting Machines.   Previous editions of this text, all within the last decade, included discussions of electromechanical accounting machines. As a result of progress in the application of electronic technology, these machines have now been replaced by electronic accounting machines. These comparatively low-cost business data processing systems are also called electronic accounting computers, office computers, electronic billing computers, or magnetic record computers. Whatever the title, these devices are especially designed to prepare a number of basic accounting records and reports. The usefulness of accounting machines is demonstrated by the fact that with a minimum of operator assistance, they can perform five data processing operations: record data, sort it into various categories, calculate, summarize by taking columnar totals, and prepare reports and documents.

Because of their close relationship to minicomputers, these machines are discussed in detail in Chapter 10.

Point-of-Service Terminals.   In this category are a variety of devices including cash registers, certainly the most widely used equipment of this type. Similar devices of varying complexity are used for many different point-of-sale and financial applications. Included are *accounting control systems,* formerly called *window posting machines,* which are especially designed for posting and controlling transactions originating at a cashier's window. They can be used, however, for any application in which it is desired to make entries on a customer's statement and at the same time to record data for accounting purposes. For example, the machine shown in Figure 4–12 prints detailed transaction data on a paper tape as it is posted to the customer's account. An optional feature of the illustrated system is the ability to record selected transaction data on magnetic tape cassettes as an automatic by-product of the basic recording operation. This information can then be sent to either a data processing center or central accounting office to generate reports of sales or financial data.

These machines have a ten-key numerical keyboard and rows of special keys, each of which is used to print an identification of the type of service, department involved, or method of payment. Keyboards are interchangeable and can be altered and color-coded to meet the user's requirements. Instead of a movable carriage, machines of the type illustrated in Figure 4–12 have a flat printing table. Ledger cards and statements are inserted into special guides on the table for printing.

Accounting control systems are used extensively in hotels for posting guests' accounts. Data from source documents showing details of charges to guests is recorded on account cards by depressing keys to enter the

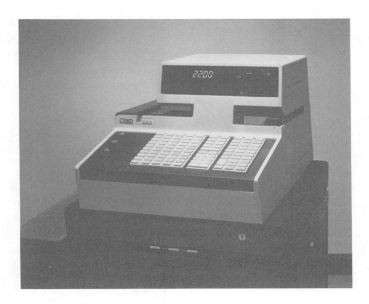

Figure 4-12. *Accounting control system.*
(Courtesy NCR Corporation.)

amount and identify the nature of each charge. While producing account cards, the machine also prepares a detailed summary of revenue classified by room rentals, food, beverages, telephone, and so on.

DATA STORAGE

Filing Systems and Equipment

Filing is the process of arranging and storing records systematically so that they may be retrieved easily and quickly when needed. Filing is an extremely important part of any business or governmental operation. It is a means of safeguarding data needed in the current operations of an organization and of preserving data that may be needed for reference in the future.

The two basic methods of arranging data in files are *alphabetical* and *numerical.* Material in an alphabetic file may be arranged by *name* of individual or organization, by *subject*, or by *geographic area.* The basic form of numeric filing is the arrangement in sequence of documents that are numbered serially, such as invoices or checks. Data may also be arranged chronologically or by code numbers. Many variations of both alphabetic and numeric methods have been devised to meet special needs. It is not uncommon to find different forms of each method used in the same organization to handle various types of data.

Filing is largely a manual operation. This is true even in systems where other operations are highly mechanized or automated. The nature of filing activity is such that materials to be filed are usually transported manually. Cabinet drawers and doors must be opened and shut, filing locations must be identified, and documents must be inserted and removed. As a result, it is estimated that as much as 80 per cent of the cost

Figure 4-13. *Lateral files.*
(Courtesy Tab Products Company.)

of operating a filing system is attributable to clerical salaries, fringe benefits, and related expenses. Thus, two of the primary objectives in designing modern filing equipment have been to reduce as much as possible
the physical effort required to file and retrieve data, and to increase the
visibility of stored materials. The conservation of space is another important factor.

A wide variety of specialized filing equipment has been developed
in recent years to meet virtually every filing need. Only a brief review
of the major classes of equipment will be included here.

Types of Files. *Vertical filing cabinets* are the most widely used type of
equipment. In this system materials are filed on edge in a vertical position from front to back. Guides are placed horizontally across the top
of folders. Letter-size and legal-size cabinets are available in single-
drawer to six-drawer models for use in filing correspondence, forms,
catalogues, and other materials. Card cabinets are made in various sizes
to accommodate checks, job tickets, address cards, index cards, punched
cards, and other small items.

Lateral files have become increasingly popular because of several advantages. With this type of file, hanging or standing folders are arranged
on open shelves in a vertical position from left to right, rather than from
front to back (Figure 4–13). This arrangement simplifies access to files,

improves visibility, and reduces significantly the space needed to house the same amount of files in a file room. Furthermore, facing cabinets do not need as wide an aisle.

Visible record files are designed so that cards or other records overlap in shingle fashion. With this arrangement, part of each record containing a name, inventory description, or other index classification is always visible. This makes it possible to locate records quickly for posting or reference purposes.

Visible record files are available in a variety of forms. Most common is the horizontal-tray type, illustrated in Figure 4–14, which forms a sloping writing surface when pulled out of the cabinet. This allows entries to be made on records without removing the cards.

Rotary card files are another type of equipment stressing visibility and quick accessibility. These units consist of a series of shelves containing trays of record cards that are suspended somewhat like the seats on a Ferris wheel. By pushing a button on the control panel of an electrically powered model, a desired tray, or set of trays, can be automatically located and positioned for use in a few seconds. Since the shelves can be revolved vertically in either direction, a selected shelf can reach the operator by the shortest route.

Rotary card files are available in a variety of models. These range from small models approximately 14 inches wide to large models capable of storing up to half a million records in approximately 26 square feet of floor area (Figure 4–15). The degree of automatic control varies with the size and type of equipment.

Rotary shelf files operate in much the same manner as rotary card files. This system of power-driven rotating shelves may be used for any type of materials that can be stored on open shelves. This may include file folders, binders, account ledgers, or electronic data processing tapes. This method has the advantage of concentrating a large volume of records in one area. For example, one model has a capacity of up to 160,000 letter-size documents.

Microfilm. Over 100 years ago it was discovered that original documents could be reproduced on film in greatly reduced size. Since that time

Figure 4-14. *Visible record file.*
(Reprinted with permission by Sperry Remington, A Division of Sperry Rand Corporation.)

Figure 4-15. *Automated records storage and retrieval unit.*

(Reprinted with permission by Sperry Remington, A Division of Sperry Rand Corporation.)

microfilm has been used for various purposes ranging from espionage to the storage of cumbersome engineering blueprints, drawings, and other documents. However, recognition of the full potential of microfilm and its countless applications has occurred only in recent years. It is now seen as a low-cost and efficient means of reproducing, manipulating, storing, retrieving, and disseminating all types of information.

Two developments stimulated the acceptance and widespread use of microfilm. First, the mountains of paper accumulating in offices and factories all over the nation created an awareness that the question was no longer where to store the paper and how to retrieve it. More pertinent was the question of whether it would be practical or economically possible to keep the paper at all. Second, important advances in microfilm technology provided a practical means of coping with the problems inherent with paper—weight, bulk, difficulty of retrieval and transfer, high mailing costs, and shortages.

The rapid growth of microfilm techniques and applications has resulted in the development of a new term, *micrographics.* This term has been partially defined as encompassing the process of producing microfilm images; reproducing the images in larger size and in various forms; the research, development, manufacture, sale, and use of microfilm and related equipment for its reproduction and use; and the use of information in the form of microfilm in combination with computers and/or telecommunications. This definition reflects the transition from a limited concept of microfilm to a much broader range of technology and applications. The use of this new term coincides with the emergence of microfilm as a major industry with vast potential for growth.

Basically, microfilming is the process by which records are photographed at a very high rate of speed and at great reduction in size. About 98 per cent of the space normally required to store records is saved when they are microfilmed. For example, it is estimated that one microfilm storage unit will hold the photographic images of the contents of 160 standard four-drawer file cabinets. Decreasing the need for filing cabinets is very important in view of estimates that business firms pay from $35 to $100 a year, depending upon location, for the rental of space occupied by just one file cabinet.

In addition to saving space, microfilming has the following advantages:

1. The cost of filing equipment needed to store materials is greatly reduced.
2. The cost of labor in maintaining files is also reduced considerably.
3. The cost of mailing or otherwise transporting materials from one location to another is decreased.
4. Retrieval time is greatly reduced.
5. Since microfilmed records occupy so little space, they can be retained indefinitely by the department using them. This eliminates the inconvenience of having to retrieve records from a storage warehouse if they are needed for reference at a later date.
6. Filmed duplicates of important records can be prepared and stored in a separate location for protection against fire or other loss.
7. With certain types of equipment, full-sized paper prints of microfilmed documents can be made easily in less than a minute. (See Figure 4–5.)

The following examples illustrate the value of microfilming not only as a storage technique, but also as a means of reproducing filmed documents for reference purposes.

At the end of each monthly accounting period, banks furnish customers with statements and the canceled checks that have been charged against their accounts. Before returning the checks, however, many banks make microfilm copies of the front and back of each check. This provides a filmed record of each transaction that can be filed and retrieved later if needed. Claims of error can be settled by viewing microfilmed records or, if necessary, by producing a full-sized print of any check in question.

Many department stores follow a similar procedure in handling monthly charge accounts. In this case the problem of filing and retaining the original sales slips prepared by clerks is avoided by microfilming each sales slip. The original copies of sales slips can then be mailed to customers along with their monthly statements. This enables the customers to check the original slips against their statements. Again, if any question about the accuracy of an account arises, transaction records can be viewed or prints of sales slips can be prepared on a microfilm reader-printer.

A basic microfilm system consists of a camera, a storage unit, and a reader for projecting images. Two types of cameras are used in microfilming: the *rotary* and the *planetary*. Rotary cameras are designed primarily for office use in recording transaction documents and business records. They are similar to office copying machines in appearance and methods of operation. Documents to be photographed are fed into a slot, either manually or automatically. They are conveyed through the machine on a revolving belt and are photographed as they pass an aperture. Documents leave the machine on the same side they entered and are stacked in a tray. Pictures are usually taken on rotary cameras with 16-millimeter or 35-millimeter film similar to that used in motion-picture cameras.

Planetary cameras are designed for filming engineering drawings, blueprints, maps, and open books. In this system a camera is mounted on a post so that it can be raised or lowered. The camera faces down on a lighted table where the material to be photographed is placed. Most planetary cameras use 35-millimeter or 70-millimeter film.

Microfilmed data is usually stored in the same form in which it was originally exposed: in long strips mounted on reels, cartridges, or cassettes. However, the unit record concept of data processing has resulted in the increased use of cut, rather than roll film. In this approach, individual pictures called frames are clipped from the roll and mounted on specially designed cards. One type of card, the *aperture card,* contains a rectangular die-cut opening designed specifically for mounting a film image (Figure 4–16). It is possible to obtain special camera-processors that photograph documents up to 18 by 24 inches and automatically produce developed films mounted on an aperture card in less than a minute. Information identifying the images can be key punched and interpreted on the cards, which can be reproduced, sorted, and collated on punched card equipment. Aperture cards are used for the storage

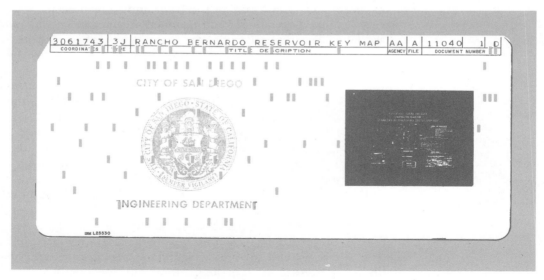

Figure 4-16. *Aperture card.*

and retrieval of a wide range of filmed documents including business records, library materials, and engineering drawings.

Groups of closely related documents, such as pages of a report or book, may also be filmed on a single sheet of microfilm called *microfiche*. (*Fiche* is an adapted French word meaning "card.") A microfiche can be any size, but is usually a standard 3 by 5, 4 by 6, or 5 by 8 inches, or the standard punched card size, 3¼ by 7⅜ inches. The number of images varies with the size of the card. For example, a 4-by-6-inch card holds 98 images, and a standard punched card size holds up to 90 images. The microfiche form generally has a legible heading (Figure 4–17).

Ultrafiche is an extension of microfiche. By reducing original material over 90 times, ultrafiche is able to pack more images in an inch than any other type of microfilm media. This level of reduction allows up to 1,000 pages to be contained in an area of 3 by 5 inches. Popular forms of ultrafiche include cards of 3 by 5 or 4 by 6 inches.

Since microfilm cannot be read with the naked eye, it must be magnified in some way. Special readers are available to project and reproduce the various types of microfilm. The unit illustrated in Figure 4–18 is designed to project two microfiche images side by side on the screen, permitting reference to related documents such as a parts list with a design drawing. To select and project a microfiche image on this model, a pointer is guided by fingertip control to the appropriate reference number on a gridded index card. A slight movement of the pointer in any direction from one index frame to another instantly brings a new image into view. Machines called *reader-printers* not only project an image on the screen but also produce a full-sized paper print of the projected document when a button is pressed (see Figure 4–5).

In spite of the advantages of microfilm in records storage, the most rapid advancement in the use of this technique is in the field of *informa-*

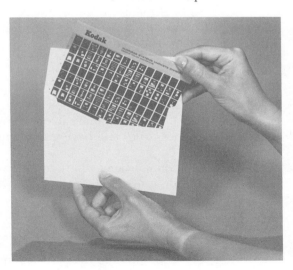

Figure 4-17. *Microfiche card.*
(Courtesy Eastman Kodak Company.)

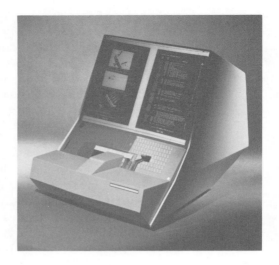

Figure 4-18. *Microfiche reader.*
(Courtesy Eastman Kodak Company.)

tion retrieval. Retrieval of microfilmed information may be accomplished in several ways. Microfiche forms are usually stored in card files from which they can be easily retrieved manually, although the index information is often stored in a computer. If aperture cards are used, they also may be manually indexed, coded, filed, and retrieved like cards in any other card file. However, in large installations, identifying data may be punched into the cards by a card punch machine. Cards can then be arranged and retrieved by a punched card sorter.

A number of highly sophisticated systems combining microfilming with electronic equipment have been developed in recent years. They are designed to accommodate a large volume of microfilmed documents, perhaps in the millions. These systems vary in concept, but in general they provide for automatic retrieval of specified microfilms, projection of the documents, and printing of reproductions—all in less than a minute.

LIMITATIONS OF MANUAL AND MECHANICAL DEVICES

In spite of the importance of manual and mechanical methods and devices and the remarkable improvements that have increased their usefulness, they still have shortnomings. Some of these are:

1. Human beings participate to some extent in most of the operations of recording, copying, classifying, sorting, calculating, and summarizing, which creates the possibility of error at each point in the cycle.
2. The limited communication that exists between many manual and mechanical devices prevents the smooth flow of data from one operation to the next. Again, human intervention in transcribing or otherwise handling data creates the risk of error.

3. The transfer of data from one location or step to another is sometimes cumbersome and time-consuming and can result in misplacement of data.
4. Although manual and mechanical devices and methods have made impressive gains in speed and efficiency, they still fail to meet the demands of large organizations for the rapid processing of vast amounts of data.

The limitations outlined above have been overcome to a great extent by electronic data processing systems, to which the remainder of this book will be devoted.

IMPORTANT WORDS AND PHRASES

unit sets	spirit process	point-of-service terminal
continuous forms	offset process	lateral file
carbonless paper	copying	visible record file
accounting board	electrostatic copying	rotary file
document control register	reverse-digit sorting	microfilm
automatic typewriter	block sorting	micrographics
word processing	edge-notched card	aperture card
duplicating	electronic calculator	microfiche
stencil process	programmable calculator	ultrafiche

REVIEW QUESTIONS

1. What are the advantages of printed forms?
2. Describe the manner in which the accounting board makes it possible to record the various steps in a transaction simultaneously.
3. In what ways do document control registers improve manual operations?
4. What are the three ways in which most automatic typewriters are controlled?
5. Describe the technique of preparing sales orders with an automatic typewriter.
6. Explain the difference between the duplicating and copying methods of reproducing.
7. What are the three principal methods of duplicating? Describe the unique characteristic of each.
8. Identify and describe the principal copying process in use today.
9. Describe the process of combining the use of copying and duplicating machines to produce multiple exact copies of documents.
10. Describe the process of reverse-digit sorting.
11. What is the purpose of block sorting? How is it accomplished?
12. Describe the pattern of notched holes used to represent each digit from 1 to 9 on an edge-notched card.
13. How many sorts would be necessary to place in sequence a group of edge-notched cards with code numbers ranging from 1 to 99?
14. Identify the three major types of electronic calculators and describe the main characteristics of each.
15. Name and describe the three functional groups of electronic calculators.

16. Describe a typical application of a point-of-service terminal.
17. What are the advantages of lateral files? How do they differ from vertical filing cabinets?
18. Describe the operation of rotary card files and rotary shelf files.
19. What are the advantages of microfilming?
20. What are the nature and function of an aperture card?
21. Describe a microfiche card.
22. What are the limitations of manual and mechanical methods and devices?

5

RECORDING DATA FOR COMPUTER PROCESSING

The ideal method of collecting data for processing in an automated system is to record it in a machine-sensible code at its point of origin. A machine-sensible code is a symbolic method of representing data in a medium such as punched tape, punched cards, or magnetic ink that can be sensed mechanically or electronically, as a means of entering and transferring the data automatically from one step to another in the data processing sequence.

Jean Emile Baudot took the first step toward the automation of source data when he built a paper tape punch and reader in the 1870s. Baudot, a French telegrapher, found that his messages were increasing faster than he could send them. In place of the telegraph key, he designed a keyboard similar to that of the typewriter. But, instead of typing on paper, his invention sent Morse code signals out over the wire. It was much faster and much easier to operate, but as the volume increased, the wire, the single link between remote points, was unable to handle the traffic. Baudot then devised an attachment to his keyboard for storing Morse code signals in punched paper tape that could then be used to transmit the messages as the line became available.

In punched code the letter *E,* a single dot in Morse code, became a single hole in the first row or channel of a five-channel punched paper tape. Other letters of the alphabet were represented by various combinations of holes in the five channels. This basic procedure, developed nearly one hundred years ago, is still used in Teletype and telegraph systems throughout the world.

Except for the use of punched cards, the development of techniques for automating source data progressed very slowly. The first accounting machine synchronized with a paper tape punch was developed in 1935. The first paper tape typewriter was introduced in the 1940s for use in automatic letter writing. A major advancement was made in the early 1950s, when the concept of integrated data processing was introduced. The term *integrated data processing* was first used to describe systems involving paperwork that was mechanized from origination to completion. The large-scale application of IDP was pioneered by the United States Steel Corporation and was first demonstrated at a special conference of the American Management Association in February 1954. Five-channel punched tape was the machine-sensible code used in that system.

Originally, IDP involved the preparation of a machine-sensible code medium, generally punched paper tape, as part of a manual recording operation. However, developments in source data automation such as optical character recognition and magnetic ink character recognition broadened the scope of applications. In addition, translating devices such as tape-to-card converters extended the range of machines that could be included in performing a continuous series of data processing operations. To illustrate, let us assume that data has been punched into paper tape as a by-product of a recording operation performed on a typewriter with a tape-punching mechanism. This data could be transmitted to another city by a tape-transmitting device. The tape produced by the receiving unit could be converted to punched cards for input to a computer. The processed information could be printed in characters that can be read by an optical character recognition (OCR) device. OCR devices can convert data into other forms including punched tape, the original recording medium of the data in this example.

This is merely one example of how data may be transferred among a variety of machines by the use of a common medium or by conversion from one medium to another. Later in this chapter we shall see additional samples of this technique.

The concept of integrated data processing became increasingly significant and resulted in two basic objectives that now dominate the field of data processing:

1. Recording data at its point of origin in a machine-sensible code
2. Completing all processing on machines capable of reading the original code or a code to which it can be converted automatically

These procedures are such a routine part of today's automatic data processing that they no longer require special identification. Thus, the descriptive term "integrated data processing" has become almost historical. However, the term "source data automation" is often used to describe the principle of recording information in a communicable medium at the point of origin.

When Jean Emile Baudot conceived the idea of a machine-sensible code, there was only one mode of recording data, the deliberate creation of punched paper tape by manually depressing the keys of a punching device. Now, as a result of today's varied equipment, three major modes are available for recording selected data in the languages of machines. Data may be recorded by deliberate action, as a by-product of another function, or by conversion from one medium to another. Some of the most commonly used codes, media, and machines used to record data are discussed and illustrated in the following sections.

PUNCHED CARDS

Since the 1890s the punched card has been the primary means of recording data for entry into data processing equipment. Recent years have seen the development of other media including magnetic tape, magnetic cards, and optical character recognition. These new techniques are challenging the punched card concept, but as yet they have failed to diminish substantially the popularity of punched cards, evidenced by the estimated 500,000 card punch machines now being used.

It is significant, however, that punched cards are now used primarily as turn-around documents and as a medium for entering data for processing by computer systems rather than by punched card machines. With the advent of low-cost computers even small organizations are finding it economically feasible to use small computers, and punched cards have proved to be an economical and effective data entry method for such systems. It is anticipated that in the next few years punched cards will be replaced to a great extent by other data entry techniques. In the meantime, they are still an important means of data entry.

Card Structure, Material, and Codes

The punched card is familiar to almost everyone because of the frequency with which it appears in such forms as payroll checks, insurance premium notices, utility bills, magazine subscription notices, money orders, and cashiers' checks.

Standard cards measure 7⅜ inches by 3¼ inches and are cut from durable card stock to provide strength and long life. Cards must meet rigorous specifications in dimension and quality to assure accuracy of

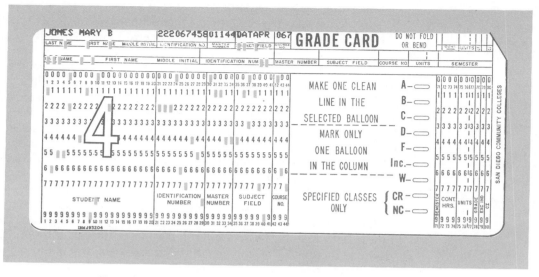

Figure 5-1. *Eighty-column card printed to assist in reading data.*

results and the proper functioning of machines. To facilitate card handling and machine processing, cards can now be obtained with round corners.

Cards are often ruled and printed with column headings to assist in reading the information that is recorded by card punch machines (Figure 5–1). To aid in identification, cards are available in a number of solid colors or with special stripes. Cut corners at the upper right or upper left provide another visual aid in detecting cards that may be backward or upside-down in the deck. Corner cuts also provide a means of visually distinguishing two classes of data. For example, accounts receivable transactions might be recorded on cards with left-corner cuts and accounts payable transactions on cards with right-corner cuts.

All of the physical characteristics just mentioned are recognizable by humans and are designed for that purpose. With one exception, they are not detectable by machines and have no influence on the machine processing of cards. The exception consists of a special device that can be installed on certain machines to mechanically recognize corner cuts.

Eighty-Column Card. The standard punched card is divided into 80 vertical areas called card columns (Figure 5–2). These are numbered 1 to 80 from the left side of the card to the right. Each column is then divided into 12 punching positions called rows, which are designated from the top to the bottom of the card. Each column of the card is used to accommodate a digit, a letter, or a special character.

Digits are recorded by holes punched in the appropriate positions of the card from 0 to 9. The top three punching positions of the card

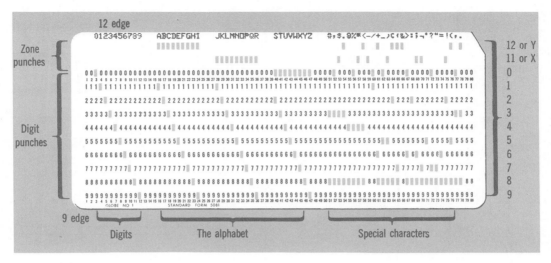

Figure 5-2. *Eighty-column card showing punching combinations for digits, letters, and special characters.*

(12, 11, and 0) are called the *zone* punching positions. (The 0 punch may be either a zone or a digit punch.) In order to accommodate any of the 26 letters of the alphabet in one column, a combination of a zone and a digit punch is used. The various combinations of punches that represent the alphabet follow a simple pattern. The first nine letters of the alphabet, *A* to *I,* are coded by the combination of a 12 zone punch and one of the digit punches from 1 to 9. Letters *J* through *R* are coded by an 11 zone punch and one of the digit punches 1 to 9. *S* through *Z* are coded by a 0 zone punch and one of the digit punches 2 to 9. The 11 special characters are recorded by one, two, or three punches in a column (Figure 5–3).

Codes. A *code* is a system of writing in which numbers or letters, or a combination of both, are used arbitrarily to condense lengthy data into a smaller space. This technique is a necessity in recording data on punched cards because of the maximum capacity of 80 columns. In addition, codes provide a convenient means of identifying and distinguishing data for classification purposes.

Although many coding techniques are used, most codes are constructed by using numerals to represent original data. The use of numerals in place of state names is a clear example of the advantage of using codes. Fourteen columns would be required to record the longest state name. Five columns would be necessary even if abbreviations were used. However, by numbering the states alphabetically from 1 to 50, only two columns would be required, leaving three to twelve additional columns available for other data.

Table of Hollerith Codes

Letters	Punches	
	Zone	Numeric
A	12	1
B	12	2
C	12	3
D	12	4
E	12	5
F	12	6
G	12	7
H	12	8
I	12	9
J	11	1
K	11	2
L	11	3
M	11	4
N	11	5
O	11	6
P	11	7
Q	11	8
R	11	9
S	0	2
T	0	3
U	0	4
V	0	5
W	0	6
X	0	7
Y	0	8
Z	0	9

Numbers	Punches	
	Zone	Numeric
0	—	0
1	—	1
2	—	2
3	—	3
4	—	4
5	—	5
6	—	6
7	—	7
8	—	8
9	—	9

Common Special Characters	Zone	Numeric
&	12	—
-	11	—
'	0	8-3
.	12	8-3
@	—	8-4
%	0	8-4

(For a complete card code for all Special Characters refer to Figure 5-2.)

Figure 5-3. *Hollerith code combinations for letters, numbers, and certain most-used special characters.*

The use of codes to express many classifications of data not only saves space, but also increases efficiency by reducing the number of card columns to be processed for certain items of data.

Card Design. Cards are divided into segments called *fields*. Each field consists of one or more consecutive columns reserved for punching a specific type of data. The length of a field is determined by the maximum length of the particular type of data to be recorded in it. For example, in a field designed to accommodate prices, a five-digit field would be planned if it were known that no price would exceed $999.99. (Dollar signs, commas, and decimals are not punched in the card.) To permit the recording of prices from $1,000.00 to $9,999.99, a six-digit field would be required.

Figure 5–1 illustrates a card that contains both alphabetic and numeric data punched in fields of various sizes.

Because the amount of data that can be entered on a single card is limited, it is essential to select the most important data to be included. The data to be recorded on a card will, of course, be largely dependent on the requirements of the reports and documents that will be prepared from it. Although the specific nature of data varies greatly, it will generally be of three types.

Type	Examples
Reference data	Invoice number, page number, identification number, or date, which indicates the original source of the data and its relationship to other data
Classification data	Occupation, organizational department, or geographic area, which permits the grouping and summarizing of comparable data
Quantitative data	Price, hours, quantity, or weight, to be used in performing calculations

The arrangement of data is not invariable, but it is considered desirable to place reference data on the left side of the card, classification data in the center, and quantitative data on the right. Other design considerations include such factors as the following:

1. The number of columns needed for each item of information should be determined.
2. The fields of the card should be arranged so that data can be punched into the card in the order in which it is read from the source document. Data would normally be read from left to right or from top to bottom on the original document.

Card Punching

The most commonly used method of converting source data into punched cards is by the use of a manually operated machine called a *card punch,* also referred to as a *key punch.* The operator of this machine reads a source document and transcribes the information into punched holes by depressing keys on a keyboard. The machine feeds, positions, and ejects cards automatically, thus enabling the operator to concentrate on depressing the proper keys in the correct sequence (Figure 5–4).

Card punch equipment is marketed by a number of manufacturers. One of the most widely used models is the IBM 29 Card Punch, described in the Appendix. The latest IBM card punch is the 129 Card Data Recorder, shown in Figure 5–5. It can be obtained in three different models. Model 1 will punch and verify cards; Model 2 will punch and print; and Model 3 will punch, print, and verify. Machines with the printing feature

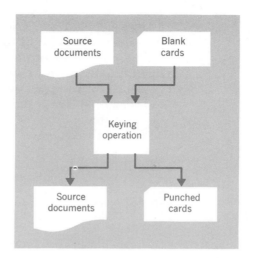

Figure 5-4. *Flowchart of card punch operation.*

Figure 5-5. *IBM 129 Card Data Recorder.*

(Courtesy International Business Machines Corporation.)

allow the data punched in the card to be printed on the face of the card immediately above the 12 zone row.

The 129 Card Data Recorder contains an electronic buffer storage area where data entered through the keyboard is first stored. If the data has been correctly recorded, the buffer storage area releases the data to the punching mechanism, where it is punched into a card. This technique permits an overlap of operations, as one card can be punched while a second card is being keyed into buffer storage. The use of buffer storage also provides the operator with an opportunity to correct self-caught errors before the card is actually punched.

The Card Data Recorder can also be used to verify the original punching of cards. In the verifying operation the image of the original card is first read and stored in buffer storage. An operator re-keys the data from the same source document used in originally punching the card. The re-keyed data is compared with the image in buffer storage, and if it agrees, the original correct card is released. If the original card was punched incorrectly, the operator can correct the error by correcting the image in buffer storage and causing a new card to be punched.

The UNIVAC 1710 Verifying Interpreting Punch (see Figure 1–3) is designed to punch data into standard 80-column cards using a buffer principle similar to that described in the preceding discussion. All key punching is initiated in the normal manner. However, instead of each keystroke causing the card to be punched, data is entered into core storage. When all information for the card is in storage, the punching operation takes place automatically, as information for the next card is being entered.

Other punches such as the one shown in Figure 5–6 are small enough for convenient location on-site where transactions occur. This data collection terminal can receive and organize information from punched cards, embossed cards, plastic identification badges, scales, and clocks as well as from its own keyboard. Depressing the punch button causes the compiled data to be punched into a standard-size 80-column card

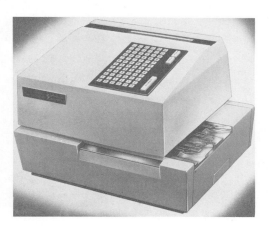

Figure 5-6. *Source record punch.*
(Courtesy Standard Register Company.)

or into a multicopy card form with interleaved carbon paper. This same operation also causes the numeric information to be printed in figures across the top of the card or form.

A detailed discussion of the IBM 29 Card Punch as well as other machines in the punched card series is presented in the Appendix.

PUNCHED TAPE

Codes

Data is recorded in paper tape by a special arrangement of punched holes along the length of the tape. Since paper tape is a continuous recording medium, as compared to punched cards, which are fixed in length, it can be used to record data in records of any length. The only limitation is that of the storage medium from which the data is received or the storage medium into which the data is to be placed.

Tapes using five, six, seven, and eight channels are available. However, only the five-, seven-, and eight-channel codes will be described here since they are the most commonly used.

Five-Channel Code. Data is recorded (punched) in five parallel channels along the length of the tape. Each row of punches across the width of the tape represents one letter, digit, or symbol. Since the five punching positions allow only 32 possible combinations of punches, a shift system is used to double the number of available codes. A *letters* code punch at the start of a section of tape indicates to the printing or conversion device that the following characters are alphabetic. When the *figures* code punch appears, the following punches are interpreted as numeric or special characters.

Figure 5–7 illustrates the manner in which characters are interpreted depending upon the shift code preceding them. The function characters—

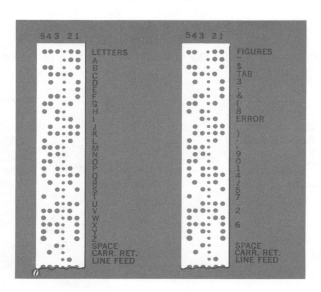

Figure 5-7. *Punched tape showing five-channel code.*

space, carriage return, and line feed—are the same in both shifts. The actual function of the carriage return and line feed characters depends upon the machine with which they are used.

Seven-Channel Code. The American Standard Code for Information Interchange (ASCII) is a seven-channel code in which the channel positions are numbered from right to left as follows:

7	6	5	4	3	2	1

Zone portion   Digit portion

The character representations of the seven channels are shown in Figure 5–8. In this illustration a "1" represents a punch and a "0" represents the absence of a punch. The eight-channel version of the ASCII code that is most commonly used in data collection and transmission systems utilizes the eighth channel as a parity check channel.

The parity check channel (CH) performs a technical function. As a means of checking accuracy each column of the tape is punched with an odd number of holes. Since some characters are expressed by an even number of punches, it is necessary to add a check punch to produce an odd number of holes. Many tape-handling devices count the number of punched holes. If the number of punches in any column does not add to an odd figure, an error in transmission is indicated. This type of checking is known as *parity checking*.

Eight-Channel Code. Data in this code is recorded (punched) in eight parallel channels along the length of the tape. As illustrated in Figure 5–9 eight channels are used as follows, reading from left to right:

Channel	Function
EL	End of line (carriage return)
X	For alphabetic characters
O	For alphabetic characters
CH	For parity check
8	Numeric channel
4	Numeric channel
2	Numeric channel
1	Numeric channel

A punch in the end-of-line (EL) channel marks the end of a record on the tape. On a typewriter equipped with a tape-sensing mechanism, a punch in the end-of-line channel causes the carriage to return.

Character	ASCII	
0	011	0000
1	011	0001
2	011	0010
3	011	0011
4	011	0100
5	011	0101
6	011	0110
7	011	0111
8	011	1000
9	011	1001
A	100	0001
B	100	0010
C	100	0011
D	100	0100
E	100	0101
F	100	0110
G	100	0111
H	100	1000
I	100	1001
J	100	1010
K	100	1011
L	100	1100
M	100	1101
N	100	1110
O	100	1111
P	101	0000
Q	101	0001
R	101	0010
S	101	0011
T	101	0100
U	101	0101
V	101	0110
W	101	0111
X	101	1000
Y	101	1001
Z	101	1010

Figure 5-8. *Character representation of the seven-channel ASCII.*

The X and O channels serve the same purpose as the zone punches in 80-column punched cards. These channels are used in combination with the numeric channels to record alphabetic and special characters.

The four channels on the right of the tape, excluding the small feed holes between the 8 and 4 channels, are the numeric channels. When used alone these channels represent digits. The numeric values of 1, 2, 4, and 8 can be expressed by a single punch. Other values are expressed by a combination of punches. For example, 3 is represented by holes

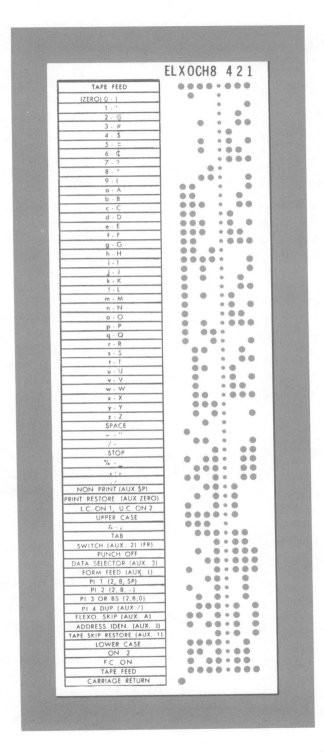

Figure 5-9. *Punched tape showing eight-channel code.*

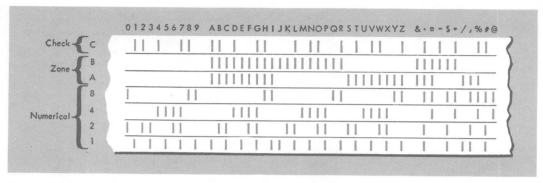

Figure 5-10. *Representation of magnetic tape showing standard binary coded decimal interchange code.*

punched in the 2 and 1 channels; 7 is represented by holes punched in the 4, 2, and 1 channels, and so on.

The CH channel is used for parity checking as described above.

Tape-Punching Devices

Automatic Typewriters. The automatic typewriter can produce an original document and at the same time punch five-, six-, seven-, or eight-channel paper tape as an automatic by-product. Tape may be punched with all of the typewritten data or with selected items only. Tape can be coded to automatically control card punching, address plate embossing, communications machines, or electronic data processing machines. When placed on the reading mechanism of the typewriter, punched tape can be used to control the operation of the typewriter itself.

Teletype Machines. Punched tape may also be prepared on Teletype machines. On most models, punching of the tape is accompanied by simultaneous production of a ribbon (hard) copy of the data on plain paper or printed forms.

MAGNETIC TAPE

Codes

Magnetic tape looks very much like the tape used in home or office tape recorders except that it is normally ½-inch wide and is manufactured to higher specifications. It is made of acetate or mylar coated with magnetizable material. Data is recorded in the form of magnetized spots or *bits* that create electrical impulses. Data recorded in this manner can be retained indefinitely.

Although it is impossible to see the magnetized spots that are recorded on magnetic tape, Figure 5–10 shows the arrangement in which the codes would appear if they were visible. Data is usually recorded in seven or nine parallel channels or tracks along the length of the tape depending on the code that is being used. Each channel can record from 100 to more than 6,000 bits an inch. Each character is represented by the presence or absence of bits in the channel positions of one column across the width of the tape.

As a means of verifying accuracy, each character may be checked for even or odd parity. Parity checking is a built-in self-checking feature utilized in most magnetic tape-coding methods. As in the case of paper tape coding, this consists of a channel in which a redundant bit is added whenever necessary to create either an odd or even parity for the character or digit represented. In some codes, each digit or character is represented by an even number of bits. Although different characters are made up of different combinations of bits, the number of bits in any valid character is always even. Thus, a character with an odd number of bits would be detected as an error. Similarly, a code may be used in which all characters must have an odd number of bits. In this case an even number of bits would indicate an error. Codes that use an odd number of bits are said to have an *odd parity*. Codes that use an even number of bits are said to have an *even parity*.

In contrast to the continuous recording of sound on tape, data is recorded as separate record units or groups of records. A record may consist of any number of characters, fields, or words. Records are separated from each other by a short segment of blank tape ⁶⁄₁₀ or ¾ inch in length for the majority of units. This blank tape is called an *inter-record gap* (Figure 5–11). During writing, a gap is automatically produced at the end of each record. During reading, the record begins with the first character sensed at the end of a gap and continues without interruption until the next gap is reached. Gaps allow the magnetic tape to stop between records and to attain proper speed before reading or writing is resumed. To save space a group of related records may be combined into a *multiple-record block*. Each of these blocks is also separated by an inter-record gap. The larger a block of records is, the more efficient the tape storage and data transfer rate will be.

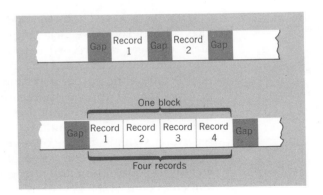

Figure 5-11. *Representation of single records and multiple-record blocks recorded on magnetic tape.*

Figure 5-12. *Magnetic tape recording device. (Reprinted with permission from Honeywell, Incorporated.)*

Data Recorders

In the past, data was generally transferred to tape from some other medium by means of a conversion device. However, by using special tape recording devices it is now possible for data to be recorded directly in a medium that has an input speed more nearly compatible with computer capabilities. For example, the unit illustrated in Figure 5–12 permits an operator to record data onto seven- or nine-channel, ½-inch magnetic tape via a keyboard. This model may also be used to verify data previously recorded on tape and to search a prerecorded tape for records specified by the operator.

Data that is keyed in by the operator is first entered into a storage device. This delay between keying and recording allows the operator to make changes in a record before it is actually written on tape. However, after data is recorded on tape, it may be easily changed by positioning the tape at the proper point and keying in new data that automatically replaces the data previously recorded.

In addition to stand-alone key-to-tape systems such as the one illustrated in Figure 5–12, multi-terminal key-to-tape and key-to-disk data recording systems may be obtained. For example, the system shown in Figure 5–13 may be composed of from one to 16 data entry units and includes a control unit and a printing device. Each operator in this system enters data via a keyboard, a record at a time. As each character of the record is entered, it is simultaneously displayed on a cathode ray

Figure 5-13. *Key-Disk/Key-Tape Data Entry System.*
(Courtesy GTE Information Systems, Inc.)

tube (CRT) screen. This permits immediate verification of each character or the entire record.

All data entered into the system is temporarily stored on an internal disk storage device, where it remains while the data is verified or otherwise manipulated. Entire batches of data in storage can be accessed and verified at one time. Characters or records of data can be selectively deleted, corrected, or inserted as the need arises.

The control unit, which is actually a minicomputer, provides coordination and control over the data entry stations. In exercising this control it permits various jobs to be entered and verified in any order. It also performs the functions of arranging, combining, and formatting of data fields and records.

After the data records have been verified and formatted, they are transferred from the temporary disk storage device to a removable magnetic tape storage device for use as high-speed input to the computer system. The recording system control unit may also be used in a telecommunication application to control the transmission of data to another location.

MAGNETIC DISKETTE

Medium

A magnetic diskette is a plastic disk that measures about 8 inches in diameter and weighs less than 2 ounces. Data is stored as magnetized spots in concentric tracks on the face of the diskette. The diskette, sometimes called a *floppy disk,* is reusable and can easily be corrected or updated. Each diskette can usually hold an entire day's output from a typical data entry station. The size, capacity, and portability of the diskette make it a convenient medium for recording and storing data that can then be transferred for processing at another location.

Data Stations

Data stations are independent units designed for the purpose of recording data at sites that are remote from the central computer system (Figure 5–14). Data is entered by an operator on a 64-character keyboard similar to the card punch keyboard that can record letters, numbers, and special characters. The numeric section of the keyboard is also available in a 10-key adding machine arrangement.

As the data is recorded through the keyboard, it is recorded on a single magnetic diskette sealed in a plastic jacket. Each recording station has a cathode ray tube (CRT) display station. This display station is directly behind the keyboard in the operator's line of sight and displays the data being entered on the diskette. Once data has been recorded on the diskette, it can be easily transported and used as direct input into the centralized computer system.

PUNCHED TAGS

Another use of punched holes to automate source data is in the price-inventory tag attached to many items in modern department stores. The

Figure 5-14. *IBM 3741 Data Station.*
(Courtesy International Business Machines Corporation.)

tag may be a single part or may consist of two or more detachable stubs. The tag generally contains a limited amount of printed information and encoded inventory data identifying the article to which the tag is attached. The encoded data required by the user for automated inventory record keeping usually includes merchandise number, vendor, style, color, size, and price (Figure 5–15).

As merchandise is sold or returned, the tags are removed by sales personnel and sent to the data processing center. Readers are available for on-line computer input of tags, but usually tags are converted to a more quickly readable computer input medium, such as magnetic tape, before processing. The computer can then produce inventory reports based on the tag-encoded transaction data and other data influencing inventory levels.

Although print-punch tags have been used primarily in the transaction-oriented merchandising industry, applications are not limited to this field. They have also been used effectively for such purposes as industrial inventory control, manufacturing records, production control, material inspection, and piecework payroll computations.

The code structure used in tags is similar to the five-channel code structure used in punched paper tape. A combination of small holes in a vertical line represents a single digit of data. Punching is numeric only.

It is possible to create holes in tags by setting the dials of a print-punch recorder (Figure 5–16). Once the dials are set, many tags containing

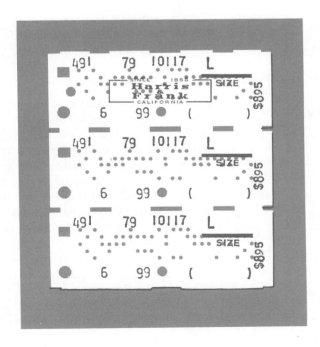

Figure 5-15. *Three-section price ticket.*
(Courtesy Harris & Frank Company.)

Figure 5-16. *Hopper-fed print-punch machine.*

the same data may be made automatically at the rate of 200 stubs a minute without resetting the dials.

In addition to the use of punched holes to encode tags, newer types of machine-readable tags utilizing magnetic coding are now available for point-of-sale data collection.

OPTICAL CHARACTERS

An increasingly important method of recording for machine processing and transmission is the one that uses optical characters. Alphabetic as well as numeric data printed with specially designed type and hand-printed characters may be read by optical character recognition (OCR) devices through a scanning process.

Type style generally plays an important role in optical character recognition. This is especially true in transferring data to sales documents from embossed credit cards such as the one shown in Figure 5–17. The embossed numbers on cards of this type are usually stylized to improve the print quality and facilitate machine recognition. For example, properly stylizing the numeral 6 prevents it from being read by a machine as the numeral 8 because of carbon or a poor impression. Some of the stylized type fonts are specifically designed for a particular method of machine reading. However, for other methods of reading, a stylized typeface may be helpful but not essential.

Figure 5-17. *Embossed plastic plate used for credit or identification purposes.*
(Courtesy Standard Oil Company of California.)

Figure 5-18. *OCR type style prepared on an IBM "Selectric" typewriter.*
(Courtesy International Business Machines Corporation.)

Optical characters are created by a variety of devices that print or type with a specially stylized typeface. For example, the type style shown in Figure 5–18, which meets the specifications of the American National Standards Institute, is available on a special element designed for use with the IBM "Selectric" typewriter. Other typewriters can also be obtained with optically readable type styles.

Optical characters can be transferred from embossed credit cards to sales transaction documents using a device such as the one shown in Figure 5–19. Embossed cards and sales documents in the form of 51- or 80-column punched card unit sets can be easily inserted into the machine illustrated. By operating a simple lever or stamping mechanism, the identifying data on the card is imprinted on the original sales form and also on the carbon copies. Variable numeric data such as the amount of sale or number of units may be recorded simultaneously on devices such as the one illustrated by setting keys.

Optical character readers eliminate the slow and costly process of manually key punching vast amounts of data from source documents in order to convert it into machine-sensible form. Depending on the model, the output of devices that read optical characters may include printed reports, magnetic tape, paper tape, or punched cards. Optical scanners may also enter data directly into a computer for immediate processing.

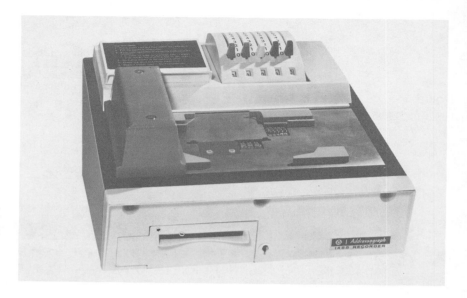

Figure 5-19. *Data recorder used to imprint cards with both human-and machine-sensible characters.*
(Courtesy Addressograph Multigraph Corporation.)

MAGNETIC INK CHARACTERS

Magnetic ink character recognition, familiarly called MICR, is a machine-sensible code adopted by the American Bankers Association as a national standard for use by banks throughout the country. This code consists of numerals and symbols imprinted by machine in a distinctive type style and with magnetic ink containing particles of iron oxide. The MICR code consists of ten digits, 0 through 9, and four special symbols. The numerals are readable by humans.

The documents on which MICR is used, primarily checks and deposit slips, may be paper or cards of various sizes. However, to make MICR a universal code, it was necessary to define a standard format for magnetic printing. The bottom ⅝ inch of a check is reserved for encoding in MICR. A space of 6 inches, measuring from the right edge of the check, is specified as the universal printing area. Specific areas within the universal 6-inch area are designated to contain certain types of data common to all banking operations (Figure 5-20).

All data except the amount can be printed before the bank issues a supply of checks to the user. Printing may be accomplished with standard duplicating or printing equipment using special iron-oxide bearing ink. Special key-operated devices are available to manually record amounts or other identifying data on checks. This data is encoded by the first bank receiving the check for processing.

The particles of iron oxide in the MICR ink are detected by reading heads in magnetic scanning equipment. Scanned data may be entered directly into a computer, or the data may be recorded on punched cards, paper tape, or magnetic tape, which can then be used as input to the computer.

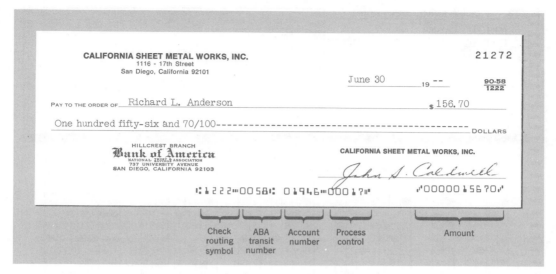

Figure 5-20. *Check with characters inscribed in magentic ink.*

OPTICAL MARK RECOGNITION

Optical mark recognition (OMR) is the process in which a machine senses the presence or absence of marks recorded on predesigned response sheets (Figure 5–21). Responses are indicated by blacking in circles or other designated areas that are read by an optical mark sense reader.

Response sheets can be custom designed to provide data collection and storage for a wide range of applications such as test scoring, class attendance reporting, student registration, inventory control, and payroll changes. Responses can be recorded on both sides of a response sheet and can be read by optical mark reader systems at the rate of 7,000 sheets an hour (Figure 5–22). The data collected and recorded by the scanner is transferred to magnetic tape for later input to the computer system.

A complete mark sense reading system consists of an OMR scanner, a scanner controller unit with an 8,000-word memory (minicomputer), a teletypewriter for interacting with the system, a cassette drive unit for programming, and an output tape unit.

BAR CODES

Bar codes were originally adopted for identification and data entry by the Association of American Railroads in 1967. The system permits the reading of codes identifying the owner and serial number of each freight car as it passes a light ray scanner at speeds up to 80 miles an hour. The bar code with its accompanying reader and/or remote scanning equipment is now being adapted to a large variety of other data entry applications.

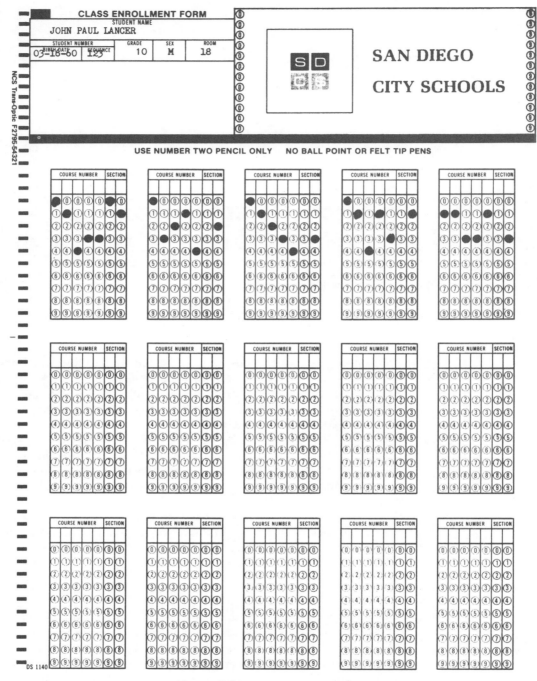

Figure 5-21. *Optical mark-sensé card.*

Figure 5-22. *Optical mark reader system.*
(Courtesy National Computer Systems, Inc.)

Figure 5-23. *Bar code.*

The most familiar use is in large food chain outlets for identification and pricing of grocery items. The code, called the Universal Product Code (UPC), consists of a block of lines that vary in width (Figure 5–23). The lines in the code represent ten numbers. The first five digits identify the producer, and the next five digits identify his product. As each grocery item is passed by the bar code scanner at the checker station, the identification code of the item is read into a computer. The computer determines the current price of the item and prepares a listing of the purchases showing the item number, item description, and price. Upon signal from the checker, the computer will add the necessary sales tax and print the total cost of all items purchased.

Bar codes and scanners for data entry are being adapted to such applications as inventory control, hospital patient records and X-ray identification, manufacturing assembly line operations, U.S. mail truck and mail bag identification and routing, and library circulation control (Figure

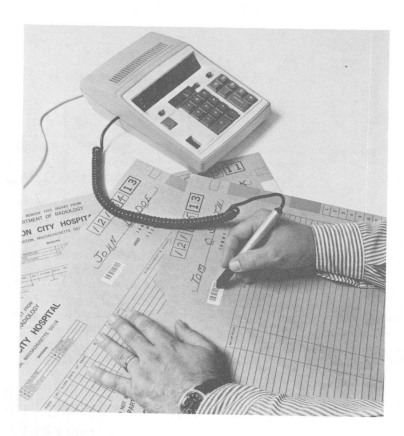

Figure 5-24. *Ames Guiding Light Systems Pen Terminal.*

(Courtesy Ames, Medical Record Systems Division.)

5–24). Bar codes can be adapted to any data entry application that requires the identification of a person, part, or item suitable for reading by a stationary or portable light ray scanner.

DATA CONVERSION

Every machine used in automatic data processing operates on a particular code. In a large system with a variety of equipment, several codes are likely to be found in use, each related to a group of machines or a specific type of machine employed in the processing cycle. Thus, the code medium in which source data is originally recorded might not be acceptable to all machines in the system. Instead it would be necessary to convert the data from one medium to another to facilitate the flow of data through the system. This might occur once or perhaps several times.

The fact that the data was recorded originally in a machine-sensible form makes it possible to convert the data automatically. For example, credit card data recorded in optical characters by the data recorder shown in Figure 5–19 can be automatically converted to magnetic tape by the use of a special device. Other equipment can be used to convert data recorded in the form of magnetic ink characters into magnetic tape.

To facilitate the use of a variety of processing or transmittal equipment, conversion of data from one medium to another can be accomplished by many other special devices in addition to the document-to-tape converters already mentioned. Other combinations include the following.

Paper tape to:	Magnetic tape Punched card Embossed card
Magnetic tape to:	Paper tape Punched card
Punched card to:	Magnetic tape Paper tape Embossed card
Print-punch tag to:	Paper tape Punched card
Edge-notched card to:	Punched card Punched tape

The large variety of machines available to complete the conversions listed above will not be described here. Instead, let it suffice to say that the code medium of almost any machine can be converted into the code media of other machines by using the proper converters. Furthermore, any new code that is developed is likely to be followed soon by devices to convert it to other forms.

IMPORTANT WORDS AND PHRASES

machine-sensible code
integrated data
  processing
card column
code
field
card punch
key punch
punched tape
magnetic tape

bit
inter-record gap
multiple-record
  block
data recorder
magnetic
  diskette
data station

punched tag
optical character
  recognition (OCR)
magnetic ink character
  recognition (MICR)
optical mark
  recognition (OMR)
bar code
data conversion

REVIEW QUESTIONS

1. What is a machine-sensible code?
2. What is the meaning of the term "integrated data processing"? When was this concept first used?
3. What principle is described by the term "source data automation"?

4. The standard punched card is divided into how many vertical columns? How many units of data may be recorded in one column?
5. Describe the 12 punching positions of a card. How are they used?
6. What punches would be needed to record the following letters and digits on a card? 2, 7, C, H, L, R, S, V.
7. Why is it necessary to use codes in recording data on punched cards? Explain how it would be possible to identify the state of Massachusetts on a punched card by using two columns only.
8. What is a card field? How is the length of a card field determined?
9. What three types of data are generally entered on a punched card?
10. What is the purpose of an inter-record gap on magnetic tape?
11. Discuss optical characters and how they are used as a data entry method.
12. Magnetic ink character recognition is commonly used for what purpose?
13. How is optical mark recognition used as a data entry medium?

6

ELECTRONIC DATA PROCESSING: INTRODUCTION

Before the twentieth century was well on its way, electrically powered business machines were turning out great volumes of data for a world that was increasingly dependent on numbers and records. It was inevitable that electricity would be used to activate calculators and that an automatic computing machine would evolve. The age of the computer began in 1939 when Dr. Howard Aiken of Harvard University completed plans for a calculating machine that embodied many of the principles used in today's computers. Dr. Aiken's machine, called the Automatic Sequence Controlled Calculator, was completed in 1944. It combined in a single integrated device the ability to receive input data, perform a sequence of calculations, and record output.

In 1946 J. Presper Eckert and John W. Mauchly, faculty members at the University of Pennsylvania, completed the first actual electronic computer, called ENIAC, an abbreviation of Electronic Numerical Integrator and Computer. It was the first computer to use vacuum tubes instead of mechanical gears or electromechanical switches to do its calculating work. Also, it had a form of built-in machine logic enabling it to solve complete problems by making decisions or choices as it went along.

Succeeding advancements have been rapid and impressive and leave little doubt that the electronic computer is one of the most significant developments of this century. The purpose of this chapter and the ensuing chapters is to survey the characteristics of this relatively new and important medium of processing data. The physical elements and functions of a computer system are outlined as well as basic programming techniques, programming systems, and electronic data processing operations.

CLASSIFICATION OF COMPUTERS

Although there are no industry standards, computers are generally classified in three ways: by purpose, by type, and by capacity.

Purpose

Depending on their flexibility in operation, computers are either special purpose or general purpose. A *special purpose* computer is one that is designed to solve a restricted class of problems. Such a computer may even be designed and built to do one job only. In this case, the steps or operations that the computer follows may be built into the hardware. Many of the computers used for military purposes are of this type. Computers specifically designed to solve navigational problems on submarines or to track airplanes or missiles are good examples of special purpose equipment. Other examples include computers used for process control applications in such industries as oil refining, chemical manufacture, steel processing, and power generation. Special purpose computers are being increasingly used to control automated manufacturing processes.

General purpose computers are designed to solve a wide variety of problems. Theoretically a general purpose computer can be adapted by means of an easily alterable set of instructions to handle any problem that can be solved by computation. There are, of course, limitations imposed by memory size, speed, and type of input and output. The versatility of general purpose computers makes it possible to use them for such widely diversified tasks as payroll, banking, sales analysis, billing, cost accounting, labor distribution, manufacturing scheduling, and inventory control (Figure 6–1).

Type

Electronic computers are basically of two types, analog and digital, according to the manner in which they represent data. An *analog computer* is so named because it performs by setting up physical situations that are analogous to mathematical situations. An analog computer operates on data in the form of continuously variable physical quantities such as pressure, temperature, revolutions, speed of sound, or voltage. Thus, an analog computer is essentially a measuring device.

The automobile speedometer is a familiar device that utilizes information in analog form. It converts the turning rate of a shaft into a numerical approximation of speed. A slide rule can also be classified as an analog device. Distances between points on the slide rule are read numerically in such a way that they provide approximate answers to multiplications, divisions, square roots, and so on.

Figure 6-1. *General purpose electronic data processing system. (Courtesy International Business Machines Corporation.)*

Since analog data is acquired through a measuring process, analog computers have the advantage of being able to accept data directly from measuring instruments without the need for an intermediate conversion to some symbol or code. This permits the high-speed collection of data at the point of origin. This feature, along with the analog computer's ability to process data at high speeds, makes these machines useful as controlling devices in oil refineries, paper mills, steel mills, and military weapons systems. Since the analog computer measures and compares quantities in one operation, it has no storage. The answers to problems are frequently read off on dials or cathode ray tubes.

Analog computers are far outnumbered in use today by digital computers. *Digital computers* operate on representations of real numbers or other characters coded numerically. The digital computer has a memory and solves problems by counting precisely, adding, subtracting, multiplying, dividing, and comparing. The ability of digital computers to handle alphabetic and numerical data with precision and speed makes them ideally suited for processing data. Therefore, the discussion in this book will be limited to computers of the digital type.

Although computers are basically of the analog or digital type, it should be recognized that a third type of computer is now being marketed. This is known as a *hybrid computer* and combines analog and digital capabilities in the same computer system. This capacity is most significant in a situation where the digital processing of data collected in analog form is desirable.

Capacity

In the early stages of electronic computer development, capacity was sometimes measured in terms of physical size. Today, however, phys-

Figure 6-2. *Condensed circuitry on silicon chip in center (1/20 inch) performs functions previously requiring surrounding components.*

(*Courtesy Radio Corporation of America.*)

ical size is not a good measure of capacity, for late models have achieved compactness as a result of such developments as paper-thin monolithic silicon circuits, no larger than the letter *o* on a typewriter. These integrated circuits perform the complete logic functions of a handful of transistors, diodes, and resistors previously used in computing systems (Figure 6–2).

Current electronic circuit technology, such as *large-scale integration* (LSI), *monolithic system technology* (MST), and *solid logic technology* (SLT), offers further improvement in component reliability and faster circuit speeds. Improvements in reliability are made possible by the increased number of circuit connections that can be made on a chip (miniature base for electronic circuits), thereby reducing the number of external connections. Improvements in circuit speed result from the reduced distance between circuits. The benefits of reduced circuit distance can be appreciated when it is realized that electric current travels about one foot in a billionth of a second (nanosecond).

An earlier development enabling increased compactness was the magnetic core. These wired discrete ferrite cores make it possible for computers to hold large amounts of data in storage, yet reach any single bit of information in a few billionths of a second.

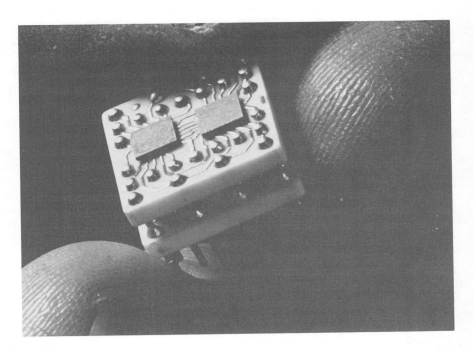

Figure 6-3. *Monolithic storage array module containing 512 bits.* *(Courtesy International Business Machines Corporation.)*

More recently the use of monolithic storage technology to store data instead of forming logic circuits has been implemented. In one example, the IBM 370, Model 145, each storage module measuring ½ inch contains 512 storage bits (Figure 6–3).

Thus, as a result of miniaturization, capacity is expressed in terms of the volume of work that a computer can handle and is not necessarily evident in the physical size of the computer.

Although there are diverse opinions as to the best criteria to be used for measuring computer performance and capacity, most authorities accept purchase price or rental charges as the standard for ranking computers in four general categories: mini, small, medium, and large. Minicomputers are generally priced below $50,000 and are usually purchased instead of rented. They have all the functions regarded as essential to larger computers and are considered "mini" only in that they have minimal input-output capabilities, and less capacity for work in a given amount of time than other computers. For this reason the characteristics that distinguish minicomputers from other computers are not entirely clear. However, because this segment of the computer industry is developing rapidly, a special discussion on minicomputers is presented in Chapter 10.

Small computers are generally priced above $50,000 and below $100,000 and may be either rented or purchased. A small computer configuration usually rents for under $7,500 a month, the average being around

$4,000. Small computers can have a variety of input-output devices attached and are likely to be more versatile and have greater performance capabilities than minicomputers.

The medium-scale computer system usually sells for over $100,000 and under $750,000, and rents for over $7,500 and under $30,000 a month. A medium-scale computer can have greater primary storage capacity with faster access, and more and faster input-output devices than are available on a small computer.

Large-scale computer systems usually sell for over $750,000 and up to $8,000,000, and rent for $30,000 to $175,000 a month. Large-scale computers may contain up to several million positions of primary storage with very fast access. These computers, as well as many medium-scale computers, also may provide for simultaneous operation of several input-output devices and concurrent execution of several programs.

The greatest number of computers in use today are in the mini and small categories. Approximately 75 per cent of all computers now in operation are classified in the lower end of the scale, about 20 per cent are medium-scale, and the remaining 5 per cent are classified as large-scale.

COMPUTER FUNCTIONS

The ability to compute is only one of the functions of an electronic data processing system. The other basic functions are data storage, control, and communication. These functions enable electronic computers to process data in the following steps:

1. The data to be processed and the instructions for processing it are recorded in an input medium such as punched paper tape, punched cards, magnetic tape, magnetic ink characters, or optical characters.

2. The instructions and data are fed into an input device, where they are automatically converted into electrical impulses. The instructions and data are then routed to the main storage or memory unit, where they are held until needed. Data also may be stored in an external or auxiliary device.

3. Instructions are accessed and interpreted by the control unit of the computer, which directs the various data processing operations by issuing commands to all components of the system.

4. In accordance with instructions, data is transferred from storage to the arithmetic-logical unit of the computer, where arithmetic operations or comparisons are performed as directed by the control unit.

5. Processed data is routed to the storage unit, where it may be held for further processing or moved to an output device, again as directed by the control unit.

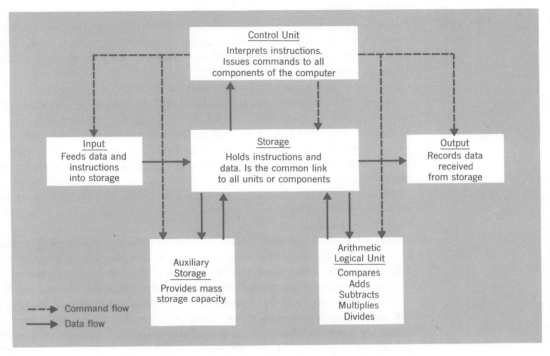

Figure 6-4. *Relationship of functions of a computer system.*

6. Data emitted from storage is recorded by an output device in a medium such as punched tape, punched cards, magnetic tape, or printed documents.

The relationship of these functions is illustrated in Figure 6–4. This diagram depicts the significance of the storage unit as a common link between all units or components of the computer. It also shows that all units operate under the direction of the control unit as it receives and interprets one instruction at a time. These functions will be described in greater detail in the following chapters.

A method of representing data that is acceptable to the system is essential for performance of the functions outlined above. We shall now consider methods of data representation.

DATA REPRESENTATION

One prerequisite for understanding digital computers is a knowledge of the manner in which they handle data. Computers are made up of many electronic components: transistors, switches, magnetic cores, wires, integrated circuits, and so on. Data is represented in these components by the presence or absence of electronic signals or indications, much as the presence or absence of holes in a punched card represents data.

Each component in a computer has only two possible states: on or off. For example, transistors are in either a conducting or nonconducting state; magnetic materials are magnetized in one direction or in the opposite direction; relays and switches are open or closed; and voltage is present or absent. With this limited number of possibilities for each component part, the computer must be capable of accepting large volumes of numeric and alphabetic data, and must store, process, and produce data as output. Because of these design characteristics, it is not feasible for the computer to utilize decimal arithmetic, which would require components to have ten states for each digit. Instead, the computer uses a form of the two-digit numbering system known as the *binary numbering system*.

To aid in understanding the binary numbering system, let us begin with the decimal system. Two important concepts in the decimal system, also applicable to other systems, are absolute value and positional value. The *absolute values* in the decimal system are the ten digits 0 to 9. Since the number of digits or absolute values used in a system determines the base (also called "radix"), the decimal system has a base of ten.

The ten numerals of the decimal system allow us to represent any quantity from zero to nine. Numbers larger than nine are handled by the concept of *positional value*. In a positional numbering system the value of each position in a multidigit number represents a specific power of the base. In the decimal system, the positions to the left of the decimal point increase by powers of ten, and the numbers to the right of the decimal point decrease by powers of ten. Consequently, the first position to the left of the decimal point has a positional value of 10^0 or 1, the second position has a value of 10^1 or 10, the third has a value of 10^2 or 100, the fourth 10^3 or 1,000, etc.

The small figure written above and at the right of another figure is called an *exponent*. The exponent indicates the power to which the number it accompanies is to be raised, i.e., how many times the number is to be multiplied by itself. Therefore, $10^2 = 10 \times 10$ or 100; $10^3 = 10 \times 10 \times 10$ or 1,000; etc. Any number raised to the zero power has the value of 1; any number raised to the first power has a value equal to that of the number itself.

Thus, each digit written in decimal notation is interpreted as having a value equal to the absolute value of the digit (1, 2, 3, 4, etc.) times the value of the position it occupies. The positions of the decimal system are commonly called units, tens, hundreds, thousands, etc. Table 6–1 illustrates the positional-value and absolute-value concepts as applied to the decimal system.

| *Binary Numbering System* | The binary system is comparable to the decimal system in using the concepts of absolute value and positional value. The difference is that the |

Table 6-1 The Decimal Numbering System

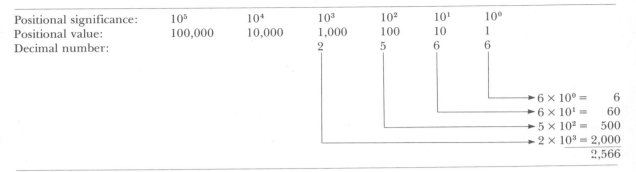

Positional significance:	10^5	10^4	10^3	10^2	10^1	10^0
Positional value:	100,000	10,000	1,000	100	10	1
Decimal number:			2	5	6	6

$$6 \times 10^0 = 6$$
$$6 \times 10^1 = 60$$
$$5 \times 10^2 = 500$$
$$2 \times 10^3 = \underline{2,000}$$
$$2,566$$

Table 6-2 The Binary Numbering System

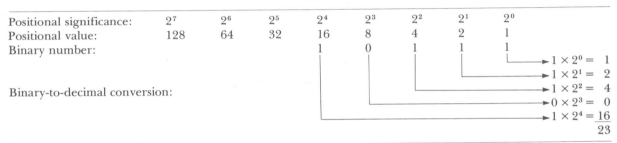

Positional significance:	2^7	2^6	2^5	2^4	2^3	2^2	2^1	2^0
Positional value:	128	64	32	16	8	4	2	1
Binary number:				1	0	1	1	1

Binary-to-decimal conversion:

$$1 \times 2^0 = 1$$
$$1 \times 2^1 = 2$$
$$1 \times 2^2 = 4$$
$$0 \times 2^3 = 0$$
$$1 \times 2^4 = \underline{16}$$
$$23$$

binary numbering system employs only two absolute values: 0 and 1. Because there are only two digits, the binary system has a base number of 2. This means that the positional significance of a binary number is based on the progression of powers of 2.

As shown in Table 6–2, the binary positional values are obtained by following the same rules discussed in the previous section on the decimal numbering system. Thus, the rightmost (least significant) position of a binary number represents the base number to the zero power and has a value of 1. The second position represents 2 raised to the first power, or 2. Progressing to the left, $2^2 = 2 \times 2$ or 4; $2^3 = 2 \times 2 \times 2$ or 8; etc. If the binary notations in Table 6–2 were continued to the left, they would have values of 256, 512, 1,024, 2,048, 4,096, 8,192, etc.

As indicated in Table 6–2, numbers are expressed in binary notation as a series of 0s and 1s, commonly referred to as bits. The 0 is described as no bit and represents an "off" condition. The 1 is described as a bit and represents an "on" condition. The lowest-order position in the binary system is called the 1-bit. The next position is called the 2-bit; the next, the 4-bit; the next, the 8-bit; and so on.

Here are some additional examples of numbers expressed in the binary system:

Value of each bit							
64	32	16	8	4	2	1	
		1	0	1	0	1	= 21
	1	0	1	1	1	1	= 47
1	0	1	0	0	0	1	= 81
1	1	1	0	0	1	0	= 144

Since binary arithmetic requires the use of only two digits, binary numbers can be easily represented in the various two-state components of electronic computers. The on condition may represent 1, and off may represent 0. For example, transistors could be used to represent the quantity 5 electronically by the following combination of on and off conditions:

It is apparent that zero would be expressed if all circuits were in an off condition. Values other than 5 could be expressed by different combinations of on and off conditions. As indicated by the preceding illustration, four computer circuits are needed in this system to represent all of the decimal digits, 0 to 9, in binary form.

Other Computer Codes

To facilitate the recording and processing of data, most computers use one of the following codes based on the binary numbering system.

Binary Coded Decimal. This code is one of the most common variations of the binary system. It employs only the first four binary positions with the respective values of 1, 2, 4, and 8. Any decimal digit from 0 to 9 can be represented by a combination of these four values. In this system a separate binary equivalent is required for each digit of the decimal number being expressed. Thus, units, tens, hundreds, thousands, etc., can be expressed as follows:

Thousands				Hundreds				Tens				Units				
8	4	2	1	8	4	2	1	8	4	2	1	8	4	2	1	
1	0	0	1	1	0	0	0	0	1	0	0	0	1	0	1	= 9,845
0	1	1	0	0	1	1	1	0	0	1	1	0	0	0	1	= 6,731

Standard Binary Coded Decimal Interchange Code (Table 6–3). This code, which is the one used by most second-generation computers, is an expansion of the binary coded decimal system. The significant difference in the standard BCD code is the use of zone bits as shown below:

Parity	Zone		Numeric			
C	B	A	8	4	2	1

The zone bits of an alphanumeric character perform a code function similar to the zone positions on a punched card. They are used in combination with digits to represent the letters of the alphabet or special characters.

The illustration above also shows a bit position on the extreme left labeled "Parity." It should be noted further that some of the codes in the third column of Table 6–3 contain a bit in the column on the extreme left and others do not. The bits recorded in this column are known as *check bits* and are used for verifying accuracy. Some computers have a built-in checking device that detects the loss or addition of bits during the transfer of data from one location to another in the computer. This process is known as a *parity check* and was explained earlier.

The addition of necessary check bits is accomplished automatically as input data is converted to binary codes. Further study of Table 6–3 will reveal that odd parity is being used in the code illustrated in the third column. Although check bits are not shown with the other codes, they are employed when these codes are used with most computers.

Whenever data is transmitted, the computer checks to determine if the necessary odd or even number of bits is present. If an error is detected, the computer will indicate that a parity error has occurred and will stop. Some computers make several attempts to transmit the data before stopping.

Extended Binary Coded Decimal Interchange Code (EBCDIC) (Table 6–3). This code, which is the one used by most computers, employs eight binary positions to represent a single character. The use of eight bits may seem inefficient. However, the extended code has some definite advantages over the standard BCD code:

1. Eight binary positions allow 256 different bit configurations (2^8) versus 64 provided by the six-position BCD code (2^6). This increase in possible bit configurations provides capacity for both upper and lower case letters, numerals, and many special characters as well as unused configurations for future use.
2. Each of the possible 256 bit combinations can be punched into one column of an 80-column card. This allows pure binary information

Table 6-3 Comparison of Selected Codes

Character	Standard Card Code	Standard BCD Interchange Code		EBCDIC*		ASCII†	
0	0	100	1010	1111	0000	011	0000
1	1	000	0001	1111	0001	011	0001
2	2	000	0010	1111	0010	011	0010
3	3	100	0011	1111	0011	011	0011
4	4	000	0100	1111	0100	011	0100
5	5	100	0101	1111	0101	011	0101
6	6	100	0110	1111	0110	011	0110
7	7	000	0111	1111	0111	011	0111
8	8	000	1000	1111	1000	011	1000
9	9	100	1001	1111	1001	011	1001
A	12-1	011	0001	1100	0001	100	0001
B	12-2	011	0010	1100	0010	100	0010
C	12-3	111	0011	1100	0011	100	0011
D	12-4	011	0100	1100	0100	100	0100
E	12-5	111	0101	1100	0101	100	0101
F	12-6	111	0110	1100	0110	100	0110
G	12-7	011	0111	1100	0111	100	0111
H	12-8	011	1000	1100	1000	100	1000
I	12-9	111	1001	1100	1001	100	1001
J	11-1	110	0001	1101	0001	100	1010
K	11-2	110	0010	1101	0010	100	1011
L	11-3	010	0011	1101	0011	100	1100
M	11-4	110	0100	1101	0100	100	1101
N	11-5	010	0101	1101	0101	100	1110
O	11-6	010	0110	1101	0110	100	1111
P	11-7	110	0111	1101	0111	101	0000
Q	11-8	110	1000	1101	1000	101	0001
R	11-9	010	1001	1101	1001	101	0010
S	0-2	101	0010	1110	0010	101	0011
T	0-3	001	0011	1110	0011	101	0100
U	0-4	101	0100	1110	0100	101	0101
V	0-5	001	0101	1110	0101	101	0110
W	0-6	001	0110	1110	0110	101	0111
X	0-7	101	0111	1110	0111	101	1000
Y	0-8	101	1000	1110	1000	101	1001
Z	0-9	001	1001	1110	1001	101	1010

*Extended Binary Coded Decimal Interchange Code.
†American Standard Code for Information Interchange.

to be punched into a card, with each column representing eight bits of binary information.

3. The eight-bit field can be used to store two decimal digits. This gives better utilization of storage facilities than the BCD format, which is capable of recording a single digit in a six-bit field.

As we have seen, most character codes are divided into zone and numeric parts. The extended binary coded decimal interchange code is no exception. To aid in understanding how this code is used, let us analyze a primary storage position typical of most of today's computers. Each storage location is known as a *byte* and consists of eight bits plus a parity bit. The EBCDIC divides the eight bits of a byte as shown below:

```
         Zone          Numeric
       ┌──────┐      ┌──────────┐
     │ 0 │ 1 │ 2 │ 3 │ 4 │ 5 │ 6 │ 7 │
```

Figure 6–5 illustrates how the zone portion, bits 0–3, of the EBCDIC byte is used to identify different characters. Bit positions 4–7 of the EBCDIC byte are the numeric portion and correspond to the numeric hole punches 0–9. Bits 4–7 are coded as a four-bit binary number. Note the similarity of the numeric portions of the standard BCD interchange code and the EBCDIC in Table 6–3.

Decimal data can be represented in binary form in either of two formats: zoned or packed. The zoned or unpacked format uses all eight bits of a byte to represent a digit, as shown in Figure 6–6. The packed format uses the numeric portion of a byte to represent one digit and the zone portion to represent a second digit, as shown below:

```
                      Numeric        Numeric
                    ┌──────────┐   ┌──────────┐
Packed byte =     │ 8 │ 4 │ 2 │ 1 │ 8 │ 4 │ 2 │ 1 │
```

Figure 6–6 shows the decimal digits 1, 2, and 3 represented in binary form in both zoned and packed formats. It should be noted in this example that the plus or minus sign is located in the zone portion of the

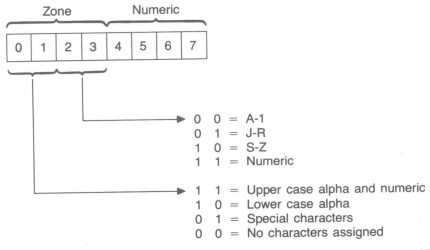

Figure 6-5. *Uses of zone portion of EBCDIC byte.*

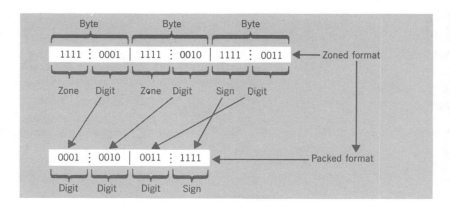

Figure 6-6. *Decimal digits 1, 2, and 3 represented in binary form in both zoned and packed formats.*

low-order byte in the zoned format, and is located in the low-order digit position in the packed format. In this code the presence of the normal zone bits "1111" is an unsigned indication assumed to be positive. If this had been a negative quantity, the zone portion would have appeared as "1101," which is a minus indication.

Packing of digits leads to efficient use of storage, increased arithmetic performance, and improved rates of data transmission. Program instructions are available to cause the computer to either pack or unpack a numeric field.

American Standard Code for Information Interchange (ASCII) (Table 6–3). This is a seven-bit binary code that can be processed by many computers. Also available is an eight-bit version of the ASCII code, which is not illustrated here. The bit identification for each format is as follows:

ASCII		7	6	5	4	3	2	1
ASCII-8	8	7	6	5	4	3	2	1

We should note that in the ASCII formats the bits are numbered from right to left, and in the EBCDIC format the bits are numbered from left to right. Today the ASCII format is most frequently used by data transmission devices.

IMPORTANT WORDS AND PHRASES

special purpose computer
general purpose computer
analog computer
digital computer
binary numbering system
binary coded decimal
check bit
parity check
Extended Binary Coded Decimal Interchange Code (EBCDIC)
byte
American Standard Code for Information Interchange (ASCII)

1. What was unique about the ENIAC?
2. Briefly describe general purpose computers.
3. What is the main difference between analog and digital computers? Which one is generally used for business data processing?
4. Name several devices that utilize information in analog form.
5. Briefly describe a hybrid computer.
6. What are the four basic functions of an electronic data processing system?
7. Why does the binary system have a base number of 2?
8. What is the decimal value of the binary number 111?
9. What are the binary notations for the following decimal values? (a) 255, (b) 83, (c) 37.
10. What does EBCDIC represent?

7

EDP CENTRAL PROCESSING UNIT

The central processing unit (CPU) is the single component that distinguishes the electronic computer from all other data handling systems. It can sequentially execute a series of programmed instructions or jump to an instruction anywhere in a program. In addition to this unique capability for accessing instructions in the desired order and for executing instructions, the CPU also controls and monitors the entire system and contains facilities for addressing primary storage, for storing or retrieving data, for initiating communications between primary storage and all other devices, and for the arithmetic and logical processing of data.

    The functions of the control unit and the arithmetic-logical unit are discussed in detail in the following sections.

CONTROL UNIT

The control unit directs and coordinates all activity of the computer including the following:

1. Control of input-output devices
2. Entry and retrieval of information from storage
3. Routing of information between storage and the arithmetic-logical section
4. Direction of arithmetic-logical operations

The performance of these operations requires a vast number of "paths" over which data and instructions may be sent. Routing data over the proper paths in the circuitry, opening and closing the right "gates" at the right time, and establishing timing sequences are major functions of the control unit.

All of these operations are under the control of a stored program. A *program* is a set of instructions indicating to the computer the exact sequence of steps it must follow in processing a given set of data. Each instruction usually includes two things:

1. An *operation code* that specifies what is to be done
2. One or more *operands* that designate the address or addresses of the data needed for the specified operation

The instructions and data required by a computer to solve a problem are generally entered through a regular input device and are stored sequentially within the computer's primary storage. The instructions must be stored in operating sequence in primary storage for the control unit to have access to them. To receive, interpret, and execute stored program instructions, the control section of the central processing unit must operate in a prescribed sequence. All stored program operations are executed in fixed intervals of time measured by regular pulses emitted from an electronic clock. The frequency of these pulses may be as high as a million or more each second. A fixed number of pulses determines the time of each basic machine cycle during which the computer can perform a specific operation.

The first machine cycle necessary to carry out an instruction is called an *instruction cycle*. The time for this cycle is known as *instruction time* or *I-time*. During *I*-time the following steps are completed:

1. A duplicate of an instruction is transmitted from a specified primary storage location to the instruction register in the control unit. The instructions in primary storage are not destroyed or altered as a result of being duplicated in the control unit and, therefore, can be used an unlimited number of times.

2. The operation part of the instruction, which tells the computer what is to be done, is decoded by the control unit—that is, it activates the particular circuits needed to carry out the instruction.

3. The operands (location of data to be operated on) are placed in address registers. This indicates what data is to be used in performing the required operation.

4. The location of the instruction to be executed next is ascertained.

I-time is followed by one or more machine cycles referred to as *execution cycles* or *E-time*. During the execution cycle, the machine actually performs the specified operation. The number of execution cycles is determined by the instruction to be executed. For example, a computer would require more machine cycles to multiply *A* times *B* than it would to add *A* plus *B*. The *E*-cycle begins by transferring from storage the data located at the address identified by the address register. This data is placed in a storage register where it is operated on according to the operation part of the instruction. In addition to the storage location of data, the address register may indicate the address of an input-output unit or a control function to be performed.

ARITHMETIC-LOGICAL UNIT

The arithmetic-logical unit performs the actual processing of data including addition, subtraction, multiplication, and division. This unit also performs certain logical operations such as comparing two numbers to see if one is larger than the other or if they are equal. In this way the computer is able to make simple decisions.

Arithmetic Operations

As indicated earlier, most computers now being produced are equally proficient at processing business or scientific problems. To satisfy both of these needs computers must be capable of handling fixed-length and variable-length data fields. They must also be capable of four classes of operations: fixed point arithmetic, floating point arithmetic, decimal arithmetic, and logical operations. Decimal arithmetic is generally associated with business applications, whereas fixed point and floating point arithmetic are generally used for scientific and engineering applications. The selection of the method to be employed is largely at the discretion of the programmer and is identified in the program instructions.

These classes of operations differ in the data formats used, the registers involved, the operations provided, and the way the field length is stated. To illustrate the four processing operations we will refer to Figure 7–1, a schematic of basic registers and data paths in the IBM System/370 computer.

Decimal Arithmetic. Computers perform decimal arithmetic on signed packed decimal numbers (see Figure 6–6) using the storage-to-storage concept employed by most business-oriented second-generation computers. In the storage-to-storage concept, variable-length data fields are

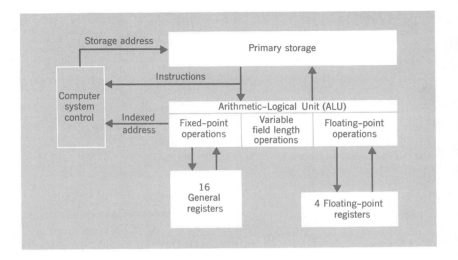

Figure 7-1. *Schematic of basic registers and data paths in the IBM System/370 computer.*

brought out of main storage, operated on by the arithmetic-logical unit, and the results are placed back into main storage. For example, let us assume that an instruction calls for the addition of a quantity in a field labeled *A* to the quantity in a field labeled *B*. As shown in Figure 7–2, the following operations would result.

1. The instruction "ADD A + B," the next instruction to be processed, is called from primary storage and goes to the computer system control unit, where the operation code representing "ADD" is translated into commands.
2. The computer control system then commands the arithmetic-logical unit (ALU) to add the data stored at the locations identified as fields *A* and *B* and to store the result in the original location of field *A*.

As this concept is important, a more detailed discussion of a sample problem is justified. Let us assume that we wish to adjust the inventory of a certain stock item by adding the stock receipts and subtracting the stock issues. The following factors are involved:

Hammer, claw	170
Stock receipts	+ 50
Stock issues	− 95
Balance on hand	125

After the beginning inventory record for claw hammers has been read by an input device and transferred to primary storage, the computer would then be instructed to perform the following steps.

1. Add stock receipts to the quantity on hand. This is accomplished by one instruction, symbolically represented as ADD QTYHD + STKRCP,

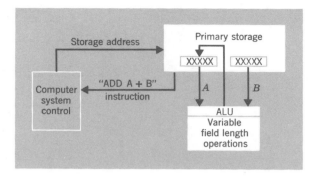

Figure 7-2. *Schematic of decimal arithmetic data paths.*

which causes the quantity on hand (170) and stock receipts (50) to be transferred to the arithmetic-logical unit where they are added together. The result (220) is returned to the quantity-on-hand field in primary storage. This causes the original quantity-on-hand amount in primary storage to be destroyed as the new quantity on hand is recorded.

2. After this ADD instruction is executed, the system control unit receives the next instruction, translates it, and then executes it. During execution the series of operations in step 3 would be performed.

3. Subtract stock issues from the quantity on hand. This is also accomplished by one instruction, symbolically represented as SUBT QTYHD − STKISS, which causes the quantity on hand (220) and the stock issues (95) to be transferred to the arithmetic-logical unit. Here the issues are subtracted from the quantity on hand and the result (125) is returned to the quantity-on-hand field in primary storage. Again this causes the previous quantity on hand (220) to be destroyed.

4. The new quantity-on-hand figure (125) is now available in primary storage for whatever use is to be made of it by the instructions that follow. Normally, the quantity on hand and its associated data would constitute a record that would be conveyed to an output device such as magnetic tape; or perhaps it would be formatted into a print line and printed, or both. After the disposition of this updated record, the next instruction would cause the succeeding record to be read by an input device and transferred to primary storage. The process just described would then be repeated.

Fixed Point Arithmetic. Fixed point arithmetic is a method of calculation in which the computer does not consider the location of the decimal point. This is similar to the situation that exists in the use of desk calculators and slide rules, which require the operator to keep track of the decimal point. With electronic computers the location of the decimal point is the programmer's responsibility.

Fixed point arithmetic uses the storage-to-accumulator or the accumulator-to-accumulator concepts that were used by most scientific-oriented second-generation computers. Fixed point arithmetic operations are performed using fixed-length binary data fields. The results of either the storage-to-accumulator or the accumulator-to-accumulator operation will be stored in either one or two general registers. Addition, subtraction, multiplication, division, and comparison operations take one operand (data field) from a register and another from either a register or storage and return the result to a general register. Figure 7–3 shows the data flow for the fixed point add instruction: "ADD field *A* to *B*." In this case let us assume that the *A* field quantity stored in general register 3 is to be added to the *B* field quantity stored in primary storage and that the result is to be returned to general register 3.

The stock inventory problem used to illustrate decimal arithmetic could also be performed using fixed point arithmetic.

Floating Point Arithmetic. For certain arithmetic operations, typically those in the scientific and engineering areas, it is helpful or even essential to let the computer assume the task of keeping track of decimal points. When using the fixed point binary or decimal instructions, it is necessary to be aware of the maximum possible sizes of all data, intermediate results, and final results. It is often necessary to know the minimum sizes as well. This awareness is essential to avoid the possibility of exceeding the capacity of a register or of a storage location. Such knowledge about problem data is often difficult and sometimes impossible to develop. Furthermore, working in fixed point requires the program-

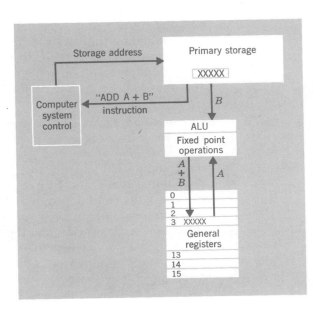

Figure 7-3. *Schematic of fixed point arithmetic data paths.*

mer to align decimal or binary points correctly throughout the process of shifting and rearranging data in order to maintain significance while avoiding capacity overflow.

For these reasons, it is a great convenience to let the computer take over the clerical details of a complete accounting for number sizes and decimal point alignment. Floating point arithmetic saves programming time and makes possible the solution of complex problems that would otherwise be almost impossible.

The basic idea of floating point numbers is that each quantity is represented as a combination of two items: a numerical fraction and a power of 16 by which the fraction is multiplied to get the number represented. The 16 applies specifically to the IBM Systems/360 and 370; other floating point systems may use binary or decimal multipliers.

Floating point operations are performed with one operand from a floating point register and another one from either a floating point register or storage, with the result placed in a floating point register.

The details of floating point arithmetic are not within the scope of this book. The purpose here is merely to introduce the concept.

Logical Operations

Nonarithmetic data manipulations, generally referred to as *logical operations,* constitute a substantial portion of today's computing task. Logical operations such as *compare, move, translate, edit, bit test,* and *bit set* are used in extracting, categorizing, transforming, rearranging, and editing data. The operations are discussed in groups that possess similar functions.

Shifting. Left- and right-shift operations are used for many of the processes of isolating, eliminating, and aligning groups of contiguous bits. Shifting consists of moving data in one storage field to another location and realigning the data within the new field. For example, shifting is often used to drop excess digits beyond the decimal point that result from multiplication, or to align the decimal points in two data fields so that they may be arithmetically operated on.

Operand-Pair Logic. Logic operations on operand pairs are primarily used for extracting, testing, modifying, and recombining bit groups. The *load, store, insert,* and *move* type of operations are the easiest to understand. The *compare* logical operations result in the setting of a condition code to one of three states: low, equal, or high. The program can check the condition code setting and as a result either branch to an alternate series of instructions or continue to process the series of instructions being processed at the time the condition code was tested.

Editing. The editing operations are generally those that perform the following:

Type of operation	Function
Move zones or move numeric	Permits the separation or recombination of zone and numeric data.
Pack and unpack	Used for packing and unpacking decimal data fields.
Edit	Permits editing of packed decimal data for printing. These operations can suppress or protect leading zeros, provide punctuation such as commas and periods, and control printing of credit or minus signs.

Conversion. The *convert to binary* and *convert to decimal* operations provide for radix conversion of address and data values.

FUNCTIONAL ELEMENTS

Functional elements may be included in the CPU as individual components or as an integral part of the control or arithmetic-logical units. Three of the more common functional elements are registers, decoders, and adders.

Register

A *register* is a device capable of receiving data, holding it, and transferring it as directed by control circuits. Registers are named according to their function as shown by the following examples.

Type of register	Function
Accumulator	A register in which the results of arithmetic or logic operations are accumulated.
Storage	Temporarily holds data taken from or being sent to storage.
Address	Holds the address of a storage location or device.
Instruction	Holds the instructions being executed.
Index	Is used in address arithmetic, i.e., to modify an instruction address and for indexing. For example, the storage address of data could be increased by the length of the record each time the instruction is executed, thereby causing the computer to read sequential records one after the other.
General	Can perform the functions of several special registers such as accumulators, storage registers, address registers, and index registers.
Floating point	Used in floating point arithmetic operations.

Certain registers hold data while related circuits analyze the data. For example, an instruction may be held by one register while associated *decoder circuits* determine the operation to be performed and locate the data to be used.

Addition is the fundamental operation performed by a computer. When a computer subtracts, multiplies, or divides, it does so by adding and shifting. The adder constitutes a major part of the arithmetic unit circuitry and forms the basis of most of the computer's arithmetic and logical functions. It receives data from two or more sources, performs the arithmetic functions, and conveys the result to a receiving register.

MAIN STORAGE

The technique of holding data and computer instructions in computer-processable form is referred to as *storage*. *Main* or *primary* storage is usually an integral physical part of the CPU and is directly controlled by the computer. Thus, data in main storage is automatically accessible to the computer.

To be accessible, each data character must be stored in an identifiable location with a unique address. Addresses usually start with zero and continue sequentially to the highest number required. Related units of data are recorded in adjoining positions in main storage. For example, the word *storage* would require seven storage positions or locations. The letter *s* would be stored in the leftmost position or address, and the letter *e* would be stored in the rightmost position with an address six numbers higher than *s*.

An important characteristic of main storage units is that each position or word must be accessible on a random basis. In other words, the computer must be able to reach any position of main storage directly. Further, it must be possible to use the data as many times as desired without erasing it from storage until such time as it is no longer needed. Data in storage is not lost as a result of the writing-out process unless the instruction is specifically a write-and-erase type. However, reading data into storage necessarily destroys data previously stored at the specified locations.

Main storage accepts data from an input unit, exchanges data with and supplies instructions to the central processing unit, and furnishes data to an output unit. Main storage is used to store the instructions in a program that the computer is executing and the data being processed by the program. In most business applications only a limited segment of the data to be processed is put into main storage at one time while it is being processed. The usual procedure in computer operations is to store the bulk of data to be processed in an auxiliary storage device, transfer portions of the data to main or working storage, process it, and then return it to auxiliary storage. This procedure is repeated until all of the data is processed.

*Magnetic Core
Storage*

Many computers use magnetic core storage. The extensive use of magnetic core storage is based on the fact that it is comparatively inexpensive

Figure 7-4. *Magnetic core storage.*
(Courtesy General Electric Company.)

to build, provides fast access to data, and is very reliable. It requires little current and can be used on either a variable or fixed word length concept.

This medium is made up of thousands of magnetic cores, about the diameter of the head of a straight pin, strung on a grid of fine wires (Figure 7–4). Each grid of wires and cores is called a *plane.* Cores are mounted with wires running through each core at right angles to each other, and magnetized by sending electrical current through the wires. By sending half the current needed to magnetize a core through each wire, only the core at the intersection of the wires is magnetized. Cores are arranged so that combinations of charges representing data are instantly accessible.

Cores are magnetized positively or negatively depending on the direction of the current. By reversing the flow of current, the magnetic state, or polarity, of a core can be changed. Thus, the two states can be used in accordance with the binary system to represent 0 or 1, yes or no, or on or off conditions. Figure 7–5 illustrates the storage of both alphabetic and numeric data in magnetic cores using the extended binary coded decimal interchange code.

Most computer instructions have the capacity to identify the location and length of a data field as well as the operation to be performed with the data. In this manner data in core storage can be accessed by addressing the high-order position of the data and stating the number of positions in the field. For example, if we wanted to use the word "clasp" in Figure 7–5, we would address storage location 1006 and state that the field contained four more positions.

Monolithic Storage

Until recently the major type of primary storage component was magnetic core. However, technological innovations in the manufacture of

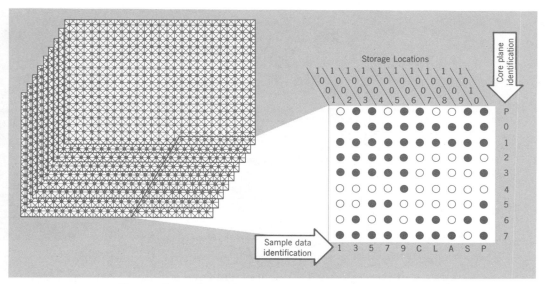

Figure 7-5. *Representation of data stored in magnetic cores.*

monolithic semiconductor circuits have led to the use of these components as primary storage units in some computers.

One common type of *monolithic storage array chip* is approximately ⅛-inch square and contains over 1,000 elementary components, transistors, resistors, etc. The components are integrated on a chip to form 128 storage bits and their associated decoding, addressing, and sensing circuitry. Two storage array chips are mounted on a half-inch square substrate (see Figure 6–3), and a pair of substrates is packaged into a storage array module. Each ½-inch square storage module, which contains 512 storage bits (4 × 128), is mounted on a storage array card as shown in Figure 7–6.

Monolithic storage units have the following advantages over magnetic core storage units:

1. They are less expensive to manufacture.
2. They have improved reliability.
3. Compact components and shorter circuits enable faster storage read-in and read-out speeds.
4. The nondestructive read-out capability of these components also contributes to faster read-out speeds. Core storage read-out is destructive and requires a regeneration cycle after the read-out process.
5. Dense component packaging reduces system space requirements.

Recently, as a result of advanced technology, large-scale integrated (LSI) semiconductor circuits have been used for main storage. These LSI

Figure 7-6. *Monolithic storage array card (left) and basic storage unit.*
(Courtesy International Business Machines Corporation.)

chips have increased storage density, which results in reduced space requirements and faster data transfer speeds.

To fully appreciate how a CPU can perform from several hundred thousand operations to more than several million operations a second, it is necessary to have a general understanding of the numbering systems and arithmetic operations that are involved. These are described in the following section.

COMPUTER NUMBERING SYSTEMS AND ARITHMETIC

In the preceding chapter we learned that a form of binary code is used in the internal operations of the computer because of design characteristics. Nevertheless, most computers can accept or deliver data in decimal form. In preparing input, data is written in standard decimal or alphabetic form. Computers automatically convert data into the proper mode for internal use. They also convert processed data into decimal and alphabetic characters when preparing output.

Because of this automatic conversion of data, a thorough understanding of the different notational systems is seldom required by business data processing personnel. However, to appreciate the manner in which computers manipulate numbers, we shall expand the discussion of numbering systems included in the preceding chapter and review some of the principles of binary computation.

Arithmetic is performed with binary numbers following the same basic rules as in the decimal system except that the binary system requires more frequent "carries." In binary there is a carry to the next column whenever the total exceeds one. In the decimal system there is a carry to the next column whenever the total exceeds nine.

Addition. In binary addition the following rules apply:

1. 0 plus 0 equals 0
2. 0 plus 1 equals 1
3. 1 plus 1 equals 0, with a 1 carry

EXAMPLE.

	Decimal	*Binary*
	9	1001
	+ 5	+0101
	14	1110

Subtraction. In binary subtraction, which is equally simple, the following rules are used:

1. 0 minus 0 equals 0
2. 1 minus 0 equals 1
3. 1 minus 1 equals 0
4. 0 minus 1 equals 1, with 1 borrowed from the left

EXAMPLE.

	Decimal	*Binary*
	13	1101
	− 6	−0110
	7	0111

Although subtraction is generally performed in the traditional way as shown, it should be understood that computers also perform subtraction by a complement addition process. Illustrations of how a computer executes subtraction by forming a complement of the subtrahend and by adding this number to the minuend are not included here, as they are not essential to understanding how a CPU functions.

Multiplication. The rules for multiplying two binary numbers are:

1. 0 times 0 equals 0
2. 0 times 1 equals 0
3. 1 times 1 equals 1

EXAMPLE.

	Decimal	*Binary*
	6	110
	× 5	×101
	30	110
		000
		110
		11110

Division. Binary division proceeds in the same manner as decimal division, except that the rules for binary multiplication and subtraction must be applied.

EXAMPLE.

	Decimal	*Binary*

$$
\begin{array}{r}
6 \\
5\,\overline{)30} \\
30 \\
\hline
00
\end{array}
\qquad
\begin{array}{r}
110 \\
101\,\overline{)11110} \\
101 \\
\hline
0101 \\
101 \\
\hline
0000
\end{array}
$$

Decimal to Binary Conversion. The conversion of a decimal number to its binary equivalent is accomplished by dividing the decimal number by two, the base of the binary system, until the quotient reaches zero. The remainder of each successive division is recorded to the right. The remainders, read in reverse, comprise the binary number.

EXAMPLE.

$$
\left.
\begin{array}{l}
2\,\overline{)57} \\
2\,\overline{)28} \text{ with the remainder 1} \\
2\,\overline{)14} \text{ with the remainder 0} \\
2\,\overline{)7} \text{ with the remainder 0} \\
2\,\overline{)3} \text{ with the remainder 1} \\
2\,\overline{)1} \text{ with the remainder 1} \\
\phantom{2\,\overline{)}}0 \text{ with the remainder 1}
\end{array}
\right\} 111001
$$

Binary to Decimal Conversion. The conversion of a binary number to its decimal equivalent is accomplished by the following steps:

1. Multiply the high-order digit of the number by its base
2. Add the next digit to the product
3. Multiply the sum by the base
4. Continue the process until the low-order digit has been added

EXAMPLE.

$$
\begin{array}{r}
1 \quad\ 1 \quad 0 \quad 1_2 \\
\times\ 2 \\
\hline
2 \\
+\ 1 \\
\hline
3 \\
\times\ 2 \\
\hline
6 \\
+\ 0 \\
\hline
6 \\
\times\ 2 \\
\hline
12 \\
+\ 1 \\
\hline
13_{10}
\end{array}
$$

Hexadecimal (a hexagon has six sides, and decimal means ten) stands for the base 16 numbering system. Most computers operate on a principle that utilizes the hexadecimal system, as it provides high utilization of computer storage and an expanded set of characters for representing data.

As we have already seen, a numbering system requires as many different symbols as there are in the base of the system. Thus, base 10 (decimal) requires ten different symbols. Base 2 (binary) requires two. In base 16 (hexadecimal) sixteen symbols are required. Because only a single character is allowed for each absolute value, the hexadecimal system uses the ten symbols of the decimal system for the values 0 through 9, and the first six letters of the alphabet to represent values 10 through 15 (Table 7–1).

Table 7-1 Decimal, Binary, and Hexadecimal Equivalents

Decimal	Binary	Hexadecimal
10 1	8 4 2 1	16 1
1	1	1
2	1 0	2
3	1 1	3
4	1 0 0	4
5	1 0 1	5
6	1 1 0	6
7	1 1 1	7
8	1 0 0 0	8
9	1 0 0 1	9
1 0	1 0 1 0	A
1 1	1 0 1 1	B
1 2	1 1 0 0	C
1 3	1 1 0 1	D
1 4	1 1 1 0	E
1 5	1 1 1 1	F
1 6	1 0 0 0 0	1 0

As illustrated in Table 7–2, the positional significance of hexadecimal symbols is based on the progression of powers of 16. The highest number that can be represented in the units position is 15. Therefore, we must carry 1 to the next position to the left to make the number 16. This then becomes the 16 position. The next number to the left is then 16 times as large, or 256; the next number is also 16 times as large, or 4,096; etc.

Table 7-2 The Hexadecimal Numbering System

Positional significance:	16^5	16^4	16^3	16^2	16^1	16^0
Positional value:	1,048,576	65,536	4,096	256	16	1

Binary-Hexadecimal Conversion. Conversion from binary to hexadecimal and vice versa is a simple process, as there is a direct 4-to-1 relationship (2^4 to 2^1) between the base 16 and base 2 systems. Thus, every four binary digits become a single hexadecimal digit, and each hexadecimal digit becomes four binary digits.

EXAMPLE.   Convert hexadecimal 2A6 to binary:

$$
\begin{array}{ccc}
2 & A & 6 \\
\downarrow & \downarrow & \downarrow \\
0010 & 1010 & 0110
\end{array}
$$

Convert binary 001010100110 to hexadecimal:

$$
\begin{array}{ccc}
0010 & 1010 & 0110 \\
\downarrow & \downarrow & \downarrow \\
2 & A & 6
\end{array}
$$

Hexadecimal Computations

Arithmetic is performed with hexadecimal numbers following the same basic rules used in the decimal system, except that hexadecimal addition does not result in a carry until the decimal value of 15 is exceeded.

EXAMPLE.

$$
\begin{array}{ll}
\text{Decimal:} & 9 + 1 = 10_{10} \\
\text{Hexadecimal:} & F + 1 = 10_{16}
\end{array}
$$

Addition. Since the hexadecimal numbering system uses sixteen symbols, it has too many possible conditions to state all the rules regarding hexadecimal addition. Instead, we will illustrate hexadecimal addition with a series of problems.

EXAMPLES.

$$
\begin{array}{ccccccc}
8 & 8 & A & F & 2A & AA & 9A \\
+7 & +8 & +3 & +F & +B1 & +C6 & +57 \\
\hline
F & 10 & D & 1E & DB & 170 & F1
\end{array}
$$

Subtraction. Subtraction in hexadecimal is just like decimal subtraction, except that when borrowing from the position to the left the value transferred is 16 rather than 10.

EXAMPLE.

Decimal

$$
\begin{array}{ll}
13 \text{ becomes} & 0(13) \\
- \ 8 & - \ \ 8 \\
\hline
 & 5
\end{array}
$$

Hexadecimal

$$
\begin{array}{ll}
13 \text{ becomes} & 0(19) \leftarrow \left(\begin{array}{l}\text{Decimal} \\ \text{value}\end{array}\right) \\
- \ 8 & - \ \ 8 \\
\hline
 & B
\end{array}
$$

Another hexadecimal example:

$$\begin{array}{ll} \text{F9A} \text{ becomes} & \text{F8(26)} \leftarrow \left(\begin{array}{l}\text{Decimal}\\ \text{value}\end{array}\right) \\ -\underline{\text{A8F}} & -\underline{\text{A8} \quad \text{F}} \\ & \quad 50 \quad \text{B} \end{array}$$

**IMPORTANT WORDS
AND PHRASES**

control unit
program
operation code
operand
instruction cycle
execution cycle
arithmetic-logical unit

fixed point
 arithmetic
floating point
 arithmetic
logical operations
register
adder

main storage
magnetic core
 storage
monolithic storage
hexadecimal
 numbering
 system

REVIEW QUESTIONS

1. What four types of activities are directed and coordinated by the control unit?
2. Define a stored program.
3. What are the functions of the arithmetic-logical unit?
4. What three classes of arithmetic operations are performed by computers?
5. Name four types of logical operations.
6. What are the functions of a register?
7. On what basis must each position of main storage be accessible?
8. What does LSI represent?
9. What are the sums of the following binary values?
   (a) 1 + 1,   (b) 101 + 10,   (c) 111 + 1.
10. What are the sums of the following hexadecimal values?
    (a) 7 + 7,   (b) 8 + 8,   (c) A + 4,   (d) C + D.

8 EDP AUXILIARY STORAGE

Auxiliary storage supplements the primary storage of a computer and usually holds much larger volumes of data. Auxiliary storage devices attached to a single computer can store from several hundred thousand to several billion characters of data. The data paths of auxiliary storage devices are always connected to primary storage. However, since data moving from or to auxiliary storage must be routed through primary storage, it is not as rapidly accessible as the data in primary storage.

There are two basic auxiliary storage techniques, sequential and random. In *sequential storage* data is recorded and accessed serially in the order in which it occurs. Thus, the search for and retrieval of a specific item of data may require the scanning of many records preceding it in storage.

In *random storage* any record can be located directly without scanning all of the other records ahead of it in sequence. Instead, the access device proceeds directly to a specified location for the purpose of reading or recording data without regard to the sequence or location of data previously read or recorded. This ability to go directly from one record to another regardless of location gives random access devices an important advantage over sequential access devices in many data processing systems.

Sequential and random processing techniques will be discussed in greater detail after the following description of auxiliary storage devices.

TYPES OF AUXILIARY STORAGE

Magnetic Disk Storage

The magnetic disk is a thin metal disk resembling a phonograph record. It is coated on both sides with a magnetic recording material. Data is stored as magnetized spots arranged in binary form in concentric tracks on each face of the disk. A characteristic of disk storage is that data is recorded serially bit by bit, eight bits per byte, along a track rather than by columns of characters as shown in the illustration of core storage (Figure 7–5).

Figure 8–1 shows data recorded serially using the extended binary coded decimal interchange code. The absence of parity bits in this illustration results from the fact that the technique of checking parity in each byte is generally not used with direct access devices. Instead these devices utilize a more efficient method of reliability checking, which will not be explained here because of its complexity.

Disks are normally mounted in a stack on a rotating vertical shaft. Enough space is left between disks to allow access arms to move in and read or record data. Access arms are usually forked and have at least two recording heads. Thus, upon entry into a stack of disks a recording head is available to read or write on either side of a disk.

As all access arms on a drive move in and out in unison, they are all positioned at the same time over comparable tracks of each of the recording surfaces. This enables data to be read or written on the same track of each recording surface without moving the access arms. This

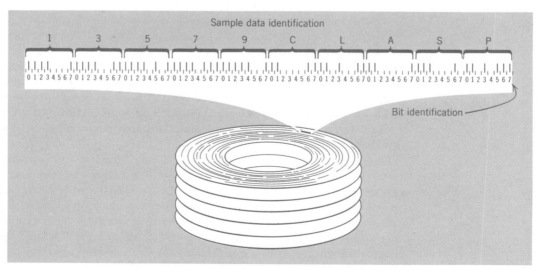

Figure 8-1. *Representation of data recorded on a disk storage device.*

significantly improves data transfer speeds, as there is no interruption in reading or writing required for the movement of the heads.

Organizing data to take advantage of this design characteristic is referred to as the *cylinder concept.* A cylinder of data is the amount of data that is accessible with one positioning of the access mechanism. Figure 8–8, a layout of an indexed sequential file, is an example of how the cylinder concept is utilized in one type of file organization.

A single magnetic disk unit is capable of storing more than 300 million characters. Usually more than one disk unit can be attached to a computer. Magnetic disk storage has an excellent cost-to-storage ratio and is very reliable. Although access speed is limited by the revolving action of disks and search movement of the arms, the average seek time (time it takes for the read-write heads to be positioned over a given track) is about 30 milliseconds, and the average rotational delay (time it takes for data within the track to reach the read-write head) is about 8.3 milliseconds. Once the data is located by the read-write head, the data transfer rate can be close to 1,200,000 bytes per second. Data recorded on magnetic disks can be randomly or sequentially accessed.

A major advantage of most disk storage devices is that disk packs, each consisting of a stack of disks, may be removed and replaced on the drive unit. This capability is helpful in several ways. First, the pack required for a particular job may be mounted before the job is started, removed when the job is completed, and replaced with the pack necessary to perform the next job. Second, if the size of a file for a particular job exceeds the capacity of a single pack, multiple packs may be used.

Recent innovations have resulted in significant increases in data storage capacity, much faster data transfer speeds, and improved reliability. Some of the disk storage units with these characteristics are manufactured with nonremovable disk packs. A unit of this type is shown in Figure 8–2. These units also may have, in addition to the moving-head access storage described above, a limited amount of fixed-head access storage, which is ideally suited for rapid access to frequently used data or instructions.

Storage capacity may be extended further by the use of multiple disk units. For example, the direct access storage facility shown in Figure 8–2 consists of two disk storage units, each with a storage capacity of over 317 million bytes.

Vast storage capacity, direct accessibility of data, and a relatively fast data transfer rate, along with other advantages, have made it very common for disk storage devices to be attached to computers.

Magnetic Drum Storage

The magnetic drum (Figure 8–3) has been used extensively as a means of storing data, especially in the early computers, many of which used the drum for primary storage. In today's larger computer systems the drum is used for rapid access to frequently used data and other auxiliary storage functions. Access to data can be on a random or sequential basis.

Figure 8-2. *IBM 3350 storage subsystem capable of storing 634 million bytes.*
(Courtesy International Business Machines Corporation.)

Figure 8-3. *Magnetic drum storage.*
(Courtesy Sperry UNIVAC, A Division of Sperry Rand Corporation.)

A drum is a cylinder with a magnetizable outer surface on which data is recorded serially in a series of bands around the drum in a manner similar to that utilized on disk storage. As the drum rotates at a constant speed, data is recorded or sensed by a set of read-write heads. The heads are positioned close enough to the surface of the drum to be able to magnetize the surface and to sense the magnetization on it. The heads contain coils of fine wire wound around tiny magnetic cores. There may be one or more heads for each drum track or one or more heads that can be moved to the various tracks. The drum may rotate up to 3,500 revolutions per minute, and the data transfer rate to or from the processing unit may be up to 1,440,000 bytes per second. The rotational delay to a specific part of the track ranges from 0 to 17 milliseconds and averages 8.5 milliseconds.

Data is stored in the form of minute magnetized spots, arranged in binary form on the individual recording tracks. Spots are magnetized by sending pulses of current through the write coil. The polarity of a spot is determined by the direction of the current flow. Thus, depending on their polarity, spots can represent either 1s or 0s, the two binary digits.

The magnetic drum storage unit is ideally suited to applications in which a very high data transfer rate for a limited amount of data is required. Recently, fixed-head disk storage modules with fixed read-write heads for each track are also being used to meet these high data transfer rate requirements.

Magnetic Bubble Storage

A new way of storing data in the form of magnetic bubbles is being evaluated for a variety of applications. The magnetic bubble device, invented at Bell Laboratories, consists of round magnetic regions whose magnetization is the opposite of the thin film of magnetic material in which they reside. The tiny bubbles can be moved around rapidly under the control of electrical signals generated in metal circuit patterns deposited on top of the magnetic film. The bubbles are used to record and store data. Figure 8–4 shows an enlargement of a magnetic bubble circuit pattern in an experimental device.

Bubble memories have a number of important advantages over existing technologies. Their production cost is low and they have low power requirements. They are highly reliable since the memory contains no moving parts. In addition, bubble memories can hold data without electricity to sustain them. Thus, data is not lost even if power fails. Data stored in the form of magnetic bubbles can be randomly accessed at speeds that are slow by semiconductor storage standards but several times faster than disk storage.

These characteristics, and potential storage densities of perhaps a billion bits per square inch, make magnetic bubble devices very promising as a replacement or supplement for magnetic drums or disks.

Figure 8-4. *Enlargement of the circuit pattern in an experimental magnetic bubble storage device at the IBM Thomas J. Watson Research Center.*
(Courtesy International Business Machines Corporation.)

Magnetic Tape Storage

Magnetic tape may be classified as auxiliary or external storage depending on the circumstances (see Figure 9–3). Active tape records mounted on tape read-write units are considered as auxiliary storage during the time that they are connected to and controlled by the computer. However, when inactive tape records are removed from the tape read-write units and stored, they are classified as external storage. In other words, they hold data in a form prescribed for the computer but they are separated from the computer. The same could be said for most magnetic disk packs.

Figure 8–5 shows how the same data represented in preceding illustrations would be recorded on magnetic tape in the extended binary coded decimal interchange code. Note that the channels on nine-track tape do not run in 0 to 7 sequence. The purpose of this is to place the most frequently used channels near the center of the tape, thereby reducing the chance of dust, dirt, or physical damage to the outer edge of the tape causing data to be lost. As shown in Figure 8–5, parity may be checked horizontally at the end of each record on magnetic tape in addition to being checked vertically by each byte.

Another method of recording data on magnetic tape is called *phase encoding*. In this method, instead of recording only 1 bits, both 0 bits and 1 bits are recorded as magnetized spots that are opposite in polarity. This method of recording allows distinction between 0 bits and absence of recording and facilitates verification of recording. Nine-track phase

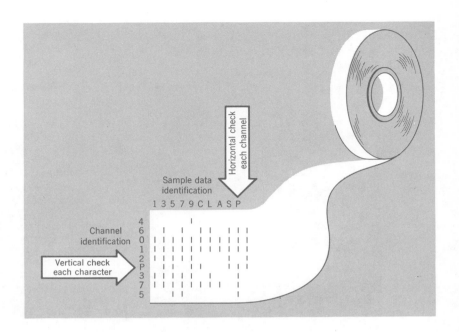

Figure 8-5. *Representation of data recorded on magnetic tape.*

encoding (PE) provides optimum performance and reliability with greater recording density and more rapid transfer of data.

Many of the newer tape drives employ the group coded recording (GCR) technique for encoding (recording) and checking data. This technique permits instantaneous correction of errors occurring in any track or in two tracks simultaneously.

Magnetic tape drives can move tape at speeds of more than 200 inches a second. The data transfer rate for magnetic tape is governed by two factors: (1) data density (bits per inch), and (2) tape speed. Slow-speed magnetic tape drives might have a data transfer rate of 15,000 characters a second, and high-speed tape drives, at 6,250 characters an inch, might have a data transfer rate of 1,250,000 characters a second. Since data is recorded on magnetic tape serially, it must be accessed sequentially.

For the medium to large computer user, the *mass storage facility,* a recent innovation, provides on-line access to a very large collection of data. The system is primarily intended to replace a large-volume magnetic tape library. The mass storage facility employs as the primary storage medium a cylindrical data cartridge, approximately 2 inches in diameter and 4 inches long, containing a 771-inch length of 3-inch wide magnetic tape. Each tape can contain up to 50 million bytes of data. The data cartridges are stored in honeycomb-shaped cells in the mass storage facility (Figure 8–6).

Magnetic disk drives serve as intermediate storage units (staging devices) between the CPU and the mass storage facility. Data cartridges

Figure 8-6. *IBM 3850 mass storage facility. (Courtesy International Business Machines Corporation.)*

are retrieved; the magnetic tape is read by an accessor mechanism; and the data is transferred to magnetic disk (staged) for access by the CPU.

Knowledge of how data is organized for storage on auxiliary storage devices is a prerequisite to understanding the value and significant contribution of auxiliary storage devices to electronic data processing. This subject is covered in the following section.

Records

As was noted earlier, a byte (composed of eight data bits and a parity bit) is the smallest addressable unit of data in the primary storage unit of a computer. A *logical record* consists of from one to several hundred bytes of data related to a unique identifier or *key*. For example, a payroll file would contain a logical record for each employee on the payroll. The key for each payroll record would probably be the employee social security number.

Two or more records that are written, read, or stored as a single unit are called a *record block*. Each block of logical records is called a *physical record*. The primary reasons for blocking records are to utilize auxiliary storage efficiently and to reduce the amount of computer time required to process a file. Figure 8–7 illustrates the organization of unblocked and blocked records on magnetic tape and shows how blocked records conserve tape space and decrease the number of interruptions in the processing of data by reducing the quantity of inter-record gaps (IRG).

It should be noted that actual processing is done on individual logical records even though the records are accessed a block at a time.

Characteristics of Files

A *file* is a collection of records organized according to some common characteristic. A file may also be referred to as a *data set*.

There are a number of important considerations in determining an efficient method of file organization. Included are:

1. The volume of records in the file. Large files must be organized very carefully to minimize the time required to locate specific records.
2. The frequency of reference to the file; that is, will the file be utilized on an hourly, daily, weekly, or monthly cycle.
3. The amount of transaction activity. Additions and deletions are of particular concern, as they can be processed far more efficiently with the appropriate method of file organization.

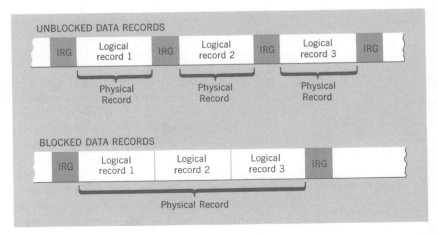

Figure 8-7. *Organization of unblocked and blocked records on magnetic tape.*

4. The distribution of activity. If a relatively low percentage of records on a large file is to be processed in a run, the file should probably be organized so that any record can be directly accessed.
5. Finally, the growth potential of the file must be kept in mind when selecting a method of organization.

File Organization Methods

The term *file organization* refers to the relationship of the key of a record to the physical location of that record in the file. The basic methods of organizing files of records are sequential and random.

Sequential File Organization.   In a sequential file the records are stored one after the other in ascending or descending order according to some key. The key may be based on the alphabet, some numerical scheme, or a combination of both. For example, a sequential customer file might utilize an alphabetical key based on names or a numerical key based on account numbers. An example of the use of a combined key would be a file of automobile licenses including both letters of the alphabet and numerals.

On direct access devices, the sequential organization and other methods to be described later usually employ the cylinder concept of recording data. The *cylinder concept* makes it possible to utilize direct access storage devices very efficiently. This is achieved by taking advantage of the fact that all access arms on a disk drive move in and out in unison. They are, therefore, all positioned at the same time over the relative track on each recording surface. This allows data to be read or written on the same track of each recording surface without interruption for head movement.

Each track represents a complete circle on the disk recording surface in which data is recorded serially bit by bit. A track is not a spiral as in the case of a phonograph record. Thus, a discrete jump of the read-write head is required to get from one disk track to the next one. To minimize the movement of the track read-write arms, data is recorded beginning in track 1 of disk surface 1 and then down through the cylinder without having to move access arms. Then with a single shift to track 2 of disk surface 1, data can again be recorded downward track by track until the area on that particular cylinder is exhausted.

Thus, it can be seen that a cylinder consists of the related tracks on all of the disks on the drive. Accordingly, a cylinder of data may be defined as the amount of data that is accessible with one positioning of all the read-write heads on an access mechanism. This design characteristic contributes significantly to processing speed since switching between read-write heads in the system is electronic rather than physical. Figure 8–8 is an example of how the cylinder concept is utilized in one type of file organization.

In addition to sequential organization, two of the most common methods of organizing files recorded on direct access devices are *indexed sequential* and *random*. The remaining discussion will be limited to these

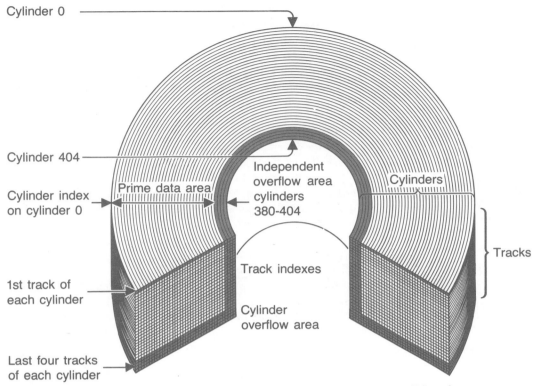

Cylinder 0

Cylinder 404

Cylinder index
on cylinder 0

Prime data area

Independent
overflow area
cylinders
380-404

Cylinders

Tracks

1st track of
each cylinder

Track indexes

Cylinder
overflow area

Last four tracks
of each cylinder

Figure 8-8. *Representation of an indexed sequential file on a disk pack.*

two file organization methods, as most of the other methods are similar in principle to one of them.

Indexed Sequential Organization. In an *indexed sequential file* the records are organized sequentially with indexes that permit quick access to individual records as well as rapid sequential processing. In order to narrow the search for a particular record, three indexes of different levels may be created and recorded as the primary sequential file is loaded onto a direct access storage device. The three levels are the *master index* pointing to a *cylinder index,* which points to a *track index,* which points to a specific data record.

The *track index,* which is the lowest level of index, identifies the contents of any given cylinder of data. The contents are, of course, identified by keys. Each cylinder in the prime data area has a track index indicating the highest record key in each track within the cylinder. This index serves as a guide in searching for the track on which a particular record is located. This is determined by searching until the high record in a track is found to be equal to or greater than the key of the record being sought. This would indicate that the desired record is located in that track. When the appropriate track is located, a sequential search is conducted to find the specific record. Each track index must be recorded on the first track or tracks of the cylinder that it indexes.

The next higher level of index is the *cylinder index*. It consists of a series of entries identifying the key of the highest record that was stored on each cylinder in the prime data area. Thus, the cylinder index indicates the contents of the entire file and serves to narrow the search for a specific record to a particular cylinder. As indicated above, the track index at the beginning of that cylinder further narrows the search to a particular track. In other words, the cylinder index indicates the range of keys within each of the cylinders in a file, and the track index indicates the range of keys within each of the tracks on a given cylinder.

The cutout in Figure 8–8 shows how an indexed sequential file might be organized on a disk pack. Note that the cylinder index is located on cylinder 0. This index points to the proper track index. Next, note that the track index appears in the first track of each cylinder reserved for the prime data area. This index points to the proper track in the cylinder. Also note that the last four cylinders have been reserved for cylinder overflow area. Files maintained in sequential fashion do not normally have space for insertion of additional records in the file. Therefore, as new records are placed in the prime data area, an existing record is usually bumped into the cylinder overflow area associated with the proper cylinder. When that area is full, added records are then placed in the independent overflow area. In both cases appropriate additions are made to the indexes, as records added to an indexed sequential file are kept in logical sequence and identified by the indexes even though they are not in physical sequence.

The *master index* is the highest level of index and may be used when the cylinder index occupies more than four tracks and a search through it would be too time-consuming. The master index is usually stored immediately before the cylinder index. It consists of one entry for each track of the cylinder index, thus reducing the search time required to locate a particular cylinder.

As the cylinder and independent overflow areas become full, the time required to locate records increases. When this occurs, or in any event when the independent overflow area becomes full, the file must be reorganized. The most common method of doing this is to sequentially record the file on another device and then reload the file in the original area. This process also causes deleted records to be dropped as the file is loaded in the prime area. Records that are to be deleted are usually flagged during normal processing of the file and then dropped from the file when it is reloaded.

The *indexed sequential access method* (ISAM) programs that are used to create indexed sequential files and add, alter, or delete records are provided by the equipment manufacturer. These programs are tailored by the user to meet his requirements. They are used together with the user's processing program to provide the necessary interface between the user-developed processing program and the auxiliary storage device on which the file is organized.

Users of one of the IBM virtual operating systems have the option of using the *virtual storage access method* (VSAM) instead of the indexed sequential access method. The VSAM, which is a more recently developed access method, offers certain advantages over the ISAM. For example, VSAM is designed to give the user options for data security and integrity and to give improved performance as a result of more efficiently organized indexes and files.

Random Organization. In a *random organization file* records are stored without regard to the sequence of the control field. A random file may be organized in several different ways, but there must be some predictable relationship between the key of a record and the direct access storage device address of the record. This relationship permits rapid access to any record. However, it may require extra processing time to obtain the address if the address must be derived.

Addresses may be determined by means of direct addressing or indirect addressing techniques. In *direct addressing* every key in the file is converted to a unique address by the application of a mathematical formula to the control field. For example, in one method the numeric record key is divided by the number of records per track; the quotient equals the track address, and the remainder plus one equals the sequential location of the record within the track. An inventory file with numeric stock numbers would probably be a good application for direct addressing of a random organization file.

Indirect addressing enables the range of keys for a file to be compressed to a smaller range of addresses by using one of the following randomizing techniques.

Randomizing method	Description
Division/remainder	A common method in which the key is divided by a prime number (a number evenly divisible only by itself and one) that is close to the number of addresses allotted to the file. Divide the remainder by the number of records per track. The quotient equals the track address and the remainder plus one equals the record number.
Digit analysis	May be employed when it is possible to make use of any existing evenness in the distribution of the keys. The number of times that each digit appears in each position of the keys is analyzed, and this information is used to determine which positions of the key may be used as the address.

Randomizing method	Description
Folding	The key is split into two or more parts, which are added together, and the sum or part of it is used as the address.
Radix	The key is transformed to a different radix or base, the excess digits are discarded, and the remaining digits are the address.

As can be seen, random file organization has considerable flexibility. However, this may appear to be a disadvantage because the user is primarily responsible for the logic and programming required to locate records in a random file.

With this understanding of file organization methods and the media on which the various types of files can best be stored, we are ready to discuss how these files may be processed.

Techniques of File Processing

Transactions (additions, deletions, and changes) may be sequentially or randomly processed against a file. Files maintained in sequential order are normally updated by the use of *sequential processing* techniques, which require that the transactions to update such files be sorted into the same order using the same key or record identifier. This enables transaction keys and master file keys to be successively compared. Each time a master file key is matched by a transaction file key, the master record is updated by the transaction, and the result is written onto the updated master file. Master records for which there are no matching transaction records are copied onto the updated file in proper sequence without change.

When magnetic tape and punched cards are used as the file media, sequential processing is the only efficient method of processing the files. These files are most efficiently processed when a majority of the records are processed each time the file is used or updated. In addition, for economic reasons sequential processing techniques dictate that data must first be accumulated in sufficient quantity and batched for processing. In other words, a number of similar items are collected, sorted, and placed in sequence for processing together. Since sequential processing generally requires the batching of data, there are many applications that cannot be handled effectively on a sequential basis. Any applications requiring immediate posting of transactions to maintain up-to-date balances or current status, for example, cannot be handled easily with the use of sequential access files.

Files stored on direct access storage devices may be sequentially or randomly processed efficiently provided the files are properly organized for the type of processing desired. Specific records in sequentially organized files recorded on direct access storage devices may be quickly located without the necessity of reading all of the preceding records. This is accomplished by a technique known as *binary search*. To perform a binary search of a file, the search key is first compared with the last record in the middle cylinder of the file. If the search key is higher than that record, the search key is next compared with the last record in the middle cylinder of the upper half of the file. However, if the search key is lower than the last record of the middle cylinder, it is next compared with the last record of the middle cylinder in the lower half of the file. The binary search continues in this manner until the cylinder with the record equal to the search key is located (Figure 8–9).

An advantage of *random processing* is that input transactions may be processed against the file in whatever order they occur, rather than having to be put in a particular sequence. This allows transactions to be processed individually and facilitates immediate updating of status or balances. For example, it is possible to process random transactions such as those generated by a teleprocessing system against a direct access file.

Another advantage of random processing is that transactions may be processed against more than one file during a run. For example, when a sale is recorded, the account receivable may be entered, an inventory adjustment may be made, etc. Since the transactions are handled less frequently, this can save sorting time, reduce processing time, and minimize control problems.

In random processing the record to be revised is copied from direct access storage, entered in main storage, updated, and then written back in the same location. This destroys the previous contents of that storage location and creates problems of file reliability that are not encountered in a batch processing system employing punched cards or magnetic tape.

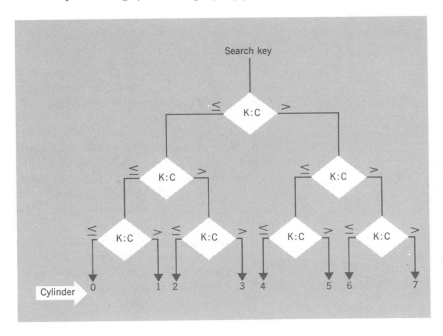

Figure 8-9. *Binary search of a sequential file.*

When these sequential media are used, the original files are still available to provide backup information after new updated files have been written. If the updating of a record in direct access storage is in error, the record that existed prior to updating is no longer available. Therefore, special transaction editing techniques are required to insure the integrity of the file.

DATA MANAGEMENT SYSTEMS

As computer processing techniques became more sophisticated, recognition of the fact that most systems performed the basic functions of adding, changing, deleting, and retrieving records led to the development of generalized data management systems. A *data management system* (DMS) is a series of computer programs used primarily to aid in the manipulation of computer files and the extraction of data from the files for report preparation. Data management systems perform these tasks by interpreting the programmer's specifications of what he wants to accomplish in the program and then producing the detailed program ready for either execution or compilation and execution.

Data management systems are designed to facilitate the development and programming of traditional systems where the approach is to organize data in files related to various applications. Although these systems have been fairly successful as an aid in developing specific applications, they are not to be confused with data base management systems that provide storage, control, and retrieval of data contained in one or a combination of files referred to as a *data base*.

DATA BASE

Remember that the term "data" is used to denote any facts, figures, letters, words, charts, or symbols that represent an idea, object, condition, or situation. Also remember that information is derived from data. Until recently information could be produced only from manual or computer files organized by function or application system. Under the new *data base* concept a collection of data is maintained in a nonredundant structure designed for use in a broad range of applications. In other words, a basic file of varied data is developed to meet the requirements of a variety of applications without the necessity of incorporating and thus repeating the data common to each application.

For example, a data base designed to handle the information requirements of the personnel-related activities of an organization will contain data regarding personnel, payroll factors, tax and other deductions, group insurance, abilities and qualifications of personnel, and so on. Let us assume that some event takes place such as an employee termination, the addition of a dependent, a promotion, or a change of address. If a data base is maintained, less computer time would be required to process the transaction than would be needed to update the same information in several files related to different applications. A data base also eliminates the necessity of maintaining controls to assure that common data in various applications files is current and complete.

Thus, the integration of data in a data base reduces redundancy, permits easier updating, improves control, and gives greater flexibility of use. Also, data bases can be structured in a number of ways so that both predictable and unanticipated information needs can be easily satisfied with both on-line and batch processing methods.

DATA BASE MANAGEMENT SYSTEM

A *data base management system* (DBMS) is comprised of complex computer programs designed to maintain and manage a volume of data in a nonredundant structure so that it is readily available for processing in multiple applications. With data base management systems, applications programs are flexible and can be easily modified in response to changing requirements without concern about the specific data involved. This results from the fact that all programs draw upon a single source of complete and current data. Likewise, changes can be made in the data base architecture without modifying existing applications programs.

This independence of data and programs frees a programmer from concern about the structure and location of data elements. Data base descriptions define the structure of data to be used in applications programs (logical data structure) and define the manner in which the data is stored in auxiliary storage (physical data structure). This enables an applications programmer to deal only with the logical data structure and never directly with a physical data structure. A DBMS generally utilizes the file organization and access methods developed by the equipment manufacturer.

A DBMS has utility programs to aid in establishing and maintaining data bases. A DBMS also provides data base integrity through control of updates to assure validity of the data base. This is accomplished by the creation of an audit trail (log) and through special programs designed to recreate or recover a damaged data base. A DBMS provides security capabilities to assist in assuring that information is available only to those entitled to it and that only authorized persons may update the data base.

Finally, a DBMS can provide the user more nearly current information than is available with batch processing. This is made possible by teleprocessing capabilities that enable remote terminal users to enter both inquiry and update transactions.

IMPORTANT WORDS AND PHRASES

sequential storage	physical record	random file
random storage	file	data management system
logical record	sequential file	data base
record block	indexed sequential file	data base management system

1. Name the three primary types of auxiliary storage devices.
2. What advantages have contributed to the widespread use of magnetic disk storage?
3. Why is magnetic tape limited to sequential processing?
4. Define a logical record and a physical record.
5. What is a record block?
6. What is the definition of a file?
7. What are the basic methods of organizing files of records?
8. How are records stored in a sequential file?
9. What is a cylinder of data?
10. What are the three index levels in an indexed sequential file?
11. What are the two advantages of random processing?
12. What is a data base?

9 EDP INPUT-OUTPUT DEVICES

The discussion at this point of input devices as well as output devices may seem questionable. However, since many of the devices used for output are actually part of a combined input-output (I/O) device, it is more practical to consider the two functions simultaneously. Also, this sequence was chosen on the assumption that it would be easier for the reader to comprehend the significance of I/O devices after having acquired an understanding of the basic functions of a computer system.

Communication with the data processing system is achieved through an input-output device linked directly to the system. Input information is converted to a form usable by the system and is transmitted to main storage. Similarly, output involves converting processed data from main storage to a form or language compatible with an output medium and recording the data through an output device. This chapter will describe these functions and the methods used for input and output of data.

Since the computer is an electronic device and input-output units are primarily electromechanical devices, the computer is capable of operating at much faster speeds. To enable the computer to operate as nearly as possible at full capacity, the transfer of data between I/O devices and the main storage unit usually takes place independently through an intermediary known as a *channel*.

The I/O channel and associated control and connecting units provide for the *buffering* (temporary storage), coordination, and transfer of I/O data. Thus, the central processing unit is relieved of the burden of communicating directly with I/O devices. This permits I/O operations to proceed concurrently with the processing of data. In other words, the computer can carry on high-speed computations while input data is being received and while output data is being transferred (Figure 9–1).

The channel that performs this function may be an independent unit complete with necessary logical and storage capabilities, in effect, a small special purpose computer capable of performing only I/O operations; or it may share central processing unit facilities and be physically integrated with the central processing unit. In either case, channel functions are identical.

In some cases a channel data path is shared by several low-speed devices such as card readers, punches, printers, and terminals. In other cases, a channel may accommodate higher data rates but may be limited to only one data transfer operation at a time.

**INPUT-OUTPUT
DEVICES**

All standard I/O devices have certain common characteristics. They are auxiliary machines connected to the computer and under control of the

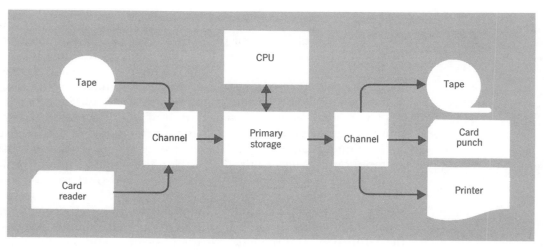

Figure 9-1. *Representation of input-output channel functions.*

central processing unit. Most I/O devices are automatic; once started, they continue to operate as directed by the stored program. These devices can transmit data to or receive data from only the main memory section of the central processing unit.

I/O devices may be used for both input and output or for just one of these functions. More than one form of input and output may be used, and different forms may be combined. For example, punched cards may be used as input and magnetic tape as output. The specific form of input and output depends on the configuration of the computer system and the functions it is designed to perform.

In addition to the standard I/O devices, the use of remotely located devices as I/O units is emerging as an important technique. Included in this category are remote job entry units, transaction recorders, point-of-sale devices, typewriter terminals, visual display units, touch-tone telephones, and voice response systems. Although they are remote from the computer, these devices can be operated on-line; that is, they may transmit data over conventional transmission facilities directly to a computer as the data is recorded at the point of origin. Traditionally, input has been regarded as the weakest link in computer systems because of the time required to record, convert, and read data for input. On-line transaction recorders, and other innovations such as optical character recognition and magnetic ink character recognition, are alleviating the "input bottleneck" by making it possible for data in machine-sensible language to be read directly into a computer.

Each of the I/O devices will be considered separately.

Punched Card Readers and Punches

The punched card is a versatile medium that can be key punched, verified, sorted, collated, and reproduced by punched card machines. It can also be read or punched by certain auxiliary computer devices. The major disadvantages of the punched card are the limit on the amount of data a single card can hold and the relatively slow data transfer rate of card readers and punches. Even so, punched cards are a very important source of data to the computer as well as a useful external storage medium.

Data to be processed is transferred from punched cards into the main storage of a computer system by means of a card reader. Output representing the results of processing may be a printed report or a new punched card file. The input file remains intact. Therefore, both the input and output files are available for further processing by the computer or by punched card machines.

Most card readers and punches use a mechanical picker knife and pinch rollers to transport cards under sensing brushes for reading and under die punches for punching. The majority of these devices read or punch an entire row at a time. Some card-reading machines use vacuum feed and belts to transport cards by the reading station. Certain card readers employ photoelectric reading stations. Most of these read the card serially a column at a time. The punch unit may be a separate device or may be combined with the read unit as a single card read-punch unit (Figure 9–2). Card-reading speeds vary from 100 to 2,000 cards a minute, and card-punching speeds vary from 100 to 300 cards a minute.

All card readers and punches operate at much slower data transfer speeds than the central processing unit. As this causes the central processing unit to lose some of its processing potential, many large installations use separate card-to-tape and tape-to-card converters to take advantage of magnetic tape's much faster data transfer speed. Another technique used to reduce this data transfer difference is the simultaneous operation of a number of input-output devices. To do this a computer must have the capacity to process several programs at the same time.

Punched Tape Readers and Punches

Although punched tape is much less widely used than cards in electronic data processing systems, it has two distinct advantages over the punched card. First, punched tape record lengths are not limited as are the lengths of punched card records. Second, tapes lend themselves to use as a "common language" medium for communication between a variety of data processing devices and computers. In fact, input tapes generally originate as a by-product of other machine operations. Machines that can

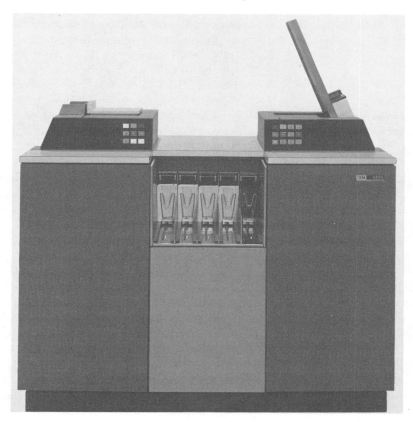

Figure 9-2. *Card read-punch unit.*
(Courtesy International Business Machines Corporation.)

produce punched tape while simultaneously recording transactions or preparing documents in another form include automatic typewriters, accounting machines, cash registers, and window posting machines.

Punched tape has several disadvantages, however. Since tape is a continuous medium, records cannot be added or deleted very easily. Further, data punched in tape cannot be sorted or collated. Consequently, the use of punched tape for file applications is limited.

Most punched tape readers are either photoelectric or electromechanical. The speed of punched tape readers ranges from 10 to 2,000 characters a second. Mechanical readers can perform reliably at speeds up to 100 characters a second. For higher speeds, photoelectric sensing techniques are generally used.

Tape-punching equipment operates more slowly than tape readers. Because of the electromechanical action required to produce the holes in tape, the maximum speed is around 300 characters a second.

Magnetic Tape Units

A single magnetic tape transport can perform both input and output functions (Figure 9–3). In either case, magnetic tape has one of the best ratios of data transfer speed to central processing unit handling speed

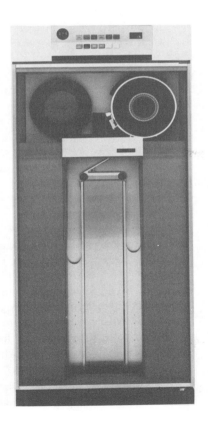

Figure 9-3. *Magnetic tape unit.*
(Courtesy International Business Machines Corporation.)

of any input-output or auxiliary storage medium. Magnetic tape can contain a large amount of data in a compact, easily erasable, and readily available form. The tape is relatively inexpensive, tolerant of many storage conditions, and usable for up to 50,000 passes through a tape read-write unit.

Magnetic tape provides a good means of storing information needed for particular computer runs. This may include programs, tables, and data needed for problem solving. Magnetic tape may also be used for storing intermediate results of computations. However, a more important use of tape is for storing large files of data. Although we are mainly interested here in the use of magnetic tape for input-output purposes, it should be remembered that magnetic tape also serves as a major auxiliary storage medium.

Magnetic tape does have several disadvantages, however. First, data recorded on it cannot be read by people. Therefore, when used as output, it requires conversion to some other medium if it is to be visually readable. Second, it is not a practical medium for random processing of data.

All tape units require two tape reels. The one containing tape to be read or written is called a *file reel* and the other is called a *take-up reel*. Magnetic tape moves from the file reel through vacuum columns and past the read-write heads to the take-up reel. Each of the vacuum columns holds a loop of tape by a controlled vacuum. The purpose of the loop is to allow the tape reels to move independently and to allow some slack between the file reel and the take-up reel. If there were no slack tape, the fast starting and speed of the take-up reel would snap the tape. Because of the vacuum columns, the file reel can release tape and the take-up reel can automatically wind tape without maintaining a constant tension.

Magnetic tape reels are equipped with a file-protection ring that can be used to safeguard data recorded on the tape. When the ring is removed, data cannot be written on the tape, but the tape data can be read for processing.

Modern magnetic tape units and associated control units have proven to be very fast, reliable, and cost-effective input-output devices. Because of these characteristics magnetic tape units have been a major contributor to the rapid growth in the use of computers.

Printers

Printing devices (Figure 9–4) prepare permanent visual records of data received from the computer system. All printing devices have a paper transport that automatically moves the continuous manifold forms as printing progresses. The majority of printing devices are *impact printers* that print by pressing the paper and the ribbon against the proper type as it "flies by" in front of the paper. This method involves the use of type that is engraved and assembled in a chain or engraved on the face of a drum or wheels. During each print cycle, all of the characters in the print

Figure 9-4. *High-speed printer.*
(Courtesy International Business Machines Corporation.)

set move past each printing position and a magnetically actuated hammer presses the paper against an inked ribbon and piece of type at the instant the selected character is in position. This combination of mechanical and electronic technology is one of the marvels of the electronic data processing system.

Most high-speed printers can print 300 to 2,000 numeric lines containing 80 to 160 print positions a minute. A few printers are slower and some can print as many as 2,000 alphanumeric lines a minute. Vertical spacing is usually controlled by a punched tape loop or by the program. The punched tape loop is known as a carriage tape.

Very often a *print buffer* that temporarily holds one line of data to be printed is provided in either the printer or central processor. This facilitates printer control and timing and frees the computer for other work while the line is being printed.

Nonimpact printers capable of printing from 4,000 to more than 13,000 lines a minute are becoming more common. These printers form an image on a drum by an electrostatic process similar to that used by many forms copying machines. A variety of fonts or character styles is used. Although these devices are unable to produce simultaneous multiple copies, they can be programmed to produce multiple copies sequentially. Some of these nonimpact printers have a form printing feature that makes it possible to print along with data the lines, headings, and other elements normally included in preprinted forms. These printers produce good quality printing, can intermix font size and style, and through the optional use of smaller fonts can print data in a smaller area, thus reducing the size of paper required.

High-speed printers used to be considered as output devices exclusively. Now, however, impact printers are capable of printing data on forms such as utility bills, renewal notices, and other documents designed to be returned to the sender. Upon return the documents can be batched and fed into an optical scanning device capable of reading the data and automatically recording it on some magnetic storage medium. In view of this turn-around capability it can be said that impact printers are capable of preparing data in machine processable form and are, therefore, no longer limited in function to producing only human-sensible output.

*Remote Job
Entry Units*

One or more input-output devices may be coupled with the primary unit of a remote job entry (RJE) station, called a communications controller. A typical RJE station will consist of a communications controller, a card reader, a card punch, and an impact printer. Other I/O units such as punched tape readers and punches also may be part of a RJE station. RJE stations are primarily used for transmitting batches of data to a remote computer and receiving batches of output from a remote computer. RJE stations allow physically separated locations to share a computer.

Microfilm Systems

Considering the mechanical process that is involved, printers operate at speeds that are truly impressive. Nevertheless, even their maximum speeds are not compatible with the processing and output capacity of computers.

One technique that is emerging as a solution to this problem employs microfilm as an output medium. This process involves several basic steps: (1) computer output is converted to letters and numbers for display on a cathode ray tube, and (2) the data on the screen is then photographed on microfilm. In contrast to the 300 to over 13,000 lines per minute capacity of printers, microfilm systems now in use can handle 7,000 to 30,000 lines a minute.

In addition to greater speed, this technique has the advantage of compactness, which facilitates the storage and retrieval of data. For example, the microfilmed images of 1,600 pages of computer-generated information can be held in the palm of one hand. By the use of reader-printers, specific microfilm frames can be viewed, and copies can be easily produced by depressing a button. (See Figure 4–5.)

Most computer output microfilm (COM) units can produce either microfilm rolls or microfiche, another concept that is gaining wide acceptance. In this technique more than 200 pages of data are recorded on a single fiche (card) usually about 4 inches wide by 6 inches long. Many makes of inexpensive microfiche viewers are available. (See Figures 4–17 and 4–18.)

*Magnetic Ink
Character Readers*

Magnetic ink character recognition (MICR) is a high-speed data input technique that reduces manual keystroke operations and allows source documents to be sorted automatically. Magnetic ink reading heads produce electrical signals when magnetic characters are passed beneath them. These signals are analyzed by special circuits and compared with stored tables to determine what character has been sensed. The data is then transmitted to the memory of the computer for processing.

By the use of a combination reader-sorter it is possible to sort documents as they are being read to provide input to the computer (Figure

Figure 9-5. *Magnetic character sorter-reader. (Courtesy NCR Corporation.)*

9–5). Such sorters may also be operated off-line, that is, independent from the computer. In a banking operation, for example, such a sorter might be used to arrange checks and deposits into customer account number order. Checks may also be sorted by Federal Reserve bank symbol or by American Bankers Association transit number. MICR reader-sorter units are capable of handling from 750 to 1,600 check-sized cards or paper documents a minute, with one line of printing on each document. The majority of MICR equipment is used by the banking industry to process checks and deposits.

Optical Character Readers

Optical character recognition devices are designed to handle sheets of paper, cards, or journal tapes. They have the ability to read marks, printed numerals, special characters, alphabetic characters, and hand-printed letters or numerals (Figure 9–6).

There are many types and makes of optical character readers. Some of these can read only journal tapes, some read only numeric data and certain characters, some read alphabetic data as well as numerals, and some can read all of these forms of data as well as certain hand-printed

Figure 9-6. *Optical reader.* (*Courtesy International Business Machines Corporation.*)

characters. Some document readers can read only standardized type styles; therefore, the type styles and sizes approved by the American National Standards Institute are used by various equipment manufacturers to produce journal tapes and other kinds of documents.

As a source document moves past the scanning device of an optical character reader, the document is flooded with light and read by a photosensitive technique. Optical character readers translate each character into a code, and either transmit the coded data directly to a computer or transcribe it onto punched cards, punched tape, or magnetic tape. These techniques promise to reduce, and in many cases eliminate, the manual keystroke operations that have been required for the preparation of computer input data.

Optical scanning applications can produce great economies of time, manpower, and money in handling source and re-entry documents. For example, documents such as insurance premium notices, charge sales invoices, and utility bills can be prepared originally by a computer in a type style that can be read by an optical scanning device. Thus, upon return with the customers' payments the same documents can be validated and re-entered for further processing. These are referred to as *turn-around documents.*

Transaction Recorders

Point-of-origin transaction recorders may be operated off-line, i.e., not in direct communication with the computer, in which case the data is normally transmitted to a converter where it is recorded on punched cards or punched tape. However, we are primarily concerned here with the on-line use of transaction recorders, which enables them to transmit data directly to a computer storage unit.

Transaction recorders are generally equipped with slots into which the operator inserts prepunched cards, inventory tags, or badges containing such data as employee numbers, job numbers, stock numbers, and so on. Variable data, such as hours worked or amount of stock removed, may be entered by setting dials, keys, or levers. Other transaction recorders utilize keyboard arrangements into which the operator punches the data to be recorded (Figure 9–7). Devices of this type are used by tellers in banks and savings institutions to process account inquiries, checking transactions, savings transactions, and loan payments.

Direct wire transfer of data from transaction recorders to a computer

Figure 9-7. *Financial terminal. (Courtesy NCR Corporation.)*

is an effective means of quickly updating account balances, payroll time records, inventory balances, and other records that must be maintained on a current basis.

Point-of-Sale Devices

Point-of-sale (POS) devices are used primarily in retail department stores and supermarkets to accelerate the checkout process and to capture vital sales information on an on-going basis (Figure 9–8). Functions that can be performed automatically by these devices include product pricing, price extensions, tax and change computation, credit authorization, and inventory update.

Data is usually entered by means of a keyboard. However, bar codes, which were discussed and illustrated in Chapter 5 (see Figure 5–23), are being used increasingly as the recording medium for point-of-sale devices. These codes can be scanned with a photoelectric light in a stationary reading station at a checkout stand or they may be read by a hand-held wand. (See Figure 5–24.)

Typewriter Terminals

Another type of on-line device capable of communication with the computer is the *printer-keyboard terminal*. Most of these devices, which are similar in appearance to electric typewriters, have a typewriter keyboard with a few additional keys, and a pin-feed platen for feeding continuous forms. Typewriter terminals can be connected by cable to the computer system. Remote units can also be connected to a computer by a variety of data transmission techniques.

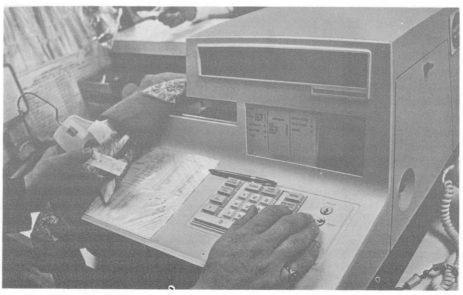

Figure 9-8. *NCR 280 point-of-sale terminal. (Courtesy NCR Corporation.)*

These devices can print from 10 to 120 characters a second and can be used to inquire into a file of data under control of the computer. They can also receive data sent under computer control in response to either terminal commands or computer instructions.

Display Stations

Display stations are similar in operation to typewriter terminals except that instead of providing printed copy these devices display data on the face of a cathode ray tube. Display stations are preferred over typewriter terminals wherever printed copy is not required. As with typewriter terminals, data can be entered through the keyboard and sent to the computer. However, an advantage of display stations is that the data keyed in can be checked on the screen for accuracy before it is transmitted to the computer (Figure 9–9).

Figure 9-9. *Information display system.*
(Courtesy International Business Machines Corporation.)

Some information display systems are equipped with light-pen attachments. These devices, which resemble a pocket flashlight, can be used to manipulate or identify a portion of displayed data. This is accomplished by simply touching the pen to the image of the data that is to be transmitted to the data processing system.

Cathode ray tube display stations may also be designed for use in scientific or technical applications. These specially designed units may display diagrams, drawings, graphs, and sketches. In the past it was often necessary for users of computers to convert drawings into numerical coordinates for computer input and to convert columns of numerical answers back into drawings or graphs in order to understand the answers. Through the use of special programming techniques and electronic controls, computer systems are now able to accept information and produce answers in graphical form.

Most display stations are used in conventional business systems. In these systems the display stations may be stand-alone units, that is one unit on a transmission line, or a few or many stations may be clustered around a control unit, which may or may not be programmable. A programmable controller may have connected to it a variety of terminals such as typewriter terminals, special purpose terminals, and display stations.

One display station model also has a hard copy printer incorporated in it. In other words, this station with a single keyboard is capable of functioning as either a display station or a typewriter terminal.

Voice Response Systems

Still another type of terminal communication device is the voice response system. This system is comprised of a message handling unit, a number of touch-tone telephone units, and standard telephone lines. The audio response unit is located near the computer and has a vocabulary tailored to the users' needs. The touch-tone telephone can be used to enter data or to inquire into a file under control of the computer (Figure 9–10). The inquiry is transmitted to the voice response unit and then accepted by the central processing unit. The computer processes the inquiry,

Figure 9-10. *Touch-tone telephone.*
(Courtesy American Telephone and Telegraph Company.)

composes a coded response, and returns the message to the voice response unit. Here the message is interpreted, and the proper words are selected from the prerecorded stored vocabulary and sent to the inquirer's telephone headset.

The major advantage of the voice response system is that it provides quick verbal responses from a computer system by means of low-cost, remotely located, and multipurpose telephone terminals. Such systems are used to provide stock quotation information, to relay weather information to airplane pilots, and to intercept incomplete telephone calls and tell the callers why their calls cannot be completed. Other voice response systems are in the planning stages or are in operation in such fields as banking, communications, transportation, retail sales, and hospitals. In banking, for example, bank account balances can be maintained in computer storage and used to provide clearance for persons desiring to cash checks. Thus, a telephone call to the automated system can produce a verbal clearance or indication of insufficient funds in response to the account number. In department stores a customer's credit standing can be verified in a similar manner by dialing the individual's account number and the amount of the sale.

Console

The console is, in effect, the external control center of a computer and is used mainly to monitor the system. The console is particularly important to the technician in testing for and locating computer failures.

The console control panel contains a series of lights that indicates to the operator the status of internal electronic switches (Figure 9–11). Also included on the console control panel is a series of keys and switches that enable the operator to start and stop the processing functions and reset the computer when error conditions cause it to stop.

Figure 9-11. *Computer central processing unit and console with visual display unit.*
(Courtesy Sperry UNIVAC, A Division of Sperry Rand Corporation.)

Most consoles also have a built-in typewriter terminal or visual display unit that can be used by the operator to issue commands to the computer. These devices also enable the computer to print messages to the operator signaling that an error condition exists or that some device requires operator attention. Other messages may furnish information to assist the operator in monitoring the system.

As a result of advancements in computer design and programming techniques, the console is used less today as an aid to computer operations. Many of the functions once relegated to the console operator are now contained in the program or are performed by circuitry and components built into the computer.

IMPORTANT WORDS AND PHRASES

channel   impact printer   turn-around document

buffering   nonimpact printer   display station

REVIEW QUESTIONS

1. What are the functions of the input-output channel?
2. Briefly describe the common characteristics of all standard input-output devices.
3. What are the advantages of punched tape as compared to punched cards?
4. A magnetic tape unit can perform what two functions?
5. What is the purpose of the magnetic tape file-protection ring?
6. What characteristics have made magnetic tape units a major contributor to the rapid growth in the use of computers?
7. Why are high-speed printers no longer limited to producing human-sensible output?
8. What basic steps are involved when microfilm is used as computer output?
9. The majority of magnetic ink character readers are used by what industry?
10. Name two turn-around documents that could be read by an optical scanning device.
11. Where are point-of-sale devices primarily used?
12. How do display stations differ from typewriter terminals?
13. What is the major advantage of voice response systems?
14. What is the primary purpose of the console?

10 MINICOMPUTERS AND MICROCOMPUTERS

A significant aspect of computer history will be the decline in size that has accompanied the computer's increased capabilities. Of perhaps greater significance is the associated decrease in price that has made the computer accessible to ever-increasing numbers of users who otherwise would not have been able to afford a computer.

In just a decade, the minicomputer industry has become firmly established, with installations numbering over 100,000. It is estimated that in the early 1980s this number will surpass one million, and, if sales predictions are correct, the value of worldwide deliveries could reach $2 billion annually.

To provide a better insight into the important role of mini and microcomputers in the field of data processing, let us consider some of their characteristics and major applications.

MINICOMPUTERS

In recent years minicomputers have received more attention than any other subject in the field of electronic data processing. There are several reasons for this:

1. Advancements in technology and production methods have allowed minicomputers with increased capabilities to be marketed at lower cost.

2. Business firms and organizations of all types are compelled to seek more efficient and economical ways of meeting their data processing requirements. They are naturally attracted by the potential and favorable prices of minicomputers.

3. Minicomputers provided the basis for a new concept in data processing systems—*distributed processing*. This approach assigns tasks in a large organization to smaller computers on the basis of location or type of task. In a distributed processing system minicomputers may augment or replace a large, centralized computer.

The concept of distributed processing is contrary to the policy of centralization that has been adopted by most large organizations. Some firms have centralized by setting up large data processing departments that provide services for the whole organization, while others have established regional data processing facilities, usually called data centers.

Centralization was based on studies showing that large computers could do the work of several small or medium ones at less cost. Other supporting factors included the advent of data base technology and the advantage of not having to provide staffs of technical personnel in several locations.

In spite of these advantages, centralized operations have not always proven entirely satisfactory. Users sometimes complain that the service received from data centers is not always timely and that the centers are not responsive to their unique needs. Consequently, management may be faced with deciding whether the economic benefits of centralized data processing are worth the consequences. If the decision is negative, there is now a viable alternative resulting from developments in minicomputer technology.

There are several advantages to a distributed computing system:

1. Many small jobs can be divided among the various processors and completed efficiently and promptly without regard to priority.
2. The system can be easily expanded in increments by adding more processors and memory modules.
3. The failure of one unit does not cause the entire system to shut down.

This is not to imply that large computers will be replaced entirely with minicomputers in the near future, but rather to indicate that there is now a practical alternative to large systems.

Minicomputer Characteristics

A minicomputer is just what the name implies—a smaller version of a standard computer, applying large computer technology to a scaled-down unit. It performs most of the operations executed by a larger computer, but it may perform less work in a given amount of time. Circuitry, storage, and other features are quite sophisticated, but reduced in scale and capacity to make them appropriate and economical for simpler or specialized applications.

A wide variety of characteristics and capabilities are available in currently produced minicomputers. Although variable configurations are available, minicomputers frequently come as standardized hardware configurations with ready-to-run software. In the IBM System/32, for example, a single desk-sized cabinet houses a central processor, 16,000 to 32,000 bytes of main memory, a disk storage unit, keyboard and diskette input-output, a printer, and a display screen (Figure 10–1). Preprogrammed industry application programs (IAPS) include such applications as construction, wholesale food, wholesale paper and office products, hospitals, and membership associations.

The physical characteristics of minicomputers afford several advantages. First, they do not have the installation requirements of a large computer—air conditioning, special wiring, raised floors, and other housing needs normally associated with big systems. Thus, a minicomputer can be installed in just about any office and can be positioned for easy access.

Second, most minicomputers are simple enough so that existing personnel can be easily and quickly trained on site to operate them. Systems generally become usable as soon as the organization's records have been entered into them in accordance with simple rules.

Minicomputer Applications

The first applications of minicomputers were mainly in engineering and research laboratories and industrial environments. Specific applications in which minicomputers have been widely used with success include

Figure 10-1. *IBM System/32.*
(Courtesy International Business Machines Corporation.)

process control, numerical control of machine tools, and direct control of machines and production lines, all of which are discussed in detail in Chapter 19. Other applications include control and analysis of laboratory experiments, analysis and interpretation of medical tests, computer-aided design, and traffic control. Other fields in which minicomputers received early acceptance were data communications and education.

Minicomputers are now being used in a much wider range of applications, especially in the area of business. Although minicomputers used for business purposes possess certain basic characteristics, they do have different configurations related to their specific applications. Thus, they can be roughly divided into three categories: accounting computers, small business computers, and remote job entry systems.

Accounting Computers.   These machines combine the capabilities of an office typewriter and printing calculator. In fact, their physical appearance may resemble that of conventional office equipment. The fact that the machines can be programmed to perform many operations automatically reduces the time and effort required to prepare invoices, payroll records, checks, journals, ledger statements, and other documents. In a billing operation, for example, the operator types alphabetic data such as name, address, item description, etc., on a typewriter keyboard. Numeric data such as product number, quantity, unit price, etc., is entered through a companion numeric keyboard. Under stored program control, the machine then performs all calculations and completes the form.

A system of this type generally includes a keyboard for data entry, a processing unit, a limited amount of storage locations, and a typewriter-style printer or line printer (Figure 10–2). Because of its basic capacity, this system is generally used for applications that are operator-oriented. This means that the machine is tended by a human operator who keys in all variable data and issues commands. The operator may also have to enter the master file or related ledger data needed to process each transaction. A familiar example is the operation of posting to the progressive balance type of ledger card. This is a three-column record showing charges (debits), credits, and current balance. There are generally four operations in posting:

1. The old balance is recorded in the machine.
2. Charges are recorded.
3. Credits are recorded.
4. A new balance is automatically recorded as a result of horizontal addition and subtraction of entries.

Ledger cards, monthly statements, and journal records may be prepared on these machines in one operation by the use of carbon paper or special carbonless forms.

Figure 10-2. *Business minicomputer. (Courtesy Burroughs Corporation.)*

A variety of auxiliary devices is also available to increase the amount of storage, to speed up input and output functions, or to add special capabilities to the system. For example, in systems with auxiliary input-output equipment, master file data can be read directly into the processor from punched cards, paper tape, magnetic ledger cards, magnetic tape, or magnetic disks. This, of course, provides higher processing speeds and greater flexibility.

Magnetic ledger cards are one of the most popular input-output media. Their principal advantage is that they enable small businesses to employ the individual visible ledger records they have traditionally used. Information about each account can be recorded on the card in printed form. In addition, machine-readable data can be recorded on magnetic stripes embodied in the card. This magnetically encoded data can be automatically machine-read and updated whenever necessary. For example, in the ledger card operation described above, data encoded magnetically on the cards allows the machine to perform automatically such functions as picking up old balances, aligning ledger cards, verifying account numbers, and recording new balances.

Accounting computers are designed mainly for organizations whose needs, although substantial, are insufficient to justify the cost of large-scale electronic data processing systems or even a general purpose mini-computer with peripheral devices. Included in this category are an estimated one-half million enterprises in the United States that have less than 150 employees. In firms of this type, common applications of accounting computers include billing, accounts receivable, inventory control, payroll, accounts payable, and general ledger. Programs for various applications are usually available from manufacturers at little or no cost, along with programming services for special applications.

Small Business Computers. Essentially these are stand-alone, general purpose computers with a minicomputer-size processor and with on-line input-output devices allowing users to instantly enter or retrieve data from large randomly accessed files. In addition to on-line data entry, such systems usually feature conventional tape or disk storage, display terminals, and multiprogramming capabilities providing for the simultaneous processing of several independent programs. This is an important feature in a company where several individuals or departments may need to access and process data stored in the computer at the same time. These computers may have communications capability, but this is incidental to their basic purpose of in-house business data processing.

The stand-alone, low-cost characteristics of minicomputers make them appropriate for a wide range of applications. There is practically no organization that cannot profit from their use to increase productivity, reduce operating costs, handle accounting functions, and improve management control of such activities as production scheduling, purchasing, and inventory control.

In addition to providing total data processing services for a small organization, minicomputers are also used by large organizations to provide a low-cost means of handling specific, smaller-sized jobs, especially those requiring keyboard entry for orders, disbursements, or other such transactions. As indicated earlier, a minicomputer may also be used as an approach to decentralized data processing in a large organization.

Remote Job Entry Systems. These systems are in effect small computers with communications capabilities. They are installed at remote locations, branch offices, or departments of a large organization, for example, where they serve two purposes. First, they may act as stand-alone computers, filling local data processing requirements. Second, they serve as so-called *intelligent terminals,* which organize and edit batched data that they transmit to, or receive from, a larger computer installed at company headquarters. The larger computer stores the central files, performs the major work, and assigns tasks and receives output from the subservient systems.

Remote systems of this type, which are also known as *remote batch processors,* are an essential part of *distributed processing systems.* As indicated earlier, this type of system is based on the concept that data processing may not be most efficiently done in large, centralized computers, but rather should be dispersed among smaller computers linked by data communications lines.

Future of Minicomputers

Continued reductions in the size and cost of minicomputers are anticipated in the next few years, along with improvements in performance. However, the most significant developments are expected to be in the growth and diversification of applications. It is clear that minicomputers will have an increasing impact on the world of business data processing. In addition, the adaptation and acceptance of minicomputers for the solution of data processing problems in hospitals, financial institutions, and many other activities will provide a growing market for many years to come.

MICROCOMPUTERS

The established status of minicomputers as a less expensive alternative to larger general purpose computers is already being challenged by a newer and even less costly class of equipment called *microcomputers*.

Microcomputer Characteristics

Microcomputers are systems based on the use of *microprocessors.* A microprocessor is a programmable large-scale integrated circuit chip containing all the elements required to process binarily encoded data. In other words, a microprocessor can perform basic arithmetic and logical as well as control functions equivalent to the central processing unit of a conventional computer. The microprocessor differs from a conventional central processing unit, however, by occupying only a single chip, or at most a few chips, of silicon. This smallest of all data processing devices, often called a *computer-on-a-chip,* packs tens of thousands of components on a single silicon chip measuring only a few millimeters in size and requiring only milliwatt power (Figure 10-3). By contrast, the central processing unit of even a minicomputer might consist of several hundred much less densely packed integrated circuits.

Microprocessors have a wide range of actual and potential applications including control functions for automobiles, household appliances, and factory machinery. Major applications in data processing encompass computer peripheral devices such as CRT terminals, printers, data entry devices, and a variety of other input-output units; telecommunications terminals; and point-of-sale units, including electronic cash registers. It is also probable that microprocessors will be used as logic components in large computers with new designs, just as adders and register stacks are being used today.

However, we are primarily concerned here with the use of microprocessors as components in microcomputers. When a microprocessor is supplemented with power supply circuitry, input-output control interfaces, and memory, it becomes a fully operational microcomputer (Fig-

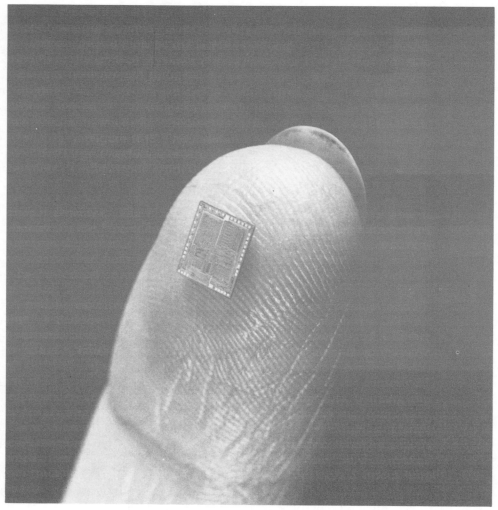

Figure 10-3. *8080 central processing unit. (Courtesy Intel Corporation.)*

ure 10–4). Actually, the distinction between a microprocessor as a component and its status as a "computer-on-a-chip" becomes somewhat hazy, particularly in view of recent microprocessor designs that incorporate all five computer subsystems on one or two chips. Although technically these chip sets could be called microcomputers, they may still be referred to as microprocessors. In any event, a microcomputer, to warrant its title, must include a microprocessor as its central processing unit.

Microcomputer memory is usually of two types. The first has a fixed content and is called *read-only memory* (ROM). A read-only memory is used to store the microcomputer's operating program. If the memory

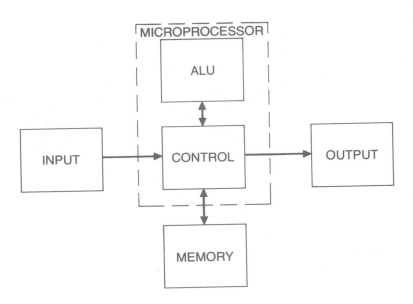

Figure 10-4. *Diagram of a microcomputer with a microprocessor CPU.*

may be programmed or reprogrammed by the user, it is known as a programmable read-only memory (PROM).

The exclusive use of read-only memories represents a major difference between microcomputers and larger, general purpose computers. While microprocessors are basically general purpose, the microcomputers built around them are usually designed for very specific applications.

The second type of memory has a variable content and is called *read-write* or *random access memory* (RAM). It is generally used to store the variable data on which the microcomputer is to act. Random access memory can also be used to store frequently changed programs.

Initially, microcomputers tended to differ from minicomputers by having smaller word size, more limited instruction sets, slower memory cycle time, a lower cost, considerably less power consumption, and custom controls for specific applications. Some of these characteristics will undoubtedly change, however, and lines of distinction may become blurred. Some microcomputers already offer capabilities quite similar to those of the smaller minicomputers. Thus, in some product lines it is difficult to differentiate between the two computers except on the basis of price.

Microcomputer Applications

Since presently available microcomputers are somewhat slower than minicomputers, they are not expected to displace minicomputers entirely. Instead microcomputers are being applied in vast new areas where even the most inexpensive minicomputers have not been economically justifiable.

The flexibility inherent in this stored program computer will enable it to be used in a multitude of different applications for which custom

Figure 10-5. *IBM 5100 Portable Computer. (Courtesy International Business Machines Corporation.)*

units will be provided at low mass-produced costs. Small, free-standing computer systems such as the one shown in Figure 10–5 provide extensive and convenient computational capabilities for individuals such as engineers and statisticians, for specialized jobs in small organizations, and for a wide range of applications in large organizations. The availability to users of a whole hierarchy of computers, from a large host machine to microcomputers performing a variety of functions throughout the organization, is expected to speed the trend toward distributed processing. As a result, some forecasters see a polarization of computers into giant systems and vast numbers of microcomputers, with a decline in the importance of medium-sized computers.

Mass applications of microprocessors and microcomputers are now underway. However, existing applications represent only a beginning when compared to estimates of 25,000 potential applications, only 10 per cent of which have been pursued. Eventually there will be a vast spectrum of applications that will dramatically affect consumers, as well as business and industrial operations. They will affect the profitability and productivity of corporations and the nature of the computer industry itself. Thus, the full exploitation of this new field promises to have social and economic consequences among the most significant in the history of data processing.

IMPORTANT WORDS AND PHRASES

minicomputer	small business computer	intelligent terminal
distributed processing	remote job entry system	microcomputer
data center	remote batch processor	microprocessor
accounting computer		

1. Define distributed processing.
2. Define data center.
3. List the main reasons for centralization of data processing services.
4. What are some of the objections to a centralized data processing facility?
5. Describe the advantages of a distributed computing system.
6. In general, what are the characteristics of a minicomputer as compared to a standard computer?
7. How do the installation requirements of minicomputers differ from those of a large computer?
8. How do accounting computers differ from small business computers?
9. Accounting computers are designed mainly for what type of organization? What are some of the common applications?
10. What are the main functions of a remote job entry system? Describe the role of the large central computer in relation to the remote system.
11. What is a microprocessor?
12. What is the basic difference between a microprocessor and a microcomputer?
13. What are the advantages of microcomputers as compared to minicomputers? The characteristics of microcomputers make them especially useful for what types of applications?

11 DATA COMMUNICATIONS

Much human progress has depended and will continue to depend on our ability to communicate. For over a hundred years electrical communication has been one of the most useful methods employed. Traditionally, electrical communication services such as the telephone and the telegraph have served primarily as a means of transmitting information between people. However, confronted with an ever-increasing need for rapid, accurate transmission of data between widely scattered business offices, government offices, and industrial plants, researchers have developed new methods of communicating. As a result, electrical communication has assumed a new role—now it is serving as a link between machines, and between people and machines.

A link of this type, consisting of devices for sending and receiving data and the medium by which the data is transmitted, is known as a *data communications system.* A data communications system represents the merging of two technologies: high-speed electrical communication and electronic data processing. The purpose of this chapter is to provide an introduction to the concepts and techniques of this rapidly growing field.

In today's complex and vigorous society, an enormous amount of information is generated daily by the activities of both public and private organizations. To achieve maximum usefulness, much of this information needs to be transmitted promptly to one or more points remote from its origin. Thus, every organization with activities in more than one location, or complex activities in a single location, must provide a system of communications for effective performance, operational efficiency, and management control. The extent to which business, government, and other large organizations are dependent on information and the movement of information is briefly discussed in the following paragraphs.

*Data Communications
in Government*

National Defense.   The U.S. Department of Defense employs what is undoubtedly the largest combination of computer and communications systems in the world. NMCS, National Military Command System, comprises more than forty Army, Navy, and Air Force systems that provide up-to-the-second information about our military status anywhere in the world.

A striking example of a huge information and control center also involved in defense is that of NORAD, the North American Air Defense Command, near Colorado Springs. NORAD's underground Combat Operations Center, housed inside Cheyenne Mountain, maintains close vigil on the airspace surrounding the North American continent. Information from a multitude of sources is transmitted to the center's 27 computers by means of a vast communications network. Among the sources are huge Ballistic Missile Early Warning System radar complexes at Clear, Alaska, at Thule, Greenland, and at Fylingdales Moor, England; the Distant Early Warning Line, a chain of radar stations stretching from Point Lay in northwest Alaska to Greenland's east coast; and dozens of other radars strategically located throughout the United States and Canada.

Data regarding more than 200,000 flights daily in North America is fed into computerized centers in the eight NORAD regions across the continent, with special attention given to some 1,500 flights that originate overseas. Information on those that cannot be identified immediately is relayed to the NORAD center inside Cheyenne Mountain. In addition, NORAD's Space Defense Center in the mountain keeps up-to-the-instant on satellites orbiting the earth. By means of data transmitted over communications lines from a variety of detection devices, NORAD maintains a comprehensive record of the positions of these satellites. The future orbits of satellites are calculated by computer, and anticipated tracks can be displayed on a screen in the Combat Operations Center. As a result, the staff can see the paths a satellite will follow for as many as nine revolutions. Figure 11–1 shows the course of a U.S.-launched weather-reconnaissance satellite as charted on the screen

Figure 11-1. *Course of weather-reconnaissance satellite charted on screen by electronic computer. (Courtesy North American Air Defense Command.)*

by an electronic computer. The traces indicate its present position as well as the course it will follow for its next two trips around the globe.

NORAD's giant computer and communications systems have the ability to cope with staggering amounts of information. Incoming information is received by an input-output data controller, which converts signals into data that can be used by the computers or stored until needed. The converter can reverse the procedure by taking data already stored and converting it back into signals for transmission to distant sites. Information processed by the center's 27 computers is translated into language symbols that can be projected in seven colors on a wall-size display board with background maps of such areas of Eurasia or North America spread out before the observers. Between the observation of an event, its digestion and interpretation by the computers, and its display on the screen or consoles, there is an insignificant delay that can be measured in millionths of a second. Thus, the observers are provided at every moment with real-time information concerning the continent's aerospace surveillance and defense status.

Federal Agencies.   The federal government employs a number of very large data communications networks in addition to those used for military purposes. For example, the U.S. Weather Bureau maintains an extensive network to collect and disseminate weather information to the Federal Aviation Agency, commercial airlines, agricultural organizations, and the general public. The Federal Aviation Agency, the Social Security Administration, and the Veterans Administration have established extensive facilities for transmitting both voice and data communications between their various locations.

The National Aeronautics and Space Administration uses a large communications network for data acquisition and tracking in connection with its activities. The success of the many phases of each space mission—design, development, test, preflight checkout, launch, injection into orbit, stabilization and control, guidance, reentry, recovery, and subsequent analysis of data—is largely dependent on the vast communications facilities employed and the power of computers to process data.

Law Enforcement.   Law enforcement activities in the United States are divided among a great many state, county, and municipal organizations that are highly interdependent. Effective law enforcement requires a flow of information between these organizations. To achieve rapid communication and ready access to records, many of the most advanced data communications techniques are used. Many states today have installed extensive communications networks to send various messages, including reports of suspects and stolen property. These networks are interconnected with those of other states to facilitate the rapid exchange of information throughout the country.

Trends in law enforcement indicate increasing dependence on data communications. This is especially evident in the tendency toward automation of police information systems and the establishment of regional record centers.

Data Communications in Business

Business is recognizing, at an ever-increasing rate, the advantages of company-wide data communications networks as a means of effectively managing widespread operations. Consequently, it has been estimated that in the late 1970s, 60 to 75 per cent of the amount spent annually on computer systems will be spent for communications terminal equipment and communications services. It has also been predicted that the volume of information transmitted in the form of digital data will eventually equal the volume transmitted by voice.

As companies grow in size, become more widely dispersed and more diverse in their operations, and at the same time try to give better service at lower prices, the problems of effective internal communication increase. Data communications plays an important role in keeping a company in touch with its own divisions as well as with its customers and suppliers. The rapid collection and transmission to a central point of data from outlying facilities such as manufacturing plants, warehouses, regional sales offices, and other branch offices provides the management of large organizations with timely information about overall operations. This technique also reduces the number of times and places at which data must be manually handled and transcribed, thus reducing clerical costs and the possibility of errors. Data generated and/or processed at a central facility can also be transmitted rapidly to outlying locations. Just as the prompt collection of data is important to a large organization, the prompt dissemination of information also plays a vital role in effective operations.

Data communications also serves to reduce operating expenses. Companies with decentralized plant operations often find it advantageous to handle payroll, purchasing, billing, and other functions on a centralized basis. By means of data communications, all branch time cards, invoices, bills, etc., can be processed at a central location, thus improving efficiency and reducing clerical operations at each of the plants.

Data communications plays an especially important role in the management of large enterprises. As a result of advances in electrical communications, business executives have almost immediate access to detailed data concerning widespread operations, formerly delayed by distance, traffic, or technical limitations. It is now possible to send information anywhere in the nation, in almost any form, with speed and accuracy. In just a few minutes, a sales, inventory, production, or financial report can be transmitted wherever needed so that a management decision can be based on timely information. Data communications can also deliver promptly all types of information vital to forecasting. Thus, an efficient communications system assures that overall planning and control are based on information that is accurate, comprehensive, and up-to-date.

Efficient data communications has been an essential element in the widespread development of on-line and real-time data processing. *On-line* means that all elements of the system, including remote terminals, are interconnected with and perform under control of a computer. Many organizations find it advantageous to establish central data files that can be randomly accessed to provide prompt responses to inquiries from outlying locations. Thus, the basic data flow pattern is in both directions. Inquiry messages are transmitted from remote terminals to the central processing facility. Appropriate responses are generated and sent back to the inquiring terminals.

The on-line inquiry processing function is often combined with real-time functions. *Real-time* means the ability of a system to collect data about transactions as they occur, and to process that data so rapidly that the resulting new information is available in time to influence the process being monitored or controlled. In a system designed for real-time updating, the central data files are modified each time a transaction occurs so that the central files always reflect the true current status of the situation involved. This provides an accurate, up-to-the-minute basis for responding to succeeding inquiries and influencing further events such as transactions, operations, special reports, or manufacturing processes.

Real-time inquiry systems are especially useful to organizations such as banks, brokerage firms, hotels, and airlines, where prompt servicing of customer inquiries is of primary importance. The reservation systems of airlines are good examples of on-line real-time information systems. When a customer wishes to make a reservation on a particular flight, the ticket agent, using a special keyboard terminal that is on-line to the computer, questions the computer about the availability of seats on that flight. The computer responds with the necessary information. If a seat is available, the agent then keys in an order for one seat. The computer records the reservation immediately and revises the inventory of seats for that flight so that following inquiries will show one less available seat.

FUNCTIONS OF DATA COMMUNICATIONS

Because system requirements differ from one organization to another, the data communications systems in use today vary widely in their functions, their structures, and their degree of complexity. However, systems generally follow three basic patterns, illustrated in Figure 11–2. In this illustration a circle represents a terminal that can send messages, receive messages, or both. The connecting lines represent the communications channel or circuit, which can be a wire, cable, radio or microwave.

Network *A* represents a simple point-to-point network, i.e., two computers or other terminal devices connected by a channel. Organizations with two or more computers in different locations may find it advantageous to connect them by a communications line of this type to facilitate computer load balancing. Thus, if one computer experiences a slack period while the other has an excessive work load, some of the excess work can be transferred to the less active computer. In addition to providing more effective utilization, communications links also make it possible for one or more computers to take over another computer's work load in the event of a breakdown. Furthermore, since each computer in such an arrangement has access to the data stored in the memory of other units, it is unnecessary to duplicate the contents of all the storage units. In this way the total amount of information that can be stored in the system is increased.

Network *B* illustrates a situation in which two terminals can communicate over channels only by passing through a third terminal. Network *B* also describes a system in which a central office can transmit data to outlying locations. A weather broadcast network that transmits weather reports to many stations is an example of this type. Conversely, outlying branches can communicate with a main office. For example, sales offices

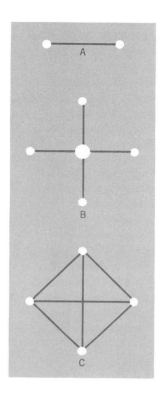

Figure 11-2. *Schematic of basic communications networks.*

may transmit orders to a centralized data processing center for further processing.

Another example of the use of a *B*-type network is for computer *time-sharing*. The purpose of a time-sharing system is to furnish continuous computing service to many users through the simultaneous use of a single facility. To accomplish this a large-capacity computer at a centralized location is tied to terminals at various remote locations by a communications link. Each remote terminal has direct and immediate access to the entire capability of the data processing facilities at the centralized location. Programs and other data can be entered into the system through each of the remote terminals. The system provides the user with a response so rapidly that he feels he has exclusive use of the computer. Actually, however, the computer services users in sequence, with the operating system allocating short "slices of time" to each user on the order of microseconds or milliseconds. Generally, when a participant's time allotment is used up, his job goes into the waiting line for a fraction of a second until its turn arrives again. This is controlled by the operating system, which causes the interrupted program and its restart point to be temporarily stored outside of main memory in an auxiliary storage unit until processing is resumed. In spite of interruptions, the high speed of the computer makes it appear that all of the users are being served simultaneously.

The basic data flow pattern in a time-sharing system is necessarily bidirectional; operating instructions and input data are transmitted from the terminals to the central computer facility and the results of processing are transmitted back to the appropriate terminals. This capability resulted in the widespread development of large centralized computer utilities providing services to a great many users.

Network *C* is the most complex of the basic distribution patterns. This is a multiterminal system in which each terminal is able to exchange information with every other point in the system.

COMMUNICATIONS MEDIA AND CODES

Data to be transmitted may originate from a number of physical forms or media. Included are handwritten or printed pages, punched cards, punched paper tape, magnetic tape, imprinted magnetic ink characters, microfilm, or computer memory, all of which have been described in preceding chapters. Although the data at the sending end may be in a form that can be transmitted, it may not satisfy requirements at the receiving end. For example, data on a printed page might be needed at the receiving office in punched card form. Thus, the data would have to be recorded on punched cards before transmission, or it could be transmitted in its original form by a facsimile system and transcribed by a card punch operator at the receiving end.

Most data transmitted is recorded in coded form. The exceptions are visual display, facsimile, and handwriting transmissions. One of the codes that has been most commonly used for communications is the five-level Baudot Code. A number of variations of the five-level code are in use as well as six-, seven-, and eight-level codes. However, a more recently developed standard code provides the basis for achieving coding uniformity of data interchanged between data processing and communications systems. In June 1967 the American National Standards Institute adopted a new data processing code, known as ASCII (American Standard Code for Information Interchange) (see Table 6–3).

The various codes other than ASCII were designed for certain types and makes of equipment and certain applications. These codes have been useful. However, with the ever-increasing scope of data processing, their differences become more restrictive because of the growing need for interchange between diverse types of equipment. For example, many data processing applications now require computer centers to process data collected from various remote points. Information at those locations may be originated by different methods and machines. Furthermore, data communications requirements may involve a wide range of terminals and multiplexers that may not be fully compatible.

Since it is not always possible for data to be recorded in the same medium and code throughout a system, some conversion may be required. It may be necessary to convert from a paper tape code to magnetic code, from a card code to magnetic tape code, etc. It is desirable to capture original data in a machine-sensible language at the source if possible. In this way any further processing, transfer, or conversion of the data can be handled automatically by machines. ASCII has made it possible to standardize the specifications and formats of each of the media used to record data, thus facilitating the conversion and general interchange of data among all kinds of data processing systems, communications systems, and associated equipment.

DATA COMMUNICATIONS EQUIPMENT

Data transmission of a basic point-to-point type is generally accomplished in five stages. The data goes from (1) an input device to (2) a transmitting terminal, then through (3) an electrical transmission link to (4) a receiving terminal and, finally, to (5) an output device. The functions performed and the facilities used in each of these stages (illustrated in Figure 11–3) are described in the following sections.

Input-Output

In most cases, data entered into a transmitting system is captured in an independent operation and then physically moved to the input terminal unit. This is true of such media as cards, magnetic tape, and paper tape. However, certain transmitting units may also accept data from a computer storage device, or data entered manually through a keyboard, by dialing, or by inserting a coded badge or card into a reading device. Thus, the input device at the transmitting terminal may be a paper tape reader, card reader, magnetic tape unit, keyboard, computer, or special data collection device.

The output device at the receiving terminal may be a tape punch, card punch, printer, magnetic tape unit, display device, or computer.

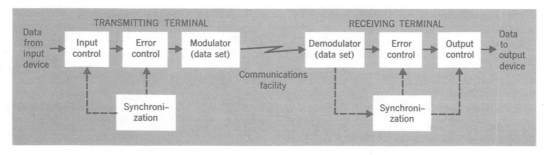

Figure 11-3. *Data Flow in a typical data communications system.*

Data communications terminals differ widely with respect to input-output media, compatibility with other equipment, speed, flexibility, and operating characteristics. However, the components of different terminals are essentially the same. As shown in Figure 11–3, these include input-output control units, error control units, synchronization units, and modulation-demodulation units. Although several of these units are generally contained in one cabinet and sold as a single communications terminal device, their individual functions will be described briefly.

The *input control unit* at the transmitting terminal controls and accepts data from the input device at a rate generally determined by the speed of the input device. The control unit stores the data temporarily by means of a buffer device and transmits it at a speed suitable to the communications facility. At the receiving terminal, the *output control unit* accepts data that is received, stores it temporarily, and transfers it to the output device at an appropriate rate.

Not all data communications terminals contain buffered input-output control units. If no buffers are used, the input, data transmission, and output functions occur simultaneously and at the same speed.

Error control units are used to detect, indicate, and possibly correct errors that occur during transmission. In most error control systems the digital data at the transmitting terminal is encoded according to some set pattern. At the receiving terminal, the data is decoded and checked to see if the data pattern meets standard requirements.

The two commonly used methods for automatic checking of data are validity checking and parity checking. A *validity check* assures the accuracy of character representation. Thus, any code configuration that does not represent a legitimate member of the character set being used is recognized as an error. *Parity checking* consists of determining whether the number of 1 bits in the characters received meets the established odd or even standard.

Since data signals are transmitted at precise time intervals, some means must be provided to assure synchronization between transmitting and receiving stations. By means of *synchronization units,* sending and receiving instruments are able to operate continuously at substantially the same frequency and are maintained, by means of correction if necessary, in a desired phase relationship.

The signals generated by terminal input devices usually have to be modified before they can be transmitted over common-carrier communications facilities. The unit used at the transmitting terminal to complete this modification is called a *modulator.* At the receiving terminal a *demodulator* is needed to convert the signals back into a form acceptable to the output device. Typically, both functions are performed by a modulation-demodulation unit used for two-way data communications. This unit is commonly called a *data set* or *modem* (Figure 11–4).

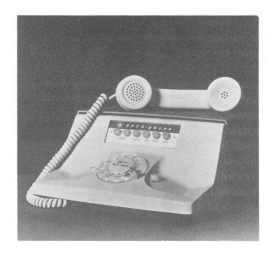

Data sets not only can convert input signals into tones the communications channels can handle but also can provide a means for dialing and setting up the connection. Data sets are furnished by the common carriers for use with many different types of communications terminals. The following section is devoted to a description of some of these terminals.

Data Transmission Terminal Equipment

Keyboard-Only Devices. Keyboard-only devices are generally used to transmit data for input to a device such as a computer or card punch. The push-button telephone is a good example of a keyboard-only device. Instead of a rotary dial, this telephone model has push buttons. These push buttons generate tones that direct calls through the telephone network (Figure 11–5).

Calls are placed by depressing the buttons corresponding to the desired telephone number. When the call has been completed, the telephone can be used to carry on a conversation or to transmit data by means of the push buttons. For example, let us assume that a call is placed from a push-button telephone to a receiving set connected to a card punch. The receiving set automatically accepts the call, transmits an answer tone, and connects the card punch to the line. Data is then entered by depressing the appropriate buttons on the telephone. Depressing the buttons creates tones that are transmitted over the line to the receiving data set. The data set converts the tones to electrical signals that are transferred to the card punch. The card punch reproduces the original data by punching holes in a card.

The telephone model illustrated in Figure 11–5 also permits automatic dialing by using punched plastic cards. Data may also be punched in the cards and transmitted to computers or other receiving devices.

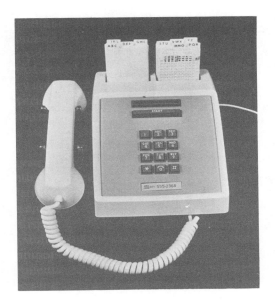

Figure 11-5. *A telephone that permits dialing and transmission of data by means of push buttons or punched card.*

(Courtesy American Telephone and Telegraph Company.)

For example, some wholesalers have installed systems that allow customers to enter orders quickly and easily. When a customer wishes to place an order, he dials the phone number of the wholesaler and identifies his company by feeding a prepunched identity card into the reading device attached to the telephone. He then feeds into the reader a punched card describing the first item he wishes to order. On a signal that the contents of the card have been transmitted, he enters the quantity desired through keys on the keyboard of the transmitting device. He then feeds in the next item card, and so on through the entire order. At the receiving end an automatic key punch, connected to the receiving device, produces a set of cards describing the complete order. No written purchase order is transmitted. At the end of the month the wholesale firm provides each customer with a listing of all orders entered.

The following example indicates how the push-button telephone is used in an audio response system at the Rohr Corporation plants in Chula Vista and Riverside, California. The system has as its basic elements the touch-tone telephone and the computer. If an employee wants to know the present location of an order for parts or material, he lifts the touch-tone receiver and on the phone keyboard presses a predetermined digit code for an order location inquiry. The audio response unit, with a prerecorded female voice, responds with a request for the "register number." The employee then enters the order register number by pressing the proper keys on the touch-tone keyboard, sending a question to the computer in the form of a series of electronic impulses. The computer then checks the register number on its disk files for status information and instructs the prerecorded voice drum to respond with appropriate and up-to-date data on the status of the order. If the order is in transit, the voice drum responds with "from location," "date," and "time," plus "to location," "date," and "time." The system could also give a priority rating for the order.

The foregoing is a simple example of a system much more expansive in its capabilities. It can deal with many facets of manufacturing such as new order inputs, history of an order, the moving of an order to a new location, quantity adjustments, and so on. It can also be applied to financial and other management problems. This use of large-scale computers coupled with audio response systems has greatly improved data processing flexibility, thus permitting current status reports and progress to be determined on a real-time basis.

Transaction™ *Telephone.*   A recent development to provide merchandising, banking, and other institutions with quick, efficient, and economical access to customer records is the Transaction telephone (Figure 11–6). The Transaction telephone was designed primarily for use in credit authorization or check verification applications. Communication with the computer at the remote data center is established when a clerk inserts a magnetically encoded dialing card. Once contact has been started, the clerk enters the customer's card, containing the customer number and expiration date. The inquiry operations are simultaneous, as the clerk can punch the amount of the transaction on the manual entry keyboard while the set is automatically making the necessary connections. To avoid errors in the inquiry operations, the set contains sequenced instructions with lights adjacent to each instruction on the face plate of the Transaction telephone unit. After contact is made and the data enters the computer, the computer answers the inquiry via an audio response unit.

Under most conditions the computer approves or disapproves the transaction. In case the computer asks for more information to clear the transaction, the clerk can enter this additional information via the manual entry keyboard. While the Transaction telephone can be used for any application requiring customer status inquiry, one of the more common applications is its use as a teller terminal for the exchange of information between the teller and the record-keeping computer in banks and savings and loan institutions.

Keyboard Printers.   Teletype machines were among the earliest and are now probably the best known of the units available for wire transmission. Teletypewriter service does for written data what the telephone does for spoken data. It is a versatile written communication system that permits transmission and receipt of messages and data between two points by telephone lines. Teletype machines will transmit direct from

Figure 11-6. *Bell Laboratories Transaction Telephone.*
(Courtesy Pacific Telephone and Telegraph Company.)

a four-row keyboard similar to that of a typewriter (Figure 11–7). Printed copy can be produced at both the sending and receiving ends. In addition, data can be transmitted and received in eight-channel punched paper tape or magnetic tape for direct input to a data processing system. Operators can also produce tape off-line for later transmission. Thus,

Figure 11-7. *Teletype Automatic Send-Receive set.*

(Reproduced by permission of Teletype Corporation.)

tapes can be prepared in advance, checked for accuracy, accumulated, and transmitted automatically at a more rapid rate than would be possible with manual typing.

Since teletypewriter equipment provides a fast means of written communication, the service is used extensively in transmitting prices, statistics, quotations, and similar data requiring written verification. Other applications include the transmission of invoices, payroll checks, personnel records, sales orders, freight bills, tracers, summaries of daily business activity, sales reports, production schedules, and other business data. For example, an associated group of gas companies set up a central service center to purchase and store supplies. Each member company uses a teletypewriter to transmit purchase requisitions to the center. The center fills requisitions from the forms received on their machine. Besides providing instant communications and a permanent record of each transaction, this procedure has enabled the group to reduce the cost of supplies by purchasing larger quantities.

Punched Tape Transmission Terminals. Punched tape transmission terminals consist of two units—a sender and a receiver. The sender includes a paper tape reader and a signal generator. As the tape passes through the reader, the punched holes are sensed by pins connected to a signal generator. The signal generator sends signals representing the sensed holes to a data set for transmission over the communications channel.

The operation is reversed at the receiver, which consists of a signal interpreter and a tape punch. As electrical signals are received, the pins in the tape punch are activated and holes are punched in tape.

Dataspeed tape-to-tape equipment, also manufactured by the Teletype Corporation, will transmit messages and data at 105 characters a second using conventional telephone lines. However, Dataspeed is strictly a tape transmission device and has no typewriter (Figure 11–8). Business data can be accumulated throughout the regular working day and transmitted at a rapid rate during nonworking hours or at intervals when the line is not in use. It is possible to alternate data transmission with voice communication on the same call.

Punched Card Transmission Terminals.   Data can be transmitted from one location to another by means of punched card transmission systems. The IBM Data Transmission System, for example, is composed of one or more sending terminals from which data is transmitted over dial or leased telephone channels. The transmission terminal contains a card reader as well as a ten-digit keyboard, functional keys, and an audio speaker (Figure 11–9). The audio speaker emits different sounds to in-

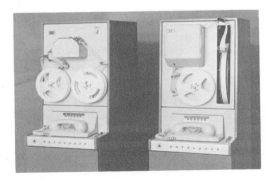

Figure 11-8. *Dataspeed Tape-to-Tape System.*

(Reproduced by permission of Teletype Corporation.)

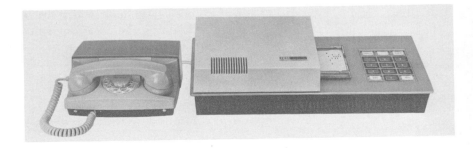

Figure 11-9. *Data transmission system showing the combination telephone, transmitting subset, and transmission terminal.*

(Courtesy International Business Machines Corporation.)

dicate (1) that a connection is established between the sending and receiving terminals, (2) that the remotely located card punch is now ready to receive, (3) that a record was correctly transmitted, or (4) that a record was incorrectly transmitted.

After a connection is made by telephone between the sending and receiving stations, the operator lifts an exclusion switch located under the handset. This disconnects the telephone and connects the transmitting terminal to the line. Numerical data can be entered into the system manually through the keyboard or automatically by inserting a prepunched card. When the operator places a card in the reader, the data is converted to audio-range frequencies. These frequencies pass over telephone channels to a receiving location where they are reconverted. A data translator located on the left side of the receiving key punch converts the codes for punching.

Magnetic Tape Transmission Terminals.   Magnetic tape transmission terminals provide direct transmission of magnetic tape data over dial or private communication circuits at the rate of 150 characters a second. Each terminal is designed to read tape for transmission or to write tape, depending on whether the toggle switch on the unit is set to send or receive. Because such terminals read or write tape with a high density of characters per inch, they are able to use tapes from or prepare tapes for the most commonly used tape devices. As a general rule there is no limitation in the length of each record transmitted, although most records are normally between 300 and 3,000 characters.

Computer Transmission Control Terminals.   It is possible for data to be transmitted directly from one computer to another by connecting special data transmission control units to the computers (Figure 11–10). Transmitting units convert data from computer storage to the transmission language used by the common-carrier equipment. The data taken from main storage may have originated as input to the computer from cards or tape and may have been rearranged, edited, printed, or computed before being sent to the transmission unit.

As a receiver, the data transmission unit converts data from the transmission language to binary coded decimal form and forwards the data to computer main storage. From this point various computer operations can be performed. These may include updating records in disk storage, rearranging and editing the data for printing, or recording the data in cards or magnetic tape.

These procedures are being used effectively in shifting large volumes of data from one computer center to another. This permits one center to back up another and allows the leveling of peak loads.

Figure 11–11 illustrates the use of a control terminal, permitting a computer to communicate with a variety of remote terminals.

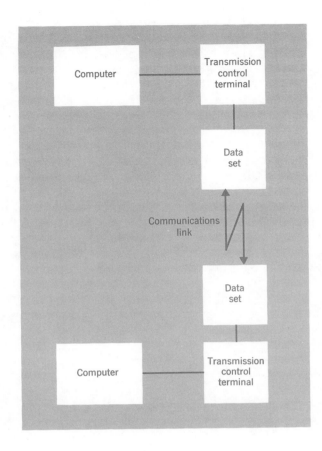

Figure 11-10. *Computer-to-computer transmission.*

Visual Display Terminals. Visual display terminals provide immediate visual access at a remote location to information stored within a computer system. The terminal consists of a keyboard, a signal generator-interpreter, a buffer, and a visual display screen (Figure 11–12).

An inquiry concerning an account, transaction, production schedule, or any such stored data can be quickly entered in the terminal keyboard. Coded signals are generated and transmitted by means of the data sets and communications channel to the computer system. The computer interprets the signals and searches its memory for the required information. The information is transmitted back to the visual display terminal in the form of coded signals. The signals are interpreted and displayed on the television-type screen. The displayed data can also be printed when models equipped with the optional printer feature are used.

Data Collection and Transmission Devices. For the most part, the terminals described above are used to transmit data previously collected,

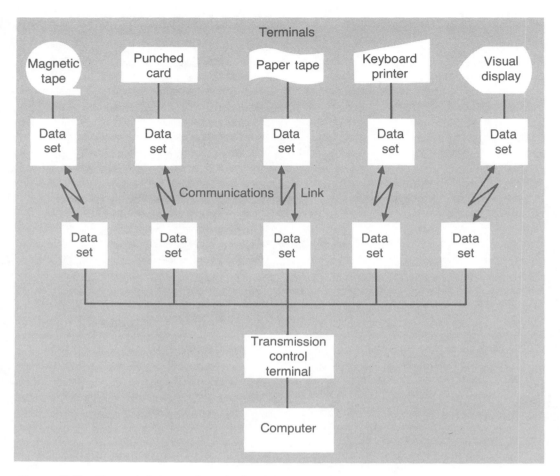

Figure 11-11. *Transmission control terminal permitting computer to communicate with a variety of remote terminals.*

recorded, or stored in other devices. A somewhat different approach is represented by the integrated data collection and transmission system.

The IBM 1030 Data Collection System is a good example of a fully integrated on-line data collection and transmission system. This system can operate within one plant or between plants. Transmission occurs over half-duplex privately owned lines or common-carrier leased private lines. The IBM 1030 system collects digital information from in-plant reporting stations and transmits it at 60 characters per second to a central computer for recording, processing, and analyzing. The system includes the following components:

Figure 11-12. *Information display terminals. (Courtesy International Business Machines Corporation.)*

Unit	Function
IBM 1031 Input Station (Figure 11–13)	Accepts alphanumeric data from 80-column punched cards, numeric data from punched plastic badges, keyed data from manual entry units, and data cartridges.
IBM 1035 Badge Reader (Figure 11–14)	Transmits numeric data from 22-column (card-stub size) badges.
IBM 1033 Printer	Provides on-line printed output at locations remote from the central computer. In combination with the input station, the printer provides full on-line inquiry and reply capabilities.

Applications of this type of system include scheduling, dispatching, attendance reporting, inventory maintenance, and labor distribution.

Figure 11-13. *Input station.*

(Courtesy International Business Machines Corporation.)

Figure 11-14. *Badge reader.*

(Courtesy International Business Machines Corporation.)

Audio Transmission Terminals. Any conventional telephone can be used as a data transmission device with the assistance of an audio terminal. An audio terminal is a keyboard device that can be used to communicate with any remote computer over voice-grade public switched telephone networks, or voice-grade leased private-line telephone service.

Most portable terminals are about the size of a portable typewriter and can be carried in a luggage-style case. The terminals may contain their own power source or may obtain their power from ordinary house current outlets. Most terminals contain the basic 60-position keyboard that provides 26 alphabetic, 10 numeric, and 13 special characters as well as function and control keys.

Portable audio terminals allow salespeople in the field to communicate immediately with the home office and production plant to obtain instant stock inventory and price data, and to place orders promptly. Other typical applications include on-line credit data inquiry, stock inventory control, central file inquiry, stock market quotations, account status inquiry, automobile warranty checks, emergency parts orders, freight car tracing, and many others.

COMMUNICATIONS FACILITIES

Broadly defined, a communications facility is a means by which data can be transmitted between two or more points. A complete range of facilities is available to suit any data communications requirement. Some of the common types of facilities and services as well as the communications companies that provide the services are presented in this section.

Common Carriers

Communications common carriers are companies authorized by the Federal Communications Commission or appropriate state agencies to furnish electrical communications services to the public. Services include communications facilities for voice, data, printed messages, and facsimile, as well as appropriate channels for television and telephoto.

The major common carriers providing interstate communications services are the American Telephone and Telegraph Company, which heads the Bell System, and the Western Union Telegraph Company. In addition, there are many independent telephone companies, the largest of which is General Telephone and Electronics Corporation. In general, the independent telephone companies offer the same types of services as the Bell System.

Communications Channels

A *channel* is a path over which data is transmitted. The agreement between the communications common carrier and the user is basically an arrangement for the use of a certain type and grade of communications channel.

Types of Channels. The three basic channel types are called simplex, half duplex, and full duplex.

Type	Description
Simplex	Transmits in one direction only
Half duplex	Transmits in both directions, but only in one direction at a time
Full duplex	Transmits in both directions at the same time

The possible volume of data communications and the flexibility of operations are greater with full-duplex channels than for half-duplex or simplex channels. However, the cost of the communications facilities and terminal equipment is also higher.

Grades of Channels. The grade or *bandwidth* of a channel indicates its capacity to transmit data. The capacity can be expressed in bits per second or a similar signal time rate.

The physical circuit or technique used may be a voice frequency circuit, a wire carrier channel, or a portion of a microwave band, depending on the facilities available in each geographical location. In any event, the user is primarily concerned with the fact that the available bandwidth is able to transmit the required volume of data.

The line speed of a channel, measured in bits per second, is directly related to the bandwidth of the channel. Thus, a high bit-per-second rate requires a wider channel or a greater number of cycles per second. The low-, medium-, and high-speed facilities are represented by three basic bandwidth classifications: narrow band, voice grade, and broadband.

Class	Description
Narrow band	A channel with a frequency less than that required for normal voice transmission. Data communications capabilities are generally in the range of 45 to 75 bits per second, although these are not specific limits. Most commonly used with low-speed teletypewriter equipment.
Voice band	A channel with a frequency from zero to approximately 4,000 cycles. Line speeds are approximately 2,400 bits per second. These circuits do not transmit data in the form of digital pulses used in data processing equipment. Therefore, data sets are required to convert the pulses or "bits" generated by data processing equipment to signals suitable for transmission. These signals are reconverted at their destination for delivery to the receiving equipment.
Broadband	A channel with a frequency greater than required for voice transmission, usually several times the 4,000-cycle bandwidth. These channels commonly use microwave transmission techniques to provide data communications at rates up to several million bits per second. The radio waves in this system tend to travel in a straight line, requiring relay stations with dishlike antennas on high buildings or towers every 20 to 35 miles.

Communication Satellites.   The U.S. Communication Satellite Act of 1962, which authorized the establishment of communication satellites, visualized their use primarily for international telephone transmissions. The satellites were intended for use as microwave transmission or relay stations in outer space.

Satellites were launched by rockets to an orbit around the earth at a distance of approximately 22,300 miles over the equator. At this distance the rotations of the earth and the satellite are the same. Thus, the satellite remains in the same spot and is synchronous with the earth's rotation.

The primary use of the satellite in today's communication networks is for retransmission of telephone and television analog signals. However, satellites make it feasible to transmit very high volumes of digital data signals almost independent of distance. Consequently, they are likely to become an important means of transmitting data communications as well as other types of communications.

Communications Services

Communications services can be obtained on a public or leased (private) basis, depending on the needs of the user. Only those services related to the transmission of data are covered here.

DATA-PHONE Service. DATA-PHONE service provides for the transmission of data between a variety of business machines using regular local or long distance telephone networks. This is accomplished by connecting a DATA-PHONE data set to a business machine terminal (see Figure 11–4). The data set converts the signals from the transmitting device into tones suitable for transmission over the telephone network and provides the means for dialing the call.

The call is answered at the receiving DATA-PHONE data set either automatically or manually. When answered by an attendant, both the sending and receiving sets are in the normal "talk" mode. When the operators have confirmed that the business machine terminals are ready to send or receive data, they switch the connection from the "talk" mode to the "data" mode by simply depressing the "data" buttons on both sets. Thus, control of the line is transferred to the business machine terminals, enabling them to transmit and receive data. At the completion of transmission, the operators disconnect the call by depressing the "talk" buttons and hanging up the telephones.

Data may also be transmitted to an unattended location by means of a DATA-PHONE data set that is arranged to answer calls automatically.

Rates for the transmission of data are the same as for ordinary telephone calls in addition to the monthly rate for the DATA-PHONE data set.

DATA-PHONE 50 Service. This is a new switched wideband message rate service for data transmission between major cities in the United States. The system transmits at speeds up to 50,000 bits per second, a 25-fold increase over the speed available in voice band DATA-PHONE service.

DATA-PHONE Digital Service. The Bell System DATA-PHONE digital service (DDS) offers an all-digital nationwide network designed and built specifically for data communications. With DATA-PHONE digital service the data signals generated by the users' terminal devices remain in their basic digital form while being transmitted over the communication channels. Previous methods required the conversion of digital signals into analog form for transmission over channels that were primarily designed for voice communications.

The new service provides private-line, point-to-point, or multipoint channels operating at speeds of up to 56,000 bits per second. The transmission of digital signals improves performance by lowering the error rate as well as being less susceptible to line interferences. The design objectives are aimed at obtaining a new high standard of performance and accuracy for transmission between approximately 100 metropolitan areas in the next few years.

Wide Area Telephone Service.   For those customers who must communicate frequently with widely scattered points, Wide Area Telephone Service (WATS) is offered. Monthly charges are based on the size of the service area in which calls are placed, not on the number or length of calls. Under the WATS plan, the United States is divided into six zones. The subscriber is billed a flat rate on a full-time or measured-time basis according to the zones to be called—the entire United States if desired. Under full-time service, the customer is provided an access line that he may use for 24 hours a day, 7 days a week. In measured-time service, the access line is also continuously available, but the basic monthly rate covers only 15 hours of service to telephones within the subscription area. WATS can be used alternately for voice communications and data transmission using DATA-PHONE service.

Teletypewriter Exchange Service.   Teletypewriter Exchange Service (TWX) provides direct-dial point-to-point connections using input-output equipment such as keyboard printers, paper tape readers, and paper tape punches. TWX calls are established in the same manner as telephone calls by dialing from one station to another. Once the connection is established, operators may type two-way written messages, or messages or data may be sent automatically by means of paper tape.

Western Union's acquisition of the Bell System's TWX service has added 42,000 terminals to Western Union's TELEX system of 35,000 terminals and has resulted in the world's largest national teleprinter network. This widely used service provides quick direct-dial two-way connections between subscribers in over 2,000 locations in the continental United States, Hawaii, and 100 other countries. Direct connections to computers and other data processing equipment are possible.

The widespread availability of both the TWX and TELEX services facilitates the use of paper tape for transmitting data to a central office for further processing.

Broadband Exchange Service.   Western Union's Broadband Exchange Service links two subscribers over transmission channels that they select as best suited to their communications needs. By means of a voice-data instrument containing ten push buttons, users can select the broadband width that will furnish optimum, economical data transmission (Figure 11–15). Type of transmission may include voice, facsimile, or digital

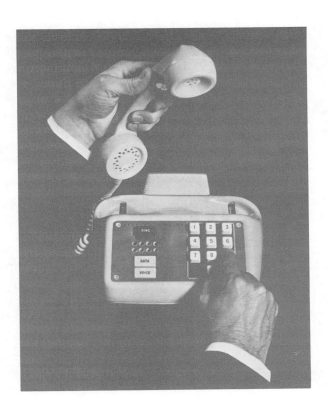

Figure 11-15. *Push-button voice-data instrument.*

(Reproduced by permission of Western Union Telegraph Company.)

data as contained in punched cards, punched tape, magnetic tape, and electronic storage devices. Thus, a firm desiring to have a problem solved could utilize the services of a computer at a remote location, possibly in a service center. Such services could be provided on a call-up basis through Broadband Exchange Service connections.

Subscribers are furnished with voice-data instruments and Datasets. The Dataset converts digital pulses from data processing equipment to frequency tones for transmission over communications circuits. When a connection has been made, both sets are switched to the data mode, and transmission can begin. If during transmission either party wishes to return to voice mode, a signal can be given. Transmission is interrupted allowing both parties to pick up the handsets and begin conversation. Most long-distance transmission is over Western Union's microwave radio network.

Private-Line Services. Both Western Union and the telephone companies provide services for the exclusive use of a single organization. Private-line voice services may be used alternately for voice communication and data transmission. Private-line teleprinter services are used with keyboard printers, paper tape readers, and paper tape punches. A private line can be set up on a two-point or multipoint basis.

TELPAK Service. TELPAK, the Bell System's broadband offering, is basically a private-line service with a bulk pricing arrangement intended for large users of communications. Users of this service have the benefit of various capacities, and the flexibility to arrange the facilities in any combination desired. For example, voice, teletypewriter, and data grade circuits may be combined within one TELPAK channel. The TELPAK capacity can also be used as a single large channel for high-speed data transmission such as facsimile, magnetic tape, and computer memory.

The rates for this service are lower than those for an equivalent number of single telephone lines.

Tariffs. For each common-carrier service provided, a tariff is published defining the service and the rate charged for that service. Tariffs may include the rates for leasing lines, for lines and subsets, or for lines, subsets, and terminals. For the most part, the categories of service outlined in this section represent different methods of pricing rather than differences in basic facilities. To a great extent the wire services now used can be employed for the transmission of voice, data, or both alternately, through the use of DATA-PHONE data sets furnished by the telephone company. This may result in savings by combining telephone and data requirements.

Communications Switching

It is possible for connections between communications terminals to be permanently established, thus allowing continuous transmission. This is, however, a costly arrangement for large networks. A more economical and flexible method is to establish temporary connections between stations wishing to exchange information. The process of temporarily connecting two stations is called *switching*. The two basic methods of performing the switching function are message switching and line switching.

Message Switching. Message switching is used to transfer messages in a leased telegraph wire system. In message switching the sending and receiving lines are not directly connected. However, all of the lines are connected to the switching center. With this method the originating station sends its message directly to the switching center together with the destination address. After the entire message is recorded on punched tape or magnetic tape at the switching center, it may be retransmitted promptly along the appropriate circuit, or it may be stored temporarily and sent out later. This is sometimes called "store and forward." Switching methods may be manual, semiautomatic, or fully automatic.

Line Switching. In line switching the communications center provides a direct connection between the two stations wishing to exchange information. The calling station first transmits to the switching center the code of the station to which information is to be sent. On the basis of the destination code, the switching center selects the line of the called sta-

Figure 11-16. *Data processing and computer switching facility maintained for General Services Administration's Advanced Record System in Romney, West Virginia.*
(Courtesy Western Union Data Services Company.)

tion and electrically connects the calling and called lines. The actual switching may be done by an operator or automatically by the use of dial equipment. The dial telephone system is an example of line switching. Only after the switching process has been completed can the transmission of data take place. Type of transmission may vary. It may be voice alone, or it may be digital data as contained in punched cards, paper tape, magnetic tape, and electronic storage devices. During communication the two stations remain in direct contact (Figure 11–16).

Line switching is generally required for on-line real-time systems. However, message switching is likely to be more economical for most other types of data communications systems. Both line and message switching methods may be used to satisfy the data communications requirements of large information systems.

IMPORTANT WORDS AND PHRASES

data communications system
on-line
real-time
time-sharing
ASCII

parity check
modem
common carrier
channel

bandwidth
broadband
message switching
line switching

REVIEW QUESTIONS

1. Briefly discuss the significance of data communications in today's society.
2. Define on-line data processing.
3. What is the significance of the American Standard Code for Information Interchange?

4. What are the five stages of data transmission?
5. Describe the function of a data set or modem.
6. List at least five different types of data transmission terminals.
7. Describe the data transmission functions that can be performed by Teletype machines.
8. What is meant by the term "common carriers"?
9. Describe the three basic types of communications channels.
10. Low-, medium-, and high-speed data transmission facilities are represented by what three basic bandwidth classifications?
11. What is DATA-PHONE service? Explain how it is used.
12. Define communications switching.
13. What is the difference between message switching and line switching?

12

EDP PROGRAM DEVELOPMENT

Computers are automatic, which means that they are able to perform long sequences of operations without human intervention. In fact, a computer may perform millions of operations without aid from an operator. A computer does, however, require instructions to direct its operations. These instructions define each basic operation to be performed and identify the data, device, or mechanism needed to carry out the operation.

The purpose of this chapter is to review the fundamentals of stored program instructions, file organization, and file processing techniques.

As indicated previously, the entire series of instructions needed to complete a given routine or procedure is called a *program*. The development of this sequence of steps is referred to as *programming*. The person who writes computer programs, a process that most authorities consider to be an art, is called a *programmer*.

The development of a computer program requires six basic steps:

1. Analyzing the problem
2. Preparing program flowcharts

3. Writing the program
4. Assembling or compiling the object program
5. Testing and correcting the program
6. Preparing the program for production

Each of these steps will be explained in this chapter.

ANALYZING THE PROBLEM

The first step in preparing an application for a computer is to define the problem precisely. In addition, program planning requires a very thorough analysis of all facets of the problem. This includes analysis of source data, the logical and practical procedures that will be needed to solve the problem, and the form of the final output. This analysis must take place before actual preparation of the program can begin. Otherwise, time may be wasted in preparing a program that will be subject to major change before it is put into operation.

PREPARING PROGRAM FLOWCHARTS

After the problem to be solved has been defined and thoroughly analyzed, it is possible to list the steps that must be followed in solving it. These steps may be written out in detail. It is more likely, however, that they will be represented by a *program flowchart,* which is a graphic illustration of what the computer is supposed to do. The flowchart is a precise and convenient means of outlining the various steps in a program. Flowcharts are not as apt to be misinterpreted as an entirely verbal presentation. Furthermore, they provide the programmer with an easy means of trying out and comparing several approaches to a problem.

Program Flowchart Symbols

Before proceeding with program flowchart development, a review of flowcharting symbols used in programming might be helpful.

The nine symbols used in programming are shown in Figure 12–1 along with a brief description of each. These nine symbols are the program flowcharting symbols recommended by the International Organization for Standardization (ISO) and are consistent with the fewer symbols adopted by the American National Standards Institute (ANSI). The two program flowcharting symbols used by ISO and not by ANSI are the preparation and the parallel mode symbols.

In addition to the flowcharting symbols shown in Figure 12–1, there is a flowcharting convention concerning modular flowcharting. *Modular flowcharting* is the process of developing a set of multilevel charts when a precise picture of program logic at a high level of detail is required. Striping a flowchart symbol signifies that a more detailed flowchart of

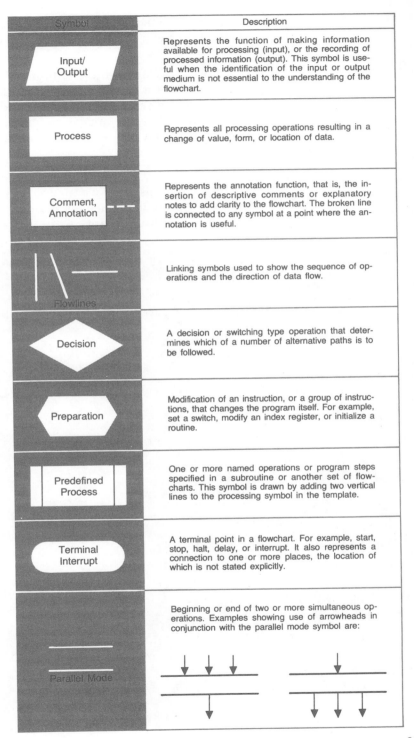

Symbol	Description
Input/ Output	Represents the function of making information available for processing (input), or the recording of processed information (output). This symbol is useful when the identification of the input or output medium is not essential to the understanding of the flowchart.
Process	Represents all processing operations resulting in a change of value, form, or location of data.
Comment, Annotation	Represents the annotation function, that is, the insertion of descriptive comments or explanatory notes to add clarity to the flowchart. The broken line is connected to any symbol at a point where the annotation is useful.
Flowlines	Linking symbols used to show the sequence of operations and the direction of data flow.
Decision	A decision or switching type operation that determines which of a number of alternative paths is to be followed.
Preparation	Modification of an instruction, or a group of instructions, that changes the program itself. For example, set a switch, modify an index register, or initialize a routine.
Predefined Process	One or more named operations or program steps specified in a subroutine or another set of flowcharts. This symbol is drawn by adding two vertical lines to the processing symbol in the template.
Terminal Interrupt	A terminal point in a flowchart. For example, start, stop, halt, delay, or interrupt. It also represents a connection to one or more places, the location of which is not stated explicitly.
Parallel Mode	Beginning or end of two or more simultaneous operations. Examples showing use of arrowheads in conjunction with the parallel mode symbol are:

Figure 12-1. *Program flow-charting symbols.*

the process or operation represented by that symbol can be found elsewhere in the same set of flowcharts. The three parts to the striping convention are:

1. A horizontal line is drawn within and near the top of the symbol.
2. An identifier is placed above the stripe in the striped symbol.
3. The detailed representation starts and ends with a terminal symbol. The same identifier appearing in the striped symbol on the original chart is placed in the entry terminal symbol in the detailed representation.

In Figure 12–2 the striping convention and certain program flowcharting standards are illustrated. The process box containing the description "Compute deductions and net pay" has a stripe across the top. An identifier, "AAA1," appears in the box above the stripe. Note that

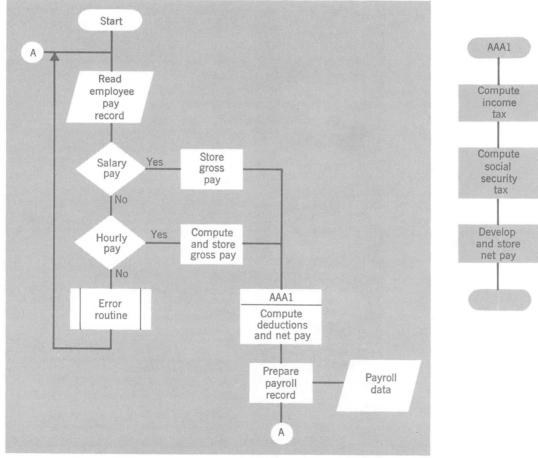

Figure 12-2. *Illustration of program flowcharting standards and conventions.*

the same identifier appears in the start terminal symbol on the accompanying chart. This illustrates how multilevel charts are related to each other.

This simple flowchart also illustrates the basic use of the predefined process symbol as opposed to the striping convention. Specifically, the predefined process symbol shown in the chart is used to identify that the error routine process is a subroutine flowcharted elsewhere. This differs from the striping process described above, as the function represented by the predefined process symbol does not require detailed representation.

Also note in Figure 12–2 the use of flowlines, the arrowhead, and connector symbols. In this example both flowline and connector symbols are used to return the flow to the beginning of the program depending on whether a normal or error routine occurs.

Program flowchart decisions are often noted in a form of *symbolic shorthand* for ease in concise flowchart preparation as well as clear understanding of the decision logic. Most of the shorthand statements in general use are as follows:

English statement	Shorthand statement
Compare A with B (where B is the common factor or constant value)	A:B
A is greater than B	A > B
A is less than B	A < B
A is equal to B	A = B
A is not greater than B (A is less than or equal to B)	A ≤ B
A is not less than B (A is greater than or equal to B)	A ≥ B
A is not equal to B	A ≠ B
Compare indicator settings	HI LO EQ
Check indicator settings	ON OFF

As can be noted in Figure 12–3, the descriptive flowchart has a brief statement in each box, and the symbolic flowchart makes liberal use of the shorthand statements. Both types have certain advantages. Generally, the descriptive flowchart is used to illustrate data manipulation programs, and symbolic flowcharts are used to illustrate complex analytical programs.

Flowchart Procedures

To illustrate the manner in which a flowchart is used in planning a program, let us assume that we wish to develop a means of preparing a current stock status report. Basically this requires:

1. Determining the beginning balance
2. Adding stock receipts
3. Deducting stock issues
4. Printing the new balance

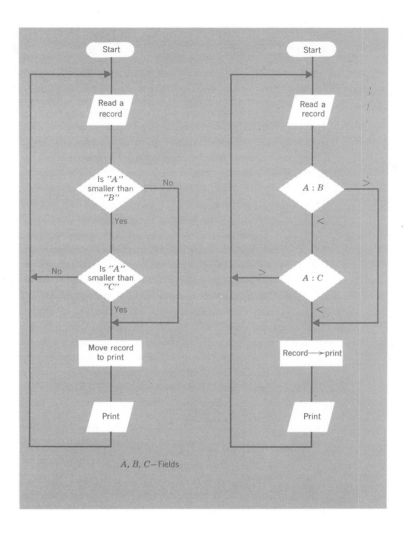

Figure 12-3. *Comparison of descriptive and symbolic flowcharts.*

A program flowchart of the solution to this problem is shown in Figure 12–4.

The following is a description of the steps shown in the flowchart:

Step 1. For each program written there are certain preliminary steps such as (a) define where in primary storage the program will be located, (b) identify input-output devices, (c) reserve storage areas and assign names to the areas, and (d) generate constant data in primary storage. Following these preliminary steps and before actual processing is started, most programming systems require that the files be opened. In this example opening the files consists of informing the program compiler that the input records in the form of punched cards are to be read by the punched card reader.

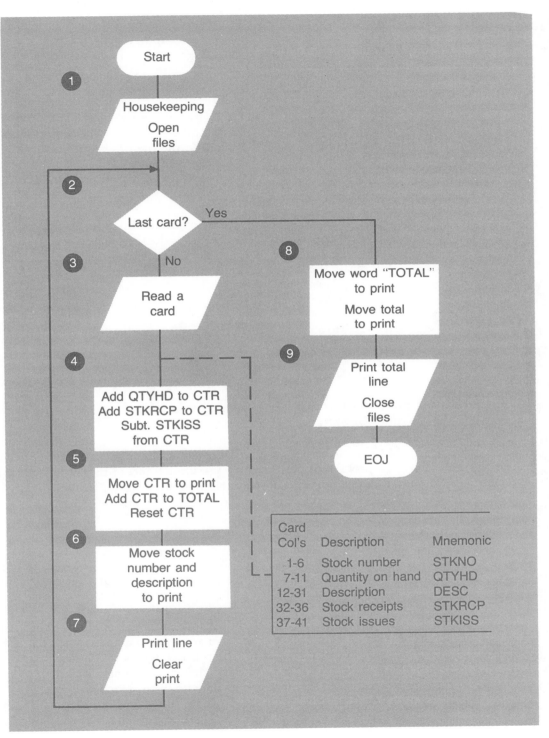

Figure 12-4. *Program flowchart.*

Step 2. Instructs the computer to determine if the last card has been processed. If the answer is no, the computer is directed to the next step. This function is automatically taken care of in some programming systems by an input-output control system (IOCS). It might at first glance appear strange that the very first step taken is to test for a last card. The primary reason for this is that if there were no data cards to be read after the program is loaded, we would not want the computer to continue with the process. The last card test in this illustration is also used to determine when the last card in the file has been processed.

Step 3. Instructs the card reader to read a card provided the last card has not been read.

Step 4. Instructs the computer to add the quantity on hand to the primary storage field labeled CTR, to add the stock receipts to the field labeled CTR, and to subtract stock issues from the field labeled CTR. In this case the label CTR is used by the programmer to identify a group of storage positions reserved to hold the factors and results of the arithmetic operations specified.

Step 5. Moves the result stored at CTR to the print area and adds it to a final total field labeled TOTAL.

Step 6. Moves the stock number and description to the print area.

Step 7. Instructs the printer to print a line and clears the print area after printing.

Step 8. If the last card indicator shows that the last card has been read and processed, the program will branch out to the end-of-job routine. This moves the final (accumulated) total to print. (This total is significant only for control purposes since it includes unrelated items.)

Step 9. Instructs the printer to print a line.

It should be pointed out that this problem was designed to illustrate certain facets of developing a program rather than to illustrate a typical stock status application.

It is essential to check each program to assure that it provides a means for handling every condition that might be encountered. For example: (1) each decision box must have at least two alternatives, and each possible result of the test must be represented by a flowline; and (2) each loop must have at least one test that can terminate it and a method for passing on to the next case if the end is not reached.

The first opportunity to perform such checking is usually when the program flowchart is complete. A thorough check of the flowchart before programming begins, perhaps by a second person, will usually reveal major defects when it is most convenient to correct them. If obscurities are detected in the review process, it is advantageous to be able to correct them before programming is started.

The checking of the flowchart does not end at this point, as minor flaws will often be revealed during the process of writing the program. These flaws are often detected during the programming process because of the need to concentrate on one part of the program at a time. For this reason, however, programming seldom helps in detecting the larger flaws in the program.

Before we proceed with the discussion on writing a program, let us first review the fundamentals of stored program instructions.

STORED PROGRAM INSTRUCTIONS

One of the most significant characteristics of electronic computers is that of internal storage. As indicated earlier, all data to be processed is initially entered into storage. In order to be processed, this data must be transmitted electronically to the other internal component, the arithmetic-logical unit. The results of the operations performed in the arithmetic-logical unit must then be routed electronically back to storage. When the results are desired, they are forwarded electronically from storage to an output device. A schematic diagram of these operations was presented in Figure 6–4.

All of these operations are under the control of a stored program. A *program* is a set of instructions indicating to the computer the exact sequence of steps it must follow in processing a given set of data.

The instructions and data required by a computer to solve a problem are both stored within the computer's main memory in numbered locations called *addresses*. Instructions are usually grouped together in main memory. They generally can be placed in any area of storage. Sequential instruction computers generally access each instruction from left to right. Therefore, each succeeding instruction is to the right of the last instruction executed unless a change in sequence of operations is dictated.

When not being operated on by the computer, a program may be stored as a deck of punched cards, or on punched tape, magnetic tape, or a random access device. When the program is required for operation, it can be read into the computer memory from any of these external storage devices. After the program is loaded into memory, the computer locates the first instruction of the program and proceeds through the sequence of instructions, operating on the data until it reaches the end of the job or is instructed to stop.

A stored program instruction is treated like any other information while stored in the computer. An instruction is not identified as an instruction until it is placed in the control section, where it is divided into its various operational segments, decoded, and then executed.

Most instructions are composed of two basic parts: (1) an operation part and (2) one or more operands.

The *operation* part designates the action to be taken such as read, write, add, subtract, compare, move data, and so on. This information is coded to have a special meaning for the computer. For example, in the programming system to be used for illustrative purposes later in this chapter, the letter A is interpreted by the computer as "add," the letter C as "compare," the letter D as "divide," SIO as "start input-output," and TR as "translate." These are, of course, merely representative of the many instructions used in this system. Furthermore, other computers may use different methods of coding to define operations.

An *operand* designates the location of data, an instruction, or an input-output unit or other device that is to be used in the execution of an operation. Thus, the operand says what to add, where to store, what to compare, and so on. The operand does not actually give the number to be added or compared. Instead, it is a symbol or label consisting of several characters or bits that give the address in storage where the data to be added or compared will be found.

There are three types of addresses:

Type of address	Purpose
Instruction	Address in memory where the instruction is located
Data	Address in memory of data to be operated upon
Device	Identification of a particular input-output device; may also refer to a certain location within the device

A computer instruction may have more than one operand. Most computers have two, and some have three. Generally, multiple-operand instructions require less storage and fewer instructions to complete a given procedure since they result in more than one operation being performed with a single instruction.

To illustrate instruction format we will use a simple *add* instruction that appears as follows:

A   5   1443

The A part of this instruction is the operation code that tells the computer it is to perform an add operation. The operand portion of the instruction contains two addresses. The first is the address of a general register, and the second is a location in primary storage. Thus, the computer is instructed to add the data at storage location 1443 to the contents of register 5.

Some computers use over 200 types of operation codes in their instruction formats and provide several methods for doing the same thing.

Other computers employ fewer (20–50) operation codes and have the capacity to perform more than one operation with a single instruction. Although all instructions will not fit into a single class, there are four basic types of instructions: (1) input-output, (2) arithmetic, (3) branching, and (4) logic and test (decision-making).

Input-Output Instructions. Input instructions direct the computer to a particular input device. Input instructions also tell the computer to read the next record and to put it into the storage locations specified. Output instructions tell the computer to send data from storage to an output device and to record it on the output medium. All input-output instructions must necessarily identify the device to be used. In some cases the device is specified by the operation part of the instruction, and in other cases it is controlled by both the operation and operand.

Other types of input-output instructions are those used in *editing*. This is the process of putting data into a more useful format. The two major editing functions are extraction of particular parts of a record for computer use or for output, and the alteration of a record into a different format. The primary editing function is the preparation of quantitative data. For example, the digits 0100135 would have limited significance if printed without editing, which could bring about the following result: $1,001.35.

The editing of quantitative data may include:

1. Eliminating all zeros to the left of the high-order significant digit.
2. Retaining zeros both to the right and left of significant digits when required.
3. Punctuating quantitative amounts with decimal and commas, and if required with the minus or credit sign. If the amount to be punctuated is expressed in dollars, then in addition to the decimal and commas, the dollar sign will be shown in accordance with accepted accounting practice. Amounts are seldom punctuated at the time of input or while operated on in the storage unit in order to conserve as much space as possible within a field or data word.

Editing may require only one instruction but will often require two or more. Usually editing is effected by first moving into the print storage area an edit word consisting of (1) the standard punctuation signs for the type of data to be printed, and (2) an indication of the point to the left of which zeros are to be dropped. This is then followed by an edit instruction that moves the data into the print storage area and eliminates the unnecessary zeros and punctuation marks.

Arithmetic Instructions. All of the basic arithmetic operations can be performed by a computer. All computers have instructions for adding and subtracting and most have instructions for multiplying and dividing.

In those computers that do not have multiply or divide instructions, these arithmetic operations can be performed through a series of additions and/or subtractions. The instructions required to perform multiply-divide operations in this manner are usually contained in a utility program called a *subroutine*. A subroutine is a set of instructions designed to direct the computer to carry out a well-defined operation—in this case an arithmetic calculation. After a self-contained subroutine of this type is written and checked, it can be used in any program that requires the operations it will perform. Sets of these subroutines are generally provided by the manufacturer of each computer as a programming aid.

Thus, when multiply or divide cannot be achieved by a standard instruction, the programmer can utilize an appropriate subroutine. This enables him to accomplish the same results without having to write all the program steps that otherwise would be required each time he found it necessary to multiply or divide. In other words, the subroutine automatically executes a series of instructions that produce the desired calculation.

In every arithmetic operation at least two factors are involved: multiplier and multiplicand, divisor and dividend, and so on. These factors are operated on by the arithmetic unit of the computer to produce a result such as a product or quotient. Therefore, at least two storage locations are needed for every calculation. Depending on the type of computer involved, these may be provided in main storage, by storage registers, accumulators, or a combination of these.

A computer has the capacity to perform numerous calculations on many factors during a series of instructions. For example, a factor may be multiplied and then other factors may be added to or subtracted from the product. The computer also has the ability to shift and round a factor or result. Shifting and rounding operations are used for adjusting, lengthening, or shortening results; and for placing the decimal point. All computers have some provision for recognizing and storing the sign associated with a factor, and for operating algebraically with the factor.

The exact rules governing the placement of factors, size of results, and so on, vary somewhat from one system to another. In all cases where it is anticipated that a result will exceed the capacity of the field or word, the programmer must arrange the data to produce partial results.

Branch Instructions. Branch instructions cause the computer to switch from one point in a program to another point, thereby controlling the sequence in which operations are performed. When a branch is executed regardless of existing conditions, it is known as an *unconditional branch*. When the execution of a branch instruction is contingent upon certain conditions being met, it is known as a *conditional branch*. Conditional branches will be discussed more fully in the following section.

Logic Instructions.   Logic (decision-making) instructions enable the computer to deviate from the normal sequence of instructions in accordance with the existence or nonexistence of certain conditions. If instructions always had to be followed sequentially in a fixed pattern, this would limit the computer to a single path of operation. The computer would not have any method of dealing with exceptions to a procedure and would be unable to select alternate paths, known as *branches,* based on conditions encountered while processing data. Moreover, a complete program would be necessary to process each record if it were not possible to repeat a given set of instructions.

The simplest of logic instructions is the *data transfer* type. Data transfer instructions are used to move data from one storage location or register to another. Included are such instructions as *plain move, move numeric data only, move zone only,* and *store address.*

A more complex type of logic operation is the *shift.* Shifting consists of moving the characters in a word columnwise to the right or left; that is, each character is moved from one column to the next. Shift operations are used to line up the characters of two words before comparing them or to line up two sets of numerals before adding them.

Shifting also may be used to isolate data. This operation is necessary in a fixed word length computer where two items of data may be stored in one computer word to save space. For example, in a computer with a fixed word length of ten characters, the assignment of a four-character item of data to a storage location would leave six unused character positions. These six positions could be used to store another item of data. However, it would be necessary to separate the items in order to isolate the one needed for a particular operation.

Another type of logic operation is to *compare* the data at one storage location with data in a register, accumulator, or other storage location. The two fields can be compared and evaluated in a specified sequence and one of four possible results will be indicated. The four results of comparisons are:

1. *A* is smaller than *B.*
2. *A* is equal to *B.*
3. *A* is not equal to *B* (the opposite of 2).
4. *A* is larger than *B* (the opposite of 1).

The comparison instruction should be followed by a *conditional branch* instruction with a provision that the branch instruction is to be executed if the comparison indicates the existence of the condition requiring the branch (Figure 12–5). If the condition does not exist, the computer executes the next in the regular sequence of instructions.

It should be noted that computers do not actually make decisions in the normal sense of the word. Instead, they follow directions that are

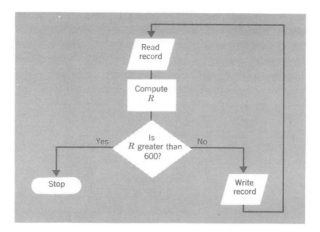

Figure 12-5. *Flowchart of a conditional branch.*

explicitly set forth in the program. In other words, the programmer decides what exceptions can arise during a program. He then establishes a set of comparisons that enable the computer to recognize the exceptions. Finally, he specifies the exact procedure the computer is to use in processing each exception.

The *test* for a certain condition is another type of logic operation involving the same techniques as the comparison instruction. Tests may be made for such conditions as a positive or negative sign for a quantity, zeros or blanks, last card, end of file, or end of job. If the condition being tested is met, the result is a branch to the designated location of another instruction. If the test is not met, the branch instruction is ignored and the next sequential instruction is accessed. Thus, branching is conditional; that is, it is dependent on the condition tested for being met.

There are other programming techniques besides branching instructions that can be used to vary the path the computer will follow through a program. No attempt will be made here to explain these techniques; however, for reference purposes, they are known as *instruction modification, address modification, indexing,* and *indirect addressing.*

With this understanding of stored program fundamentals, we can now proceed with the third step in program development, writing the program.

WRITING THE PROGRAM

After the steps for solving a problem have been set down, usually in a flowchart, a detailed series of instructions called a *program* is written. A stored program is the method of conveying to the computer, in a language that the computer can interpret, the operations it is to perform.

Only during the first few years were computer programs prepared in actual machine language or codes. Today most computer programs are first written in some symbolic language convenient to the programmer and then translated by the computer to machine-processable codes.

The program written in symbolic form is called the *source program.* This program is usually punched into cards and read into the computer, where it is translated into machine language by a *processor program,* commonly called a *compiler* or *language translator,* previously stored in the computer. The machine-language program produced as output from the compiler is called the *object program.* The object program is used in operation of the routine or procedure that was programmed originally in symbolic form.

Types of Source Program Statements

A computer is directed to perform its operations by a series of actual machine instructions stored in primary storage following their translation from the source program. These instructions usually originate as one-line statements on the coding form. There are three types of source program statements:

Statement	Description
Machine instruction	One-for-one symbolic representation of a machine instruction.
Macro instruction	Causes the compiler to retrieve a specially coded symbolic routine from the macro library, modify the routine according to the information in the macro instruction, and insert the modified routine into the source program for translation into machine language. A macro may be defined as "involving large quantities." Thus, for one macro instruction, many instructions may be assembled.
Processor instruction	Specifies auxiliary functions to be performed by the processor and, with a few exceptions, does not result in the generation of any machine-language code. The auxiliary functions assist the programmer in checking and documenting programs, in controlling storage-address assignments, in program sectioning and linking, in data and storage-field definition, and in controlling the processor program.

In order to go into greater detail about writing a program we will use a specific programming system. As the IBM Assembler Language is the most popular machine-oriented programming language now in use, we have selected it to illustrate basic programming concepts. Although Assembler Language is a very complete and powerful language, we will use a very limited number of its instructions, as the goal here is to illustrate the basics of programming and not the capacity of the language.

Coding Forms

Figure 12–6 illustrates the coding of the procedure depicted by the program flowchart in Figure 12–4. To assist the reader in understanding

IBM

PROGRAM	SAMPLE		PUNCHING INSTRUCTIONS	GRAPHIC	Ø	O				PAGE 1 OF 3
PROGRAMMER		DATE		PUNCH	NUM	ALPHA				CARD ELECTRO NUMBER

Name	Operation	Operand	Comments	Identification Sequence
SAMPLE	START	Ø	START PROG RELATIVE TO CORE LOC Ø	SAMØ1ØØØ
	PRINT	NOGEN		SAMØ1Ø1Ø
	STM	14,12,12(13)	SAVE REGISTERS	SAMØ1Ø2Ø
	BALR	9,Ø	LOAD BASE REG WITH PROG LOC	SAMØ1Ø3Ø
	USING	*,9	DEFINE REG 9 AS BASE REGISTER	SAMØ1Ø4Ø
	ST	13,SAVE13	SAVE VALUE IN REG 13	SAMØ1Ø5Ø
	LA	13,REGSAVE	LOAD REG 13 - ADDR OF PROG SAVEAREA	SAMØ1Ø6Ø
	B	PROC	BRANCH AROUND DCBS.	SAMØ1Ø7Ø
CARDIN	DCB	DDNAME=SYSIN,		XSAMØ1Ø8Ø
		RECFM=F,		XSAMØ1Ø9Ø
		LRECL=80,		XSAMØ11ØØ
		BLKSIZE=80,		XSAMØ111Ø
		DSORG=PS,		XSAMØ112Ø
		EODAD=LCARD,		XSAMØ113Ø
		MACRF=(GM)		SAMØ114Ø
PRTOUT	DCB	DDNAME=SYSPRINT,		XSAMØ115Ø
		RECFM=FA,		XSAMØ116Ø
		LRECL=133,		XSAMØ117Ø
		BLKSIZE=133,		XSAMØ118Ø
		DSORG=PS,		XSAMØ119Ø
		MACRF=(PM)		SAMØ12ØØ
RECIN	DS	ØCL80	DEFINE CARD INPUT AREA	SAMØ2ØØØ
STKNO	DS	CL6	STOCK NUMBER COLS 1-6	SAMØ2Ø1Ø
QTYHD	DS	CL5	QUANTITY ON HAND COLS 7-11	SAMØ2Ø2Ø
DESC	DS	CL2Ø	DESCRIPTION COLS 12-31	SAMØ2Ø3Ø
STKRCP	DS	CL5	STOCK RECEIPTS COLS 32-36	SAMØ2Ø4Ø
STKISS	DS	CL5	STOCK ISSUES COLS 37-41	SAMØ2Ø5Ø
BLANK	DS	CL39	REST OF CARD COLS 42-80	SAMØ2Ø6Ø
PRLINE	DS	ØCL133	DEFINE PRINT LINE	SAMØ2Ø7Ø
CTLCAR	DC	CL1' '	DEFINE CONTROL CHARACTER	SAMØ2Ø8Ø
RCOUT	DC	CL132' '	DEFINE PRINTER OUTPUT AREA	SAMØ2Ø9Ø
PQTY	DS	CL3	RESERVE 3 BYTES FOR QTY (PACKED)	SAMØ21ØØ
PSRCP	DS	CL3	RESERVE 3 BYTES FOR RCP (PACKED)	SAMØ211Ø
PSISS	DS	CL3	RESERVE 3 BYTES FOR ISS (PACKED)	SAMØ212Ø
CTR	DC	P'+ØØØØØØØ'	DEFINE 4 BYTE PACKED DEC COUNTER	SAMØ213Ø
TOTAL	DC	P'+ØØØØØØØ'	DEFINE 4 BYTE PACKED DEC TOTAL CTR	SAMØ214Ø
TOTCON	DC	CL5'TOTAL'	DEFINE A CONSTANT OF TOTAL	SAMØ215Ø
SAVE13	DS	F	DEFINE 4 BYTES FOR VALUE IN REG 13	SAMØ216Ø
REGSAVE	DS	18F	DEFINE 18 FULLWORDS FOR REG VALUES	SAMØ217Ø
PROC	OPEN	(CARDIN,(INPUT))	OPEN CARD DATA SET	SAMØ3ØØØ
	OPEN	(PRTOUT,(OUTPUT))	OPEN PRINTER DATA SET	SAMØ3ØØ5
GETCD	GET	CARDIN,RECIN	READ A CARD	SAMØ3Ø1Ø
	PACK	PQTY,QTYHD	CONVERT QTY ON HAND TO PACKED DEC	SAMØ3Ø2Ø
	PACK	PSRCP,STKRCP	CONVERT STOCK RECPT TO PACKED DEC	SAMØ3Ø3Ø
	PACK	PSISS,STKISS	CONVERT STOCK ISSUE TO PACKED DEC	SAMØ3Ø4Ø
	AP	CTR,PQTY	ADD QTY ON HAND TO COUNTER	SAMØ3Ø5Ø
	AP	CTR,PSRCP	ADD STOCK RECEIPTS TO COUNTER	SAMØ3Ø6Ø
	SP	CTR,PSISS	SUBTRACT STOCK ISSUES FROM COUNTER	SAMØ3Ø7Ø
	UNPK	RECOUT+79(6),CTR	UNPACK CTR INTO PRINT AREA	SAMØ3Ø8Ø
	AP	TOTAL,CTR	ADD COUNTER TO TOTAL COUNTER	SAMØ3Ø9Ø
	SP	CTR,CTR	CLEAR COUNTER	SAMØ31ØØ
	MVC	RECOUT+24(6),STKNO	MOVE STOCK NO TO PRINT AREA	SAMØ311Ø
	MVC	RECOUT+39(20),DESC	MOVE DESCRIPTION TO PRINT AREA	SAMØ312Ø
	PUT	PRTOUT,PRLINE	PRINT A LINE	SAMØ313Ø
	MVI	RECOUT,X'4Ø'	MOVE A BLANK TO PRINT AREA	SAMØ314Ø
	MVC	RECOUT+1(131),RECOUT	MOVE 131 SPACES TO CLEAR PRINT AREA	SAMØ315Ø
	B	GETCD	BRANCH TO READ THE NEXT CARD	SAMØ316Ø
LCARD	MVC	RECOUT+89(5),TOTCON	MOVE THE WORD TOTAL TO PRINT AREA	SAMØ317Ø
	UNPK	RECOUT+99(7),TOTAL	UNPACK TOTAL INTO PRINT AREA	SAMØ318Ø
	PUT	PRTOUT	PRINT TOTAL LINE	SAMØ319Ø
	CLOSE	CARDIN	CLOSE CARD FILE	SAMØ32ØØ
	CLOSE	PRTOUT	CLOSE PRINTER FILE	SAMØ321Ø
	L	13,SAVE13	RESTORE REGS 13	SAMØ3212
	LM	14,12,12(13)	RELOAD REGS WITH ORIGINAL VALUES	SAMØ3214
	LA	15,Ø	LOAD REG 15 WITH RETURN CODE = Ø	SAMØ3216
	BR	14	END OF JOB	SAMØ3218
	END	SAMPLE		SAMØ322Ø

Figure 12-6. *Source program written in IBM Assembler Language (related to Figure 12-4).*

the program shown in Figure 12–6, let us first describe the various fields, and columns on the form used for coding in this language.

1. The intended use of the various sections in the form heading should be obvious. The reason for the punching instructions is to identify for the card punch operator how certain graphics are to be punched. The instructions indicate, for example, that the Ø represents a zero and the unslashed 0 represents the letter *O*. This prevents errors in reading and key punching these similar characters. Since modern programming languages of this type use more letters than numerals, the programmer has chosen to slash zeros, as this requires less effort. It should be noted, however, that other programmers may prefer to use the opposite approach and to slash letters rather than numerals. In this case, Zs may also be slashed to distinguish them from 2s.

2. The name field is used to assign a symbolic name to a statement. A name allows other statements to refer to the statement by that name. If a name is given, it must begin in column 1 and must not extend beyond column 8. SAMPLE and CARDIN in Figure 12–6 are examples of names in the name field.

3. The operation field is used to specify the mnemonic operation code of a machine or assembler instruction or a macro. This field may begin in any column to the right of column 1 if the name field is blank. If the name field is not blank, at least one blank must separate the name and operation fields. In our example we have consistently started the operation codes in column 10, as this makes the program easier to follow and is the technique used by most programmers.

4. The operand field provides the assembler with additional information about the instruction specified in the operation field. If a machine instruction has been specified, the operand field contains information required by the assembler (processor program) to generate the machine instruction. The operand field specifies registers, storage addresses, input-output devices, and storage-area lengths. The operand field may begin in any column to the right of the operation field, provided at least one blank space separates it from the last character of the operation mnemonic. If there is no operand field but there is a comments field, the absence of the operand field must be indicated by a comma, preceded and followed by one or more blanks.

    Depending on the instruction, the operand field may be composed of one or more subfields called operands. Operands must be separated by commas, and a blank space must not intervene between operands and commas, as a blank space sets the limits of the field. Note on the illustration that each operand field has been started in column 16. Again, this is a preferred technique and not required.

5. The comments field is provided for the convenience of the programmer and permits any number of lines of descriptive information about

the program to be inserted into the object program list, which is printed out after the program is assembled (Figure 12–19). Comments appear only in the program list and have no effect on the assembled object program. The comments field must appear to the right of the operand field and be preceded by at least one blank. The entire line can be used for comments by placing an asterisk in column 1. The comments fields in the program illustration have been very liberally used in order to make the program as easy as possible to follow. A programmer would not normally be so verbose.

6. The *X* in column 72 is used to identify the continuation of entries on the following line. Notice that lines 1080 through 1130 have *SX*'s in column 72 and that the last, DCB entry for CARDIN on line 1140 does not have an *X* in column 72.

7. The identification-sequence field may be used for program identification and statement sequence numbers. (Each line on the coding form is a statement.)

Program Coding

Now that the assembler coding form has been described, we shall consider the program coding illustrated in Figure 12–6. The program shown is an actual program written in accordance with the program flowchart in Figure 12–4. This flowchart should serve as an aid in following the program. The operation codes and mnemonic operands, which are intended to aid the programmer, should also be helpful in interpreting the program. This is because they may be easily associated with the operations they actually represent. For example, the operation code B on line 1070 of the sample program represents a branch instruction, and the operand "PROC" is a mnemonic operand selected by the programmer to represent the beginning of the actual procedure that starts on line 3000.

The following numbered comments can be related to each block on the flowchart in Figure 12–4 by the corresponding numbers. To facilitate reference to particular lines on the coding sheets, excerpts from the coding sheets will be shown on the pages where the specific instructions are described. However, an occasional reference to the complete coding sheets in Figure 12–6 may be necessary to fully comprehend explanations involving other sections of the program.

1. The first seven lines are standard IBM operating system linkage conventions (Figure 12–7). The next statement on line 1070 is a branch instruction that will cause the computer to jump to the instruction with the name PROC shown on line 3000. In other words, as the compiled program is first executed, the branch instruction causes the computer to go around the series of processor instructions to the first procedure instruction on line 3000.

Name	Operation	Operand	Comments	Identification-Sequence
SAMPLE	START	∅	START PROG RELATIVE TO CORE LOC ∅	SAM∅1∅∅∅
	PRINT	NOGEN		SAM∅1∅1∅
	STM	14,12,12(13)	SAVE REGISTERS	SAM∅1∅2∅
	BALR	9,∅	LOAD BASE REG WITH PROG LOC	SAM∅1∅3∅
	USING	*,9	DEFINE REG 9 AS BASE REGISTER	SAM∅1∅4∅
	ST	13,SAVE13	SAVE VALUE IN REG 13	SAM∅1∅5∅
	LA	13,REGSAME	LOAD REG 13 - ADDR OF PROG SAVEAREA	SAM∅1∅6∅
	B	PROC	BRANCH AROUND DCBS,	SAM∅1∅7∅

Figure 12-7.

Name	Operation	Operand	Identification-Sequence
CARDIN	DCB	DDNAME=SYSIN,	SAM∅1∅8∅
		RECFM=F,	SAM∅1∅9∅
		LRECL=8∅,	SAM∅11∅∅
		BLKSIZE=8∅,	SAM∅111∅
		DSORG=PS,	SAM∅112∅
		EODAD=LCARD,	SAM∅113∅
		MACRF=(GM)	SAM∅114∅

Figure 12-8.

Name	Operation	Operand	Identification-Sequence
PRTOUT	DCB	DDNAME=SYSPRINT,	SAM∅115∅
		RECFM=FA,	SAM∅116∅
		LRECL=133,	SAM∅117∅
		BLKSIZE=133,	SAM∅118∅
		DSORG=PS,	SAM∅119∅
		MACRF=(PM)	SAM∅12∅∅

Figure 12-9.

The next series of instructions, 1080 through 1200, are standard DCB (data control block) instructions used to define the characteristics of the specified file to be processed. In this case the first DCB macro on lines 1080 through 1140 defines the characteristics of that card file for the processor program (Figure 12–8).

The second DCB macro on lines 1150 through 1200 defines the characteristics of the printer file for the processor program (Figure 12–9). These two series of macro statements will cause the processor program to insert a series of instructions and constants into the object program.

The statements on lines 2000 through 2150 are used to reserve areas of primary storage and to define and enter constant data into the program (Figure 12–10). DS stands for "define storage" and is used to reserve storage areas and to assign names to the areas. For example, statement 2000 assigns the name RECIN to an 80-position card input area, and statement 2010 assigns the name STKNO to a six-position field within the 80-position area. The DC statements are used to generate constant data and to place it in primary storage. For

RECIN	DS	ØCL8Ø	DEFINE CARD INPUT AREA	SAMØ2ØØØ
STKNO	DS	CL6	STOCK NUMBER COLS 1-6	SAMØ2ØIØ
QTYHD	DS	CL5	QUANTITY ON HAND COLS 7-11	SAMØ2Ø2Ø
DESC	DS	CL2Ø	DESCRIPTION COLS 12-31	SAMØ2Ø3Ø
STKRCP	DS	CL5	STOCK RECEIPTS COLS 32-36	SAMØ2Ø4Ø
STKISS	DS	CL5	STOCK ISSUES COLS 37-41	SAMØ2Ø5Ø
BLANK	DS	CL39	REST OF CARD COLS 42-80	SAMØ2Ø6Ø
PRLINE	DS	ØCL133	DEFINE PRINT LINE	SAMØ2Ø7Ø
CTLCAR	DC	CLI' '	DEFINE CONTROL CHARACTER	SAMØ2Ø8Ø
RCOUT	DC	CLI32' '	DEFINE PRINTER OUTPUT AREA	SAMØ2Ø9Ø
PQTY	DS	CL3	RESERVE 3 BYTES FOR QTY (PACKED)	SAMØ2IØØ
PSRCP	DS	CL3	RESERVE 3 BYTES FOR RCP (PACKED)	SAMØ2IIØ
PSISS	DS	CL3	RESERVE 3 BYTES FOR ISS (PACKED)	SAMØ2I2Ø
CTR	DS	P'+ØØØØØØØ'	DEFINE 4 BYTE PACKED DEC COUNTER	SAMØ2I3Ø
TOTAL	DC	P'+ØØØØØØØ'	DEFINE 4 BYTE PACKED DEC TOTAL CTR	SAMØ2I4Ø
TOTCON	DC	CL5'TOTAL'	DEFINE A CONSTANT OF TOTAL	SAMØ2I5Ø
SAVEI3	DS	F	DEFINE 4 BYTES FOR VALUE IN REG 13	SAMØ2I6Ø
REGSAVE	DS	18F	DEFINE 18 FULLWORDS FOR REG VALUES	SAMØ2I7Ø

Figure 12-10.

PROC	OPEN	(CARDIN,(INPUT))	OPEN CARD DATA SET	SAMØ3ØØØ
	OPEN	(PRTOUT,(OUTPUT))	OPEN PRINTER DATA SET	SAMØ3ØØ5

Figure 12-11.

GETCD	GET	CARDIN,RECIN	READ A CARD	SAMØ3ØIØ

Figure 12-12.

example, the DS statement on line 2130 assigns the name CTR to a four-position packed field containing seven zeros and a plus sign. The statement on line 2150 assigns the name TOTCON to a five-position field containing the word TOTAL. The comments field should be helpful in understanding the other DS and DC statements.

The statements on lines 3000 and 3005 prepare the card reader and printer for operation (Figure 12–11). This completes all of the "housekeeping" functions, and we are now ready to begin the procedure or processing part of the program.

2. The last card test is made by the input-output control system (IOCS) as instructed by the statement on line 1130. Since this statement automatically instructs the IOCS to insert into the object program all of the necessary instructions for this operation, no other statements need be entered by the programmer.

3. The statement on line 3010 has a GET macro and CARDIN and RECIN operands (Figure 12–12). This instruction makes the next consecutive record from the file named CARDIN available for processing in the area defined as RECIN. The mnemonic CARDIN will refer the processor program to the statement with the name CARDIN. This statement is on line 1040 and is the first of several statements describing the card-read device.

	PACK	PQTY,QTYHD		CONVERT QTY ON HAND TO PACKED DEC	SAM03020
	PACK	PSRCP,STKRCP		CONVERT STOCK RECPT TO PACKED DEC	SAM03030
	PACK	PSISS,STKISS		CONVERT STOCK ISSUE TO PACKED DEC	SAM03040
	AP	CTR,PQTY		ADD QTY ON HAND TO COUNTER	SAM03050
	AP	CTR,PSRCP		ADD STOCK RECEIPTS TO COUNTER	SAM03060
	SP	CTR,PSISS		SUBTRACT STOCK ISSUES FROM COUNTER	SAM03070

Figure 12-13.

	UNPK	RECOUT+79(6),CTR		UNPACK CTR INTO PRINT AREA	SAM03080
	AP	TOTAL,CTR		ADD COUNTER TO TOTAL COUNTER	SAM03090
	SP	CTR,CTR		CLEAR COUNTER	SAM03100

Figure 12-14.

4. Before performing decimal arithmetic we must pack the data, as decimal arithmetic instructions are intended for use only with packed decimal data. Therefore, the instructions on lines 3020 through 3040 will cause the decimal data just read into storage to be packed and placed at new locations (Figure 12–13). For example, the pack instruction on line 3020 will cause the data located at QTYHD to be packed and stored at location PQTY. The operand QTYHD represents the "quantity on hand" field in card columns 7 through 11 as it is named and described on line 2020. The operation AP on line 3050 represents an "add packed decimal" instruction. The operand CTR represents a reserved storage location defined on line 2130, and the operand PQTY represents the reserved storage location defined on line 2100. This statement on 3050 is translated into program instructions by the processor program, which causes the computer to add the sum at the location named PQTY to the sum at the location named CTR. With this understanding it should be possible to follow the statements on lines 3060 and 3070.

5. To print a packed-decimal sum we must first change it to an unpacked or zoned format and move it into the assigned print area. The statement on line 3080 causes the sum at the storage location named CTR to be unpacked and placed in the print area named RECOUT (record out) plus 79 (Figure 12–14). RECOUT + 79 identifies where in the print output area the six-position sum should be placed. RECOUT + 79 is translated by the processor program into an actual storage address 79 greater than the actual address of RECOUT.

The statement on line 3090 causes the sum at CTR to be added to the sum at TOTAL. The following instruction on line 3100 causes the sum at CTR to be subtracted from itself; thus, the storage location named CTR will be reset to zero.

6. The statement on line 3110 will cause the data at the storage location named STKNO to be moved to the print area at RECOUT + 24. The

next statement will cause the data at the storage location named DESC to be moved to the print area at RECOUT + 39 (Figure 12–15).

7. The PUT macro on line 3130 is the opposite of the GET macro on line 3010 (Figure 12–16). The PUT macro causes the output device named PRTOUT (print out) to print a line. The statements on lines 3140 and 3150 will cause a blank first to be placed at RECOUT and then to be moved to the other 131 print-area positions. These operations clear the 132-position print area of the data just printed. As shown on the flowchart, the next step should be to test for a last card and, if the last card has not been read, to read a card. The B operation on line 3160 is a branch (jump) instruction telling the computer to get its next instruction at GETCD, the name of the statement on line 3010.

8. When the input-output control system (IOCS) recognizes that the last card has been read, it will cause the computer to branch to the instruction named LCARD. This name was given to the EODAD (end of data address) statement on line 1080 as part of the DCB specifications. The statement named LCARD is on line 3170 and will cause the constant (TOTAL) named TOTCON to be moved to the print area at RECOUT + 89 (Figure 12–17). The next instruction will cause the sum at storage location named TOTAL to be unpacked and moved to the print area at RECOUT + 99.

| | MVC | RECOUT+24(6),STKNO | MOVE STOCK NO TO PRINT AREA | SAM∅311∅ |
| | MVC | RECOUT+39(2∅),DESC | MOVE DESCRIPTION TO PRINT AREA | SAM∅312∅ |

Figure 12-15.

	PUT	PRTOUT,PRLINE	PRINT A LINE			SAM∅313∅
	MVI	RECOUT,X'4∅'	MOVE A BLANK TO PRINT AREA			SAM∅314∅
	MVC	RECOUT+1(131),RECOUT	MOVE 131 SPACES TO CLEAR PRINT AREA	SAM∅315∅
	B	GETCO	BRANCH TO READ THE NEXT CARD			SAM∅316∅

Figure 12-16.

| LCARD | MVC | RECOUT+89(5),TOTCON | MOVE THE WORD TOTAL TO PRINT AREA | SAM∅317∅ |
| | UNPK | RECOUT+99(7),TOTAL | UNPACK TOTAL INTO PRINT AREA | SAM∅318∅ |

Figure 12-17.

	PUT	PRTOUT		PRINT TOTAL LINE			SAM∅319∅
	CLOSE	CARDIN		CLOSE CARD FILE			SAM∅32∅∅
	CLOSE	PRTOUT		CLOSE PRINTER FILE			SAM∅321∅
	L	13,SAVE13		RESTORE REGS 13			SAM∅3212
	LM	14,12,12(13)		RELOAD REGS WITH ORIGINAL VALVES	SAM∅3214
	LA	15,∅		LOAD REG 15 WITH RETURN CODE = ∅	SAM∅3216
	BR	14		END OF JOB			SAM∅3218
	END	SAMPLE					SAM∅322∅

Figure 12-18.

9. The statement on line 3190 will cause the output device named PRTOUT to print a line (Figure 12–18). The close statements on lines 3200 and 3210 are the opposite of the open statements and will cause the card reader and printer devices to discontinue service as input and output file processing devices for this job. The statements on lines 3212–3218 are return linkage statements that turn control back to the operating system.

The last statement on the coding sheet (3220) causes two functions to be performed. First, it instructs the processor program to terminate the assembly of the object program. Second, it designates a point in the program to which control will be transferred after the object program has been loaded. In this program, control will be transferred to the first instruction in the object program.

ASSEMBLING OR COMPILING THE OBJECT PROGRAM

After the program has been written and checked, and usually punched into cards (note that each line can contain a maximum of 80 characters), it is ready for translation into an object program.

As indicated above, a source program is prepared in a language that is convenient to the programmer but that is not meaningful to the computer. Consequently, it is necessary to translate the source program from symbolic language to a machine language. This is accomplished by a program called a *processor* that is usually furnished by the computer manufacturer for use with a particular computer.

The processor is loaded into the computer prior to the reading of the source program, which is written in a language common to the programmer and the processor. Then as the source program is read, the processor automatically translates it to a machine-language program known as an *object program* (Figure 12–19). In other words, the processor treats the source program as input data and produces an object program as output data. The object program may be recorded on punched cards, magnetic tape, or another auxiliary storage medium. Since the object program is in a language that is meaningful to the computer, it may then be loaded into memory and used by the computer to perform the planned operations.

After the object program has been assembled, a printed list of the program is usually prepared. This program list is a helpful programming aid, as it lists, in addition to the information contained on the coding sheets, the machine-language instructions and the addresses in storage where the instructions are located. These storage locations are assigned automatically by the processor. The program list also flags many of the programmer errors by listing an error notification code on any line that has an error in the source statement.

Figure 12–19 illustrates the assembled program list of the program shown on the flowchart in Figure 12–4, and on the coding sheets in

```
  LOC  OBJECT CODE     ADDR1 ADDR2  STMT    SOURCE STATEMENT                                    F04MAR74   9/01/76

 000000                                   1 SAMPLE   START 0                    START PROG RELATIVE TO CORE LOC 0    SAM01000
                                          2          PRINT NOGEN                                                     SAM01010
 000000 90EC D00C        0000C            3          STM   14,12,12(13)         SAVE REGISTERS                       SAM01020
 000004 0590                              4          BALR  9,0                  LOAD BASE REG WITH PROG LOC          SAM01030
 000006                                   5          USING *,9                  DEFINE REG 9 AS BASE REGISTER        SAM01040
 000006 50D0 91BE        001C4            6          ST    13,SAVE13            SAVE VALUE IN REG 13                 SAM01050
 00000A 41D0 91C2        001C8            7          LA    13,REGSAVE           LOAD REG 13 - ADDR OF PROG SAVEAREA  SAM01060
 00000E 47F0 920A        00210            8          B     PROC                 BRANCH AROUND DCBS.                  SAM01070
                                          9 CARDIN   DCB   DDNAME=SYSIN,                                            *SAM01080
                                                           RECFM=F,                                                *SAM01090
                                                           LRECL=80,                                               *SAM01100
                                                           BLKSIZE=80,                                             *SAM01110
                                                           DSORG=PS,                                               *SAM01120
                                                           EODAD=LCARD,                                            *SAM01130
                                                           MACRF=(GM)                                               SAM01140
                                         63 PRTOUT   DCB   DDNAME=SYSPRINT,                                        *SAM01150
                                                           RECFM=FA,                                               *SAM01160
                                                           LRECL=133,                                              *SAM01170
                                                           BLKSIZE=133,                                            *SAM01180
                                                           DSORG=PS,                                               *SAM01190
                                                           MACRF=(PM)                                               SAM01200
 0000D4                                 117 RECIN    DS    0CL80                DEFINE CARD INPUT AREA               SAM02000
 0000D4                                 118 STKNO    DS    CL6                  STOCK NUMBER COLS 1-6                SAM02010
 0000DA                                 119 QTYHD    DS    CL5                  QUANTITY ON HAND COLS 7-11           SAM02020
 0000DF                                 120 DESC     DS    CL20                 DESCRIPTION COLS 12-31               SAM02030
 0000F3                                 121 STKRCP   DS    CL5                  STOCK RECEIPTS COLS 32-36            SAM02040
 0000F8                                 122 STKISS   DS    CL5                  STOCK ISSUES COLS 37-41              SAM02050
 0000FD                                 123 BLANK    DS    CL39                 REST OF CARD COLS 42-80              SAM02060
 000124                                 124 PRLINE   DS    0CL133               DEFINE PRINT LINE                    SAM02070
 000124 40                              125 CTLCAR   DC    CL1' '               DEFINE CONTROL CHARACTER             SAM02080
 000125 4040404040404040               126 RECOUT   DC    CL132' '             DEFINE PRINTER OUTPUT AREA           SAM02090
 0001A9                                 127 PQTY     DS    CL3                  RESERVE 3 BYTES FOR QTY (PACKED)     SAM02100
 0001AC                                 128 PSRCP    DS    CL3                  RESERVE 3 BYTES FOR RCP (PACKED)     SAM02110
 0001AF                                 129 PSISS    DS    CL3                  RESERVE 3 BYTES FOR ISS (PACKED)     SAM02120
 0001B2 000000000C                     130 CTR      DC    P'00000000'          DEFINE 4 BYTE PACKED DEC COUNTER     SAM02130
 0001B7 000000000C                     131 TOTAL    DC    P'00000000'          DEFINE 4 BYTE PACKED DEC TOTAL CTR   SAM02140
 0001BC E3D6E3C1D3                     132 TOTCON   DC    CL5'TOTAL'           DEFINE A CONSTANT OF TOTAL           SAM02150
 0001C4                                 133 SAVE13   DS    F                    DEFINE 4 BYTES FOR VALUE IN REG 13   SAM02160
 0001C8                                 134 REGSAVE  DS    18F                  DEFINE 18 FULLWORDS FOR REG VALUES   SAM02170
                                       135 PROC     OPEN  (CARDIN,(INPUT))     OPEN CARD DATA SET                   SAM03000
                                       141          OPEN  (PRTOUT,(OUTPUT))    OPEN PRINTER DATA SET                SAM03005
                                       147 GETCD    GET   CARDIN,RECIN         READ A CARD                          SAM03010
 000234 F224 91A3 90D4  001A9 000DA    152          PACK  PQTY,QTYHD           CONVERT QTY ON HAND TO PACKED DEC    SAM03020
 00023A F224 91A6 90ED  001AC 000F3    153          PACK  PSRCP,STKRCP         CONVERT STOCK RECPT TO PACKED DEC    SAM03030
 000240 F224 9149 90F2  001AF 000F8    154          PACK  PSISS,STKISS         CONVERT STOCK ISSUE TO PACKED DEC    SAM03040
 000246 FA42 91A3 001B2 001A9          155          AP    CTR,PQTY             ADD QTY ON HAND TO COUNTER           SAM03050
 00024C FA42 91A6 001B2 001AC          156          AP    CTR,PSRCP            ADD STOCK RECEIPTS TO COUNTER        SAM03060
 000252 FB42 91AC 91A9 001B2 001AF     157          SP    CTR,PSISS            SUBTRACT STOCK ISSUES FROM COUNTER   SAM03070
 000258 F354 916E 91AC 00174 001B2     158          UNPK  RECOUT+79(6),CTR     UNPACK CTR INTO PRINT AREA           SAM03080
 00025E FA44 91B1 91AC 001B7 001B2     159          AP    TOTAL,CTR            ADD COUNTER TO TOTAL COUNTER         SAM03090
 000264 FB44 91AC 91AC 001B2 001B2     160          SP    CTR,CTR              CLEAR COUNTER                        SAM03100
 00026A D205 9137 90CE 0013D 000D4     161          MVC   RECOUT+24(6),STKNO   MOVE STOCK NO TO PRINT AREA          SAM03110
 000270 D213 9146 90D9 0014C 000DF     162          MVC   RECOUT+39(20),DESC   MOVE DESCRIPTION TO PRINT AREA       SAM03120
                                       163          PUT   PRTOUT,PRLINE        PRINT A LINE                         SAM03130
 000284 9240 911F        00125        168          MVI   RECOUT,X'40'         MOVE A BLANK TO PRINT AREA           SAM03140
```

```
  LOC  OBJECT CODE     ADDR1 ADDR2  STMT    SOURCE STATEMENT                                    F04MAR74   9/01/76

 000288 D282 9120 911F  00126 00125   169          MVC   RECOUT+1(131),RECOUT MOVE 131 SPACES TO CLEAR PRINT AREA SAM03150
 00028E 47F0 9220        00226        170          B     GETCD                BRANCH TO READ THE NEXT CARD         SAM03160
 000292 D204 9178 91B6  0017E 001BC   171 LCARD    MVC   RECOUT+89(5),TOTCON  MOVE THE WORD TOTAL TO PRINT AREA    SAM03170
 000298 F364 9182 91B1  00188 001B7   172          UNPK  RECOUT+99(7),TOTAL   UNPACK TOTAL INTO PRINT AREA         SAM03180
                                      173          PUT   PRTOUT,PRLINE        PRINT TOTAL LINE                     SAM03190
                                      178          CLOSE CARDIN               CLOSE CARD FILE                      SAM03200
                                      184          CLOSE PRTOUT               CLOSE PRINTER FILE                   SAM03210
 0002C2 58D0 91BE        001C4        190          L     13,SAVE13            RESTORE REG 13                       SAM03212
 0002C6 98EC D00C        0000C        191          LM    14,12,12(13)         RELOAD REGS WITH ORIGINAL VALUES     SAM03214
 0002CA 41F0 0000        00000        192          LA    15,0                 LOAD REG 15 WITH RETURN CODE = 0     SAM03216
 0002CE 07FE                          193          BR    14                   END OF JOB                           SAM03218
 000000                               194          END   SAMPLE                                                    SAM03220
```

Figure 12-19. *Assembled program list (related to Figure 12-6).*

Figure 12–6. At the top of the program lists are field headings that are defined as follows:

1. The field headed LOC (location) contains the high-order byte storage address assigned to each machine-language instruction generated by the processor. Storage addresses are actually in binary form; however, for ease of reading, they are printed on these lists in hexadecimal.

2. The field headed OBJECT CODE, ADDR 1 ADDR 2 (addresses 1 and 2) contains all of the actual machine instructions generated by the processor program in hexadecimal representation.

3. The STMT (statement) field is used to number sequentially all the statements in the program. The statements inserted by the processor program, although assigned sequential statement numbers, are not shown in the listing because the optional statement PRINT NOGEN was included in this program for brevity.

4. The SOURCE STATEMENT field contains each statement line as it was key punched from the coding form. Note that the statements beginning with statement 9 (identification sequence 1080 through 1140) have been assigned only one statement number. The reason is that this group of entries made by the programmer is regarded as one continuous statement since all but the first statement have an X in column 72.

With the aid of the flowchart in Figure 12–4, it should be possible to follow most of the program steps. It should be noted that the location and object code data are represented in hexadecimal and that the procedure part of the program starts with statement 135.

Most program lists are accompanied by a supplemental list such as a cross-reference list or symbol table. This list will show, usually in alphabetical order, the name given a statement, the length of the field represented, the location in storage where the definition appears, the statement number of the definition entry, and the statement number of each statement making reference to it. This list is another helpful aid to the programmer when reviewing the program, locating errors, and correcting or making a change in the program.

TESTING AND CORRECTING THE PROGRAM

Flowchart preparation and program coding are major steps in developing a program. The other major step is to test the program by processing test data. Often the preparation of test data will require more time than the writing of the program. Therefore, an experienced programmer will usually make test data notes as items to be tested come to mind during the design of the flowchart and writing of the program.

A good test will contain examples of every conceivable condition that could occur during actual operation. Test material may include (1) copies of the actual data the program is intended to process, (2) hypothetical data designed to simulate conditions that will be encountered in processing actual data, or (3) a combination of actual and hypothetical data.

In testing large or complicated programs, it is usually best to first test a segment (module) of the program at a time and then test the complete program. Segmenting large programs for testing aids the programmer in finding errors, as the more errors there are in a program, the more difficult they are to find since one error may obscure clues to another error. A program test, whether it is designed for a segment or the entire program, should first test the organization of the program with a simple test that follows the typical flow of the program. It should then test all of the normal conditions in the program. The exceptions should be tested next and finally the extreme cases, usually related to incomplete or incorrect input. An error in a program can be identified through incorrect output or more frequently through the computer stopping as a result of trying to operate on an invalid instruction.

The primary aid to locating the cause of an error is to print out the data in storage related to the program being tested. This process, which is called a *storage dump* or sometimes a *storage print,* produces a "snapshot" image of the following:

1. Contents of the permanently assigned storage area. These are the first few positions of primary storage.
2. Contents of the registers.
3. As much of the primary storage above the permanently assigned storage as is allowed to print. This should include the entire program and all of the data as it existed in primary storage at the time the dump occurred.

The storage dump is used by the programmer as an aid in detecting program errors without tying up the computer. This procedure of getting the bad program off the computer is better than trying to locate and correct errors through manual operation at the computer console. Locating an error can often be more challenging to the programmer than programming itself.

Many programs will suddenly fail after being in production for as long as several months. This is invariably the result of a condition occurring that was not anticipated while preparing the program or during program testing. Thus, program testing can be every bit as important as program preparation.

| PREPARING THE PROGRAM FOR PRODUCTION | The final step is the preparation of the program for production. This consists of completing the system documentation and the operating instructions. Normally a system is comprised of one or more procedures |

that may contain one or more programs. These programs may be run individually or grouped into one or more jobs. The system documentation and the operating instructions usually contain the following:

1. A narrative description of the system. This is usually a general description of the total system and is used by interested persons such as computer operators and programmers who need to understand the system.
2. A system flowchart showing the flow of data through the system. This is helpful, as it relates various data to its origin and destination.
3. A procedure definition. This is a narrative description of each procedure in the system.
4. A procedure flowchart showing the steps for each procedure in the system.
5. Job definition and job step instructions.
6. Job control cards for execution of the job.

The system documentation usually contains the following additional items.

1. Copies of all the correspondence and notes relative to the system.
2. Copies of all card layouts, record layouts, storage layouts, input-output analysis layouts, and file analysis layouts.
3. Program flowcharts and/or decision tables for each program. The final program flowchart may be printed by a computer using the program source deck as input.
4. A program list for each program written.
5. Sample reports, report layouts, and printer carriage tape if required.
6. Source program, object program, and job control card decks.

As we can see from the list of items in the systems documentation and operating instructions, considerable time and effort are required in their preparation. Most programmers would much rather proceed with the next project than spend the time that good documentation requires. Therefore, one of the responsibilities of management is to see that documentation standards are developed and that all programmers and systems analysts comply with them.

Figure 12–20 is a graphic representation of the programming steps discussed in this chapter. This may be helpful as a general review of the steps in developing a computer program.

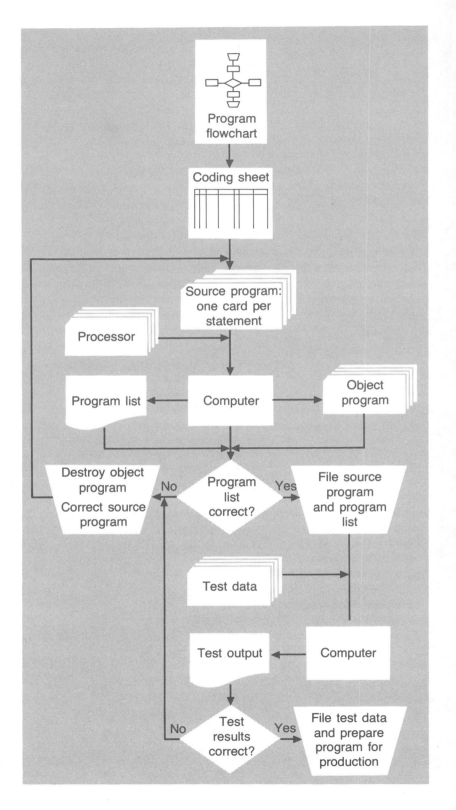

Figure 12-20. *Relationship of programming steps.*

IMPORTANT WORDS AND PHRASES

program flowchart
modular flowcharting
program
address
operation
operand

editing
subroutine
branch instruction
source program
processor program

object program
machine instruction
macro instruction
processor instruction
storage dump

REVIEW QUESTIONS

1. What are the various facets of problem analysis that precede the development of a computer program?
2. What are the advantages of the program flowchart as a programming aid?
3. What does striping a flowchart symbol signify?
4. Name and define the two basic parts contained in most instructions.
5. Name the three types of address that an operand may contain.
6. Name the four basic types of instructions.
7. Briefly describe the primary editing function.
8. What is a branch instruction?
9. When is a conditional branch instruction ignored?
10. Why are logic instructions important to the successful operation of a computer?
11. Why are most of today's programs written in some sort of symbolic language?
12. Distinguish between a source program, a processor program, and an object program.
13. How does the programmer distinguish between a zero and an alphabetic O?
14. What is the purpose of the comments field on the Assembler Language coding form?
15. How is an object program produced?
16. What will a good program test contain?
17. What is the final step in the preparation of a program for production?

13　PROGRAMMING SYSTEMS

In the preceding chapter it was stated that even though a computer program can be written in machine language, very few of them actually are. Writing a program in machine language is difficult for the following reasons:

1. Each instruction must be written using actual machine codes. For computers that use pure binary representation this is almost impossible.
2. The instructions must be arranged in the exact sequence in which they are to be executed. Each time an instruction is omitted through error or oversight, all succeeding instructions must be relocated to make room for the insertion in storage of the omitted instruction. This requires the programmer to keep a detailed record of where in storage each instruction is located.
3. Revising an existing program is usually impractical and very time-consuming because of the need to reassign the locations of the instructions affected.
4. The programmer must fully understand the basic operations of the computer and the functions of each operation code.
5. Including proven routines or segments of other programs in a new program is quite difficult unless each instruction can be automatically

located in storage in proper sequence within the new program. When a machine language is used, the programmer must assign the storage locations for the routine.

ELEMENTS OF PROGRAMMING SYSTEMS

Many of the difficulties and objections to writing a program in actual computer codes have been eliminated by the development of programming systems. These systems were made possible by the use of symbolic languages enabling the programmer and the computer to communicate in a language that is much simpler for the programmer to use. A programming system consists of two parts, a *language* and a *processor,* which are described in the following sections.

Programming Language

The basic purpose of a programming language is to allow a data processing program to be written with a minimum of burden on the programmer and a maximum of burden on the computer. Thus, the language is composed of abbreviated words or symbols that can be easily associated with the regular language of the programmer and that also can be translated into machine language by the computer. The use of symbolic language also makes it easier for persons who are not familiar with the program to read and understand it. All programming languages, like other languages, have certain established rules of grammar and punctuation. Each one also has a vocabulary of its own.

A data processing procedure is first written in the programming language; this is called a *source program.* The source program must be written in precise form according to the rules of the language to convey to the computer exactly what it is to do. The source program is then recorded on a computer input medium such as punched cards or magnetic tape and read into the computer for translation by the processor.

Processor

A *processor,* frequently called a *compiler* or *translator,* is a program usually supplied by the equipment manufacturer for creating machine-language programs. A processor previously stored in the computer receives the source program written in symbolic language by the programmer and translates the instructions into machine-language instructions acceptable to the computer. This machine-language program is called an *object program.*

While translating the source program into an object program, the processor performs these functions:

1. Refers to a table containing all mnemonic abbreviations used by the programmer to specify operations and selects the equivalent machine codes.
2. Assigns storage locations to mnemonic names (labels) and indexes them for future reference. This relieves the programmer of a great amount of clerical work in assigning memory.

3. Calculates the amount of storage needed to store each instruction and assigns the necessary storage addresses.
4. Refers to stored constants and other data as required by the source program.
5. Usually prints messages that note names not referenced elsewhere in the program, references to nonexistent names, invalid mnemonic operations, and other discrepancies. This aids the programmer in the development of an operable program.
6. Usually prepares the instructions necessary to load the object program into computer storage and refers the computer to the first step in the program after it is loaded.

As the object program is developed, it is recorded on a storage medium as explained in the preceding chapter.

The more powerful the computer, the more assistance the programming system can provide in the preparation of programs. For example, in the more powerful systems, previously written routines for checking, input-output, restart, etc., may be inserted into the object program by the processor as specified by the programmer.

Because of characteristics such as those described above, as well as others to be described later, a good programming system offers the following advantages:

1. The programmer can concentrate more fully on the problem being programmed rather than on the computer.
2. Program preparation time is reduced, thus making a programmer many times more productive.
3. The human-machine communication problem is overcome, and there is less opportunity for human error.
4. The programmer is able to utilize program techniques and routines that have been developed previously by himself or by other programmers and that have proved to be satisfactory.
5. It is easy for a program to be modified as the need arises.
6. Program testing requires far less machine time since a programming system aids in reducing programming errors.

All programming systems are translators since they translate language written by the programmer into language understood by the computer. All of these translators treat the source program as input data, manipulate it, and create a machine program. There are, nevertheless, different levels of sophistication in the method of operation and effectiveness of programming systems. This will be apparent in the following discussion.

PROGRAMMING SYSTEM AIDS

The complexities of equipment and the development of powerful programming systems have resulted in programming subspecialties. Although there is and probably always will be an overlap, *application programmers* write programs designed to do specific jobs; for example, the one illustrated in the preceding chapter. *Systems programmers* write the programs that run the computer system and aid the application programmer in performing his task. Most of these programs are originally developed by the manufacturers of the various computer systems. The programs are usually written in a generalized fashion encompassing all of the necessary components or features of the equipment marketed in a given product family and are supplied along with the equipment. The user's systems programmers then modify or tailor these vendor-supplied programs to meet unique requirements and to give maximum efficiency of computer operation. Many of these programs, commonly referred to as *software*, will be described here or in later chapters.

Subroutines

A *subroutine* is a standard sequence of instructions designed to direct the computer to carry out a specified operation. Originally these basic routines recorded in a computer input medium were included in the source program at the proper place and assembled along with the rest of the program. In other words, the subroutines had to be inserted at each point that they were needed in a routine as shown in Figure 13–1.

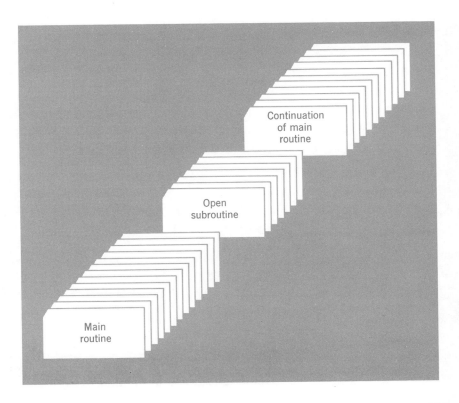

Figure 13-1. *Program using an open subroutine.*

As a result they were included in the main operational sequence of the object program. These are known as *open subroutines.*

A *closed subroutine* is one that requires programming only once since it may be entered from several points in a program. As a means of avoiding repetition of the same sequence of instructions in different places in the main routine, control may be transferred to a closed subroutine from more than one place in the main routine. Multiplication is a typical example of an operation that can be performed whenever needed by the use of a subroutine.

To utilize a closed subroutine it is necessary to provide linkage from the main routine to the subroutine. This is accomplished by means of a *branch instruction.* Since a subroutine may be entered several times, some provision must be made for returning to the main program each time the subroutine is used. Consequently, before branching occurs, the return instruction in the subroutine must be modified so that at the end of the operation it will effect a return to the appropriate point in the main routine (Figure 13–2).

Macro Instructions

Instructions that have the capability of generating more than one machine-language instruction are called *macro instructions.* A macro instruction is a method of describing in a one-line statement a function, or functions, to be performed by the object program. Macro instructions enable the programmer to write one instruction such as "read a tape," and the processor will then automatically insert the corresponding detailed series of machine instructions. In this manner the programmer avoids, in still a better way, the task of writing one instruction for every machine step. This increases programmer productivity because sequences of instructions that are repeated frequently can be called for by a simple macro statement, thereby relegating still another clerical task to the computer.

A macro instruction is actually a *pseudo instruction* that is not translated into a machine instruction. Instead, the macro instruction causes the automatic insertion of an open subroutine. The macro routine may differ from the standard subroutine, however. The standard subroutine is a self-contained routine that is available in a fixed form. The macro routine, on the other hand, may be formed when the macro instruction is encountered and may be tailored to meet the data requirements of the program being processed. Such routines are inserted in the source program automatically wherever a macro statement appears. The basic subroutines used in this process are drawn from a library of subroutines usually held in auxiliary storage until called for.

In its simplest form, a macro instruction may result in merely including in the main program a fixed subroutine from a library. This is known as *macro substitution.* The use of this type of macro generally imposes upon the user the task of designing or selecting the proper library routine. Subroutines are typically used to perform detailed operations such as multiplication and division.

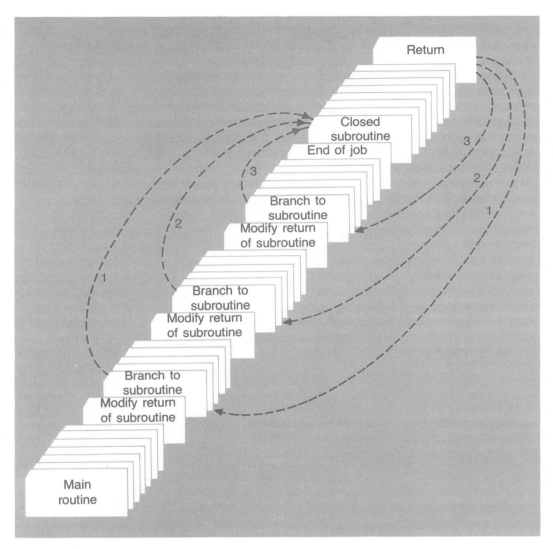

Figure 13-2. *Program using a closed subroutine.*

By the use of a more advanced technique known as *macro generation,* the user need only specify the type of function he wishes to perform. In other words, he merely describes in a one-line statement an operation to be performed at a certain point by the object program. The statement does not indicate how the operation is to be performed. This is determined by the compiler, which selects the proper routine and generates a set of instructions tailored to meet the specific requirements of the program.

The subroutine that results from the use of either a substitute or generative macro consists of a sequence of symbolic instructions. These symbolic instructions are merged into the source program as it is assembled. The processor then produces the object program by translating the symbolic instructions into machine instructions.

*Input-Output
Control Systems*

A computer program can be divided into three segments:

1. Input—the entering of data into the computer
2. Processing—the internal manipulation of data
3. Output—the writing of the results

A large portion of each program deals with the input-output segments. Therefore, *input-output control systems* (IOCS) were developed to relieve the programmer of all equipment and timing considerations involved in these functions, thus allowing him to concentrate on the processing portion of his program. The input-output control system accomplishes this by means of a group of programmed routines that control the reading of input data and the writing of output data. The IOCS also performs the following functions:

1. Checks for equipment error while reading or writing and initiates reread or rewrite procedures if possible.
2. Generates end-of-reel (EOR) and end-of-file (EOF) procedures as required.
3. Checks the labels on input tapes and writes the labels on output tapes. Labels can also be written and checked on disk files.
4. Controls the organization and transfer of records to and from magnetic tape or disk files.
5. Allows simultaneous reading, computing, and writing on those computers capable of simultaneous processing.
6. Provides for priority processing, and when requested prepares records to indicate the point at which an interrupted program should be restarted.

The ability of IOCS to perform these functions reduces the programmer writing, checking, and testing effort required to produce a working program. The use of IOCS also produces standard input-output routines and formats, which are most helpful when several programmers are working on different parts of the same program or on several programs within an application. IOCS can also be helpful in adapting existing programs to a different configuration of the same computer or to an entirely new computer system.

To use IOCS the programmer first must describe in coded form the equipment on which the program will be processed. Then the files must be defined, also in coded form. Following this, the programmer can employ certain macros such as *get, put, open,* and *close* to generate instructions that make a record available to the object program for input or output. Some IOCS also provide other features such as priority interrupt, checkpoint for restart, and real-time routines, which will be described later.

IOCS are especially important in the utilization of random processing techniques. Random access storage devices can provide vastly increased storage capacity to a computer system. They also present a greater challenge in the effective storage and retrieval of data. IOCS provide the special techniques necessary for the optimum processing of data stored on a random basis.

Sort and Merge Programs

Sort Programs.   Sorting files consumes a large percentage of computer time in any application requiring the sequential processing of records. It is fairly easy to sort punched cards and other individual documents because the records can be physically rearranged. However, the problem of rearranging the sequence of items on magnetic tape or disks is somewhat different. Fortunately, it is possible to use the computer itself to perform the complex sorting and merging operations necessary to arrange records on such media in either ascending or descending sequence.

Nearly every computer has a *generalized sort program* consisting of two parts: the assignment program and the actual sort program. The *assignment program* converts the generalized sort program to a specific program that will efficiently sort a particular file of records. In other words, the generalized sort program has an overall structure that can be modified to handle files of various formats. Variable characteristics such as record length, location, and length of control fields (keys), and number of records in each block may be entered into the computer. This data may then be used to modify the structure of the basic program, thereby producing a program to do the specific sort.

The *sort program* is normally divided into three operating sections called *phases*.

Phase 1.   As most files being sorted are too large to fit into main storage at one time, the sort program causes as many records to be read into storage as capacity will permit. The records are sorted internally and written out onto intermediate work tapes, or disk areas if this type of storage is being used. The next batch of records is then read from the input file, and the process continues until the entire file has been read, partially sorted, and rerecorded on intermediate work tapes or disk areas. After phase 1 is completed, two or more tapes or disk areas containing many series of sequenced records are ready for the merge passes to be performed during phases 2 and 3.

Phase 2.   During phase 2 all merging except the last merge takes place. Through a series of merges the relatively small strings of sequenced records are merged into successively longer strings. A two-way merge is the minimum merge possible. Depending on the number of tape drives available, three- or four-way (or more) merges are possible. The more tapes used in the merge process, the faster the sort will be.

Phase 3. During phase 3 the final merge of two or more strings of information into a single sequence takes place. At the same time most programs provide for the restoration of each record to its original format. This would be necessary if the original record format was rearranged during phase 1 to facilitate the sorting operation. It is also possible through added programming for records to be summarized, deleted, or altered during phase 3.

To illustrate the process of sorting records on magnetic tape, let us assume that the key words in Figure 13–3 are recorded on a tape in the order shown. It should be recognized that these are only the control words and that in actual practice each would be associated with an entire record. Our objective is to sort the records so that they will be in sequence according to the key words.

In phase 1 the records on tape *A* are sorted, three records at a time, and placed alternately on tapes *C* and *D* as shown in Figure 13–4.

Phase 2 merges tapes *C* and *D* and alternately places them on tapes *A* and *B* as shown in Figure 13–5. It should be noted that in writing

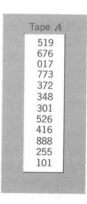

Figure 13-3.

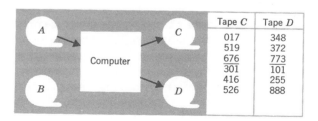

Figure 13-4. *Phase 1 sort.*

records a change is made from one tape to another when a stepdown occurs. A stepdown is a number followed by a smaller number. Thus, records were written on tape *A* until a stepdown occurred between key words 773 and 101, at which time output was switched to tape *B*.

As illustrated in Figure 13–6, phase 3 is the final merge of all records into a single string of records in sequence. Records may also be prepared for the next operation as this final pass is completed.

At the end of phase 1 the tapes ordinarily would have to be rewound in order to become input to phase 2. During phase 2 the tapes would have to be rewound before each of the many passes necessary to complete the merging process. There are, however, some computers that can read records from tape in either direction and can merge records without rewinding. In an actual sort, phase 1 would handle many more records on each sort, and phase 2 would require many passes to complete the merge.

Data sorting is increasingly being accomplished on random access devices. Since all of the strings of records on random access devices are readily available, it is possible to use other sorting techniques that are more efficient than tape-sorting procedures like the one described above.

Merge Programs. Merge programs are similar to phase 3 of the sort program. They are generalized and also have an assignment phase during which they may be modified in accordance with user specifications. Merge programs can be used to merge many strings of records into a

Tape *A*	Tape *B*
017	101
348	255
372	301
519	416
676	526
773	888

Figure 13-5. *Phase 2 sort.*

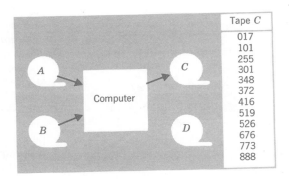

Tape *C*
017
101
255
301
348
372
416
519
526
676
773
888

Figure 13-6. *Phase 3 sort.*

single sequence and at the same time check the sequence of the records on each file as it is merged. Examples of how a merge program might be used are:

1. Files that are too large to be sorted on the available equipment as a single file may be sorted in sections and then merged.
2. Several transaction files may be merged at the end of a processing period such as weekly, monthly, or quarterly.

Sort and merge programs are usually classed as utility programs. However, they have been covered here separately because of the major role sorting plays in most computer facilities.

Utility Programs

Utility programs are generally used to assist in the operation of a data processing system. They relieve the computer user of the need to prepare programs to do routine things such as clear disk storage, write from disk to tape, write from tape to cards, and write from tape to print. The functions of a data processing facility are to compile and test programs, and to perform production runs. Utility programs are used to support and augment both of these functions.

Utility programs are general purpose programs that can be grouped into the following six general classifications.

Classification	Function
Sorting and merging programs	Perform the functions described in the preceding section.
Simulators	Routines that run on one computer and imitate the operations of another computer.
Translators	Programs whose input is a sequence of statements in some language and whose output is an equivalent sequence of statements in another language.
Housekeeping routines	Used to set storage to an initial condition (blanks or zeros) or to cause data to be placed into or read out of storage. For example, *clear storage, print storage,* and *punch storage* are names of some of the more common housekeeping routines.
File conversion routines	Used to move data from one external or auxiliary storage device to another. *Tape to disk, card to tape,* and *tape duplicate* are the names of three of the more common file conversion routines.
Program-testing aids	Designed to make program testing easier and to aid in error detection. Most medium- to large-scale computers have utility programs that provide automatic program testing. That is, when the computer is under control of this program, it may assemble and load a program, then feed in the test data, and test the pro-

Classification	Function
	gram. Any errors during assembly or test are indicated as printed output, and the computer automatically produces a display of storage (storage dump) at end of job or at point of error. The computer then automatically assembles and loads the next program to to be tested.

TYPES OF PROGRAMMING LANGUAGES

Machine-Oriented Programming Languages

Instructions written in a computer-oriented language reflect the composition of the machine instructions required by the particular computer being used. The number of letters that can be used in a word, the set of acronyms such as BAL (branch and link), and the order of fields within an instruction are fixed in accordance with the order and size of the fields in a machine instruction. In short, a machine-oriented language is designed for a specific computer and is not intended for use on other types of computers. The assembler language discussed in the preceding chapter exemplifies a machine-oriented programming language.

A machine-oriented programming language allows the programmer to take advantage of all the features and capacities of the computer system for which it was designed. It also is capable of producing the most efficient object program insofar as storage requirements and operating speeds are concerned. For these reasons, most vendor-supplied software is written in a machine-oriented language.

The primary reasons that most application or production programs are not written in a machine-oriented language are:

1. Being such a complete language, it is a more difficult language to learn, to use, and to debug.
2. Being machine-oriented, any extensive additions or deletions of equipment on which the program is to be run will usually require considerable reprogramming before the program will operate on the changed configuration. This is one of the major reasons for using a problem-oriented language in writing application programs.

Problem-Oriented Programming Languages

In a problem-oriented language, the notations reflect the type of problem being solved rather than the computer on which the program is to be run. For example, the notations used to write a program in COBOL resemble English; FORTRAN notations resemble the language of mathematics; PL/I notations combine the features of both COBOL and FORTRAN.

Just as restrictions exist in the notation of English and of mathematics, there also exist restrictions in the notation of problem-oriented languages. Only a specified set of numbers, letters, and special characters may be used in writing a program; and special rules must be observed for punctuation and for the use of blanks. Nevertheless a program written in a problem-oriented language is written in a more flexible form than one in a machine-oriented language.

The problem-oriented processor is designed to scan the source program, character by character, recognize the intended meaning of the words or symbols, and generate the instructions required to perform the designated functions. In doing this, the compiler uses techniques that enable it to produce a number of machine-language instructions from a single statement in the source program. This is known as a one-to-many translation as opposed to the one-to-one translation that generally occurs in a machine-oriented program.

Problem-oriented programming languages have several advantages.

1. They are easier to use than most machine-oriented languages and, therefore, generally enable the programmer to finsh a job much sooner.
2. They are easier to learn, thus enabling specialists other than programmers to write computer programs.
3. They are more durable because they are easier to modify. This is especially helpful if the program must be modified by someone other than the original programmer.
4. They can be compiled and run on a variety of computers. In addition, they may require only minor modification and recompiling when major changes are made in the computer configuration.

In the next chapter a problem-oriented language especially designed for educational purposes will be discussed in depth. The BASIC programming system will be used to demonstrate the principles of computer program preparation as well as the advantages of a problem-oriented programming language.

IMPORTANT WORDS AND PHRASES

programming language
source program
processor
object program
application programmer
systems programmer
software

subroutine
open subroutine
closed subroutine
branch instruction
macro instruction
input-output control system (IOCS)

sort program
merge program
utility program
machine-oriented language
problem-oriented language

REVIEW QUESTIONS

1. A programming system consists of what two parts? Describe the basic purpose of each part.
2. Distinguish between application programmers and systems programmers.

3. How does a closed subroutine differ from an open subroutine?
4. What is a macro instruction?
5. What are the primary purposes of input-output control systems? How do they aid the programmer?
6. Outline briefly the magnetic tape-sorting procedure described in this chapter.
7. What is the basic purpose of utility programs? Name the six general classifications of utility programs.
8. What are the two basic types of programming languages? What is the main difference between the two?
9. Most application or production programs are not written in a machine-oriented language for what reasons?
10. What are the advantages of problem-oriented programming languages?

14 BASIC PROGRAMMING SYSTEM

The BASIC (Beginner's All-purpose Symbolic Instruction Code) programming language developed at Dartmouth College, Hanover, New Hampshire, is a mathematical problem-oriented language designed for use by beginning programmers. Since its development in the early 1960s, BASIC has undergone divergent modification and enhancement. That is, many persons have attempted to make BASIC look more and more like FORTRAN, which will be described in the next chapter. Others have added extensions to the BASIC language that widen its scope of applicability. As a result, there are in existence today many BASIC "dialects" that will not be discussed here, as this chapter is not intended to be a complete coverage of the language. Instead, the fundamentals of computer programming will be demonstrated through the use of BASIC programming statements that should be common to all BASIC systems.

In addition to being simple and easy to use, BASIC is also designed to facilitate communication between humans and the computer in a time-sharing system. Therefore, before discussing the details of the BASIC programming language, let us review the characteristics and procedures of the time-sharing environment in which BASIC is likely to be used.

TIME-SHARING

Time-sharing allows a large number of users at various remote terminals to simultaneously use a centrally located computer for problem solving.

Each user operates independently and receives such fast response that he has no awareness of the use of the facility by others.

A time-sharing system generally has the following characteristics:

1. Each user has one or more terminals such as Teletype machines connected to the central computer by data communications lines.
2. Each user acts independently of the others sharing the system. He may enter, modify, and execute programs within minutes, and may receive error messages during program entry and execution. He also may enter data.
3. A master program called the "supervisor" keeps track of the work each user is doing and determines the order in which terminals are served. Supervisory functions include scheduling of users' requests, transferring control of the central processor from one user to another, moving programs in and out of main memory, and managing the users' private files. In effect, the computer gives recurring spurts of attention to users on a rotational basis. Ordinarily the elapsed time between spurts of attention to any one problem is so brief that the user has the impression he alone is being served.
4. Each user may develop his own set of programs or may utilize standard routines provided by the time-sharing service.
5. The user's data files may be maintained at the computer center. Each user's files are uniquely identified and are accessible only to him through the use of specific instructions.

Of particular significance in time-sharing systems is the speed of the computer, which enables many terminal operators to use the system at the same time without interfering with each other. This results in an economic advantage, which is a primary reason for the extensive use of time-sharing today.

Terminal Operating Procedures

Before attempting to use a terminal, the operator should study the guide for that particular terminal, as there are many different makes of typewriter terminals, each with certain operating characteristics. To establish communication with the computer, the following procedures are generally followed:

1. If there is a mode switch, it is set for communication.
2. The operator turns the power on.
3. If the terminal is equipped with a dial-up mechanism, the next steps are as follows; if not, number 4 is the next step.
   a. The operator depresses the TALK button on the data set telephone.
   b. He lifts the receiver and dials the number that has been assigned to the computer.
   c. When a steady, high-pitched tone is heard on the receiver, the operator depresses the DATA button firmly for a moment and

then releases it; the DATA button should light and remain lit as long as the terminal is connected to the computer.

   d. The telephone receiver is then replaced.

4. If the terminal is equipped with an acoustic coupler mechanism, the next steps are as follows; if not, number 5 is the next step.

   a. The operator lifts the receiver of a standard telephone and dials the number that has been assigned to the computer.

   b. When a steady, high-pitched tone is heard on the receiver, he places the receiver firmly in the acoustic coupler mechanism. The terminal is now ready for communication with the computer.

5. When the ATTN (attention) key is depressed the computer will usually type LOGON inviting the user to identify himself by typing his identification code on the same line with the LOGON statement. If there is no attention key, the operator types in the word HELLO followed by his identification code. After typing his identification code, he must press the carriage return key to notify the computer that he has finished that line.

6. The computer will usually respond to the identification code with an acknowledgment that may include the date and time followed on the next line by the statement READY. Next the operator types the name of his program and the key word BASIC.

7. The program is then entered, and the word RUN is typed below the END statement to signal the computer to run the program.

8. When the operator finishes his work, he disconnects the terminal from the computer by typing the LOGOFF or BYE statement.

9. The terminal power switch is then turned off.

THE BASIC PROGRAMMING LANGUAGE

Fundamentals of Coding and Compilation

A BASIC program consists of a group of statements, each of which is limited to one line. Each statement must be prefaced by a number that can be up to five digits in length. Statement numbers serve a dual purpose in BASIC. One purpose is to provide a label or tag for each statement. The other is to identify the sequence in which the statements will be executed. There can be no blanks between the digits in the statement number; however, at least one blank space must separate the statement number from the BASIC statement that follows.

The recommended statement numbering method is to increment each number by ten (10, 20, 30, 40, 50) at the time that the program is originally written. This leaves numbers for later use if it should be necessary to insert additional statements. Statements can be recorded or entered into the computer in any sequence, as the BASIC compiler will place the statements in ascending statement number sequence before executing the program. Also, if more than one statement has the same number, only the last statement will be used by the compiler. In a time-sharing environment this procedure is very helpful, as it enables us to modify a statement by merely retyping it using the same statement number. A statement may be deleted by simply retyping the statement number with nothing after it.

The following example shows how an original program would be re-ordered by the computer. Note particularly that statements 30 and 35 have been placed in ascending sequence, and that statement "40 PRINT X" has been replaced by "40 PRINT Y".

Program as written	Program when compiled
30 LET X=A+B+C+D	10 READ A,B,C,D
10 READ A,B,C,D	20 DATA 100,200,300,400
20 DATA 100,200,300,400	30 LET X=A+B+C+D
40 PRINT X	35 LET Y=X/4
50 END	40 PRINT Y
35 LET Y=X/4	50 END
40 PRINT Y	

Writing Statements

The primary elements of a BASIC statement are identifiers and operators. *Identifiers* represent values that may be either constant or variable. A *string* of characters (a sequence of letters of the alphabet, numbers, or special characters) whose value cannot be changed throughout program execution is called a *constant* and may be included in a program statement or referenced in a statement through the use of a valid symbol.

Values that can vary during program execution are called *variables* and must be represented by valid symbols. The programmer may only refer to variable data through the use of symbols, as the actual primary storage locations for each value (data item) are assigned by the BASIC compiler. To do this the BASIC system develops a cross-reference table for the symbolic identifiers and the primary storage locations for every data item. A valid BASIC identifier symbol can be either a single alphabetic letter (*A* through *Z*) or it can be a single letter followed by a single digit or a dollar sign.

Operators specify mathematical operations to be performed or relational comparisons to be made. Accordingly, operators are noted in a BASIC statement as either arithmetic or relational symbols. The symbols used to denote arithmetic operators are listed in order of priority of execution.

Arithmetic operator	Definition	Priority
** or ↑	Exponentiation	1
*	Multiplication	}2
/	Division	
+	Addition	}3
−	Subtraction	

Arithmetic expressions are evaluated in order of operator priority. If more than one symbol with the same level of priority appears in an expression, the leftmost operator will be performed first.

The symbols used to denote relational operators are:

Relational operator	Definition	Example
=	Equal	A = B
< >	Not equal	A < > B
> =	Greater than or equal to	A > = B
< =	Less than or equal to	A < = B
>	Greater than	A > B
<	Less than	A < B

The portion of a statement that is to the right of an equal sign specifies the value to be assigned to the variable on the left of the equal sign and is called an *expression*. An expression is composed of identifiers and operators and can be very simple, involving no calculations, or it can be quite complicated, involving several variables and operators.

The following BASIC statements, with the exception of FILES, will be used in the sample programs that appear later in this chapter.

Statement	Function
REM	Enables the placement of comments in a program list to facilitate understanding. REM (remarks) statements in no way affect program execution, as they are ignored.
	EXAMPLE: 10 REM THIS PROGRAM COMPUTES UNIT PRICE
READ	Specifies variables whose values are supplied by DATA statements. A comma must separate each of the variables. A numeric variable can be either an alphabetic letter or a letter followed by a numeral and can only be assigned a decimal number value. A string variable can only be an alphabetic letter followed by a dollar sign and can be assigned a string value of 0 to 72 teleprinter characters.
	EXAMPLE: 20 READ A,B1,C$,D
DATA	Supplies values for variables named in the READ statement. A comma must separate each of the values.
	EXAMPLE: 30 DATA 163,99.9,"XYZ123",30
	NOTE: Prior to program execution, two data tables are constructed that contain the values in all the

DATA statements in order of appearance in the program. One table contains numeric values, and the other table contains string values. A string value, which must be enclosed in quotation marks, is a series of letters and/or numerals generally used for descriptive statements such as stock descriptions, employee names, or other types of indicative data.

A data table pointer is set to the next succeeding item in the data table as the preceding data item is drawn from the data table. The data table is a form of data input to the program that is unique to BASIC. This enables the programmer to incorporate the input data with the program that will use the data. A READ statement can draw data from more than one DATA statement.

INPUT

The READ and DATA statements provide for the entering of data at the time the program is entered into the computer. On certain occasions it may be desirable to enter data for computations at the time of program execution. The INPUT statement provides this capability. When the computer encounters an INPUT statement at execution time, the computer stops with a request for the entry of data. The programmer can then enter the values of the variables specified in the INPUT statement.

EXAMPLE: 20 INPUT A,B,C,D

FILES

Another method of introducing data into the computer at execution time is through the use of the FILES statement. It is important to note that only files that have been previously established and stored in memory of the computer can be introduced into the computer by the use of the FILES statement. In the process of establishing files for use with a BASIC program, files must be assigned an identifying file name. The file name is composed of one to six alphabetic characters. When establishing a file with a BASIC program, the data is stored with the use of the DATA statement. This permits the retrieval of items of data in sequence from records within the file by the assignment and use of variable names.

EXAMPLE: 10 FILES INPUT

DIM

Specifies the maximum string size (dimension) and causes storage space to be reserved for the string variable. Each string having more than one character must be mentioned in a DIM statement.

EXAMPLE: 100 DIM C$(6)

NOTE: In the example above the string variable C$ has been assigned a string variable maximum size of six positions.

LET — Causes the value of an expression to be assigned to one or more variables. The expression is evaluated by using the current values of the variables that appear in the expression.

EXAMPLE: 40 LET X=A+5

NOTE: The LET statement is the principal method in BASIC for performing arithmetic operations, or assigning a symbol to a constant. LET is optional, as the statement will be executed whether or not it includes the word LET. However, for ease of understanding, it is best to include the word LET in the statement.

GOTO — Causes control to be unconditionally transferred to a specific statement. Whenever the GOTO statement is encountered during program execution, it causes the statement identified by the statement number following the GOTO to be executed next. GOTO is the statement used to unconditionally alter the sequence of program execution by branching to other than the next sequential statement.

EXAMPLE: 50 GOTO 10

IF-THEN — Tests a relational expression and, if the relation is true, transfers control to the specified statement; if the statement is false, the next sequential statement is executed. IF is the statement used to conditionally alter the sequence of program execution.

EXAMPLE: 60 IF X=1000 THEN 200

NOTE: In the example above, when the numeric variable X equals 1000, program control will be transferred to statement 200.

FOR — Initiates a program loop and causes repeated execution of the statements that numerically follow, up to and including a matching NEXT statement. FOR and NEXT statements must be paired and are matched when the same simple arithmetic variable is specified for each of the two statements. The simple arithmetic variable is the loop control variable. It is followed by an equals sign and two expressions or symbols separated by the key word TO. The expression to the left of the key word TO will be incremented by the value defined by the STEP option until the expression to the left of the key word TO becomes greater than the expression to the right of the key word TO.

EXAMPLE: 70 FOR N= A TO B STEP 2

NOTE: FOR N identifies the start of a loop and A is the variable that will be incremented by 2 until the loop has been executed enough times for the A variable to exceed the B variable. (The STEP 2 indicates that 2 will be added to the variable A each time the loop is executed. If STEP is omitted, an increment of 1 is assumed.) Program loops will be illustrated in the programming examples that follow.

NEXT   Identifies the last statement of a FOR/NEXT loop. The NEXT variable must be the same as the simple arithmetic variable specified in the associated FOR statement. The first time through the loop when the NEXT statement is executed, the simple arithmetic variable (A in the preceding example) will be increased by the value designated by STEP, and, if the new value for the simple arithmetic variable is no greater than the variable to the right of the key word TO in the FOR statement, program control will return to the FOR statement. When the variable to the left of TO becomes greater than the variable to the right of TO, program control proceeds to the statement following the NEXT statement.

EXAMPLE: 90 NEXT N

PRINT   Causes the values of the specified arithmetic and character expressions to be printed. The format of the print line is to a large extent controlled by BASIC: 5 fields per line when commas are used as variable separators, and 12 fields per line when semicolons are used as variable separators. The value of the first expression after the statement PRINT will be printed in the first field, and the second value will be printed in the seond field, and so on. Each expression or constant in the PRINT statement is separated from the following expression or constant by either a comma or a semicolon. PRINT constants must be enclosed in quotation marks and will be printed exactly as shown in the PRINT statement. A comma at the end of a PRINT statement indicates that the information in the next PRINT statement is to be printed on the same line to the right of the last information in the preceding PRINT statement. A PRINT statement without any expressions or constants will cause a blank line on the report. Blank PRINT statements are used to separate printed lines in the report where this is desirable.

EXAMPLE: 80 PRINT A, "AVERAGE";B

| IMAGE | The IMAGE statement is used to specify a format to be used in a PRINT USING statement. The IMAGE statement consists of symbols that represent types of data, written in the order and quantity in which the data is to be printed. The symbol D specifies numeric data. The period (.) specifies a decimal point within the numeric data. A decimal field is specified by using a period in conjunction with the symbol D. Blank spaces are specified by the symbol X. |

EXAMPLE: 100 USING DDD,DD

| PRINT USING | The PRINT USING statement is used to print output data according to a specified format in the IMAGE statement to which it refers. |

EXAMPLE: 150 PRINT USING 100; A

| END | Indicates the end of a program. Most BASIC compliers require an END statement for successful execution. The END statement can be followed with a comment that will have no affect on program execution; however, the comment may be provided to make the program easier to understand. |

EXAMPLE: 220 END

These BASIC statements will be used in the following programming examples. Although most BASIC compilers utilize additional statements, these statements, if used in accordance with the above guidelines, should be executed by any BASIC system.

Program Errors

BASIC has very few syntax rules that when violated will result in a fatal error condition. However, if mistakes are made while entering a program, BASIC responds with an ERROR message indicating that something is wrong with the last statement entered. When this occurs, the error can be corrected by reentering the statement in proper form. Other program errors can be encountered during program execution. When this occurs, program execution will be halted, and a diagnostic message indicating the reason for halting the program will be printed.

BASIC PROGRAMS

Using the BASIC statements described above and a few others that will be introduced later, the fundamentals of BASIC will be demonstrated through discussion of several sample programs.

The first sample program, shown in Figure 14–1, is designed to cal-

Figure 14-1. *BASIC*
program to calculate the
average of four numbers.

```
10  READ A,B,C,D
20  DATA 111,222,333,444
30  LET X=(A+B+C+D)/4
40  PRINT X
50  END
```

culate the average of four numbers. The following discussion will assist
in understanding the program:

Statement number	Function
10	Specifies four variables that will be assigned values supplied in the data statement.
20	Supplies the values for variables specified in the READ statement. The variable A will be assigned the value 111, etc. Remember that DATA statements may appear anywhere in the program, as prior to program execution a data table is constructed that contains the values in the DATA statements in order of appearance.
30	A LET statement that causes the expression to the right of the equal sign to be evaluated and the value to be assigned to the variable to the left of the equal sign. In this example the variables A, B, C, and D will be added together, the result will be divided by 4, and the quotient will be assigned to the variable X.
40	Causes the value assigned to the variable X to be printed.
50	This is an END statement, which must always be used to identify the end of the program.

```
10  LET N=1
20  IF N>10 THEN 60
30  PRINT N,N*2
40  LET N=N+1
50  GOTO 20
60  END
```

Figure 14-2. *Illustration of*
program loop in BASIC.

The second program, shown in Figure 14–2, illustrates a program loop.
All program loops must contain a test that will cause control of the program to be transferred to a statement outside the loop. If this were not
so, once a loop was entered there would be no way to terminate execution
of the statements within the loop. The details of this program are as
follows:

Statement number	Function
10	Specifies that the variable N is to be assigned the value of 1.
20	An IF statement that tests the relational expression $N > 10$. If the relation is true, program control is

Statement number	Function
	transferred to the statement number specified after the word THEN. If the statement is false, the next executable statement is executed. In this program, statement 20 is the test that will eventually cause control of the program to be transferred to statement 60 and thereby terminate execution of the program.
30	Causes two values to be printed. This statement illustrates that calculations can be contained in a print statement. The first time this program is executed N will be assigned the value of 1. This is not greater than 10, so control will pass from statement 20 to 30. Statement 30 will cause 1 and 1×2, or 2, to be printed.
40	Will cause N to be added to 1 and the sum to be assigned to N. The value assigned to N before the execution of statement 40 was 1. Therefore, 1 plus 1 equals 2, the value that will be assigned to N after statement 40 is executed the first time.
50	Unconditionally tranfers program control to statement 20. Whenever a GOTO statement is encountered, program control will be transferred to the statement specified in the instruction. In this case, each time that statement 50 is encountered, program control will be transferred to statement 20. The second time that statement 20 is executed, the variable N will have a value of 2. This is still not more than 10, so statement 30 will cause the values 2 and 2×2, or 4, to be printed. The second time that statement 40 is executed the current value of the variable N, 2 will be added to 1 and the sum, 3, will be assigned to N. This pattern will continue until the value assigned to N is greater than 10. When this occurs, program control will be transferred to statement 60, and program execution will terminate. The results produced by this program are shown in Figure 14–3.
60	This is the END statement terminating program execution.

The main purpose of this example is to illustrate a *program loop,* a very important fundamental of computer programs. If it were not possible to cause repetitive execution of program segments (reiteration), use of the computer would be very limited. For example, if it were not possible to alter the strict sequential processing of statements, ten PRINT and ten LET statements would have been required to produce the desired results in this program. Let us suppose that instead of listing the numbers 1 through 10, we wanted to list the numbers 1 through 1,000. If we could not loop through the PRINT and LET statements, it is clear that the program would be very long, tedious to write, and inefficient

```
RUN

1        2
2        4
3        6
4        8
5        10
6        12
7        14
8        16
9        18
10       20

DØNE
```

Figure 14-3. *Results of BASIC program shown in Figure 14-2.*

to execute on a computer because of the large amount of primary storage required.

The program shown in Figure 14–4 illustrates a more concise method of structuring a loop. Following is a description of the program.

Figure 14-4. *Concise method of structuring a program loop in BASIC.*

```
10    FØR N=1 TØ 10
20    PRINT N;"SQUARED =";N↑2
30    NEXT N
40    END
```

Statement number	Function
10	A FOR statement that causes repeated execution of the statements that follow, up to and including the matching NEXT statement. As there could be more than one set of FOR-NEXT statements in the program, the same arithmetic variable must be assigned to related FOR-NEXT statements. In this example, the variable N relates the FOR to the NEXT statement.
	Until such time that the variable N exceeds the value to the right of the key word TO, each time statement 10 is encountered it will pass program control to statement 20. When the variable N exceeds the value to the right of the key word TO, program control will be transferred to the statement following the related NEXT statement; in this case statement 40. Comparison of this program with the preceding example shows that the FOR-NEXT method of causing repeated execution of the statements between the controlling statements (FOR-NEXT) requires two less instructions than the IF-GOTO statements. The IF-GOTO and the FOR-NEXT statements are the two primary methods of altering the sequential execution of statements. The method used is largely dependent on the data and relationships to be tested.

Statement number	Function
20	A PRINT statement that will cause the printing of the value assigned to variable N followed by the string of characters "SQUARED=" followed by the value of N squared. Note how constant data can be included in a PRINT statement and that a constant (fixed string of characters that, as opposed to a variable, cannot be changed during program execution) is identified by being enclosed within quotation marks. Also note the use of semicolons instead of commas as field separators. Semicolons cause the printed output to be more tightly packed than commas and can be interspersed with commas in the same PRINT statement. Finally, note that the arithmetic computation (N↑2) will result in the square of N being printed.
30	A NEXT statement that will, each time it is executed, cause the value 1 to be added to variable N since no STEP value is indicated. Program control will be transferred to the related FOR statement, in this case statement 10.
40	An END statement terminating program execution.

Figure 14–5 shows the results of running the program illustrated in Figure 14–4.

The sample program discussed, flowcharted, and programmed in Assembler Language in Chapter 12 is programmed in BASIC and shown in Figure 14–6. This program illustrates most of the primary BASIC statements as well as several fundamentals of programming. The following discussion will assist in understanding the program.

Statement number	Function
10–40	Remarks statements used to identify the program and the variables assigned to the data fields.
50–80	Cause the report title and field headings to be printed. Note how the PRINT statements that have nothing following them (60 and 80) cause a blank line to appear in the report shown in Figure 14–7.
90	Assigns the value of zero to the variable Y. This statement is required, as the first time that statement 130 is executed the variable Y to the right of the equal sign must have a value assigned to it. This is in accordance with the BASIC rule that all variables in an expression must be assigned a value.
100	A READ statement that assigns the DATA statement values to the specified variables. The first DATA statement fields will be assigned to the variables as follows:

$$A\$ = 123456$$
$$B\ \ = 100$$

```
                            RUN

                            1      SQUARED  =  1
                            2      SQUARED  =  4
                            3      SQUARED  =  9
                            4      SQUARED  =  16
                            5      SQUARED  =  25
                            6      SQUARED  =  36
                            7      SQUARED  =  49
                            8      SQUARED  =  64
                            9      SQUARED  =  81
                            10     SQUARED  =  100

                            DØNE
```

Figure 14-5. *Results of BASIC program shown in Figure 14-4.*

```
10    REM                        INVENTØRY CØNTRØL UPDATE PRØGRAM
20    REM                       FLØWCHARTED IN CHAPTER 12
30    REM      A$=STØCK NUMBER, B=QUANTITY ØN HAND, C$=DESCRIPTIØN
40    REM      D=STØCK RECEIPTS, E=STØCK ISSUES, Y=TØTAL.
50    PRINT "          INVENTØRY CØNTRØL REPØRT"
60    PRINT
70    PRINT "STØCK NUMBER          DESCRIPTIØN                   QUANTITY"
71    PRINT "------------          ------------------            --------"
80    PRINT
90    LET Y=0
100   READ A$,B,C$,D,E
110   IF A$="0" THEN 220
120   LET X=B+D-E
130   LET Y=Y+X
140   PRINT A$,C$,X
150   GØTØ 100
160   DIM A$[6],C$[20]
170   DATA "123456",100,"HAMMER-BALL PEAN",50,25
180   DATA "123457",88,"HAMMER-CLAW        ",20,53
190   DATA "123458",226,"HAMMER-SLEDGE 20 LB",144,362
200   DATA "123459",50,"HAMMER-SLEDGE 10 LB",10,50
210   DATA "0",0,"0",0,0
220   PRINT
230   PRINT "                     TØTAL";Y
240   END
```

Figure 14-6. *Inventory control update program written in BASIC.*

```
                        INVENTØRY CØNTRØL REPØRT

            STØCK NUMBER          DESCRIPTIØN                QUANTITY
            ------------          ------------------         --------

            123456                HAMMER-BALL PEAN              125
            123457                HAMMER-CLAW                    55
            123458                HAMMER-SLEDGE 20 LB             8
            123459                HAMMER-SLEDGE 10 LB            10

                                  TØTAL  198

            DØNE
```

Figure 14-7. *Inventory control report resulting from program shown in Figure 14-6.*

Statement number	Function
	C$ = HAMMER-BALL PEAN
	D = 50
	E = 25

The first time the READ statement is executed, DATA statement 170 will provide the values to be assigned to the READ statement variables. The next time the READ statement is executed, DATA statement 180 will provide the values to be assigned to the READ statement variables, and so on, until the values in the last DATA statement are assigned to the READ statement variables.

Note that the first and third variables (A$ and C$) consist of a letter followed by a dollar sign. This is how string variables as opposed to numeric variables are identified. Note also that the first and third DATA statement fields are enclosed in quotation marks. This is how string values as opposed to numeric values are identified. In statement 160, a DIM statement, the string variable A$ has 6 storage positions reserved for it and the string variable C$ has 20 storage positions reserved for it.

Now follow the relationships of the string variable, the dimension, and the string values in this program. Six storage positions have been reserved for the variable A$, and the first field of each data statement enclosed in quotation marks will be the value assigned to the variable by being stored in the storage positions reserved for it.

110	An IF statement that will cause program control to be transferred to statement 220 when the variable A$ is equal to zero. Note that the first field of the last DATA statement contains a zero. Therefore, until the last DATA statement provides the values to the variables when the IF statement is encountered, the variable A$ will not be equal to zero and the following statement (120) will be executed.
120	A LET statement that causes the variable E to be subtracted from the sum of variables B and D, and the result to be assigned to the variable X.
130	Another LET statement that causes the sum of the variables Y and X to be assigned to the variable Y.
140	A PRINT statement that will cause the variable strings, A$ and C$, and the variable X to be printed, as illustrated in the sample report produced by this program in Figure 14–7.
150	A GOTO statement that will cause program control to be transferred to statement 100.
160	See discussion under statement 100 above.

Statement number	Function
170–210	See discussion under statement 100 above.
220–230	When the last DATA statement values have been assigned to the variables specified in the READ statement, the IF statement will cause program control to be transferred to statement 220. Statement 220, a PRINT statement without variables, will cause a blank line to follow the last printed line. Statement 230, another PRINT statement, will cause the string value TOTAL to be printed, followed by the value of Y. Note in the sample report how the semicolon before the variable Y causes the value assigned to the variable Y to be printed close to the string value TOTAL.
240	An END statement that causes execution of the program to be terminated.

Since in actual practice there would probably be many more input records than are shown in the preceding example, BASIC provides other methods for handling them. For example, if the terminal were provided with a punched tape unit, the input data could be fed to the program from the paper tape reader. Another method would be to have the input provided from a sequential or random access file established at the computer facility and accessible by the computer.

There is also another method of data input through the terminal. This method uses the INPUT statement and is illustrated in the BASIC program in Figure 14–8. This program will compute the square root of a number that is provided to the program through the terminal. The following discussion of the program shows how the INPUT statement is used.

```
10   REM                    -SQUARE ROOT PROGRAM-
20   REM        THIS PROGRAM COMPUTES THE SQUARE ROOT OF A NUMBER WHICH
30   REM        IS ENTERED INTO THE PROGRAM THROUGH THE TERMINAL.
40   REM
50   REM        THE PROGRAM WILL CONTINUE TO EXPECT INPUT UNTIL THE
60   REM        QUESTION "DO YOU WISH TO COMPUTE THE SQUARE ROOT OF
70   REM        ANOTHER NUMBER?" IS ANSWERED WITH OTHER THAN YES.
75   REM
80   PRINT "ENTER THE NUMBER WHOSE SQUARE ROOT IS DESIRED ";
90   INPUT N
100   PRINT "THE SQUARE ROOT OF ";N;"IS";SQR(N)
110   PRINT
120   PRINT "DO YOU WISH TO COMPUTE THE SQUARE ROOT OF"
130   PRINT "ANOTHER NUMBER? ANSWER YES OR NO."
140   INPUT N$
150   IF N$="YES" THEN 80
160   DIM N$[3]
170   END
```

Figure 14-8. *Square root program written in BASIC.*

Statement number	Function
10–75	Remarks statements that describe the program.
80	Causes the character string to be printed. Because the statement ends with a semicolon, the terminal carriage will not be returned. Instead, the question mark that is provided by BASIC to indicate the need for input will be printed on the same line during program execution, and the program will pause until the input specifications of the program have been met.
90	An INPUT statement that specifies one variable (N) that will be assigned the value entered on the terminal during program execution after the question mark is typed and the terminal pauses. A single INPUT statement can specify more than one variable that can be either a numeric or string type.
100	A PRINT statement that causes the character string to be printed, followed by the value of the variable N (the number to be squared), followed by another character string (IS), followed by the square root of the variable N to be printed. SQR is the symbolic identification of the square root function. This function is just one of several that can be specified in BASIC by including the symbol along with a numeric variable in the statement.
120–130	Cause two character strings to be printed.
140	Another INPUT statement that specifies a string variable (N$). This shows that, as with READ statements, either numeric or string variables may be specified in an INPUT statement. Again, this statement will cause a question mark to be printed and the terminal to pause until the data has been typed in. Statement 160, a DIM statement, must be used to specify the field size of an INPUT string variable, just as it was required for a READ string variable.
150	An IF statement that compares the string variable (N$) with the character string YES; if it is equal, program control is transferred to statement 80. At such time that other than YES is assigned to the string variable (N$), the IF statement will not transfer control to statement 80. Instead, program control will go to the next sequential statement. As statement 160 is not an executable statement, program control will go to the next statement, and the program execution will terminate.
160	See discussion under statement 140 above.
170	The END statement that terminates program execution.

Figure 14–9 illustrates the results produced by the square root program decribed above.

BASIC functions such as SQR are performed in the following manner. When the function symbol is encountered, it transfers program control to the proper BASIC function subroutine, and after that has been executed, program control is transferred back to the statement from which control was originally transferred. Generally, function references are convenient time savers for programmers. They can be placed anywhere in a BASIC statement that an arithmetic variable or constant may be used.

In addition to the function subroutines provided by BASIC, the programmer may also develop his own subroutines. The GOSUB and RETURN statements enable a programmer to place a segment of a program that is to be repeated at different points in the program into a subroutine that can be executed whenever that series of statements is needed. The GOSUB and RETURN statements provide a method of transferring program control to the subroutine and back to the program.

```
RUN

ENTER THE NUMBER WHØSE SQUARE RØØT IS DESIRED ?81
THE SQUARE RØØT ØF   81    IS 9

DØ YØU WISH TØ CØMPUTE THE SQUARE RØØT ØF
ANØTHER NUMBER? ANSWER YES ØR NØ.
?YES
ENTER THE NUMBER WHØSE SQUARE RØØT IS DESIRED ?256
THE SQUARE RØØT ØF   256   IS 16

DØ YØU WISH TØ CØMPUTE THE SQUARE RØØT ØF
ANØTHER NUMBER? ANSWER YES ØR NØ.
?YES
ENTER THE NUMBER WHØSE SQUARE RØØT IS DESIRED ?4096
THE SQUARE RØØT ØF   4096    IS 64

DØ YØU WISH TØ CØMPUTE THE SQUARE RØØT ØF
ANØTHER NUMBER? ANSWER YES ØR NØ.
?NØ

DØNE
```

Figure 14-9. *Results of square root program shown in Figure 14-8.*

The two remaining examples illustrate business applications programmed in BASIC. The sample program shown in Figure 14–10 is designed to calculate the depreciation and book value for 20 years of an item with an initial value of $10,000 using the standard depreciation formula. Following is a description of the program.

```
LIST
DEPREC

100   REM ACCOUNTING PROBLEM
110   REM COMPUTE DEPRECIATION
120   REM C=INITIAL CAPITAL INVESTMENT
130   REM Y=NUMBER OF YEARS
140   PRINT "YEAR","DEPRECIATION","BOOK VALUE",LIN(1)
150   READ C,Y
155   T=0
160   FOR N=1 TO Y
170   LET D=2*C/Y
175   T=T+D
180   LET C=C-D
190   PRINT  USING 195;N,D,C
195   IMAGE 2D,13X,DDDD.DD,8X,DDDD.DD
200   NEXT N
202   PRINT
204   PRINT  USING 206;T
206   IMAGE "TOTAL DEP. =     ",DDDD.DD
210   DATA 10000,20
9999  END
```

Figure 14-10. *BASIC program to compute depreciation.*

Statement number	Function
100–130	Remarks statements used to identify the program and variables assigned to data fields.
140	Causes field headings to be printed.
150	A READ statement that assigns the DATA statement values to the specified variables.
155	Establishes a counter for the accumulation of the total depreciation column.
160	A FOR statement that causes repeated execution of the statements that follow, up to and including the matching NEXT statement.
170	A LET statement that causes the constant 2 to be multiplied by the variable C, the results of which are divided by the variable Y. The final result is placed in variable D.
175	The arithmetic statement that accumulates the total depreciation.
180	A LET statement that causes the variable D to be subtracted from the variable C, the results of which are in turn stored in the variable C.
190	A PRINT USING statement that causes the variable string N, D, and C to be printed.
195	The IMAGE statement to be used in PRINT USING statement 190.
200	A NEXT statement that will, each time it is executed, cause the value 1 to be added to variable N since no

Statement number	Function
	STEP value is indicated. Program control will be transferred to the related FOR statement, in this case 160.
202	A PRINT statement that will create one blank line before the total depreciation is printed.
204	A PRINT USING statement that causes total depreciation to be printed.
206	The IMAGE statement to be used in PRINT USING statement 204.
210	A DATA statement that supplies the values of the variables specified in the READ statement.
9999	This is an END statement, which must always be used to identify the end of the program.

```
RUN
DEPREC

YEAR              DEPRECIATION      BOOK VALUE
  1                 1000.00          9000.00
  2                  900.00          8100.00
  3                  810.00          7290.00
  4                  729.00          6561.00
  5                  656.10          5904.90
  6                  590.49          5314.41
  7                  531.44          4782.97
  8                  478.30          4304.67
  9                  430.47          3874.20
 10                  387.42          3486.78
 11                  348.68          3138.11
 12                  313.81          2824.30
 13                  282.43          2541.87
 14                  254.19          2287.68
 15                  228.77          2058.91
 16                  205.89          1853.02
 17                  185.30          1667.72
 18                  166.77          1500.95
 19                  150.09          1350.85
 20                  135.09          1215.77

TOTAL DEP. =     8784.23

DONE
```

Figure 14-11. *Results of BASIC program shown in Figure 14-10.*

Figure 14–11 shows the results of running the program illustrated in Figure 14–10.

Another example of a business problem programmed in BASIC is shown in Figure 14–12. This program is designed to calculate the compound interest on $1,000 for 20 years at 7 per cent. A detailed description of the program statements follows.

```
LIST
COMPIN

100  REM COMPUTE COMPOUND INTEREST
110  REM FOR 1 TO 20 YEARS
120  REM P=PRINCIPAL, I=INTEREST, N=NO OF YEARS, A=AMOUNT
130  PRINT "YEAR","AMOUNT",LIN(1)
140  READ P,I
150  FOR N=1 TO 20
160  LET A=P*(1+I/100)↑N
170  PRINT  USING 175;N,A
175  IMAGE 2D,13X,DDDDD.DD
180  NEXT N
190  DATA 1000,7
9999  END
```

Figure 14-12. *BASIC program to compute compound interest.*

Statement number	Function
100–120	Remarks statements used to identify the program and variables assigned to data fields.
130	Causes field headings to be printed.
140	A READ statement that assigns DATA statement values to the specified variables.
150	A FOR statement that causes repeated execution of the statements that follow, up to and including the matching NEXT statement.
160	A LET statement that causes the execution of the formula used to compute compound interest.
170	A PRINT USING statement that causes the variable string N and A to be printed.
175	The IMAGE statement to be used in the PRINT USING statement 170.
180	A NEXT statement that will, each time it is executed, cause the value of 1 to be added to variable N since no STEP value is indicated. Program control will be transferred to the related FOR statement, in this case 150.
190	A DATA statement that supplies the values of the variables specified in the READ statement.
9999	This is an END statement, which must always be used to identify the end of the program.

The results of the program shown in Figure 14–12 appear in Figure 14–13.

This description of BASIC should help you understand the problem-oriented languages in the next chapter, especially FORTRAN, which is more extensive but similar in form to BASIC.

```
                                RUN
                                COMPIN


                                YEAR                    AMOUNT


                                  1                     1070.00
                                  2                     1144.90
                                  3                     1225.04
                                  4                     1310.80
                                  5                     1402.55
                                  6                     1500.73
                                  7                     1605.78
                                  8                     1718.19
                                  9                     1838.46
                                 10                     1967.15
                                 11                     2104.85
                                 12                     2252.19
                                 13                     2409.84
                                 14                     2578.53
                                 15                     2759.03
                                 16                     2952.16
                                 17                     3158.81
                                 18                     3379.93
                                 19                     3616.52
                                 20                     3869.68


                                DONE
```

Figure 14-13. *Results of BASIC program shown in Figure 14-12.*

IMPORTANT WORDS AND PHRASES

BASIC	string	operator
time-sharing	constant	expression
identifier	variable	program loop

REVIEW QUESTIONS

1. What are the general characteristics of a time-sharing system?
2. Statement numbers serve what two purposes in BASIC?
3. Describe the recommended method of numbering statements.
4. How are program statements modified or deleted when using a time-sharing system?
5. What are the two primary elements of a BASIC statement? Define each.
6. What is the difference between the status of a *constant* and a *variable* during program execution?
7. What are the main functions of the READ, DATA, and LET statements?
8. Describe the functions of the GOTO, IF-THEN, and FOR-NEXT statements.
9. Describe the error procedure that occurs if mistakes are made while entering a BASIC program.
10. What is the purpose of the GOSUB and RETURN statements?

15

PROBLEM-ORIENTED PROGRAMMING LANGUAGES

The preceding chapter was devoted to a problem-oriented programming language originally designed for educational use. In this chapter, four of the most widely used problem-oriented languages will be described and illustrated. Included are FORTRAN, COBOL, Programming Language I, and Report Program Generator.

The program used to illustrate each of these languages is based on the same problem used to illustrate programming in Chapter 12. Therefore, the program flowchart shown in Figure 12–4 should be helpful in interpreting each program. Furthermore, a comparison of the four programs in this chapter with each other and with the Assembler Language program shown in Figure 12–19 and the BASIC program in Figure 14–6 will provide an opportunity to compare six different methods of programming the same problem.

FORTRAN

The name FORTRAN is a derivative of the original title, *Formula Translation*. FORTRAN is a programming system that makes it possible to state a problem to be programmed in terms approximating mathematical notation. Except for a general knowledge of computer operating principles and the types of input and output that can be handled, the programmer need not be concerned with the characteristics of the computer while writing a FORTRAN program.

The advantage of the FORTRAN programming system is that it provides a language in which any mathematical problem can be stated and then compiled and executed on many kinds of computers. As a result, several hundred thousand people are currently using the FORTRAN programming language as their primary method of communicating with a computer.

A FORTRAN source program is composed of statements that may cause data to be read, processing to be performed, and results to be recorded. These statements in the source program provide information to the FORTRAN processor for object program preparation. The FORTRAN programming language is composed of statements consisting of operation symbols (+ or −) and expressions (A + B − C). Statements may be divided into the following groups:

Statements	Functions
Input-output	Describe the operations that are necessary to bring in data and to write or punch the results of the program.
Control	May determine the sequence in which statements will be followed or may provide the program with the ability to handle predefined exceptions to the procedure.
Arithmetic	Specify the mathematical calculations to be performed. These statements very closely resemble a conventional arithmetic formula; for example, X = Y + Z is a valid statement.
Specification	Provide certain additional facts such as the size of the input data that is read by the program, or the placement of alphabetical and numerical information on the printed page.
Subprogram	Enable the user to name and define functions and subroutines that are to be included in the object program.

Unless the FORTRAN processor provides for source language program check-out, the programmer will need the ability to check out and remove errors in the object program. This requires that the programmer know the details of the computer and materially reduces one of the primary advantages of any programming system.

The process of converting the source program into a machine-language (object) program is called *compiling*. As there are probably no two compilers that use identical logic, it is difficult to describe a FORTRAN processor without identifying it with a particular machine. The most common compiling technique is to first convert the source program notations into a one-for-one symbolic program. This program is then converted to an object program by an assembly system. Other compilers convert the FORTRAN language directly to machine language in one pass.

Figure 15–1 shows a printed list of a program processed with a FORTRAN compiler. As mentioned earier, this program is based on the same problem used for illustrative purposes in Chapter 12. A flowchart of the problem appears in Figure 12–4.

```
                    C       FORTRAN IV
                    C
                    C       THE ASSUMPTION IS MADE THAT 000000 IS NOT A VALID STOCK NUMBER.
                    C       AS SUCH, 000000 WILL BE USED TO SIGNIFY LAST CARD.
                    C
0001                        DIMENSION DESC(20)
0002                        TOTAL=0
                    C       READ A CARD
0003                  10 READ (5,15) STKNO,QTYHD,DESC,SRCPT,SISS
0004                  15 FORMAT (F6.0,F5.0,20A1,2F5.0)
                    C       TEST FOR LAST CARD
0005                        IF (STKNO-0.0) 20,1000,20
                    C       PERFORM CALCULATIONS
0006                  20 CTR=QTYHD+SRCPT-SISS
0007                        TOTAL=TOTAL+CTR
                    C       WRITE DETAIL LINE
0008                        WRITE (6,25) STKNO,DESC,CTR
0009                  25 FORMAT (1H0,24X,F6.0,9X,20A1,19X,F6.0)
0010                        GO TO 10
                    C       END OF JOB ROUTINE
0011                1000 WRITE (6,35) TOTAL
0012                  35 FORMAT (1H0,88X,5HTOTAL,5X,F7.0)
0013                        END
```

Figure 15-1. *Printed list of program written in FORTRAN.*

In order to discuss the FORTRAN program, let us first examine the FORTRAN list format. The line numbers to the left in Figure 15–1 were added to the program by the FORTRAN compiler. The statements originally written in the source program are to the right of the compiler statement numbers.

Note on the program list the letter *C* in column 1 on the first statement line. This is how comments are identified in a FORTRAN program. In this example the first five statement lines are comments and are preceded by a *C*. Note also that lines 2 and 5 are blank comment lines inserted to make the program easier to follow.

The following analysis of the program will be referenced to the compiler statement numbers shown on the program list.

0001. Establishes a single-dimension array called DESC consisting of 20 elements. This array will be used to read in the 20-character description field.

0002. Sets the variable element TOTAL to zero.

0003–0004. Causes reading of a card and describes how the fields are to be interpreted. For example:

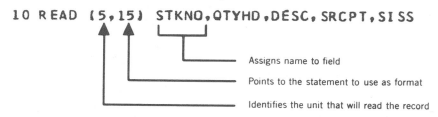

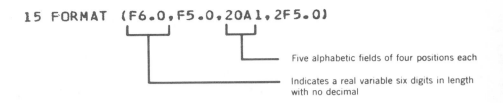

`15 FORMAT (F6.0,F5.0,20A1,2F5.0)`

Five alphabetic fields of four positions each

Indicates a real variable six digits in length with no decimal

0005. Tests for last card by subtracting zero from STKNO, and if the result is zero (meaning the last card has been read), branches to statement 1000; otherwise, goes to statement 20, the next sequential statement.

0006. Adds QTYHD and SRCPT, and subtracts SISS giving a variable called CTR.

0007. Updates TOTAL by adding CTR to it.

0008–0009. Causes printing of output and describes how printing is to take place. For example:

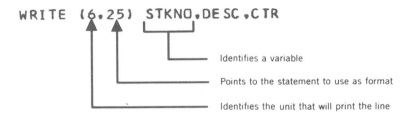

`WRITE (6,25) STKNO,DESC,CTR`

Identifies a variable

Points to the statement to use as format

Identifies the unit that will print the line

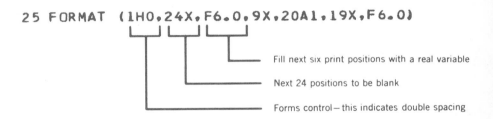

`25 FORMAT (1H0,24X,F6.0,9X,20A1,19X,F6.0)`

Fill next six print positions with a real variable

Next 24 positions to be blank

Forms control—this indicates double spacing

0010. Unconditional branch to statement 10 READ.

0011–0012. Causes printing of final total line.

0013. Returns control of the computer to the operating system supervisor program.

This example illustrates how a very simple problem can be programmed in FORTRAN, a very powerful programming system.

During the period when FORTRAN was developed in this country, ALGOL was being developed in Europe. They are similar, as some exchange of ideas occurred during the development of these two programming systems. FORTRAN, in a general sense, is an engineering language, and ALGOL is more nearly a true mathematical language. International Algebraic Language (IAL) was the forerunner of the Algorithmic Oriented Language (ALGOL). Today the language is most frequently referred to as ALGOL and on occasion IAS/ALGOL.

A very large library of FORTRAN programs has resulted from the fact that FORTRAN is the most widely used language. However, those using the ALGOL language contend that it is easier to learn, capable of expressing a wide variety of problems, and superior to FORTRAN in all respects.

COBOL

The name COBOL is derived from Common Business Oriented Language. The COBOL system was developed in 1959 by a committee composed of government users and computer manufacturers. Additional organizations have since participated in the refinement, improvement, and maintenance of COBOL. COBOL is the first major attempt to produce a truly common business-oriented programming language. It has not fully met that goal. For example, the COBOL programming approach for a binary or octal computer differs from that for a binary coded decimal computer. Even so, it is a widely used programming language.

The COBOL character set is composed of the 26 letters of the alphabet, the numerals 0 through 9, and 12 special characters. The COBOL language consists of names to identify things; constants and literals; operators that specify some action or relationship; key words essential to the meaning of a statement; expressions consisting of names, constants, operators, or key words; statements containing a verb and an item to be acted on; and sentences composed of one or more statements properly punctuated.

A COBOL program list is illustrated in Figure 15–2. This sample program list shows that source statements may start at either of two margins. In general, margin A (the leftmost margin) is used to locate major subdivisions of the program, while margin B (the indented margin) locates subordinate items and continuations of items from one line to another. Thus, the names of divisions, sections, and paragraphs are placed at margin A, as are the main entries of the data division. Most other items are placed at margin B. Names may contain from 1 to 30 characters and must not contain blanks. For this reason names very frequently contain one or more hyphens, as this allows for the use of descriptive names without violation of the rules, e.g., QTY-ON-HAND.

The source program for this problem was written in COBOL and was key punched into cards that were used to produce the program list shown in Figure 15–2. In this case the source program written by the programmer is not shown because in COBOL there is very little dif-

```
00001    001000  IDENTIFICATION DIVISION.
00002    001010  PROGRAM-ID.
00003    001020        SAMPLE.
00004    001030  REMARKS.
00005    001040        SAMPLE COBOL PROGRAM.
00006    001050        READS CARDS AND ADDS STOCK RECEIPTS TO QTY ON HAND BALANCE
00007    001060        SUBTRACTS STOCK ISSUES AND DEVELOPS A NEW ON HAND BALANCE.
00008    001070  ENVIRONMENT DIVISION.
00009    001080  CONFIGURATION SECTION.
00010    001090  SOURCE-COMPUTER.
00011    001100        IBM-360.
00012    001110  OBJECT-COMPUTER.
00013    001120        IBM-360.
00014    001130  INPUT-OUTPUT SECTION.
00015    001140  FILE-CONTROL.
00016    001150        SELECT CARD-INPUT    ASSIGN UT-S-SYSIN.
00017    001160        SELECT PRINT-OUTPUT ASSIGN UT-S-SYSPRINT.
00018    001170  DATA DIVISION.
00019    001180  FILE SECTION.
00020    001190  FD   CARD-INPUT
00021    001200        RECORDING MODE IS F
00022    001210        RECORD CONTAINS 80 CHARACTERS
00023    001220        LABEL RECORDS ARE OMITTED
00024    001230        DATA RECORD IS RECORD-IN.
00025    001240  01   RECORD-IN.
00026    001250        05   STOCK-NUMBER     PIC X(6).
00027    001260        05   QTY-ON-HAND      PIC 9(5).
00028    001270        05   DESCRIPTION      PIC X(20).
00029    001280        05   STOCK-RECEIPTS   PIC 9(5).
00030    001290        05   STOCK-ISSUES     PIC 9(5).
00031    001300        05   FILLER           PIC X(39).
00032    001310  FD   PRINT-OUTPUT
00033    001320        RECORDING MODE IS F
00034    001330        RECORD CONTAINS 133 CHARACTERS
00035    001340        LABEL RECORDS ARE OMITTED
00036    001350        DATA RECORD IS PRINT-LINE.
00037    001360  01   PRINT-LINE.
00038    001370        05   FILLER            PIC X(25).
00039    001380        05   PRT-STOCK-NUMBER  PIC X(6).
00040    001390        05   FILLER            PIC X(9).
00041    001400        05   PRT-DESCRIPTION   PIC X(20).
00042    001410        05   FILLER            PIC X(19).
00043    001420        05   PRT-NEW-BALANCE   PIC 9(6).
00044    001430        05   FILLER            PIC X(4).
00045    001440        05   PRT-WORD-TOTAL    PIC X(5).
00046    001450        05   FILLER            PIC X(5).
00047    001460        05   PRT-TOTAL         PIC 9(7).
00048    001470        05   FILLER            PIC X(27).
00049    001480  WORKING-STORAGE SECTION.
00050    001490  77   WORKING-COUNTER    PIC 9(6)    VALUE ZEROS    COMP-3.
00051    001500  77   TOTAL-COUNTER      PIC 9(7)    VALUE ZEROS    COMP-3.
00052    001510  PROCEDURE DIVISION.
00053    001520  START-PROG.
00054    001530        OPEN INPUT CARD-INPUT    OUTPUT PRINT-OUTPUT.
00055    001540        MOVE SPACES TO PRINT-LINE.
00056    001550  READ-A-CARD.
00057    001560        READ CARD-INPUT    AT END GO TO LAST-CARD.
00058    001570        ADD QTY-ON-HAND TO WORKING-COUNTER.
00059    001580        ADD STOCK-RECEIPTS TO WORKING-COUNTER.
00060    001590        SUBTRACT STOCK-ISSUES FROM WORKING-COUNTER.
00061    001600        MOVE WORKING-COUNTER TO PRT-NEW-BALANCE.
00062    001610        ADD WORKING-COUNTER TO TOTAL-COUNTER.
00063    001620        MOVE ZEROS TO WORKING-COUNTER.
00064    001630        MOVE STOCK-NUMBER TO PRT-STOCK-NUMBER.
00065    001640        MOVE DESCRIPTION TO PRT-DESCRIPTION.
00066    001650        WRITE PRINT-LINE AFTER POSITIONING 1.
00067    001660        MOVE SPACES TO PRINT-LINE.
```

Figure 15-2. *Printed list of program written in COBOL.*

```
00069    001680 LAST-CARD.
00070    001690       MOVE 'TOTAL' TO PRT-WORD-TOTAL.
00071    001700       MOVE TOTAL-COUNTER TO PRT-TOTAL.
00072    001710       WRITE PRINT-LINE AFTER POSITIONING 1.
00073    001720       CLOSE CARD-INPUT  PRINT-OUTPUT.
00074    001730       GOBACK.
```

Figure 15-2. (continued)

ference between the source statements and the statements appearing on the printed list. Again, the program flowchart in Figure 12–4 may be helpful in following the COBOL program discussion since the same problem is being used for all programming illustrations.

COBOL programs are divided into four divisions. The functions of these divisions and the program instructions for this problem that fall within each division are described below.

1. The *identification division* is used to attach a unique identification such as program name, program number, program version, etc., to the program.

    In the sample program excerpt shown in Figure 15–3, the identification division contains the name of the program on line 3 and a brief description of the program. These remarks can be very helpful to someone trying to comprehend the program for the first time.

```
00001    001000 IDENTIFICATION DIVISION.
00002    001010 PROGRAM-ID.
00003    001020       SAMPLE.
00004    001030 REMARKS.
00005    001040       SAMPLE COBOL PROGRAM.
00006    001050       READS CARDS AND ADDS STOCK RECEIPTS TO QTY ON HAND BALANCE
00007    001060       SUBTRACTS STOCK ISSUES AND DEVELOPS A NEW ON HAND BALANCE.
```

Figure 15-3.

2. The *environment division* is used to acquaint the processor with the computer on which the program is to be compiled and executed.

    The configuration section of the environment division in the sample program, lines 9 through 13, identifies the IBM 360 as the computer that will be used to compile the program and to operate the object program (Figure 15–4).

```
00008    001070 ENVIRONMENT DIVISION.
00009    001080 CONFIGURATION SECTION.
00010    001090 SOURCE-COMPUTER.
00011    001100       IBM-360.
00012    001110 OBJECT-COMPUTER.
00013    001120       IBM-360.
00014    001130 INPUT-OUTPUT SECTION.
00015    001140 FILE-CONTROL.
00016    001150       SELECT CARD-INPUT   ASSIGN UT-S-SYSIN.
00017    001160       SELECT PRINT-OUTPUT ASSIGN UT-S-SYSPRINT.
```

Figure 15-4.

The input-output section, also shown in Figure 15–4, is used to name each file, identify its media, and assign it to one or more input-output devices. The statements on lines 14 through 17 describe the card-input device as a card reader identified as SYS007 and the print-output device as a line printer identified as SYS009.

3. The *data division* is used to define the characteristics and format of the data to be processed. Every data name referred to in the procedure division except figurative constants must be described in the data division. Items and records are described by record description entries, and files are described by file description entries. The data division of this program is composed of two sections, the file section and the working-storage section.

The file section, lines 19 through 48, has two file description (FD) entries. The first, statements 20 through 24, describes the card-input as a file consisting of fixed-length unblocked records, each 80 characters in length, without labels, and known as CARD-INPUT (Figure 15–5).

```
00018    001170 DATA DIVISION.
00019    001180 FILE SECTION.
00020    001190 FD  CARD-INPUT
00021    001200     RECORDING MODE IS F
00022    001210     RECORD CONTAINS 80 CHARACTERS
00023    001220     LABEL RECORDS ARE OMITTED
00024    001230     DATA RECORD IS RECORD-IN.
```

Figure 15-5.

The card-input file, statements 25 through 31, contains records identified as RECORD-IN (Figure 15–6). The record is subdivided into its various fields such as STOCK-NUMBER and described by a picture clause. The term "picture" is used to identify a coded description of a data item (field). For example, the picture clause X(6) on line 26 describes STOCK-NUMBER as a six-position field containing alphanumeric data. The picture clause 9(5) on line 27 identifies QTY-ON-HAND as a five-position field containing numeric data. The remainder of the RECORD-IN statements should be easy to translate.

```
00025    001240 01  RECORD-IN.
00026    001250     05  STOCK-NUMBER    PIC X(6).
00027    001260     05  QTY-ON-HAND     PIC 9(5).
00028    001270     05  DESCRIPTION     PIC X(20).
00029    001280     05  STOCK-RECEIPTS  PIC 9(5).
00030    001290     05  STOCK-ISSUES    PIC 9(5).
00031    001300     05  FILLER          PIC X(39).
```

Figure 15-6.

The statements on lines 32 through 48 describe the printer file, known as PRINT-OUTPUT, and its associated records identified by PRINT-LINE (Figure 15–7).

```
00032   001310 FD   PRINT-OUTPUT
00033   001320      RECORDING MODE IS F
00034   001330      RECORD CONTAINS 133 CHARACTERS
00035   001340      LABEL RECORDS ARE OMITTED
00036   001350      DATA RECORD IS PRINT-LINE.
00037   001360 01   PRINT-LINE.
00038   001370      05  FILLER             PIC X(25).
00039   001380      05  PRT-STOCK-NUMBER   PIC X(6).
00040   001390      05  FILLER             PIC X(9).
00041   001400      05  PRT-DESCRIPTION    PIC X(20).
00042   001410      05  FILLER             PIC X(19).
00043   001420      05  PRT-NEW-BALANCE    PIC 9(6).
00044   001430      05  FILLER             PIC X(4).
00045   001440      05  PRT-WORD-TOTAL     PIC X(5).
00046   001450      05  FILLER             PIC X(5).
00047   001460      05  PRT-TOTAL          PIC 9(7).
00048   001470      05  FILLER             PIC X(27).
```

Figure 15-7.

The working-storage section, lines 49 through 51, identifies reserved storage locations for two fields known as WORKING-COUNTER and TOTAL-COUNTER, and describes them as numeric fields originally containing zeros (Figure 15–8).

```
00049   001480 WORKING-STORAGE SECTION.
00050   001490 77  WORKING-COUNTER   PIC 9(6)   VALUE ZEROS   COMP-3.
00051   001500 77  TOTAL-COUNTER     PIC 9(7)   VALUE ZEROS   COMP-3.
```

Figure 15-8.

4. The *procedure division* is used to describe the internal processing that is to take place. All input-output operations, logical decisions, data movement, and computing operations must be defined in the procedure division.

Just as verbs in the English language designate action, so it is with the COBOL verbs. Whereas the entries in the other divisions of a COBOL source program describe or define things, the verbs specify action, or procedures, to be carried out. Accordingly, the COBOL verbs form the basis of the procedure division of a source program.

The smallest unit of expression in the procedure division is the statement. Sentences, paragraphs, and sections are the larger units of expression. A statement consists of a COBOL verb or the word IF or ON, followed by any appropriate operands (data-names, file-names, or literals) and other COBOL words that are necessary for the completion of the statement. There are four types of statements:

Statement	Function
Compiler-directing	Directs the compiler to take certain actions at compilation time.
Imperative	Specifies unconditional actions to be taken by the object program.

Statement	Function
Conditional	Contains a condition that is tested to determine which alternate path in the program flow is to be taken.
Note (comment)	Makes it easier for programmers to understand and follow the program. These statements are not included in the object program.

A sentence is a single statement or a series of statements terminated by a period and followed by a space. Paragraphs consist of one or more sentences. A section is composed of one or more successive paragraphs and must begin with a section-header.

In the sample program the procedure division starts on line 52 and ends on line 74. There are no section headings in the sample program. The first paragraph heading appearing on line 53 in the procedure division reads START-PROG. In this paragraph the input and output files are opened, and the PRINT-LINE is cleared of any data that may be there at the time the program is loaded (Figure 15–9).

In the next paragraph, headed READ-A-CARD, the following steps are programmed:

1. The statement on line 57 says to read a card and, when the last card has been read, to go to (branch) the LAST-CARD paragraph (Figure 15–10).
2. The next three statements (lines 58 to 60) say to add quantity on hand to the storage area named WORKING-COUNTER, add stock receipts to WORKING-COUNTER, and subtract stock issued from WORKING-COUNTER (Figure 15–11).
3. The next statements (lines 61 and 62) say to move the sum stored at WORKING-COUNTER to a storage field known as PRT-NEW-

```
00052    001510 PROCEDURE DIVISION.
00053    001520 START-PROG.
00054    001530     OPEN INPUT CARD-INPUT    OUTPUT PRINT-OUTPUT.
00055    001540     MOVE SPACES TO PRINT-LINE.
```
Figure 15-9.

```
00056    001550 READ-A-CARD.
00057    001560     READ CARD-INPUT    AT END GO TO LAST-CARD.
```
Figure 15-10.

```
00058    001570     ADD QTY-ON-HAND TO WORKING-COUNTER.
00059    001580     ADD STOCK-RECEIPTS TO WORKING-COUNTER.
00060    001590     SUBTRACT STOCK-ISSUES FROM WORKING-COUNTER.
```
Figure 15-11.

BALANCE, and to add the sum stored at WORKING-COUNTER to the storage field known as TOTAL-COUNTER. The next statement (line 63) says to clear the storage field known as WORKING-COUNTER by moving zeros into that field (Figure 15–12).

4. The next two statements (lines 64 and 65) cause indicative fields in the RECORD-IN file section to be moved to the PRINT-OUTPUT PRINT-LINE (Figure 15–13). It should be noted that the statement names shown on lines 64 and 65 can be related to the names in the file section of the data division.

5. The next three statements (lines 66, 67, and 68) cause the paper to be spaced, a line to be printed, the print line to be cleared, and the program to branch to the paragraph headed READ-A-CARD (Figure 15–14).

6. The instructions in the LAST-CARD paragraph (lines 69 to 74) will be activated by a branch operation that occurs after the last card has been read. This LAST-CARD paragraph says to move the literal TOTAL to the print line, move the data at TOTAL-COUNTER to the print line, space the paper, write the PRINT-LINE, close the CARD-INPUT and PRINT-OUTPUT files, and stop the job by returning control to the computer operating system (Figure 15–15).

In addition to the list shown in Figure 15–2, the COBOL compiler may also produce a data division map showing each data name and the storage address it represents, and a procedure division map showing

```
00061   001600   MOVE WORKING-COUNTER TO PRT-NEW-BALANCE.
00062   001610   ADD WORKING-COUNTER TO TOTAL-COUNTER.
00063   001620   MOVE ZEROS TO WORKING-COUNTER.
```

Figure 15-12.

```
00064   001630   MOVE STOCK-NUMBER TO PRT-STOCK-NUMBER.
00065   001640   MOVE DESCRIPTION TO PRT-DESCRIPTION.
```

Figure 15-13.

```
00066   001650   WRITE PRINT-LINE AFTER POSITIONING 1.
00067   001660   MOVE SPACES TO PRINT-LINE.
00068   001670   GO TO READ-A-CARD.
```

Figure 15-14.

```
00069   001680 LAST-CARD.
00070   001690   MOVE 'TOTAL' TO PRT-WORD-TOTAL.
00071   001700   MOVE TOTAL-COUNTER TO PRT-TOTAL.
00072   001710   WRITE PRINT-LINE AFTER POSITIONING 1.
00073   001720   CLOSE CARD-INPUT  PRINT-OUTPUT.
00074   001730   GOBACK.
```

Figure 15-15.

machine-language instructions and their storage addresses. These instructions are also referenced to their source statement line number. In most cases several machine-language instructions are generated for each source statement.

Although COBOL has not attained perfect commonality, there are advantages to its use as a programming system. Among these advantages are:

1. The chance for clerical errors is reduced, as the program is written in a language familiar to the programmer.
2. Internal processing functions are stated in English. This eliminates the need for the programmer to be familiar with the machine instructions.
3. The processor will automatically insert the required input-output control system segments into the object program.
4. Standard input-output format definitions improve communications between programmers working on several interdependent programs.

Most of the arguments against COBOL in its present form are:

1. An experienced programmer can write a more efficient program in a machine-oriented language than in COBOL, although it may require more programming time.
2. Since COBOL processors are very complex, they require more computer time to compile the program. Even though the more powerful computers require less time for compiling, the time consumed is still relatively greater than that required for less complicated processors.
3. Failure to fully understand the limits of the so-called computer independence of COBOL has led some into thinking that once a problem has been programmed in COBOL it can be used with any computer without reprogramming. In reality, if a COBOL program is to be efficient, the programmer writing the program must be familiar with the characteristics of the specific computer to be used.

PROGRAMMING LANGUAGE I

Programming Language I (PL/I) is a multipurpose, high-level programming language that enables the programming not only of business and scientific applications but also of real-time and systems applications. Program preparation is simpler because PL/I does not impose rigid form rules on the programmer. In addition, no special coding forms are required. This free form reduces transcription errors because programs are not bound by card column restrictions as in previous languages.

PL/I uses basic building blocks called procedures. A procedure is a block of instructions designed to perform a specific function such as the calculation of overtime pay in a payroll application. Programmers build application programs by employing procedures as functional blocks. The use of procedures as functional blocks simplifies the programmer's task because he can revise an existing program by changing individual procedures without having to change others. He can also write a number of short procedures and combine them into a complete program.

Certain procedures may be applicable in different programs. Thus, seldom-used procedures can be held in auxiliary storage and called into main storage when needed. This conserves working storage for operations of higher priority.

A PL/I program consists of words and/or delimiters. *Words* belong to one of two categories: identifiers or constants. An *identifier* can be a word used to identify a file, a dáta item, or all or any part of a program. This type of identifier is known as a *key word.* An example of a key word would be the word DECLARE shown in card 1020 in the sample program (Figure 15–16). *Constants* name data items that will actually appear within a PL/I program and, consequently, are immediately available for use in the program. The word TOTAL on line 2160 of the sample program is an example of a constant.

There are two types of *delimiters:* separators and operators. *Separators* include the comma, semicolon, colon, period, and parenthesis. They are used to separate elements of a list, terminate statements, separate name qualifiers, and enclose lists. *Operators* are comprised of a series of the following:

Operators	Function
Arithmetic	Signs used to denote the various arithmetic functions such as add, subtract, multiply, and divide
Comparison	Signs used to denote greater than, not greater than, greater than or equal to, equal to, etc.
Logical	Signs used to denote *and, not,* and *or*

Comments may be used anywhere that a blank is permitted, except within a character-string constant or a picture specification. Comments must be preceded by a slash and an asterisk and must be followed by an asterisk and a slash. The first line of the sample PL/I program is an example of how comments are bracketed (Figure 15–16).

Figure 15–16 shows the PL/I source text for the problem flowcharted in Figure 12–4. Although PL/I can be written in free form, it is written in this example on a standard sheet designed for key punching the data into 80-column cards. Card columns 2 through 72 are used for source text, and 73 through 80 are used to identify the program and as a sequence number field. To demonstrate the flexibility of the PL/I language, the first part of the program ending on line 2070 is written in a blocked format similar to that of COBOL; the remainder of the program is written in a formula format similar to that of FORTRAN.

JOB	SAMPLE		PUNCHING INSTRUCTIONS
BY		DATE	WRITTEN AS: Ø O
			PUNCH AS: NUM ALPHA

NOTES:

```
SAMPLE: PROCEDURE OPTIONS (MAIN); /* SAMPLE PROG IN PL/I */          SAMØ1Ø1Ø
     DECLARE 1 CARDIN,   /* CARD INPUT AREA */                       SAMØ1Ø2Ø
               2 STOCKNO,      CHARACTER (6),                        SAMØ1Ø3Ø
               2 QTYONHD       PICTURE '99999',                      SAMØ1Ø4Ø
               2 DESC          CHARACTER (2Ø),                       SAMØ1Ø5Ø
               2 STKRCPTS      PICTURE '99999',                      SAMØ1Ø6Ø
               2 STKISS        PICTURE '99999',                      SAMØ1Ø7Ø
               2 FILL          CHARACTER (39),                       SAMØ1Ø8Ø
             1 PRTOUT,    /* PRINTER OUTPUT AREA */                  SAMØ1Ø9Ø
               2 FILL1         CHARACTER (24),                       SAMØ11ØØ
               2 PSTOCKNO       CHARACTER (6),                       SAMØ111Ø
               2 FILL2         CHARACTER (9),                        SAMØ112Ø
               2 PDESC         CHARACTER (2Ø),                       SAMØ113Ø
               2 FILL3         CHARACTER (19),                       SAMØ114Ø
               2 PTOT          PICTURE '999999',                     SAMØ115Ø
               2 FILL4         CHARACTER (48),                       SAMØ116Ø
             1 PRTTOT,    /* FINAL TOTAL LINE */                     SAMØ117Ø
               2 FILL5         CHARACTER (88),                       SAMØ118Ø
               2 TOTWORD       CHARACTER (5),                        SAMØ119Ø
               2 FILL6         CHARACTER (5),                        SAMØ12ØØ
               2 FTOT          PICTURE '9999999',                    SAMØ12Ø3
               2 FILL7         CHARACTER (27);                       SAMØ12Ø6
     /* THE NEXT TWO FIELDS ARE USED AS COUNTERS */                 SAMØ1219
         WCTR      FIXED DECIMAL (6),                                SAMØ122Ø
         FCTR      FIXED DECIMAL (7),                                SAMØ123Ø
     /* FILE DECLARATION FOR CARD AND PRINTER FILES */              SAMØ124Ø
         CARD FILE INPUT RECORD  BUFFERED                           SAMØ125Ø
              ENVIRONMENT (F(8Ø) MEDIUM (SYSØØ7,254Ø)),             SAMØ126Ø
         PRINT FILE OUTPUT RECORD BUFFERED                          SAMØ127Ø
              ENVIRONMENT (F(132) MEDIUM (SYSØØ9,14Ø3));            SAMØ128Ø
     /* END OF DATA DECLARATIONS. LOGIC OF PROGRAM BEGINS */        SAMØ129Ø
/* INITIALIZE CTRS TO ZERO */                                       SAMØ2Ø1Ø
     START:    FCTR = Ø;                                             SAMØ2Ø2Ø
/* OPEN RECORD FILES EXPLICITLY */                                  SAMØ2Ø3Ø
     OPEN FILE (CARD), FILE (PRINT);                                SAMØ2Ø4Ø
     ON ENDFILE (CARD) GO TO EOJ;                                   SAMØ2Ø5Ø
/* READ CARD AND PROCESS */                                         SAMØ2Ø6Ø
     GETCARD: READ FILE (CARD) INTO (CARDIN);                       SAMØ2Ø7Ø
         WCTR = QTYONHD + STKRCPTS - STKISS;                        SAMØ2Ø8Ø
         PTOT = WCTR;                                               SAMØ2Ø9Ø
         FCTR = FCTR + WCTR;                                        SAMØ21ØØ
         PSTOCKNO = STOCKNO;                                        SAMØ211Ø
         PDESC = DESC;                                              SAMØ212Ø
         WRITE FILE (PRINT) FROM (PRTOUT);                          SAMØ213Ø
         GO TO GETCARD;                                             SAMØ214Ø
/* END OF JOB ROUTINE */                                            SAMØ215Ø
     EOJ: TOTWORD = 'TOTAL';                                        SAMØ216Ø
         FTOT = FCTR;                                               SAMØ217Ø
         WRITE FILE (PRINT) FROM (PRTTOT);                          SAMØ218Ø
         CLOSE FILE (CARD), FILE (PRINT);                           SAMØ219Ø
END; /* END OF PROG */                                              SAMØ22ØØ
```

Figure 15-16. *Source program written in PL/I.*

The sample PL/I program shown in Figure 15–16 is described in the following paragraphs.

Explicit descriptions of data characteristics are written in the form of DECLARE statements used to describe named data as it is represented within the internal storage of a computer. The properties that characterize a data item are called attributes and are specified by key words. The DECLARE statements shown in cards 1020 through 1206 describe the CARDIN, PRTOUT, and PRTTOT records as they will exist in the primary storage unit of the computer (Figure 15–17).

The WCTR and FCTR statements on lines 1220 and 1230 name two counters, identify their attributes, and fix their size (Figure 15–18).

Cards 1250 and 1260 contain the DECLARE statements defining the card file as buffered and read by a model 2540 card reader with the system name SYS007. ("Buffered" indicates that data in a record being transmitted to and from a file is to be placed into an intermediate storage area known as a buffer.) The statements also identify the records (cards) as being 80 characters in length and in a file with no label (Figure 15–19).

Cards 1270 and 1280 contain the DECLARE statements defining the printer file as buffered with 132-position records printed by a 1403 model printer with the system name SYS009 (Figure 15–20). The semicolon at the end of the statement on card 1280 indicates the end of a state-

```
 SAMPLE  PROCEDURE OPTIONS (MAIN); /* SAMPLE PROG IN PL/I. */           SAM01010
    DECLARE 1 CARDIN,  /* CARD INPUT AREA */                            SAM01020
           2 STOCKNO       CHARACTER (6),                               SAM01030
           2 QTYONHD       PICTURE '99999',                             SAM01040
           2 DESC          CHARACTER (20),                              SAM01050
           2 STKRCPTS      PICTURE '99999',                             SAM01060
           2 STKISS        PICTURE '99999',                             SAM01070
           2 FILL          CHARACTER (39),                              SAM01080
         1 PRTOUT,  /* PRINTER OUTPUT AREA */                           SAM01090
           2 FILL1         CHARACTER (24),                              SAM01100
           2 PSTOCKNO      CHARACTER (6),                               SAM01110
           2 FILL2         CHARACTER (9),                               SAM01120
           2 PDESC         CHARACTER (20),                              SAM01130
           2 FILL3         CHARACTER (19),                              SAM01140
           2 PTOT          PICTURE '999999',                            SAM01150
           2 FILL4         CHARACTER (48),                              SAM01160
         1 PRTTOT,  /* FINAL TOTAL LINE */                              SAM01170
           2 FILL5         CHARACTER (88),                              SAM01180
           2 TOTWORD       CHARACTER (5),                               SAM01190
           2 FILL6         CHARACTER (5),                               SAM01200
           2 FTOT          PICTURE '9999999',                           SAM01203
           2 FILL7         CHARACTER (27),                              SAM01206
```

Figure 15-17.

```
   /* THE NEXT TWO FIELDS ARE USED AS COUNTERS */                       SAM01210
      WCTR       FIXED DECIMAL (6),                                     SAM01220
      FCTR       FIXED DECIMAL (7),                                     SAM01230
```

Figure 15-18.

ment or a series of statements; in this case it marks the end of the DE-CLARE statements.

The processing part of the program actually starts with card 2020. The first step in this problem is to be sure that the FCTR counter is set to zero by stating that the counter is to be made equal to zero (Figure 15–21).

Cards 2040 and 2050 specify that the card and print files are to be opened and that after the last card has been processed the computer is to go to the EOJ (end-of-job) routine (Figure 15–22). The file-opening statements cause about the same instructions to be inserted into the PL/I object program as were generated by the COBOL and Assembler Language processors.

Card 2070 states that a card record is to be read into the primary storage location named CARDIN (Figure 15–23). The next statement specifies that QTYONHD and STKRCPTS are to be added and the result entered into the area named WCTR, and that STKISS is to be subtracted from

```
/* FILE DECLARATION FOR CARD AND PRINTER FILES */               SAM01240
    CARD FILE INPUT RECORD BUFFERED                              SAM01250
        ENVIRONMENT (F(80) MEDIUM (SYS007,2540)),                SAM01260
```

Figure 15-19.

```
    PRINT FILE OUTPUT RECORD BUFFERED                            SAM01270
        ENVIRONMENT (F(132) MEDIUM (SYS009,1403));               SAM01280
/* END OF DATA DECLARATIONS, LOGIC OF PROGRAM BEGINS */          SAM01290
```

Figure 15-20.

```
/* INITIALIZE CTRS TO ZERO */                                    SAM02010
    START:    FCTR = 0;                                          SAM02020
```

Figure 15-21.

```
/* OPEN RECORD FILES EXPLICITLY */                               SAM02030
    OPEN FILE (CARD), FILE (PRINT);                              SAM02040
    ON ENDFILE (CARD) GO TO EOJ;                                 SAM02050
```

Figure 15-22.

```
/* READ CARD AND PROCESS */                                      SAM02060
    GETCARD: READ FILE (CARD) INTO (CARDIN);                     SAM02070
        WCTR = QTYONHD + STKRCPTS - STKISS;                      SAM02080
        PTOT = WCTR;                                             SAM02090
        FCTR = FCTR + WCTR;                                      SAM02100
        PSTOCKNO = STOCKNO;                                      SAM02110
        PDESC = DESC;                                            SAM02120
        WRITE FILE (PRINT) FROM (PRTOUT);                        SAM02130
        GO TO GETCARD;                                           SAM02140
```

Figure 15-23.

```
/* END OF JOB ROUTINE */                                          SAM02150
      EOJ: TOTWORD = 'TOTAL';                                     SAM02160
           FTOT = FCTR;                                           SAM02170
           WRITE FILE (PRINT) FROM (PRTTOT);                      SAM02180
           CLOSE FILE (CARD) , FILE (PRINT);                      SAM02190
END;   /* END OF PROG */                                          SAM02200
```

Figure 15-24.

the sum at WCTR. Card 2090 specifies that the sum at WCTR is to be moved into PTOT. The next statement specifies that the sum at WCTR is to be added to the sum at FCTR and the result is to remain at FCTR. The next two statements, cards 2110 and 2120, cause STOCKNO to be moved to PSTOCKNO and DESC to be moved to PDESC. The next two statements, cards 2130 and 2140, cause a line to be printed as formatted in the PRTOUT declarations and the program to branch back to GET-CARD, the statement that causes the computer to read a card.

The program will continue to move through this loop—read a card, process, print a line, branch to read-a-card, and so on—until the last card has been read. After the last card has been processed, the IOCS will cause the program to branch to the end-of-job routine statements starting in card 2160 (Figure 15–24). The end-of-job statements cause the word TOTAL to be moved to TOTWORD, FCTR to be moved to FTOT, the line to be printed, and the files to be closed.

PL/I has not been as widely used as COBOL or FORTRAN because it is a relatively new programming system developed by one equipment manufacturer, IBM. However, it is likely that the advantages of PL/I will cause it to become more widely used.

REPORT PROGRAM GENERATOR

Report Program Generator (RPG) is designed to provide users with an efficient, easy-to-use technique for generating programs. RPG uses a set of simple and largely self-explanatory specification sheets on which the user makes entries. Although technically RPG may not be considered a programming system, it is a very important program producing technique. As its vast capabilities include many functions in addition to report preparation, its name is a misnomer and fails to do it justice. When RPG is used, the computer actually performs two separate functions: program generation and data processing.

In the first function, program specifications, defined by the user, produce machine-language instructions. Storage areas are automatically assigned; constants or other reference factors are included; and linkage to routines for checking, for input-output operations, and for other functions are produced.

In the second function, the machine-language instructions created in the first function are executed under control of the RPG. The user's input data files are utilized to produce the desired reports or output files.

The preparation of a report by means of RPG consists of the general operations illustrated in Figure 15–25 and described in the ensuing paragraphs.

The programmer must evaluate the report requirements to determine the format of the input files and the desired appearance of the finished report. Then he must make the required entries on the various specification sheets. To illustrate this we have prepared RPG specification sheets for the same basic problem programmed in each of the previously discussed programming systems. The functions of the RPG specification sheets are as follows.

The *file description* sheet is used to describe all files used by the object program: input files, output files, table files, etc. (Figure 15–26). In the sample problem there are two files: a card input file and a printed report. The entries in columns 15 through 27 of line 10 indicate that the card input file named CARDIN is an input file, is a primary file, is to be checked for end-of-file condition, is in ascending sequence, and has a fixed file format containing 80-position unblocked records.

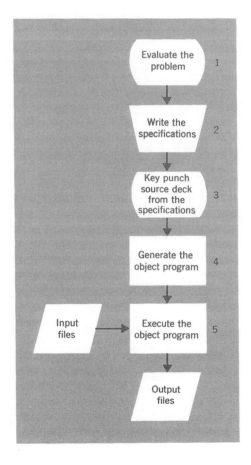

Figure 15-25. *Report Program Generator preparation steps.*

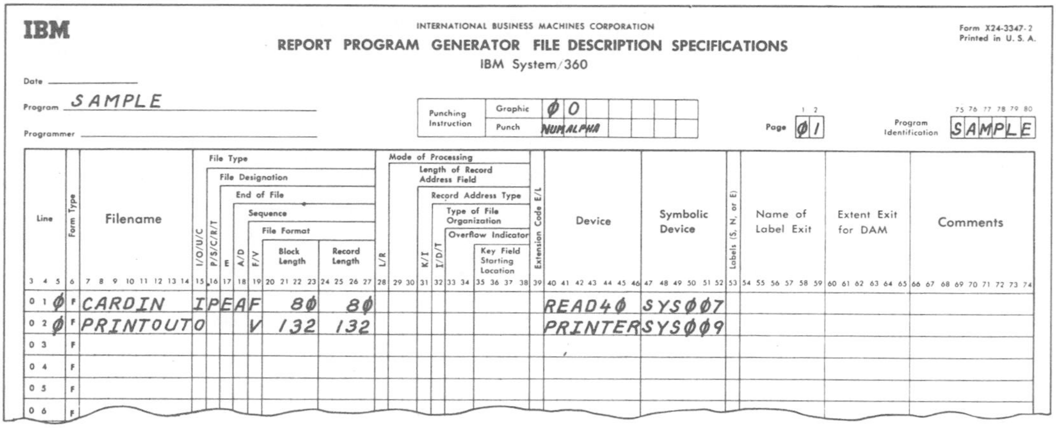

IBM INTERNATIONAL BUSINESS MACHINES CORPORATION
REPORT PROGRAM GENERATOR FILE DESCRIPTION SPECIFICATIONS
IBM System/360
Form X24-3347-2 Printed in U. S. A.

Date
Program SAMPLE
Programmer

Punching Instruction: Graphic Ø O; Punch NUM ALPHA
Page Ø1
Program Identification SAMPLE

Line	Form Type	Filename	File Type	File Designation	End of File	Sequence	File Format	Block Length	Record Length	Device	Symbolic Device
01Ø	F	CARDIN	I	P	E	A	F	8Ø	8Ø	READ4Ø	SYSØØ7
02Ø	F	PRINTOUT	O				V	132	132	PRINTER	SYSØØ9
03	F										
04	F										
05	F										
06	F										

Figure 15-26. *RPG file description specifications.*

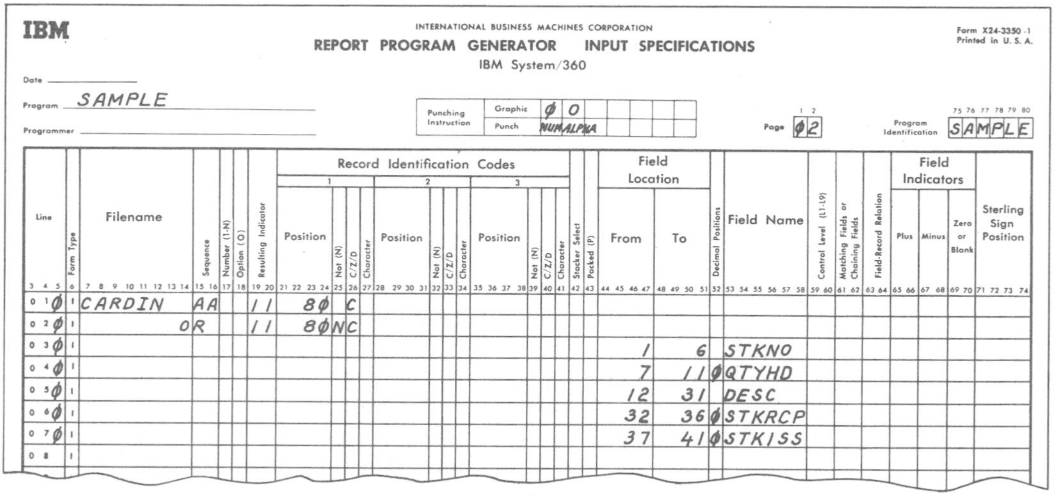

IBM INTERNATIONAL BUSINESS MACHINES CORPORATION
REPORT PROGRAM GENERATOR INPUT SPECIFICATIONS
IBM System/360
Form X24-3350-1 Printed in U. S. A.

Date
Program SAMPLE
Programmer

Punching Instruction: Graphic Ø O; Punch NUM ALPHA
Page Ø2
Program Identification SAMPLE

Line	Form Type	Filename	Sequence	Resulting Indicator	Position	Not (N)	C/Z/D	Field Location From	Field Location To	Decimal Positions	Field Name
01Ø	I	CARDIN	AA	11	8Ø		C				
02Ø	I	OR		11	8Ø	N	C				
03Ø	I							1	6		STKNO
04Ø	I							7	11	Ø	QTYHD
05Ø	I							12	31		DESC
06Ø	I							32	36	Ø	STKRCP
07Ø	I							37	41	Ø	STKISS
08	I										

Figure 15-27. *RPG input specifications.*

Columns 40 to 52 of line 10 show that the device is a model 2540 card reader assigned the symbolic name SYS007. The report output file named PRINTOUT is identified on line 20 as an output file containing a variable number of positions up to 132. The printer is assigned the symbolic name SYS009.

The *input specification* sheet is used to describe the input: record layouts, field used, etc. (Figure 15–27). The first two lines on the sample input sheet define two types of records associated with the file named CARDIN. Lines 30 through 70 define and name the various fields in the card record.

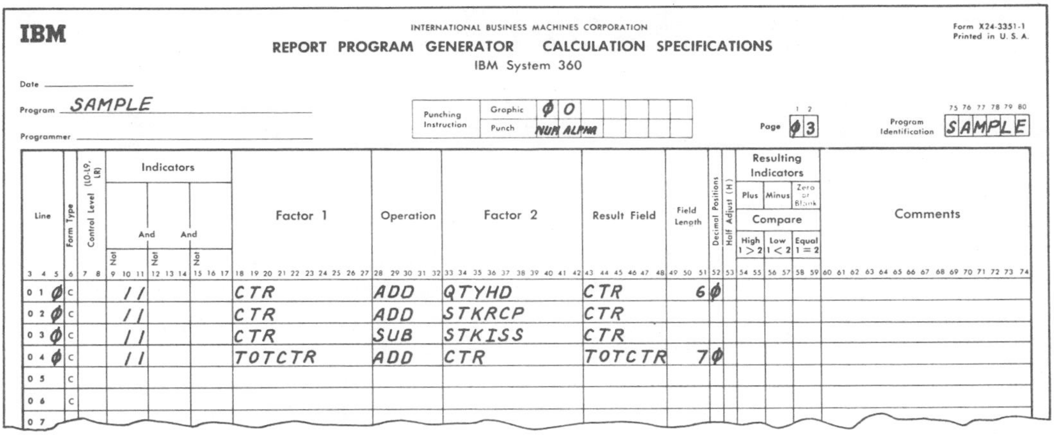

Figure 15-28. *RPG calculation specifications.*

Figure 15-29. *RPG output-format specifications.*

The *calculation specification* sheet is used to describe the processing steps: add, subtract, multiply. The sample sheet specifies that QTYHD is to be added to CTR; STKRCP is to be added to CTR; STKISS is to be subtracted from CTR; and CTR is to be added to TOTCTR (Figure 15–28).

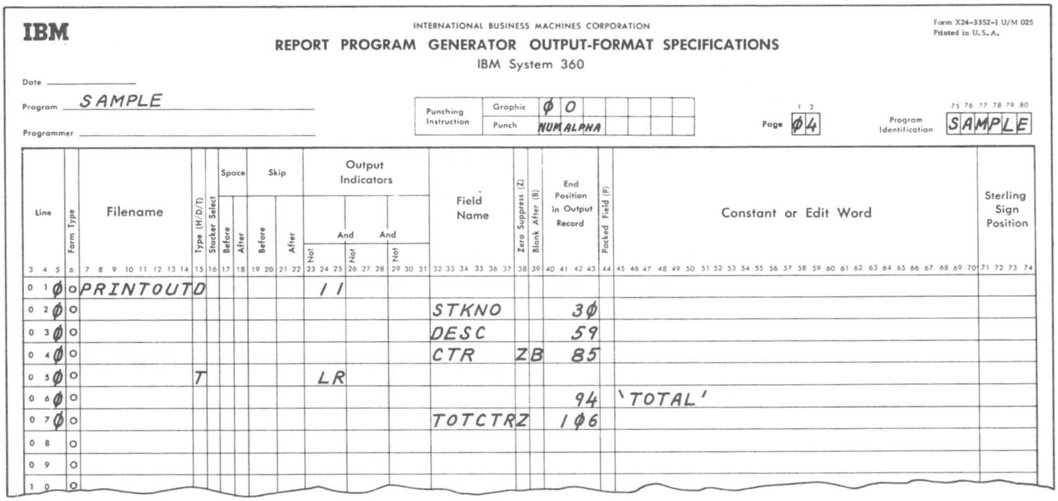

The *output-format specification* sheet is used to identify the printing positions, carriage control, etc., that will establish the format of the report (Figure 15–29). In the sample, the file named PRINTOUT obtains its data from a detail record or from the result of calculations and causes

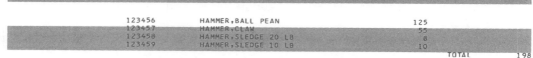

```
123456        HAMMER,BALL PEAN                    125
123457        HAMMER,CLAW                          55
123458        HAMMER,SLEDGE 20 LB                   8
123459        HAMMER,SLEDGE 10 LB                  10
                                          TOTAL    198
```

Figure 15-30. *Report resulting from RPG program.*

the data in the fields named STKNO, DESC, and CTR to print as specified. The entries on lines 50 through 70 state that the word TOTAL and the sum in the field named TOTCTR with zeros suppressed are to be printed after the last record has been processed.

Note that mnemonic names similar to those used in the Assembler Language may be used in RPG. This is one of the important features that help to make RPG the valuable program-generating technique that it is.

After the specifications have been written on the appropriate forms, cards are key punched with the data from the forms. These punched cards, called a *source deck,* are combined with the processor control card and the job control cards. The source deck and the control cards are supplied to an input device and are processed.

At the end of the processing run, known as a *compilation run,* a program capable of preparing the report specified by the programmer has been produced. This program, known as an *object program,* contains all of the computer instructions and linkages to the control system necessary to prepare the desired report.

The input files can then be read into the system, and processing of the program will begin. This is known as the *object run.* At the end of the object run, the report has been prepared, and any other functions, such as file updating, are completed. Figure 15–30 shows the results of the sample run produced by the RPG program shown in the four preceding illustrations.

IMPORTANT WORDS AND PHRASES

FORTRAN
compiling

COBOL
Programming Language I(PL/I)

Report Program Generator (RPG)

REVIEW QUESTIONS

1. What is the primary advantage of a FORTRAN programming system?
2. Name the four divisions of a COBOL program.
3. In which COBOL division is the computer that will be used identified?
4. Name the four types of COBOL procedure division statements.
5. What are the advantages of the use of COBOL?
6. What are the arguments against the use of COBOL?
7. What types of applications can be programmed with PL/I?
8. Briefly describe the functions performed by Report Program Generator.

16

ELECTRONIC DATA PROCESSING OPERATIONS

Although electronic data processing organizations may vary in structure, they all must perform comparable functions. These functions can be divided into five major categories: systems planning, research, training, programming, and the actual operation of EDP equipment.

Electronic data processing operations encompass many important activities: data is transcribed from human-readable documents to computer-language documents; machine operations are performed; files of data are maintained; and accuracy controls are exercised. These and other facets of EDP operations will be considered in this chapter.

An electronic data processing facility consists of one or more processing units and associated input-output devices, as well as certain auxiliary support equipment and files. Insofar as the arrangement of the equipment is concerned, most manufacturers have a suggested layout. The computer components should be arranged close so as to keep operator travel to a minimum and yet spread out so as not to cause congestion of personnel, documents, or supplies.

In addition to the equipment, the facility will have a certain amount of space for the supervisors, document control group, programming personnel, card punch operations, storage of records and supplies, and equipment maintenance. The arrangement of the various activities should be one that is best from a total performance point of view.

As the components of a computer system have interconnecting cables for supply of power and transmission of data, it is advisable that the equipment be placed on a raised floor 12 to 18 inches above the regular floor. This provides room for all of the cables to run under the raised floor. Air conditioning and humidity control equipment that will maintain the environment within the computer manufacturers' specifications is also essential.

DATA FLOW

Input Preparation and Control

The majority of data entering business data processing systems must be converted to a computer language compatible with the equipment being used. The bulk of this transcribing from human-readable documents to computer language is performed by operators using data entry devices. Most documents are received by data processing in groups or stacks called *batches*. These batches should have associated with them a *control* or *batch ticket* that shows from whom the documents were received, the date, perhaps the time, and a document count (Figure 16–1).

Control totals of quantitative data may also be provided. A *control total* is the sum of the quantitative data recorded in a common field of each record in a batch of records. In Figure 16–1, for example, the control total is the sum of the amount fields in the accompanying purchase orders and material requisitions. If control totals are not provided, they should be developed by the control clerks in the data processing facility. Normally the control clerks check the source documents for completeness and accuracy. The clerks also protect the source documents and batch or control tickets against loss or destruction while they are in the custody of the EDP facility. Finally, the control clerks see that the input and output schedules stated in the procedures are met.

Input Handling Procedures

After the source data has been transcribed into computer language, both the source data and resulting media are usually conveyed to the EDP control section. Each batch of computer-language records should

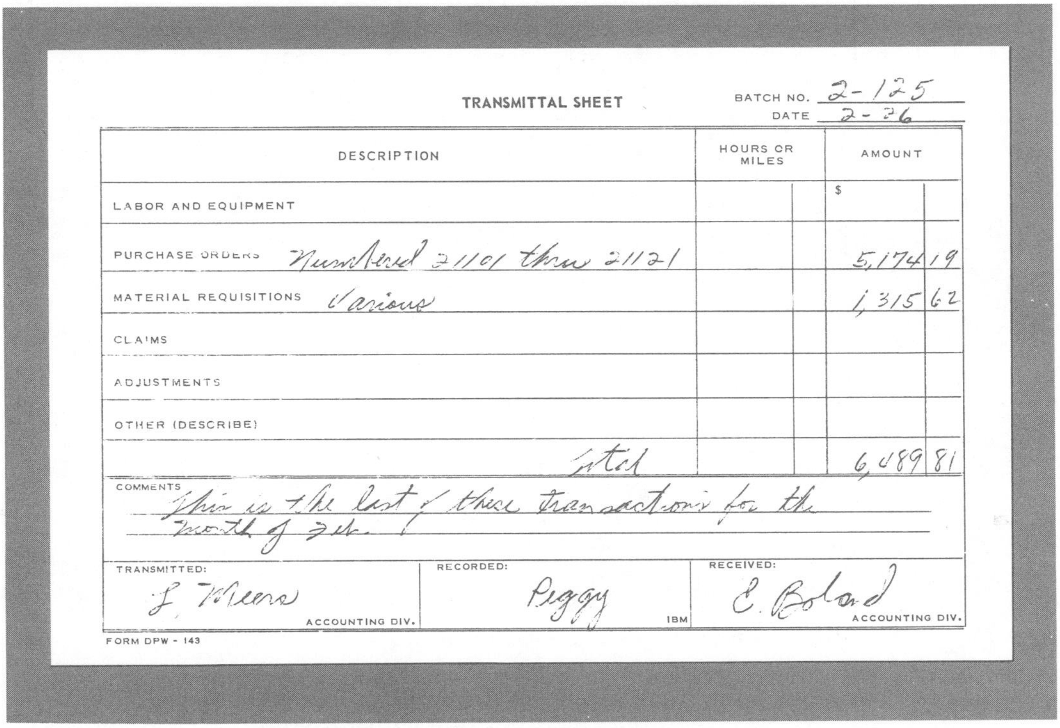

TRANSMITTAL SHEET

BATCH NO. 2-125
DATE 2-26

DESCRIPTION	HOURS OR MILES	AMOUNT
LABOR AND EQUIPMENT		$
PURCHASE ORDERS Numbered 21101 thru 21121		5,174 19
MATERIAL REQUISITIONS Various		1,315 62
CLAIMS		
ADJUSTMENTS		
OTHER (DESCRIBE)		
total		6,489 81

COMMENTS This is the last of these transactions for the month of Feb.

TRANSMITTED:	RECORDED:	RECEIVED:
L. Meers ACCOUNTING DIV.	Peggy IBM	E. Boland ACCOUNTING DIV.

FORM DPW - 143

Figure 16-1. *Combined batch ticket and transmittal sheet.*

have some sort of human-language identification (Figure 16–2). Each batch may also have some sort of machine-language identification, usually in the form of a header record containing all of the batch control data including quantitative totals. These batches can first be audited and balanced by the computer. All batches that do not balance can be flagged and returned to the control section for corrective action.

Another and often preferred approach is to have the computer list on an error sheet during the edit run the items of input data that do not have valid indicative data or the quantitative totals that do not equal the batch control totals. This approach allows the computer to continue with the normal process without operator intervention and allows the control clerks at a later time to adjust for the errors by creating new entries, one to revise out the error, and another to re-enter the transaction correctly. Whatever the approach, all reasonable effort should be made to insure the accuracy of the computer-language input. Invalid or inaccurate data can quickly destroy user confidence in the reliability of the output of the system.

Once the accuracy of the input data is established, there may be a limited amount of auxiliary processing required before the actual production run. This may include sorting, sequencing, or merging. All data,

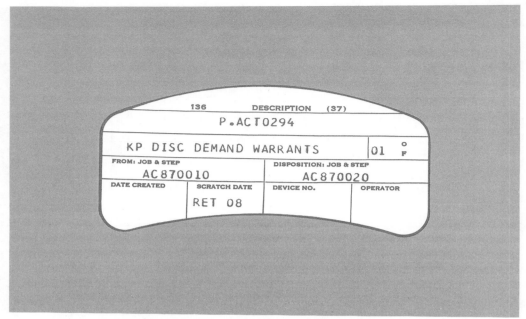

Figure 16-2. *Magnetic tape label from a key-to-disk operation.*

whether in tape, card, or other form, should be clearly identified at all times. The identification should show what it is and what the next step should be.

With EDP procedures it is important that processed data be retained as long as required to replace current to-date records in the event they are lost or destroyed. Most organizations maintain a log reflecting data in storage and use this for aid in replacing records or as a basis for purging stored data no longer required. Control must also be maintained over data that is temporarily stored for scheduled use at a later date. There are several commercially available automated tape management systems that are useful in managing large magnetic tape libraries.

Output Handling Procedures

Computer output can be in the form of human-readable information to be distributed to users, or computer-language records to be retained in the data processing facility for a following operation or for reuse at a later date. If data is in printed form, it may be balanced to control totals. Printed forms may also need to be prepared for distribution to the users. This may include separating carbon paper from multicopy forms, detaching or bursting continuous forms, and possibly inserting them into envelopes. If it were necessary to separate and detach hundreds or thousands of multicopy forms by hand, the task would be tedious and costly. To solve this problem a variety of forms-handling equipment is available, including the following.

Figure 16-3. *Multicopy continuous forms decollator.* *(Courtesy Moore Business Forms, Inc.)*

Decollator. This machine (Figure 16–3) separates multicopy continuous forms and refolds the parts continuously into individual sets. At the same time, carbon paper is removed and wound individually on removable spindles. Certain models will remove one copy and one carbon from a multicopy set and leave the remainder of the set intact.

Burster or Detacher. This type of equipment splits individual sets of continuous forms into single forms. This operation is known as "bursting." Excess margins can be removed by a power slitter (Figure 16–4).

Imprinter. This device imprints on continuous forms a limited amount of constant data such as dates, consecutive numbers, or signatures. For example, a series of pay checks in continuous form could be signed automatically on an imprinter by using a signature plate. Imprinting may be performed as a separate operation, or on certain models it may be combined with bursting.

Storage of Computer-Language Data

Computer-language output is usually entered in a log and stored in or near the data processing facility in the space provided. This may be a magnetic tape vault, a card file, or storage rack for removable random storage units. Again, all output media require some sort of control as to date and time of completion and accuracy.

Most recently the tendency is to meet large output requirements by providing computer-language data instead of, or in addition to, human-language data. This can be very beneficial to the receiver of the data, as he will be saved the cost of converting the human-readable data to computer-language data. It also reduces the opportunity for discrepancies between the originator and the user of the data. Examples of this are the fulfillment of certain federal and state information requirements such as quarterly reports on earnings, social security deductions, and unemployment insurance contributions by sending this data to the governing agencies on magnetic tape.

Figure 16-4. *Forms detacher. (Courtesy Moore Business Forms, Inc.)*

Scheduling

Scheduling can be the most arduous and frustrating part of managing an EDP operation unless a carefully conceived plan for scheduling is installed and followed with integrity. Too often EDP management expects the input always to be on schedule, and yet shows no concern if the output is delayed. If dependability of input is to be required, there must be comparable reliability of output. Some of the problems that make scheduling difficult are:

1. Users often require their reports at about the same time, generally at the end of the month, quarter, or year.
2. The volumes of data to be processed tend to vary from one time to the next.
3. A minimum of input and output devices is usually all that is available for reasons of economy. Therefore, any increase in volume of one job may cause a delay in the start of the next job.

4. Equipment breakdowns cannot be scheduled, even though with the best of equipment they occasionally do occur. In some critical operations a second standby computer may be justified in order to insure continuity of performance.

The total computer time available must be scheduled for reruns and restarts, program assembly and testing, and preventive maintenance in addition to the regular scheduled and nonscheduled production runs. One method for successful scheduling is to assign a certain period of time each day to program assembly and testing, and another to reruns. Also, a definite period may be set for preventive maintenance. The majority of the remaining time should be available for scheduling of production runs. Another plan for handling the scheduling problem is to schedule most of the production runs during the second shift and thereby leave the prime shift open for program assembly and testing, maintenance, reruns, and high-priority special runs. The duties and responsibilities of a work process scheduler will be covered later in this chapter in the descriptions of EDP operations positions.

CONSOLE OPERATION

The operator console is often a part of the central processing unit. However, on the larger systems especially, the console may be a separate unit at which the computer operator can sit. The power on and off switches are located on the console. In addition to the regular power off switch, there is also an emergency off switch that is to be used only in the event of a real emergency such as a fire. The start key is used to initiate or resume operations. The stop key is used to stop the computer at the completion of the instruction in process. On many computers additional start and stop keys are located on other input-output units for operator convenience.

Other control switches on the computer console start or stop various operations including the loading of a program from cards, tape, etc. Some consoles also contain a built-in or attached visual display unit or electric typewriter that can be used by the operator to communicate with the central processing unit control program, usually referred to as the operating system supervisor (Figure 16–5).

The setting of the mode switch or switches determines the mode of operation; that is, run, alter, character display, storage print out, address stop, etc. Most computers have a set of switches or dials for manual address operations. For example, they may be used to cause data at a specific location to be displayed on the console. The manual address switches can be used only in conjunction with certain mode switch settings.

Computers generally provide a method for manually entering data into storage. This is usually accomplished through a series of switches

Figure 16-5. *Computer central processing unit and console with typewriter.*
(Courtesy International Business Machines Corporation.)

that are used to set up the character to be entered. These switches or dials are generally operated after the destination in storage is identified in a storage address register.

Various types of registers are capable of receiving information from primary storage, storing it, and transferring it as directed by control circuits within the system. The condition of these registers at any particular time during processing can be displayed by lights and keys on the console. The *I*-address containing the address of an instruction, the data addresses of the information to be operated upon, and the storage location affected on each machine cycle all may be displayed on the console for operator use as required. In addition to the address registers there may be single-character registers that can be displayed.

Normally there is another group of lights that signals adder error conditions, arithmetic overflow, and results of a comparison. These lights are usually called logic lights. Still another set of lights indicates that an input or output device requires operator attention. Some of the newer computers display this information on the console visual display station or typewriter instead of using indicator lights on the console.

The console operator has control over the computer and all of its input or output devices. He or she usually is the one who coordinates the input process and output operations of each procedure. The console operator generally follows the procedures as set out on the operating instructions sheet (Figure 16–6). This sheet serves as a check list of operations to be performed in preparing the computer for performance under control of the proper program.

The operating instructions sheet is prepared by the programmer and is his means of conveying to the operator what he must know to proceed with the processing operation. For example, the operating instructions tell the operator which program tape reels or disk packs to use, which forms to use in the printer, and how to continue with the processing when departures from conventional procedures are necessary.

The console operator usually is responsible for having the computer read in the correct program, read in the correct input data, and produce the proper output. The console operator also must cause the proper procedures to be performed in the event of computer malfunctions, input inaccuracies, operator errors, or program mistakes.

If the computer stops because of a program or equipment malfunction, a storage print out (dump) at the point of failure should normally be made. If the computer stopped because of a program error, the output, storage print out, and console readings at the time of the stop should be recorded and delivered to the programmer, at which point another job can be put into operation. In case of equipment failure, the equipment must be repaired and tested before operation can continue. Some computers have more internal checking systems than others. Those with good checking systems will stop at the point of malfunction or record on the console or console typewriter the information required to diagnose the type of malfunction and its cause.

The console operator should also keep a computer operations log (Figure 16–7). This log should show the start, stop, and lapsed time for each job. The log may require other information deemed of value to management. This may include such things as maintenance and rerun times. Time recording machines may be used by the operator to record the various times. The primary use of the information captured on the computer operations log is for the production of user billings and information for management.

Computers with printer keyboard consoles that operate under control of an operating system may automatically prepare the computer operations log. This type of log usually shows the job number, job name, job start time, any interruptions to the process, and job stop time. In addition to providing operating information, this type of log may also be used for job accounting and job auditing activities. It also provides a means of communication between the computer and the operator and between the computer and the programmer. The communication

EDP SERVICES
OS CPU RUN SHEET

PROCEDURE NAME: <u>PROVIDE ARMS BUDGET DATA</u>   PAGE NUMBER <u>1</u> OF <u>1</u>
PROCEDURE <u>AC-98</u> TASK <u>1</u> OF <u>1</u>   ANALYST <u>K. BAILEY</u>
FREQUENCY: <u>ANNUAL</u>
STEP(S) INCLUDED: <u>20-28</u>

ESTIMATED EXECUTION TIME: <u>10 MIN</u>	TAPE DRIVES <u>2</u> CORE SIZE <u>35 K</u>
RESTART —	X	START OVER	**DASD AND TAPE FILES USED**
		REF RESTART INST	TYPE / NUMBER / DESCRIPTION VOLSER / CREATION STEP / DISPOSITION / RETENTION INFO

READER/PUNCH NAME OF FILE/ORIGIN DISPOSITION	DASD AND TAPE FILES USED
	I/ACT0035/BUDGET FILES -/LIBRARY/LIBRARY/-
R1	O/ACT0274/BUDGET ARMS DATA -/AC980020/LIBRARY/60 DAYS
R2 ALPHA CARD/CPU0020 SALVAGE IMMEDIATELY	O/PCT0019/PY FIXED ASSETS MSTR -/AC980024/LIBRARY/RET 4
P2	O/PCT0005/FIXED ASSETS MSTR -/PY980028/LIBRARY/RET 4
P1	
PRINTER FORMS REQUIRED: #0001	
FORMS DISPOSITION: CTL0030	
SPECIAL INSTRUCTIONS AND/OR PROGRAMMED CONSOLE HALTS AND REPLIES	

Figure 16-6. *Computer operating instruction sheet.*

S H I F T	DATE		WORKWEEK	SECTION			PAGE NO.	MACHINE NUMBER	
	10 – 14 – 71			5			2	340	
	CLOCK		EMPLOYEE NUMBER	JOB NUMBER		ACT. CODE	RUN CODE	STEP	FREQ.
	START	STOP		DEPT.	PROC.				
1	1327	1334	89134	DP	TTT		8	0002	Ø
1	1334	1347	89134	SS	TTT		8	1334	Ø
	1350	1355		5600	00		0	040	9
	1355	1425		AC	08		0	025	1
	1425	1453		AC	68		3	170	9
	1453	1514		AC	68		3	180	9
1	1533	1549	89134	PY	TTT		8	TPPR	Ø
	1549	1551		HE	TTT		8	9999	O
2	1607	1638	89290	0003	01		0	40	0
	1638	1653		05	07			10	
	1711	1723		0003	01			150	
	1723	1813		DP	01			10	
	1813	1815		0304	12			35	4
	1815	1820		0003	01			190	0
	1820	1821		0302	10			130	0
	1821	1841		0304	13			10	4
	1841	1842		0304	13			10	4
	1842	1852		PL	13			40	2
	1852	1855		0001	06			160	2
	1855	1902		0001	07			20	2
	1902	1904		0600	91			40	0
	1904	1912		0600	91			40	0
	1912	1931		DP	56			50	4
	1931	2009		RV	17			120	9
	2009	2033		RV	17			140	9
	2033	2038		MC	14			71	0
	2038	2207		ST	TTT		8	1948	0
	2210	2211		A	49		0	50	1
	2211	2212		0304	03		0	30	0
	2212	2231		AC	07			25	
	2231	2244		AC	41			19	
	2244	2245						21	
	2245	2255						23	
	2255	2308						25	
	2308	2317		CL	02			105	
	2317	2325		0304	02			20	

Form 9 (Rev. 5-71) DATA PROCESSING DIVISION

Figure 16-7. *Computer operations log.*

between computer and operator may occur from the computer to the operator or from the operator to the computer via commands issued by the operator at the printer keyboard.

Even though a console might technically be classed with the input-output devices to be discussed in the next section, it has been covered separately because of its special relationship to the whole EDP system.

OPERATION OF INPUT-OUTPUT UNITS

Card Readers and Punches

Card readers and punches may be either separate or combined machines. They all require operator attention. That is, the operator must place cards in the hopper where the machine may pick, feed, and read one card at a time. Further, when the stacker becomes full, the operator must remove the cards that were placed there after being read. Some card readers have a file feed device capable of holding up to 3,000 cards at a time. However, many card readers and punches have hoppers that can hold only about 1,000 cards at a time.

Most card readers and punches provide easy access to a jammed card in the hopper or transport mechanism. The operator need only remove or dismantle certain parts to gain access to the one or more cards fouled in the feed mechanism. After removal of the fouled cards, the removed transport parts are replaced, the damaged cards are made over and inserted in their proper place, and the job is restarted at the point of interruption. The majority of card readers and punches provide for restarting at the point of failure rather than requiring that the job be started over at the beginning. At the end of a job, the operator may have to run out the last one or two cards inside the unit by depressing the appropriate key. Many card readers and punches have an end-of-file button that may be depressed after the last cards have been placed in the hopper or file feed.

Magnetic Tape Units

The various makes and types of magnetic tape units are similar in general appearance and operation. They differ primarily in the speed at which the tape is moved past the read-write heads, and in the quantity of data recorded on an inch of tape (Figure 16–8).

Various keys and switches are used to open and close the head assembly, to position the tape for reading or writing the first record, and to rewind the tape onto the file reel for unloading.

Most magnetic tape drives have a fixed three-character device address. The first character refers to the input-output channel, and the second and third characters identify the specific tape drive. This device addressing technique and a standard set of symbolic names used by the programmers allow a symbolic name to be assigned to, or identified with, any available magnetic tape drive.

Tape unit heads write and erase information by magnetizing extremely small areas on the tape. Because of the speed at which tape moves past the heads and because of the small size of these areas, magnetic tape

Figure 16-8. *Magnetic tape units.*
(Courtesy International Business Machines Corporation.)

requires careful handling to protect it from foreign particles, nicks, and kinks.

Disk Storage Units

The magnetic disk storage units produced by different manufacturers are similar in general appearance and operation. They differ primarily in the quantity of data recorded (density) and the speed at which data may be transferred to or from primary storage. Magnetic disk storage units are generally referred to as direct access storage devices (DASD).

On some of the newer magnetic disk storage units the disk pack may be removed only by a manufacturer's service representative. The devices that have disk packs removable by the operator have switches to open and close the units for disk pack placement or removal.

Disk unit heads float very close to the spinning surface of the disk pack and write or erase data by magnetizing extremely small areas on the disk surfaces. Consequently, careful disk pack handling procedures are required to assure that no dirt or dust is allowed to enter the opened disk storage units. Even a particle of smoke may be large enough to cause damage to the disk pack and read-write head.

Most magnetic disk storage units have controls that enable the operator to change device addresses and to activate or deactivate the units.

Magnetic Character Readers

Magnetic character readers operate in three basic modes: (1) reader off-line, (2) reader on-line, and (3) central processing unit on-line. In the off-line mode, document feeding, reading, and sorting are controlled by the keys on the operator's panel of the magnetic character reader. In the on-line mode, the central processing unit controls document feeding and reading, while document distribution remains under the sorter operator's control. In the CPU on-line mode, document feeding, reading, and distribution are all under control of the stored program.

Magnetic character readers handle intermixed card and paper documents. Except for the document-feeding methods and the advanced technique used to read and recognize characters, the operating principles closely parallel those of conventional punched card sorters.

Printers

Most impact printers have knobs, dials, or switches that enable manual adjustment of vertical and lateral print alignment, print density, continuous forms feeding, and starting point alignments. Normal spacing during printing is in increments of six lines or eight lines an inch. This adjustment is controlled by a knob located on the printer or tractor feed device. Line spacing can be either single, double, or triple and is under control of the program.

Any movement of paper other than normal spacing is controlled by a paper or plastic tape with its two ends attached in the form of a belt. The tape with the proper punched holes for control of the form must be installed on the printer before the job can be started. The tape moves around the tape read mechanism in unison with the feeding of the continuous form. The punched holes in the tape, under program control, cause the tape and form to skip or stop skipping as instructed in the program. Some impact printers utilize a form control buffer capable of storing an image of a carriage control tape. This capability replaces the carriage tape and provides forms spacing and skipping control by a stored program.

All forms are moved past the print area by a forms tractor with pins that fit into marginally punched holes in the form. Forms are started into the printer by the operator, and when the printer has run out of paper, another stack of forms can be started with a minimum of effort and delay. Printers also provide controls for forms feeding and stacking. Most printers are designed so that the operator can change the inked ribbon when it needs replacing (Figure 16–9).

THE OPERATOR'S DUTIES

To operate a computer system the operator must be knowledgeable in three areas:

1. The mechanical details of each component or unit. He or she must know how to load a reel of tape on a tape unit, how to load a disk pack into the disk unit, how to load blank forms into the line printer, and how to operate any of the other auxiliary units. These tasks are basic and easily learned. After the operator has performed such tasks once or twice, he can perform them without difficulty.

2. The particular job being run on the computer. Information concerning the nature of each program and what is required of the operator is supplied in the operating procedures.

3. Computer manufacturer supplied programs. The operator must know how to use compiler programs, utility programs, and control programs. The control program and the associated processing programs supplied by the vendor are commonly called a programming system. If the programming system has the ability to monitor the relatively uninterrupted execution of a number of programs, it is called an *operating* or *executive system,* which will be discussed in the following section.

Figure 16-9. *High-speed impact printer.*
(Courtesy International Business Machines Corporation.)

EDP OPERATING SYSTEMS

During the past few years the trend in computer systems has been toward higher speeds, increased storage, and greater computing capability. These improvements in equipment capabilities and their associated costs have created a great deal of interest in the efficiency with which systems are operated.

In many computer installations idle processing time may run as high as 65 per cent of the total available time. The input-output devices and associated control units often are utilized only 5 to 30 per cent of the time. These percentages of utilization should make it obvious that the processing speed for which the user is paying will seldom be properly exploited without some sort of internally stored master control program. Such a program is more commonly known as an *operating* or *executive system*.

The operating system is designed to control the processing of various jobs individually or concurrently. An operating system is basically a program that supervises the running of other programs. It includes such programming aids as program compilers, program testers, an input-output control system, a report program generator, a generalized sort-merge program, and various utility programs. In general, the operating system integrates these various types of programs into a single consistent system.

The primary purpose of operating systems is to reduce the cost of running programs by increasing the utilization of the various computer components and by avoiding lost time. The main sources of lost time that all operating systems are designed to reduce are:

1. Job changing and the mounting and removal of files. This source of lost time is especially apparent when the setup time exceeds the processing time required by a small job.
2. Operator intervention to analyze error conditions and to initiate corrective action. If the operator is required to determine the cause of an error by consulting either the operator's manual or the programmer and then to initiate corrective action, this is certain to result in lost computer time.
3. Operator intervention required in the processing of service routines such as tape-handling, program selection, and data or program correction routines.
4. Imbalance between the time required for central processor and input-output functions.

Some of the secondary objectives of an operating system are:

1. Increased programmer productivity
2. Adaptability of programs to changing system components

3. Expandability of the functional capabilities of the operating system to meet changing circumstances
4. Improved response times that will more readily meet real-time requirements

Operating System Functions

Through the use of operating systems part of the burden of improved electronic data processing efficiency is delegated to the computer itself. For an operating system to achieve the high efficiencies that present-day electronic data processing systems are capable of, it should:

1. Provide for efficient utilization of the processing unit as well as all input-output devices on the system. The operating system accomplishes this by scheduling jobs in such a way that their input-output and processing time requirements are balanced, thus reducing idle processing unit time.
2. Provide for the automatic scheduling and loading of programs into primary storage.
3. Provide for the processing of jobs in the input job file, in accordance with control card instructions, by (a) scheduling jobs, (b) overlapping jobs requiring operator action with jobs requiring no operator action, and (c) issuing messages to the operator.
4. Provide for the queuing and dispatching of input-output results.
5. Provide for the receiving, processing, and dispatching of remote messages.
6. Provide a means of exercising control after a program is interrupted, saving the status of the interrupted program, and determining the routine required to process the interrupt condition.
7. Include, as part of itself, standard error-handling procedures, thus assuring that operator intervention is kept to a minimum. It should also include a method whereby programs that require long processing times need not be restarted from the beginning when an error occurs, but only from a previous checkpoint. This allows programs with errors to be interrupted and saved until the error condition is corrected. Other programs can then be processed pending continuance of the interrupted program.
8. Furnish a record (log) of what happened during processing for all programs and the time required for each job.
9. Include the ability to generate and maintain an operating system that meets the requirements of a particular installation. For example, if certain segments of the operating system have not been used recently, it will cause them to be stored in more remote areas, thereby making that prime storage area available for more useful routines.
10. Provide a program tester that enables a program or part of a program to be loaded and tested in accordance with simple and concise specifications. The specifications are comprised of symbols and definitions appearing in the original source program.

11. Provide an interruption-handling program that coordinates transfer of control between programs after an interruption. The five types of interruption that must be covered are input-output, external, program, machine, and those that are required by the operating system. The interruptions should aid the operating system in optimizing use of all the peripheral equipment as well as the processing unit. A comprehensive interrupt system allows several programs to share memory at the same time. Idle processing unit time is reduced to a minimum, and input-output operations for several jobs can be processed simultaneously while processing of another job is taking place.

Programs that are to be used with an operating system may be written without regard to absolute memory locations and physical input-output units. Thus, should the user add any peripheral equipment to his system, the operating system adjusts to the change automatically. This provides maximum benefits from the increased input-output capacity without necessitating any change in the program.

The Operating System in Operation

The operating system is actually a composite of many programs that can be united in a variety of combinations. Therefore, before the operating system is ready for operation, it must be tailored to the requirements of the installation and the jobs to be performed. This tailoring of the operating system is achieved by a segment of the system generally referred to as a *system librarian*. The system librarian also has the ability to modify, add, delete, and replace programs in the system to reflect changes in the installation's input-output equipment and storage size, the user's objectives, and other needs.

Once the operating system is generated and stored in the computer, it is ready for operation. The sequence of events required to compile and execute a typical job might be:

1. Clear the computer for the next job to be processed.
2. Read control cards and make input-output and scratch (working) tape assignments.
3. Load the program compiler into primary storage.
4. Process the source program, generate the object program, store the object program in the system library maintained in auxiliary storage, and transfer the object program from the system library to primary storage for execution. This is an exception to the procedure of recording the object program in an external storage medium such as punched cards or magnetic tape.
5. Pass control to the object program, which reads data, performs the necessary processing, and produces output.
6. Return control to the operating system when processing of the object program is completed.

This is a "job-at-a-time" or one-phase illustration. A similar cycle would be entered for the next job to be processed.

Another concept is the three-phase system. As almost all computer programs involve three functions, input data reading, computation or processing, and output result writing, it is logical for the operating system to handle each job in three separate phases. During phase one, input data is converted if necessary—decimal to binary, for example. Conversion requirements are specified by control cards or control codes in the data cards. Also, program translation may take place during phase one.

During phase two the programs go into execution, and the results are recorded on a medium such as magnetic tape or disk in a language basic to the computer.

During phase three the output results recorded during phase two may be converted for printing or punching. Also, debugging (error identification) data may be converted to symbolic formats to facilitate analysis by the programmer.

Other operating system features, in addition to the ability to execute programs in any of the three phases, include tape error recovery procedures, data input-output channel supervision, and standard or special handling of automatic computer branches (called traps) and error conditions. All of these utilize overlap features of the computer without detailed concern by the programmer. In short, the operating system enables the stacking and overlapping of jobs and computer functions.

Multiprogramming with the Operating System

Multiprogramming is the technique whereby more than one program can reside in primary storage at the same time and be executed concurrently. Although only one program can be executed at a time, the supervisor program rapidly switches control between the programs and gives the effect of simultaneous operation. For example, one program might be processing a batch job, another program might be performing a utility function, and a third program might be handling a remote terminal operation. The supervisor program would monitor the concurrent processing of these three programs so that the utility program would be executed with minimal interruption to the processing of the batch program, and the remote terminal program would be executed on request by the terminal operator.

To accomplish this interweaving of programs, the control program and equipment must be capable of recognizing the point at which a program being executed must wait for the completion of some auxiliary processing phase. At that point, the control program begins another processing task that is ready for execution. When that is done, the control program must be able to proceed to another task or return to the previous unfinished program, if it is ready to continue. Since several programs may be in stages of partial completion, multiprogramming usually requires that levels of priority be specified for different tasks.

The efficient operation of most organizations depends on a consistent flow of a wide variety of timely information. For effective decision-making the right kind of information must be at the right place, in the right form, and at the right time. To speed the information flow and reduce the data-to-decision time to a minimum in a large organization, an efficient remote message processing network is necessary.

Remote message processing is, in effect, an extension of the full power of the data processing and programming facilities of the operating system to remote locations. By extending the services of the operating system directly to the user of a remote terminal, the turn-around or response time of the system is reduced to seconds. Consequently, the system can directly control and participate in activities taking place in various parts of an organization. Remote message processing has the additional advantage of enabling centralized records to be updated instantaneously as transactions occur at different locations.

The operating system has the ability to process messages received from remote locations by means of communication lines and special equipment. Processing of remote messages differs from other types of data processing mainly in the way in which information enters and leaves the computer. Messages from remote locations enter the system in random order at unpredictable intervals and often demand a response within a few seconds. This ability to receive and process data so rapidly that the results are available in time to influence operations that are still in progress is commonly called *real-time* data processing.

The EDP system may be engaged in performing other functions when a remote message is received. Therefore, some means must be provided for interrupting the program in operation to allow the receipt and processing of the remote message and the dispatch of a return message, if necessary. As indicated before, the interrupt procedure and control of the interrupted program are functions of the operating system. The operating system will on command:

1. Interrupt the job in process provided it has a lower priority than that of the request
2. Cause the interrupted program and its restart point to be temporarily stored outside of the main memory in an auxiliary storage
3. Cause the proper program for handling the interrupt request to be loaded into main memory
4. Process the requirements of the request
5. Return the interrupted program to main memory
6. Restart the program at its point of interruption

All of this process, known as *roll-out* and *roll-in,* could take place in less than a second. If the above tasks were performed under the control of a virtual operating system, the roll-out and roll-in actions would probably not be required because of the much greater virtual storage capacity available.

**VIRTUAL STORAGE
OPERATING SYSTEM**

Virtual storage is a concept by which primary storage capacity is increased beyond that available in the computer by storing segments of programs and data in auxiliary devices. The program segments and data are brought into primary storage under control of the virtual operating system as they are needed for execution by the computer. In this way a virtual storage operating system simulates a primary storage space much larger than the primary storage capacity of the computer with which the system is used. For example, a virtual storage system may have 16 million bytes of virtual storage and operate very effectively on a computer with 4 million positions of primary storage. This is accomplished by transferring into primary storage only the program segments, called pages, that are actually being used at any given time. Thus, primary storage is dynamically shared and managed by the virtual storage operating system.

The primary advantages of virtual storage operating systems are:

1. Programs can be written without regard for the amount of primary storage space available.
2. Virtual storage operating systems allow a given size computer to run a greater number of programs concurrently and thereby effectively increase use of the CPU and the amount of work performed.
3. They make scheduling and operating a computer easier.

**EDP OPERATIONS
ORGANIZATION**

Effective operation of a computer facility is dependent upon a good organization and staff. Obviously the type of organization and number of positions will be related to the size and complexity of the computer facility, which, in turn, reflects the nature and extent of services that must be performed.

A typical EDP organization is shown in Figure 16–10. A brief description of the duties and responsibilities assigned to operations positions shown in the chart will give an understanding of the variety of knowledge and skills required for the successful operation of a medium-size computer facility.

Excluded from the following descriptions are the duties and responsibilities of a systems analyst, which will be covered in Chapter 17, and the duties and responsibilities of a computer programmer, which were discussed in Chapter 12.

Job Descriptions

Manager of Computer Operations. Plans, organizes, and controls the computer operations and related activities. Reviews new systems and computer programs, and projects their effect on equipment operation. Reports to the manager of data processing.

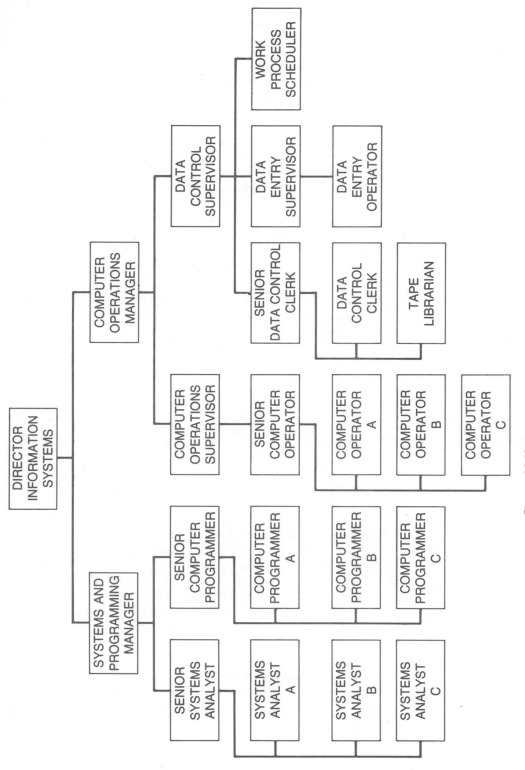

Figure 16-10. *Positions in a typical EDP organization.*

Responsibilities:
Provides technical advice in equipment evaluation, selection, and installation
Evaluates personnel performance
Participates in selection of operations personnel
Maintains accurate records on equipment utilization
Maintains good customer (user) relations

Computer Operations Supervisor.   Supervises the operation of computer equipment. Assigns and instructions operations personnel.

Responsibilities:
Meets scheduled processing requirements
Evaluates personnel performance
Controls integrity of all data files
Implements operations procedures and techniques to improve efficiency of operation
Participates in selection of operations personnel

Computer Operator.   Studies operating procedures, consults with technical staff when necessary. May supervise subordinate operators if more than one operator is required.

Responsibilities:
Prepares computer for operation as required
Operates the computer console and peripheral equipment
Loads programs and processes data in accordance with operating procedures
Controls computer operations and takes corrective action as defined in operating procedures
Verifies that reports and other outputs are complete
Records time and equipment use
Notifies supervisor of equipment malfunction
Maintains a neat and orderly equipment area

Data Control Supervisor.   Plans, schedules, and supervises the data control activities. Performs a quality control function for input and output.

Responsibilities:
Reviews input and determines its acceptability
Maintains control of input received
Reviews quality of output
Insures that all steps of processing are completed
Dispatches acceptable material to users
Notifies affected users of delays in schedule or inadequacies of input
Participates in selection of data control personnel

Data Control Clerk. Assists in supervising data control activities. Performs a quality control function for input and output and prepares output for distribution.

Responsibilities:
Reviews input and determines its acceptability
Maintains control of input received
Reviews quality of output
Operates forms separator and detacher
Dispatches acceptable material to users

Tape Librarian. Maintains and controls magnetic tape library. Maintains charge-out records. Inspects tape for wear or damage.

Responsibilities:
Provides magnetic tape files to operations in accordance with production schedule
Records circulation of magnetic tape files
Inspects and cleans magnetic tape

Work Process Scheduler. Schedules operating time of the operations activities.

Responsibilities:
Maintains long-range schedule
Prepares daily processing schedule
Negotiates processing commitments
Keeps overall utilization high and idle time to a minimum

Data Entry Supervisor. Supervises all personnel engaged in data entry and verification.

Responsibilities:
Schedules work load
Distributes work assignments
Checks accuracy of work
Evaluates data entry personnel performance
Maintains control of data and source documents

Data Entry Operator. Operates keyboard device to record and verify data.

Responsibilities:
Key records data in accordance with instructions
Maintains sequence and control of source documents
Detects data entry errors and corrects data

The duties and responsibilities described above are fairly typical for these positions. However, as new technologies and operating concepts are implemented, the duties and responsibilities of EDP operations personnel may change.

IMPORTANT WORDS AND PHRASES

batch	bursting	real-time data processing
control	operating system	virtual storage operating
total	multiprogramming	system

REVIEW QUESTIONS

1. What is the function of batch tickets?
2. What are the functions of forms separators and forms detachers?
3. Briefly describe one method for successful scheduling.
4. What is the principal responsibility of the console operator?
5. What is the primary use of the information recorded on the computer operations log?
6. Why does magnetic tape require careful handling?
7. What is an operating system?
8. How do operating systems improve data processing efficiency?
9. What is the function of the operating system librarian?
10. What is multiprogramming?
11. Define the term "real-time data processing."
12. What are the advantages of a virtual storage operating system?

17

SYSTEMS STUDY AND DESIGN: TOOLS AND TECHNIQUES

In Chapter 1 some of the problems that created the need for more efficient data processing techniques were discussed. Subsequent chapters were devoted to the various methods that have been devised to solve these problems. Regardless of the methods employed, however, the benefits derived from a data processing system are primarily dependent on the effectiveness of the system.

This chapter and the next one will introduce the techniques that are used in the study and design of a business system, which may be defined as a combination of personnel, equipment, and other facilities operating under a set of procedures designed to accomplish the objectives of an organization. Although the discussion in these chapters is related mainly to business systems, it should be noted that the techniques are generally applicable to systems development in any type of organization, regardless of differences in objectives.

EVOLUTION OF BUSINESS SYSTEMS

Today's business systems are based upon principles that originated during the Industrial Revolution. Many of the operating concepts, such as assembly lines, were first perfected in the factory and have since been employed in the office. The industrial engineering work in factories that provided the basis for industrial automation was paralleled by the application of similar techniques leading to the automation of office activities.

Five stages of advancement are apparent in the development of business systems. The first stage consisted of the simplification of manual operations through the use of techniques known as work simplification. The second stage was that of mechanization, which facilitated the combination of two or more functions in one operation. For example, the addition of tape mechanisms to adding machines and cash registers gave them the ability to record and summarize as well as to calculate.

Punched card equipment, which represented the third stage, introduced compatibility of machines that could perform a variety of functions through the use of standard punched cards.

In the fourth stage, integrated data processing extended the principle of compatibility to a wide range of equipment. Integrated data processing techniques made it possible for typewriters, accounting machines, addressing machines, and other equipment to be used with each other and with punched card equipment.

In the fifth stage of development, electronic computers enhanced the integrated data processing concept by providing the means of processing vast amounts of data at far greater speeds.

As these new and improved techniques developed, there was a tendency to apply them on a piecemeal basis as substitutes for the older methods of performing specific operations. Since the older methods were generally manual, the use of equipment was often restricted by systems concepts based on the capacity of humans. Thus, the greater versatility and capacity of the new equipment were not fully exploited.

The increased use of computers under the integrated data processing concept led to the realization that in some cases the new techniques were not being employed to the greatest advantage and that the decision-making ability of the computer could be put to far greater use. Out of this came the idea of regarding the entire business system as a unified entity that should be designed to take full advantage of equipment capabilities and new information processing techniques as a better means of attaining business goals.

Under this approach the business system is viewed as a whole rather than as an organization composed of individual operations. This is the *total systems concept,* which is the underlying principle of systems work today.

THE SYSTEMS ANALYST

As business systems requirements developed during the first half of the twentieth century, the office manager, controller, or accountant was responsible for the design and installation of new systems and procedures. During the 1950s the use of analytic methods for solving operational problems was developed. These techniques, called *operations research,* originated in Great Britain during World War II. After the war, leaders in business, industry, and government modified and applied operations research methods to solving other problems.

The persons applying these techniques to business systems became known as *methods engineers.* During the 1950s it was customary to have methods engineers design, or oversee the design of new business systems. To do this competently the operations research departments had to employ data processing technicians and accountants as advisors. As a result it was common practice to form committees of several persons, each an expert in his field, and assign a project to this group for study. The ability of a committee to function efficiently in a creative endeavor such as this was often restricted. Many times the strongest rather than the ablest personality dominated the group, making the measuring of performance and planning of a work program difficult.

The managers of data processing departments thought that they also should have a voice in the design of new systems, since they were responsible for making the systems work. Out of this developed a new profession originally titled *systems and procedures analyst,* and now more frequently called *systems analyst.* The systems analyst may be assigned to a separate department responsible to either the controller, methods engineer, or administrative manager. However, as experience has shown, when systems analysts are under the control of a data processing manager reporting to the executive level, the systems installed usually meet more of the objectives of a good business system.

The systems analyst is ordinarily the key figure in the systems program. This does not mean that he or she carries out the program alone. He is, however, a specialist who generally has the full-time responsibility for carrying out the continuing program of improvement. To succeed in this endeavor, he should enjoy working with people. He must be enthusiastic about his work and be recognized as an authority who can understand and improve the situation. He should have a basic curiosity, along with the innate ability to think beyond the immediate, to challenge precedent, and to create something new. He must be able to consider a problem without injecting personalities, emotions, or prejudices. He must be familiar with the organization and the philosophy of its management. He must be good in the communicative arts. That is, he must be capable of making clear and concise statements that cannot be misinterpreted. Finally, the systems analyst must have an understanding of human nature and the ability to deal with people on all levels, as the best designed system will never be a success without the understanding and cooperation of those concerned with its operation.

Before considering the actual conduct of systems study and design, let us first outline the major tools and techniques used to assist in analyzing and interpreting existing conditions and new design proposals.

SYSTEMS STUDY AIDS

Organization Charts

The main value of the organization chart to the analyst is to show who is responsible to whom, and who has what personnel resources at his disposal. When a current organization chart is not available, the systems analyst should prepare one.

The formal organization chart should clearly show lines of responsibility. Solid lines on the chart indicate lines of authority, and broken lines may be used to show advisory contact. Preferably, each box on the chart should have only one line entering it; otherwise the chart conveys more than one line of authority, which is a sign of poor management. Names may appear on the chart or be omitted, but if they are included the chart will require more frequent change than if only titles are used. A typical chart of a line-and-staff organization is shown in Figure 17–1.

Flowcharts

To study and plan the use of data processing equipment, it is necessary to employ some method of depicting the flow of data through a system and the sequence of operations performed. Because of the many interrelating elements, pictorial descriptions of systems are generally

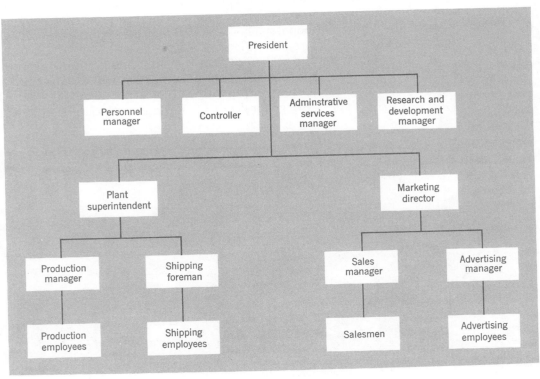

Figure 17-1. *Chart of a line-and-staff organization.*

better than narrative descriptions. Thus, flowcharts are used to outline the flow of data and operations so that they are easy to visualize and follow. Flowcharts are as essential to a systems analyst as blueprints are to an architect.

To promote uniformity in the meaning and use of specific symbols, the International Organization for Standardization (ISO) has established standard flowchart symbols for information processing. These symbols are consistent with the fewer symbols adopted by the American National Standards Institute (ANSI). The flowchart symbols used throughout this text conform with the ISO standards.

Plastic flowchart templates are available from the major equipment manufacturers and many of the business forms printing companies. These templates are used as a guide in drawing symbols. Figure 17–2 shows one such template that contains all of the ISO symbols.

Some equipment manufacturers provide a few symbols in addition to the recommended ISO symbols. For example, the IBM template has three more symbols than the Standard Register template shown in the preceding illustration.

The four basic flowchart symbols are shown in Figure 17–3. These symbols are used in all types of flowcharts, as data input, processing, and output functions are common to all data processing systems.

Three additional symbols are used to make flowcharts easier to follow. They are illustrated in Figure 17–4.

The general direction of flow is from top to bottom and from left to right. Only flow opposed to the general direction must be clarified with arrowheads. Otherwise, arrowheads are not normally used. Figure 17–5 depicts the general use of flowlines and arrowheads. Note that

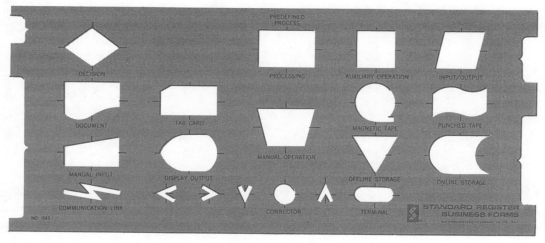

Figure 17-2. *Flowchart template. (Courtesy The Standard Register Company.)*

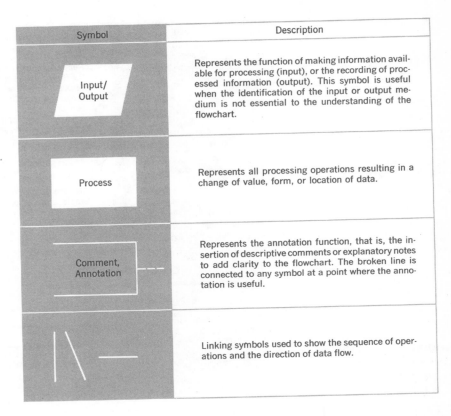

Symbol	Description
Input/ Output	Represents the function of making information available for processing (input), or the recording of processed information (output). This symbol is useful when the identification of the input or output medium is not essential to the understanding of the flowchart.
Process	Represents all processing operations resulting in a change of value, form, or location of data.
Comment, Annotation	Represents the annotation function, that is, the insertion of descriptive comments or explanatory notes to add clarity to the flowchart. The broken line is connected to any symbol at a point where the annotation is useful.
	Linking symbols used to show the sequence of operations and the direction of data flow.

Figure 17-3. *Basic flowchart symbols.*

two or more unrelated flowlines may cross, meaning that they have no logical interrelation, or that two or more related lines may join and enter a common flowline.

Flowcharts are used for various purposes including the illustration of computer programs, discussed in preceding chapters. In this chapter we are primarily concerned with the *systems flowchart,* which represents the broadest approach.

The systems flowchart is a very good tool for showing the total picture of a business system, and can be most helpful while studying the present system or designing a new one. The system flowchart illustrates in a general manner the flow of data and operations. The details are outlined on supplementary documents and are referenced by a numeric or alphabetic code. The system flowchart can be used to depict manual, mechanical, or computer operations or any mixture of these. However, emphasis is usually given to the flow of data throughout the system and the general sequence of operations rather than to how the operations are performed.

A payroll application has been selected to illustrate the use of the three basic symbols in preparing a systems flowchart. The problem is one of automating a portion of an organization's payroll function. The flow-

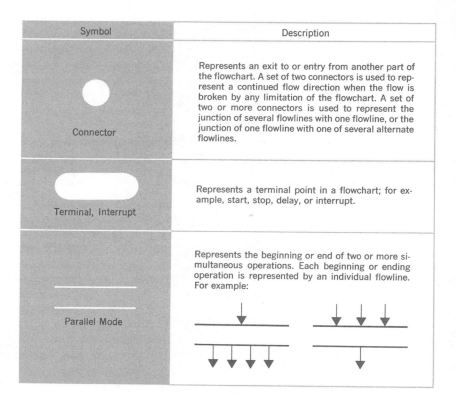

Symbol	Description
Connector	Represents an exit to or entry from another part of the flowchart. A set of two connectors is used to represent a continued flow direction when the flow is broken by any limitation of the flowchart. A set of two or more connectors is used to represent the junction of several flowlines with one flowline, or the junction of one flowline with one of several alternate flowlines.
Terminal, Interrupt	Represents a terminal point in a flowchart; for example, start, stop, delay, or interrupt.
Parallel Mode	Represents the beginning or end of two or more simultaneous operations. Each beginning or ending operation is represented by an individual flowline. For example:

Figure 17-4. *Additional symbols used to make flowcharts easier to follow.*

| Top to bottom | Left to right | Right to left | Bottom to top | No logical interrelation | Logical union |

Figure 17-5. *General use of flowlines and arrowheads.*

chart of this application shown in Figure 17–6 is typical of those used to graphically illustrate data flow in an existing system or in a system being designed. It may be described as being at the macro level; that is, it stresses the flow of data with minimum regard for the details of the operations involved.

The following explanation outlines the available facts about the problem and includes references to related process symbols on the flowchart:

Payroll master data is recorded in a magnetic tape file containing employee name, employee number, department number, salary rate, tax class, year-to-date gross earnings, year-to-date federal withholding tax, year-to-date FICA (social security deductions), and current gross pay.

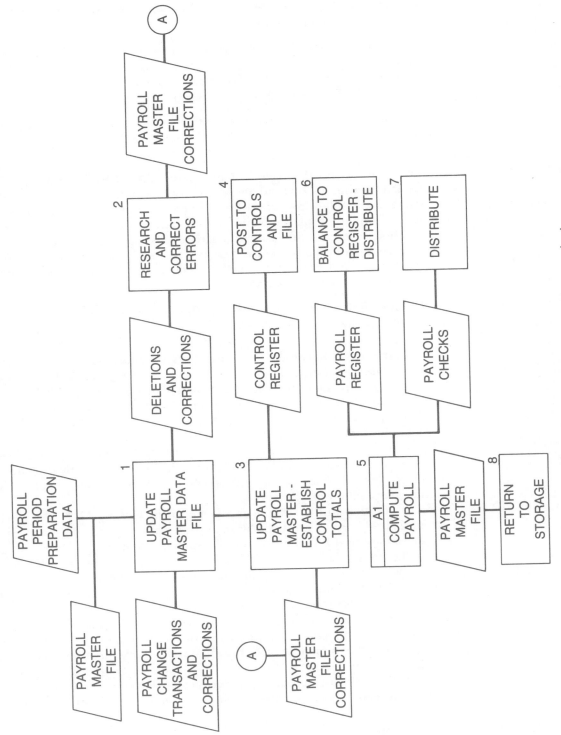

Figure 17-6. Systems flowchart at the macro level.

Payroll change transactions and corrections data are recorded in a punched card transaction file.

Each pay period the payroll master data file requires updating by applying the current change transactions. Errors detected during this application are researched and corrected. The corrections are re-entered into the file (Figure 17–6, steps 1 and 2).

Each pay period the payroll master file is updated by applying the corrected transactions from the previous step, the file is audited, and a control register is prepared (Figure 17–6, steps 3 and 4).

Each pay period the payroll master data file is used to compute the period payroll. At this time the payroll register is prepared. The register contains the following items of information: employee number, department number, employee name, year-to-date gross, year-to-date federal withholding, year-to-date FICA, current gross pay, and net pay. The information from the register is balanced to the previously prepared control ledger. At the same time payroll checks are prepared for distribution (Figure 17–6, steps 5, 6, and 7).

Upon completion of the processing, the payroll master file is returned to storage (Figure 17–6, step 8).

As previously illustrated in Figure 12–2, the process symbol described as *compute payroll* and identified as A1 in Figure 17–6 includes a stripe across the top. This characteristic indicates that a more detailed representation of this function is to be found elsewhere in the same set of flowcharts. The identification between the stripe and the top of the symbol refers to the related micro level flowchart. The supplementary flowchart, Figure 17–7, starts with a terminal symbol containing the same identification number and ends with a blank terminal symbol. Thus, this flowchart outlines explicitly the steps that are involved in the computation of payroll.

In addition to the seven symbols shown in Figures 17–3 and 17–4, specialized symbols are available to illustrate more specifically the media, operations, and functions involved in processing data.

The 14 symbols in Figure 17–8 are specialized input-output (I/O) symbols that may be used when it is desirable to identify the medium on which the data is recorded or the manner of handling the data, or both. They also represent the I/O function effectively. For example, the punched card I/O symbol, which may be used to represent either the reading of a punched card (input) or the punching of a card (output), illustrates the punched card I/O operation more precisely than the parallelogram.

Any of the nine specialized process symbols in Figure 17–9 may be used instead of the basic process symbol whenever it is desirable to iden-

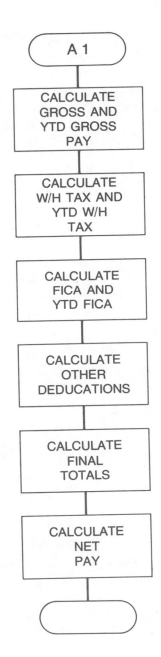

Figure 17-7. *Systems flow-chart at the micro level.*

tify more specifically the type of operation performed. For example, the decision symbol represents a decision or switching-type operation that determines which of a number of alternative paths is to be followed. The shape of the decision symbol is readily associated with the decision operation.

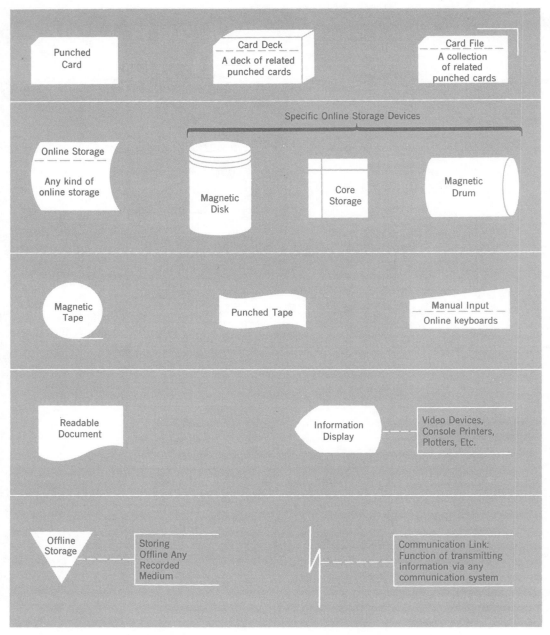

Figure 17-8. *Specialized input-output flowcharting symbols.*

Symbol	Description
Decision	A decision or switching-type operation that determines which of a number of alternative paths is to be followed.
Predefined Process	One or more named operations or program steps specified in a subroutine or another set of flowcharts.
Preparation	Modification of an instruction or a group of instructions that changes the program itself; for example, set a switch, modify an index register, or initialize a routine.
Manual Operation Offline Process	Any offline process geared to the speed of a human being, without using mechanical aid.
Auxiliary Operation	Offline performance on equipment not under direct control of the central processing unit.
Merge	Combining two or more sets of items into one set.
Extract	Removal of one or more specific items from a set.
Sort	Arranging a set of items into ascending or descending sequence.
Collate	Merging and extracting; forming two or more sets of items from two or more other sets.

Figure 17-9. *Specialized process flowcharting symbols.*

Computer programs are flowcharted with three of these symbols—the decision, preparation, and predefined process—along with the seven symbols illustrated in Figures 17–3 and 17–4. A discussion of the use of programming flowchart symbols appears in Chapter 12.

All data processing systems utilizing any of the methods—manual, mechanical, punched card, and computer—can be flowcharted with the four basic symbols. However, these symbols may be supplemented by specialized symbols in systems and procedures flowcharts when they make the flowchart easier to understand. For example, many of the specialized I/O symbols are used in drawing punched card procedure flowcharts.

Figure 17–10 demonstrates the use of various symbols and flowcharting techniques in a more detailed type of systems flowchart depicting an inventory application. It should be noted that the flow of the system is in the same general direction—top to bottom—and that arrowheads are used only when needed to keep the flow clear.

The following general principles should be applied when drawing a flowchart:

1. An effort should be made to anticipate the readers' problems in understanding the chart.
2. The main line of the flowchart should be easily recognizable.
3. There should be no attempt to chart every detail.

HIPO

In addition to the conventional flowcharting techniques described above, an alternate means of developing and documenting system specifications is available. This is the method known as *HIPO,* which is an acronym for *Heirarchy* plus *Input, Process,* and *Output.*

The development of an effective data processing system requires a precise definition of user requirements, usually called *specifications.* The conventional method of developing specifications is for the user to prepare a written list of all requirements, usually with assistance from a systems analyst. This may include a description of what the system is to accomplish, and details of requirements for input, output, stored data, logical processing, control, testing, performance, and documentation. These completed specifications are transformed by a systems analyst into system design and programming specifications, which are given to programmers for implementation and coding.

HIPO provides an alternate means of documenting user specifications in a format that facilitates completeness and correctness. It accomplishes this by its graphical representation of functions, its organized grouping of increasing detail, and the illustration of input and output of data items at each level.

A HIPO package is composed of a set of diagrams designed to graphically describe functions from the general level to the detail level. Each

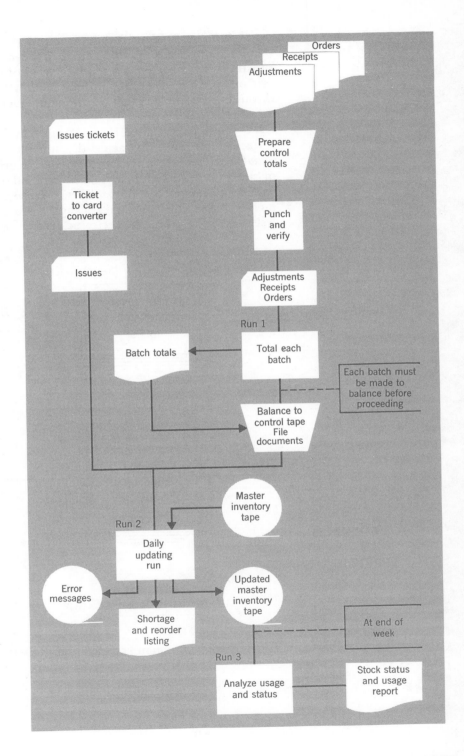

Figure 17-10. *System flowchart of an inventory application.*

major function is identified and then subdivided into lower-level functions. Computer programs can then be developed starting with the functions described in the topmost level of diagrams. HIPO diagrams can provide the necessary documentation from the start of a project through final implementation and subsequent maintenance.

HIPO Packages. Each HIPO package may, in the overall scheme, have a distinct purpose, characteristic, and audience (Figure 17–11). The *initial design package* is prepared by a design group at the start of a project or study. It describes the overall functional design of the project and is used as a design aid. The *detail design package* is prepared by a development group using the initial package as a base. In this package the analysts and programmers specify in greater detail the functional design

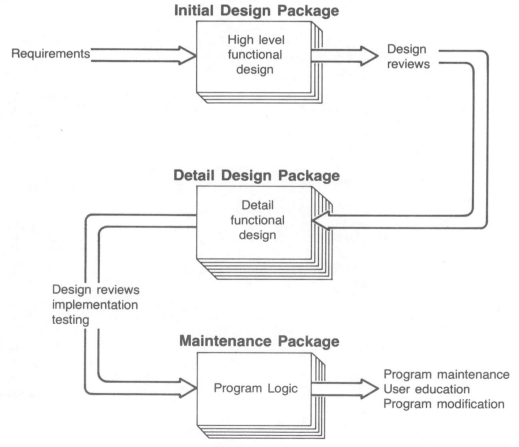

Figure 17-11. *Scheme showing the three kinds of HIPO packages.*
(Adapted by permission from International Business Machines Corporation.)

of the solution. The *maintenance package* is used to make corrections, changes, and additions to the systems solution.

HIPO Diagrams. In addition to the standard flowchart symbols shown in Figure 17–2, specialized HIPO symbols, Figure 17–12, are designed as an aid in drawing HIPO diagrams.

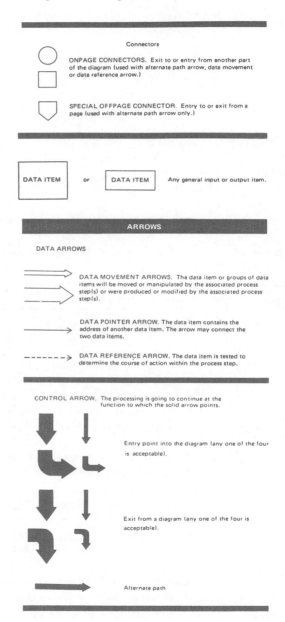

Figure 17-12. *Specialized HIPO symbols.*

(Adapted by permission from International Business Machines Corporation.)

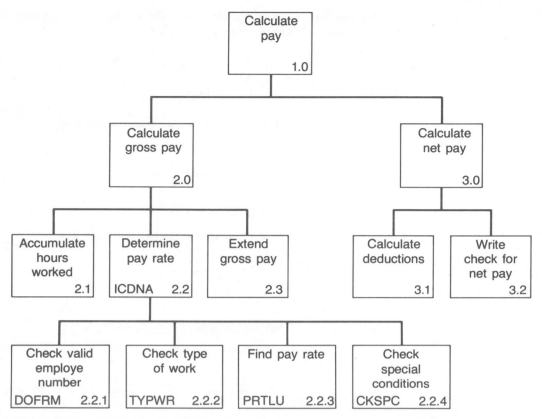

Figure 17-13. *HIPO visual table of contents. (Adapted by permission from International Business Machines Corporation.)*

A HIPO package contains three kinds of diagrams: visual table of contents, overview, and detail. The *visual table of contents* shows the major functions to be performed by the system and their relationship to each other (Figure 17–13). This is a tree-like structure similar to an organization chart. It is composed of functions or actions. Each function is represented as a box with a description consisting of a verb (action) and an object (data affected). Thus, this format names as well as defines the function to be performed.

The top box in the visual table states the overall function of the system. In the example shown in Figure 17–13 the overall function is *calculate pay.* The next level breaks that function down into logical subfunctions. Each additional level creates a more detailed degree of subfunction. Generally, only four to five levels are necessary in the initial design phase. Each box in the table refers to a diagram whose description and identification numbers are shown in the box. A legend may be added to the table as an aid to indicate the various symbols used and what they mean.

The *overview diagram* provides more general knowledge of the func-

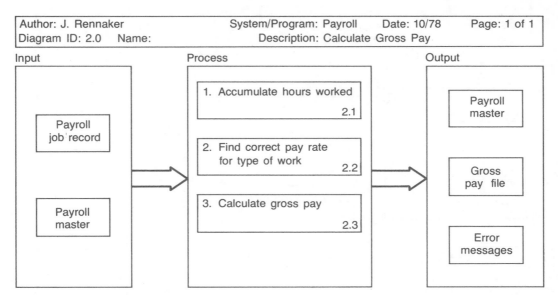

| Author: J. Rennaker | System/Program: Payroll | Date: 10/78 | Page: 1 of 1 |
| Diagram ID: 2.0 Name: | Description: Calculate Gross Pay | | |

Input

Payroll job record

Payroll master

Process

1. Accumulate hours worked
   2.1

2. Find correct pay rate for type of work
   2.2

3. Calculate gross pay
   2.3

Output

Payroll master

Gross pay file

Error messages

Figure 17-14. *HIPO overview diagram. (Adapted by permission from International Business Machines Corporation.)*

tions stated in the visual table of contents (Figure 17–14). The overview diagram introduces a greater degree of detail that must reflect all major input and output items to be included in any lower-level diagrams. While specific input and output devices need not be identified at this level, they may, if known, be noted with appropriate symbols. Note that the process steps in the overview diagram are related to the steps in the visual table by means of descriptive notation and identification numbers in the right-hand corner of each box.

While the overview and detail diagrams are graphically similar, the purpose of the *detail diagram* is to provide the explicit information necessary to fully understand the functions specified (Figure 17–15). As with the overview diagram, the detailed diagram consists of three blocks or boxes: input, process, and output. The major difference is the degree of detail documented. Note in the heading that the description (Determine Pay Rate) and diagram ID (2.2) refer to the process blocks in the overview diagram. In addition to the inputs, processes, and outputs, there is an optional extended description section that can be used to record more details than can be put in a process step. This consists primarily of notes for future implementation.

Although HIPO has a number of advantages as described above, it is apparent that the documentation of all levels of HIPO does require a significant amount of time and effort.

Decision Tables

Another aid in the study and design of systems is the *decision table*. The purpose of a decision table is to provide information concerning prob-

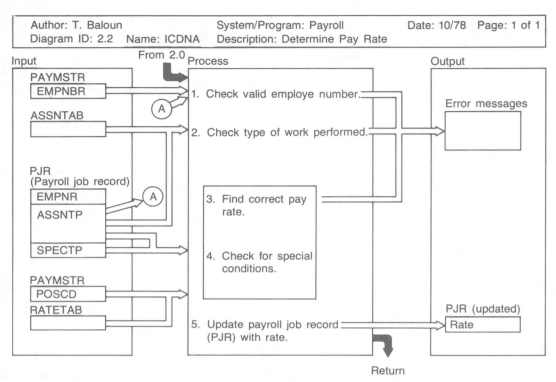

| Author: T. Baloun | System/Program: Payroll | Date: 10/78 Page: 1 of 1 |
| Diagram ID: 2.2 Name: ICDNA | Description: Determine Pay Rate | |

Input

From 2.0 **Process**

PAYMSTR
EMPNBR

ASSNTAB

PJR
(Payroll job record)
EMPNR
ASSNTP

SPECTP

PAYMSTR
POSCD
RATETAB

1. Check valid employe number.

2. Check type of work performed.

3. Find correct pay rate.

4. Check for special conditions.

5. Update payroll job record (PJR) with rate.

Output

Error messages

PJR (updated)
Rate

Return

Figure 17-15. *HIPO detail diagram. (Adapted by permission from International Business Machines Corporation.)*

lems and solutions in a concise format that is easy to read and understand. This tabular approach is used to express complex decision logic in a manner that encourages the analyst to reduce a problem to its simplest form by arranging and presenting logical alternatives under various conditions. Decision tables can be used independently of, or to complement, flowcharts.

A decision table defines all conditions (the prerequisites for an action) and separates them from all actions. Further, it relates given conditions to the appropriate actions. Alternative conditions that result in different actions constitute other rules, which are written side by side.

Figure 17–16 illustrates an airlines reservations decision table. The first rule in this table states: if the request is for first class (condition 1) and first-class space is available (condition 3), then issue a first-class ticket (action 1), and subtract 1 from the first-class seats available (action 3). In rule 2 the request is for first class, but no first-class seats are available. Tourist space is open, and the passenger will accept tourist accommodations. The actions call for the issuance of a tourist ticket and the subtraction of 1 from the number of tourist seats available.

Two characteristics of decision tables are evident in the table shown in Figure 17–16. First, not only is the combination of entries for each

		Rules							
		1	2	3	4	5	6	7	8
Conditions	1 First class request	Y	Y	Y	Y				
	2 Tourist request					Y	Y	Y	Y
	3 First class open	Y	N	N	N		Y	N	
	4 Tourist open		Y	N		Y	N	N	N
	5 Alternate class acceptable		Y	Y	N		Y	Y	N
Actions	1 Issue first class ticket	X					X		
	2 Issue tourist ticket		X			X			
	3 Subtract one from first class avail	X					X		
	4 Subtract one from tourist avail		X			X			
	5 Place on tourist wait list			X				X	X
	6 Place on first class wait list			X	X			X	

Figure 17-16. *Decision table for handling airlines reservations.*

Y = Yes   N = No

rule different from that for all other rules, but also there is no combination of entries that satisfies the conditions of more than one rule. This is a decision table convention. Second, each detail of the decision-making process has been explicitly stated and every condition considered in a direct way. The decision table format clearly shows the relationships between problems and solutions.

IMPORTANT WORDS AND PHRASES

total systems concept
operations research

systems analyst
organization chart
flowchart

system flowchart
HIPO
decision table

REVIEW QUESTIONS

1. What were the five stages of advancement in the development of business systems?
2. Define the total systems concept.
3. What is the primary responsibility of the systems analyst?
4. Why are flowcharts essential to a systems analyst?
5. How is the systems flowchart helpful in the study of an existing system?
6. Describe the four basic symbols used in a systems flowchart.
7. What is the general purpose of a HIPO package?
8. What is the primary purpose of a decision table?

18

SYSTEMS STUDY AND DESIGN: PRINCIPLES

The preceding chapter included descriptions of the major tools used by the analyst to define an existing system or design a new system. In this chapter we will consider the various steps in studying and designing a system.

OBJECTIVES OF SYSTEMS STUDY AND DESIGN

The general objectives of systems study and design are met by developing new procedures or improving existing procedures so as to increase the effectiveness of operations and, if possible, to bring about greater economy.

Systems improvement can meet the objective of increased effectiveness in the following ways:

1. Improving service to customers
2. Improving public relations
3. Improving the quantity, quality, and form of information provided to management
4. Eliminating conflicting or overlapping services

5. Obtaining greater speed and accuracy in the processing of data and the preparation of reports
6. Increasing executive efficiency
7. Improving coordination of various operating units and personnel
8. Obtaining greater operating efficiency by making possible quicker action on management decisions

Greater economy would result from the following accomplishments:

1. Increasing clerical productivity
2. Reducing operating and clerical costs
3. Eliminating unnecessary functions and activities
4. Reducing inventory and other working-capital requirements
5. Effecting maximum utilization of personnel and equipment

The study and design of a system require three major phases. First, it is necessary to acquire an understanding of the present system. Second, the results that are desired from the system must be determined. Finally, equipment must be selected and procedures devised to efficiently attain those results (Figure 18–1).

The success of systems work depends to a great extent on the thoroughness and skill with which these three phases are completed.

PLANNING THE SYSTEMS STUDY

Before beginning the actual systems study, several preliminary steps should be taken. The first step is to define the objectives of the study. Has the development of new techniques or equipment made a change in the system necessary? Is the organization striving for a smoother operation, earlier reports, new reports, better reports, or improved economy of operation?

The next step is to outline the scope of the study. Is the study to include the entire system or be limited to a portion of the system? What people may be affected? Who has to be satisfied? After answering these questions, a time schedule, estimate of the facilities and funds required, and a plan of action can be prepared.

Management of the design, development, and implementation of complex systems projects is aided by such techniques as the Project Control System. PCS is a refinement of the Program Evaluation and Review Technique (PERT), which is a refinement of the Critical Path Method (CPM).

Basically, these are flow diagrams illustrating a series of activities that must be accomplished in order to complete a project, along with the time and resource requirements for each activity.

The activities are arranged in the form of a network showing logical sequences of events, interdependencies, and interrelationships. Events are indicated as circles or blocks, numbered for identification. An event

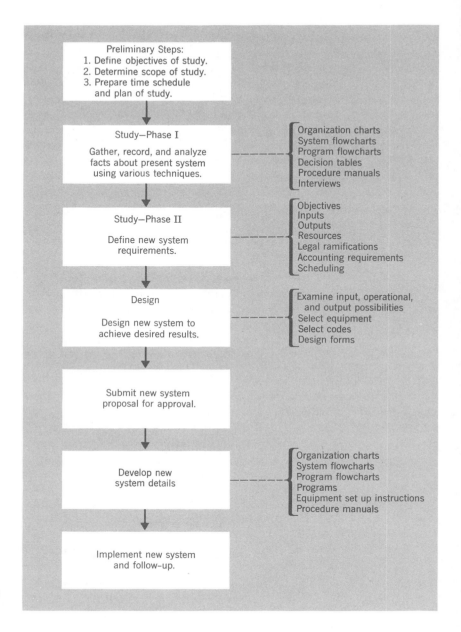

Figure 18-1. *Steps in systems study and design.*

does not represent the performance of work, but rather the point in time at which the event is accomplished, i.e., a milestone or checkpoint. Events are connected by arrows reflecting the activities required to complete the events (Figure 18–2).

PCS techniques aid in controlling projects, evaluating progress during their execution, and recognizing implications of project schedules. For

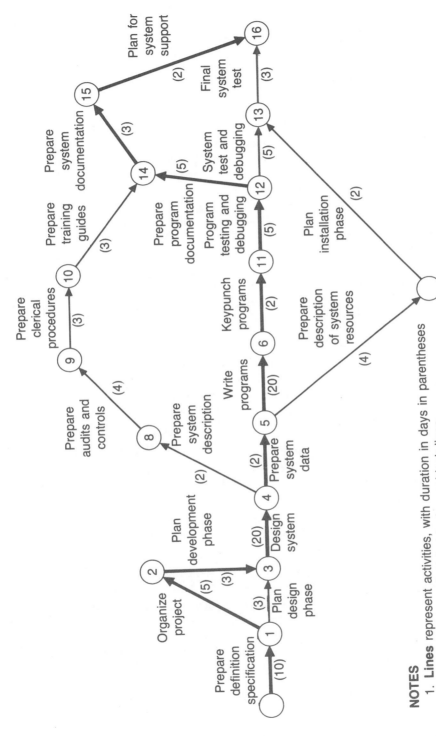

NOTES
1. **Lines** represent activities, with duration in days in parentheses
2. **Critical Path** is depicted by heavy black lines

Figure 18-2. *Example of project control system for design and development of an EDP system.*

example, analysis of a diagram may reveal that it will not be possible to complete a project as soon as desired, that some activities have been overlooked, or that the activities planned during some period of time require more resources than are available.

Emphasis is generally on time scheduling, as shown in the critical path network in Figure 18–2. However, advanced versions of PCS also include cost estimates. Thus, in addition to monitoring the progress of the project, the manager is able to compare continuously the actual cost expenditures with those estimated during the planning stage.

PCS, PERT, and CPM have proved highly useful in scheduling and controlling major construction projects, research and development programs, and other large projects, as well as the design and development of systems projects.

ANALYZING THE PRESENT SYSTEM

To acquire an understanding of the present system, the analyst must first define the resources used in the system. The personnel, equipment, facilities, and finances must be noted in a manner that will clearly show their relation to the system. To gather this information the analyst will have to:

1. Analyze the organization charts and determine that they represent the actual lines of authority, and then identify the personnel operating the present system. If there is an informal organization that overlaps the formal structure, it also must be recognized.

2. Review operating procedures and verify that the procedure manuals represent the actual operations and identify the equipment and facilities used in the system. When up-to-date procedure manuals do not exist, the analyst will have to spend more time with the managers operating the system in order to find out what resources are being used.

3. Prepare a system flowchart that reflects the resources used in the system. While developing the flowchart, the analyst may need to discuss certain operations with the people actually operating the system.

4. Interview personnel in order to obtain pertinent facts about various aspects of the system. Effective interviewing requires special skill. The interview procedure is facilitated if the analyst is recognized as an authority who can improve the situation. However, while gathering information from the operators, he should ask them for their ideas on how the system could be improved. This is important, as it gives a feeling of participation that can make it easier to install the new system.. It is also possible that a good idea may be brought to light. Either during the interview or following it the analyst should make concise notes about the interview and the subject discussed.

5. Record details of the present system. These details may include:

Inputs. The sources of data entering the system: how much, how often, and from where does it come?

Resources. Equipment, personnel, finances, facilities, and inventories used in the system.

Outputs. The reports produced: how often are they prepared, who uses them, and how are they used?

DEFINING SYSTEM REQUIREMENTS

Both while gathering information about the present system and afterwards, the analyst must define the actual requirements of the system. A good analyst must be aware of management's general policies, attitudes, and objectives for the present and future. At this point in the survey the analyst should determine:

1. Where the particular system being studied fits into the total business system of making a product or performing a service
2. What the system must do
3. What inputs it must accept
4. What outputs it must produce
5. What resources it must use

Next to management objectives, the knowledge of laws and regulations concerning the system under study is most important. Many of today's business systems were created primarily to satisfy one or more governmental requirements. The main legal responsibility of the systems analyst is to avoid any violation of laws or regulations in the business system being designed or changed.

While designing any business system the analyst must constantly be alert to the rules governing good accounting practices: the rules on debit and credit entries, for example. Moreover, the analyst should have knowledge of the accounting doctrines, such as the doctrine of consistency. Simply stated, the accountant starts with source data and builds toward final results, whereas the auditor starts with the final results and tracks back to the source. Therefore, a trail must always be left for the auditor to travel; otherwise, he may have to exert a great amount of effort to do his job.

A good system also provides for balancing to control figures at the proper places in the procedure, and provides instructions for correcting out-of-balance conditions. Avoiding errors often requires a great amount of special effort, and detecting errors often requires duplication of manual effort. It must be determined whether the degree of accuracy is sufficiently critical to justify the cost of avoiding and detecting errors.

Another requirement of a good system is that it be straightforward and easily followed by operating personnel. The more exceptions there are in a procedure, the more opportunity there is for operator error. As work progresses, certain interruptions arise for checking, questioning, making minor adjustments, and receiving instructions. These are variable factors that are present, to some degree, in all operations. However, the fewer of these interruptions and questions there are in a system, the more efficient the operation will be.

Finally, a good system requires the effective scheduling of operations. The effectiveness of data processing operations is determined by the coordination of machines, personnel, and work. While scheduling may take many forms, the broad objective as it applies to data processing is to produce the desired reports on time, with a minimum number of machines and personnel. The more difficult it is to schedule the jobs, the more important it is to do so.

DESIGNING THE NEW SYSTEM

Determining Input, Operational, and Output Methods

The first step in designing the new system is to examine the various ways in which source data can be entered into a system, operated on, and reported or recorded. Source data can first be recorded on magnetic tape, punched into cards or paper tape, recorded by mark-sensed notation or magnetic ink, or read by an optical character recognition device. Also, it is becoming more common to have data entered directly into a computer-controlled file. For example, the many airline reservation systems accept passenger bookings directly from remote terminals at various locations where reservations can be made. These terminals are connected to the computer through telephone lines.

Output alternatives available are printed reports, punched cards, paper tape, or data transmission to a remote terminal such as that used by the airline industry.

File possibilities include magnetic tapes, disks, drums, or punched cards. The operations (the process between input and output) can be performed in a number of ways, discussed in detail in preceding chapters.

The analyst also must examine the possibility of combining minor operations or splitting oversized operations. He must decide what audit and control requirements should be imposed and with what frequency the operations need to be performed.

Selecting Equipment

The selection of equipment is a complex and challenging task. Sound decisions require careful consideration of such factors as general requirements of the system, volumes of data, anticipated future expansion, available financial resources, and relative cost of various methods.

Equipment selection is generally based on the following principles:

1. Lack of repetition in an application dicates that the operation be done manually with mechanical assistance where helpful.

2. If the operation is highly repetitive or requires considerable calculating within each repetitive cycle, it will probably be most practical to use a computer.

These principles make it apparent that not all applications belong on a computer. For example, the criterion of repetition necessary for selection of a computer could not be met by an organization that processes ten invoices a day. This is not sufficient repetition to justify a method other than manual or mechanical. However, the processing of a large quantity of invoices each day might justify a computer, particularly if there were numerous calculations to be performed on each invoice. The scale of the computer and types of peripheral devices required would be determined by such factors as the complexity of the task, volume of transactions, and frequency of processing. It should also be pointed out that if a type of computer is installed with a capacity in excess of the basic requirements, the available time may be used for additional applications that are desirable but that would not otherwise have been considered.

Another consideration in the selection of equipment is the decision of whether to rent or purchase the equipment proposed. Occasionally the equipment will be rented for several years, and then, when it and the system have proved satisfactory, it may be purchased. Some of the rent versus purchase factors are:

1. Rented equipment can readily be replaced by newer equipment as it is developed.
2. Equipment rental rates generally include maintenance provisions.
3. Purchase contracts usually do not provide for maintenance beyond a short warranty period.
4. The purchase cost of equipment can usually be recovered in from five to seven years, provided the equipment has not been made obsolete by technological advancements.
5. Cash or credit conditions of the company may be a major factor.
6. Income tax and property tax considerations can also be an important factor.

These considerations make it apparent that the decision of whether to rent or purchase equipment is most frequently made at the executive or corporate levels of management.

Selecting Codes

One of the most important considerations in designing a new system is the selection of coding methods. The use of an inappropriate or inadequate code can contribute to the ineffectiveness of a system.

Events or transactions must be classified in many ways so that the data may be used for as many management purposes as required. Therefore, in constructing codes full consideration must be given to the purpose such codes will serve. The proper code for a specific application will save space in the record, assist in identifying data, and facilitate the machine processing required before and during the preparation of a desired report.

To be effective a code should include the following characteristics:

1. Flexibility—it should be possible to make additional entries of coded data in proper sequence.
2. Scope—it should be possible to expand the code to include additional categories.
3. Operation—the code should be adequate to cover all of the necessary segregations within the established categories.
4. Convenience—the code should be easy to apply.
5. Construction—the code should meet all applications requirements with the least possible number of digits.
6. Identification—if possible, the code should provide for visual identification.

Most codes are constructed of numbers of letters, or a combination of both. The use of numerals in place of names is one example of how space in a record can be saved through the use of a two-digit code. Another example would be to use two letters to identify each state, i.e., the letters CA could represent California. This code assists the user in translation, as it provides visual identification between the code and the state.

Consecutively numbering the states 1 through 50 would be considered a type of *sequence code*. The use of two alphabetic characters associated with each state would be considered a type of *mnemonic code,* as it assists the user in memorizing the codes. Following are some of the other most commonly used coding methods.

In *group classification codes* the major and minor classifications are coded in groups of thousands, hundreds, and tens. Various categories under each classification are represented by the assignment of succeeding digits. This method is suitable for coding all classes of products, accounts, and items in which division of groups under a major heading is the primary objective. For example,

2000	Packaging materials
2100	Paper
2110	Kraft
2111	Plain
2112	Laminated
2120	Tissue
etc.	

The *block code* method involves the assignment of numbers in sequence by groups of various sizes other than tens, hundreds, and thousands. Instead, a block can consist of any quantity of numbers necessary to cover the items in a particular classification. In the original design of the code, a few blank numbers may be left in each block to provide for later additions.

In the *significant digit code* method, all or part of the numbers are related to some characteristic of the data such as weight, dimension, distance, capacity, or other significant factor. This type of coding reduces the work of decoding by providing a code number that is inherently descriptive. This method is suitable for coding long lists of items where complete decoding would be laborious or impractical. The following example illustrates the application of significant digit coding to packaged products so that the last two digits represent package weights.

1000	Sugar, sacks
1005	5-pound sacks
1010	10-pound sacks
1020	20-pound sacks
1050	50-pound sacks

Designing Forms

Another important consideration in the design of a new system is forms design. Many factors affect the design of both input and output forms. When considering a new form the first questions should be:

1. Is this form really necessary?
2. What form(s), if any, will it replace?
3. Can existing forms be revised to include the new information?
4. How was this information previously supplied?

After gathering satisfactory answers to these questions the analyst can proceed with the design of the new form.

The most important principle of form design is to plan the form with the user(s) in mind. Other considerations are:

1. How many copies are to be prepared?
2. Will the form be permanent?
3. Is it for internal or external use?
4. What quality of paper and size of form should be used?
5. Is the form simple and easy to understand?
6. Is the make-up of the form straightforward and in accordance with accepted accounting practice?
7. If the form is to be read by optical character recognition equipment, does it conform to the requirements of the intended OCR unit?

The following principles contribute to good forms design:

1. Bold type should be used to emphasize important information.
2. In columns for money, sufficient space for the largest amount must be provided.

3. If writing is near the binding edge, it should be visible.
4. Filing information should be near the top of the form.
5. Every form should have a title.
6. Headings should be as small as possible, leaving sufficient space for written data.
7. A good printing style should be selected to make the form attractive in appearance.
8. The form should include only essential information.
9. The form should be designed so that a minimum of recording and recopying is required.
10. If the form precedes another form, or is dependent on another form, the same general sequénce and arrangement should be followed so that recopying and recording can easily be accomplished.

After the form is designed, it should be analyzed to determine whether it is sufficiently clear and all necessary instructions are printed on the form. Final analysis should take into consideration all principles of good forms design.

If the form is designed for completion by other than manual means, one of the ways of assuring that the printed information will be aligned within the form is to lay out the data to be printed on a spacing chart. Spacing charts are usually furnished by the forms manufacturer or the manufacturer of the printing device, e.g., typewriter, accounting machine, or computer printer.

NEW SYSTEM PROPOSAL

After all alternatives have been considered, the analyst must then put the ideal segments together to form a sensible systems approach that will accomplish the objectives of the organization. One reason for examining all of the alternatives is to insure that the new system will not be restricted by the limitations of the past.

When a general plan of the new system has been prepared, a final review of the system should be made to determine its feasibility. The review should include consideration of the following questions:

1. Will the plan work in actual practice?
2. Can the company afford the approach?
3. Will management go along with the changes required?
4. Will the supervisors and workers recognize it as a better way of doing the work?
5. Does it conform to all legal requirements?
6. Will the new system be simple and easy to understand?
7. Will it do the job completely?

After finding and testing the best concept for the new system, and prior to the final drafts of procedures, forms, formats, resource requirements, and so on, a report should be prepared. This report should describe the purpose of the particular system being studied and its relation to other systems in the application area. The new system should be outlined briefly, with estimated volumes of work and proposed schedules. Resources that will be required by the system must be described, and estimates of the cost of implementation must be made. This report, sometimes called an intent agreement, management abstract, or system proposal, should be agreed to by all responsible parties concerned. Often these people are noncommital during the survey; then when asked to endorse the final report, they become wary and have a few final thoughts that could cause a change in the approach. It is much better to find out about necessary changes before many hours have been spent documenting the system.

NEW SYSTEM PLAN

The techniques for describing the new system in detail vary in degree and complexity. No other facet of data processing has as little uniformity or as few standards. There is, however, a certain sequence to the methods for documenting a system that will prove most practical. It is as follows:

1. Construct a flowchart of the system. Prepare a narrative statement for each complex step shown in the flowchart.
2. Prepare formats of, and specifications for, the forms required. Input and output forms can best be laid out on a forms design space chart.
3. Prepare charts showing organizational changes. Support the charts with detailed duties statements for each new type of position.
4. Describe other resources such as facilities and equipment required by the new system. Lay out floor plans or forms flowcharts if necessary.

At this point some concerns have the systems analyst turn the job over to a programmer or data processing analyst for completion. In other concerns the systems analyst will complete the documentation and installation plans. There are advantages to either way. However, the latter is probably the better approach, as the analyst can better realize a sense of accomplishment. Also, he can remain knowledgeable about all facets of data processing and thereby be more versatile and valuable to the company.

The final steps for completing a new computer-oriented system usually take approximately 70 per cent of the total time required to design and implement a new system. These final steps are:

1. Prepare computer program flowcharts.
2. Write and test programs. A good aid in developing a test for a program is to make notes of requirements and conditions to be met as the system is being designed and as the programs are being flowcharted or written.

3. Produce setup instructions for each job step or program.
4. Write procedure manuals. These procedures can be in narrative form, flowchart form, or a combination of the two. Better yet, individual job instruction sheets may be used. The techniques for preparing manuals are a matter of management choice.

NEW SYSTEM IN OPERATION

The first part of the plan for installing the new system is to determine whether the system may be installed in part or all at once, and then set the installation schedule. The next steps are to order equipment and schedule the preparation of the facilities; plan for the training or recruiting of personnel; and order forms, cards, and supplies. The best plan will bring together resources, personnel, and supplies at approximately the same time, just before the planned system's starting date.

At the start of any new system the analyst should be available to the operating personnel, as there will be certain minor adjustments to be made in the procedures. Some planned work loads may be too heavy or too light, certain operations may require reappraisal, and schedules may require adjustment. The analyst should remain in close contact with the new system until all problems appear to be resolved.

In looking back, it can be seen that the systems analyst is engrossed in the new system from its design through its successful installation. No detail may be ignored without creating a problem at some stage of the installation process. The ease with which a new system is installed is an indication of the analyst's ability.

The job of the systems analyst does not end with the installation of the new system, however. His work is not complete until there has been a follow-up to verify the adequacy of the system. During the follow-up the analyst must:

1. Determine that all parts of the new system are operating efficiently
2. Make any modifications or refinements in the system or in written procedures that may be required by operating experience
3. Determine that the objectives of the system are being met

If final evaluation reveals that anticipated savings are being realized, that output of the system is on schedule, and that the quantity and quality of information are fulfilling management requirements, then it can be assumed that the system was well planned and implemented.

IMPORTANT WORDS AND PHRASES

project control system	mnemonic code	block code
sequence code	group classification code	significant digit code

1. What are the general objectives of systems study and design?
2. What are the three major phases of systems study and design?
3. Briefly describe the five steps in analyzing the present system.
4. What is the first step in designing a new system?
5. Equipment selection is generally based on what two principles?
6. What are the characteristics of a good code?
7. What is the most important principle of forms design?
8. Explain the four methods that may be used in documenting a new system plan.
9. What are the final steps in completing a new system?

19

COMPUTERS AND AUTOMATION

CHAPTER PREVIEW

The industrial use of computers encompasses a great variety of purposes ranging from routine administrative applications to the control of manufacturing operations and production systems. Modern industrial organizations use the computer for the full scope of their accounting activities—payrolls, billing, accounts payable, accounts receivable, financial planning, budgetary control, cost accounting, personnel accounting, management information systems, and so on. However, since business applications of this type are covered in other chapters, the discussion here will stress applications that are typical of industrial enterprises.

PRODUCTION
PLANNING AND
CONTROL

In manufacturing companies, the scheduling of production and control of inventory are of prime importance. Production scheduling computations are typically of such volume as to make them difficult to perform manually. Furthermore, since more than one satisfactory schedule may be possible, the computer is very useful in performing the complex calculations necessary to discover the best schedule for reducing costs and most effectively utilizing scarce production resources. Computer scheduling is also more dynamic since it facilitates quick responses to changes in the availability of or demand for materials and facilities after production has started.

In production planning it is necessary to ascertain in complete detail the number and skill of the workers needed, machine requirements, and all of the raw material and parts that will be required for the manufacture of every item. After the volume of production has been determined, a series of calculations of material requirements is carried out. Assemblies are broken down into subassemblies, subassemblies into parts, and so on, resulting in a complete list of every item required. This list is compared with existing inventories, and, if raw materails, parts, or subassemblies must be procured, purchase requisitions and orders are issued.

Production control requires the careful coordination of people, machines, and materials. Computers are used to control overall production, and they also have the capacity to cater to each individual order. In the automobile industry, for example, many cars are built to fill specific orders from dealers or customers who may choose from among many thousands of combinations of colors, accessories, and optional equipment. In some plants customers' orders are recorded on punched cards, and the data is fed into a computer. By using data collection devices, the computer controls the movement of the proper parts along feeder lines throughout the plant, thus assuring that the correct part gets to the right worker at precisely the right time.

INDUSTRIAL AUTOMATION

We have had the words *automatic* and *automaton* for a long time, but the word *automation* did not enter our language until about 1947. It soon captured the public imagination and is now familiar to nearly everyone—familiar but not always clearly understood. Perhaps this is because the word is relatively new. More likely, however, it is because the word has been subjected to various interpretations and has been associated with a number of controversial ideas, both technical and sociological.

Basically, automation involves the use of various technological devices and methods in performing manufacturing operations, or any other processes, without the direct intervention of the human hand. In a broader and more technical definition, automation has been described as "the substitution of mechanical, hydraulic, pneumatic, electrical and electronic devices for human organs of observation, decision and effort, so as to increase productivity, control quality and reduce cost."*

When the term *automation* first came into existence, it was usually associated with manufacturing operations. As applied to the industrial movement that started in the United States in the early 1950s, automa-

*Arnold, Pauline, and Percival White, *The Automation Age,* Holiday House, Pound Ridge, New York, 1963, p. 14.

tion was defined as a production technique: the integration of machine tools into a fully automatic and, in some cases, self-regulating system. Today automation represents considerably more than the integration of a series of automatic machines. Automation is now being applied diversely in all levels of industry as well as in government and business. In fact, almost every activity is now affected to some extent by the use of automatically controlled devices and systems.

THE FOUNDATIONS OF INDUSTRIAL AUTOMATION

Historical developments in the mechanization and automation of data processing operations were outlined in Chapter 2. One of these developments, the electronic computer, has contributed most significantly to industrial automation. Here it has been combined effectively with other machines and processes that also have an interesting historical background, for present-day industrial automation did not develop spontaneously. Instead, it comprises elements of other stages of technological growth. It embodies the mechanization of the Industrial Revolution, the mass production principles of the early twentieth century, and the automatic control principles that have developed since World War II. Before considering the role of the computer in industrial automation, let us briefly review the nature and origin of these other elements.

Mechanization

Since the beginning of history, human beings have sought ways of transferring to machines the burden of strenuous, repetitious, monotonous work. For centuries, people devised many ingenious and increasingly complex methods of utilizing their own muscular energy more effectively. What was needed eventually, though, was a new source of energy that could augment or supplant human energy, as well as the energy provided by harnessing water power and using domesticated draft animals. This was achieved by the important inventions and technological advancements of the Industrial Revolution, beginning around 1760, which enabled humanity to exploit in a major way the latent energy found in nature.

Industrial production was first mechanized by the steam engine; later the process of mechanization was extended much further by electric motors. The introduction of central-station power in 1881 made possible a multitude of inventions that, in turn, made modern mass production and automation possible.

Continuous Process

The early twentieth century witnessed a major technological advancement based on the principle of mass production. An essential element of mass production is the use of the continuous flow concept. This concept was known in the eighteenth century and was occasionally used in industry—flour mills, for example—but it was not widely used until this century.

A significant application of the mass-production principle occurred in the automobile industries of both Europe and the United States in the early 1900s. It was discovered that if workers moved from one car to another repeating the same task, this job specialization speeded production enormously. Soon it was recognized that it would be even better to have the workers stay put and have the jobs move by them. This assembly-line idea was adopted from the meat-packing industry, which had used moving conveyors in Chicago since the 1870s. Thus, increased productivity, or output per worker hour, was brought about by reorganizing the production process itself—an accomplishment that did not necessarily involve the introduction of new machines or new power sources.

During World War II the evolution of mass-production technology was completed by the development of automatic-transfer machines. A transfer-machine production line consists of a series of machines linked by mechanical handling equipment that moves parts automatically from station to station along the line. Under electronic control these machines can accept a piece of work, position it properly and fasten it in place, perform some operation on it, release it, transfer it to the next stage, and accept the next piece. All of this is accomplished without any direct human intervention. Consequently, transfer machines can perform in a single, integrated, automatically controlled process what was previously a series of individual job operations.

Automatic Control

The ability of machines to regulate themselves, which is a fundamental aspect of automation, is made possible by the technology of feedback. *Feedback* is accomplished by routing part of the output, or result, of a process back to the device that regulates the input of the process. Thus, if analysis of the feedback shows that the output is greater than it should be, the regulating device slows down the input; if the output is less than required, input will be increased.

Feedback principles have been known and applied for over a century. However, it was not until World War II that developments in the field of electronics permitted the manufacture of truly automatic control devices with wide applicability and highly efficient operation. These total automatic control systems are known as *servomechanisms*. A servomechanism is not a single instrument but a closely coordinated system of many instruments including sensing, measuring, transmitting, and control devices.

Among the sensing techniques employed are photoelectric cells, infrared cells, high-frequency devices, and X-ray components. The sensing unit, usually located near the output end of an automated system, observes the operations or finished products continuously. Information about what is being accomplished is transmitted to the measuring unit, which compares the information it receives with the performance requirements stored in its memory. Any difference between the two, called an error, is determined, and this information is relayed to the control unit. The control unit automatically activates forces that make the necessary adjustments to correct the error.

This cycle of continuous operations is called a "closed loop" because it is performed entirely by units built directly into the automated system. Thus, an automated system with a self-controlling closed-loop feedback has no need for a human operator to make corrections or adjustments in its performance. This contrasts with open-loop controls, where an operator receives information about the results of a process, compares it with the desired performance, and makes adjustments in the input, if needed, to correct an error.

A good example of closed-loop feedback is the simple circuit used to control temperature in an electric oven. In this case the processing unit is the oven, the sensing device is the thermostat, and the control unit is the on-off oven heat switch. The control knob is set for a desired oven temperature, which will then be held automatically as follows: when the thermostat senses that the oven temperature has risen above the level set by the position of the knob, the control device, or switch, corrects the error by switching off the electricity; similarly, when the thermostat senses that the temperature has fallen below the desired level, the control device switches the current on again.

This is an example of a simple form of what is called "on-off" control. Industrial applications normally require a more sophisticated type of control whereby the quantity being controlled is regulated automatically and continuously rather than by being switched on and off.

COMPUTERS AND AUTOMATIC CONTROL

Probably the most significant postwar technological development and the most important of all units employed in automation is the electronic computer. In addition to making a host of engineering and technical calculations never before feasible, the computer has become a significant factor in automatic control. Several of the outstanding roles of computers are described in the following sections.

Numerical Control of Machine Tools

One of the most important aspects of automation is *numerical control*, which is a means of automatically controlling the positioning and operation of machine tools. These tools are used to cut, drill, grind, press, turn, punch, mill, and otherwise alter the shape of metal pieces. In conventional methods this demands the constant attention of a skilled machine operator, especially if the part to be formed has an irregular contour. However, the metalworking industry is increasingly installing numerical control systems to produce metal parts automatically.

A numerical control system is one in which actions are controlled by the use of numerical data. The numerical control system reads numbers, translates them into instructions, directs the machine tool to perform the instructions, and compares machine performance with the instructions. Thus, numerically controlled machinery is more than automatic machining; it is *automatic data handling*. "Data" comprises all of the numbers and mathematics used to describe a manufactured item.

The data used in controlling machine operations is generally recorded on a punched tape. In the early stages of numerical control, the preparation of control tapes was almost entirely a manual process. On all but the simplest parts, it was time-consuming and error-prone because of the need for the part programmer to reduce all the necessary geometric equations to digital approximations and to perform the many thousands of calculations needed. The high level of mathematics required to define complex tool operations was quite prohibitive in terms of programming manpower when the only aid was a desk calculator.

The availability of electronic computers as calculating aids significantly reduced the time required to produce error-free control tapes. Further assistance was provided by the development of special problem-oriented numerical control programming languages that permit direct computer calculation and automatic control tape preparation. Two examples of the available English-like languages are APT (*A*utomatically *P*rogrammed *Tools*), and IBM's AUTOSPOT (*AUTO*matic *S*ystem for *PO*sitioning *Tools*).

Figure 19–1 illustrates a computer-assisted numerical control operation using the APT system. As shown in the flowchart, the operation begins with a conventional engineering drawing of a part to be machined. From the drawing the part programmer writes a set of instructions that describe the operations necessary to produce the desired part. The program specifies the requirements of each machine-tool operation and includes statements defining the geometrical characteristics of the surfaces, required cutting operations, and machine-tool capabilities. These statements, written on coding sheets, form the source program. This program is punched into cards that are read into the computer. The processor program then converts the source statements into an intermediate format and calculates the detailed motions required for the accurate, proper positioning of the machine tool and for the necessary cutting and drilling. Many thousands of calculations may be necessary to translate these statements into a sequence of error-free instructions meaningful to the machine-tool controller. By means of a user-written post-processor program, this intermediate data is then converted to a series of detailed instructions coded in numerical values, generally in the form of punched tape that can be read by the machine-tool controller. The data is stored until needed and then fed into the machine-tool control unit that converts the data into actual machine motions (Figure 19–2). In some large installations, magnetic tape is used as the input medium for the machine-tool controller.

Under development are systems in which the computer is used as an integral, on-line element of the total numerical control system. In this

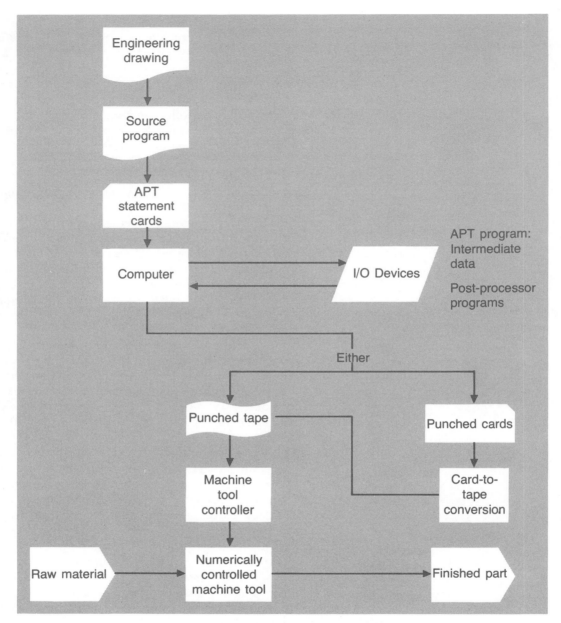

Figure 19-1. *APT system flowchart.*

Figure 19-2. *Computer-assisted numerical control operation.*
(Courtesy International Business Machines Corporation.)

case the computer actually controls and monitors machine-tool operations directly. Thus, through a feedback process the computer is able not only to regulate machine operations in response to variable conditions, but also to obtain information about production results. In this way, data for production control and accounting purposes may be developed as a by-product of manufacturing operations.

Numerical control is not restricted to machining alone. The fundamentals of control by numbers are being applied increasingly to many other fields. For example, metal-forming equipment such as punch presses, tube or pipe benders, and metal fabricators have been equipped with controllers and are being operated under numerical control. Flame-cutting machines are used in the shipbuilding and steel industries to cut large steel plates under punched tape control, and numerically controlled inspection equipment has been built.

Process Control

In contrast with numerical control, which provides automation of discrete operations, *process control* provides automation of continuous operations. The process industries were the first to use computer control on a large scale. These are industries in which ingredients flow continuously through all stages of a process as they are converted from raw materials to an end product or group of products. Included in this category are petroleum refining, steel processing, electric power generation, and the manufacture of paper, chemicals, steel, cement, and food products.

Computer process control is being used increasingly in such industries to automate the manufacturing process and to control a large number of variables impossible for a person to control simultaneously. Factors occurring in production processes of this type, including variables such as time, weight, pressure, temperature, size, volume, and revolutions per minute, are monitored at critical places in the factory. By means of an analog to digital converter these continuous physical measurements are changed into discrete numbers. This data is instantly relayed to the computer for comparison with standards or planned results programmed into the computer beforehand. If there is a discrepancy between the two, the computer decides what adjustments are necessary and sends an appropriate command to the control mechanism in order to bring operations back to standard (Figure 19–3).

Since the computer continuously receives readings from process instruments, it may also print out relevant data at regular intervals. This data may include not only raw instrument readings but also computed yields and efficiencies for use by the process engineers or average and total flows for the accounting department. Thus, the control computer also serves as a data logger part of the time (Figure 19–4).

In many control systems today humans still read and compare measurements and make decisions about necessary corrections in the production process. However, in many factories the processing of raw materials involves sequences of decisions for which all of the alternative

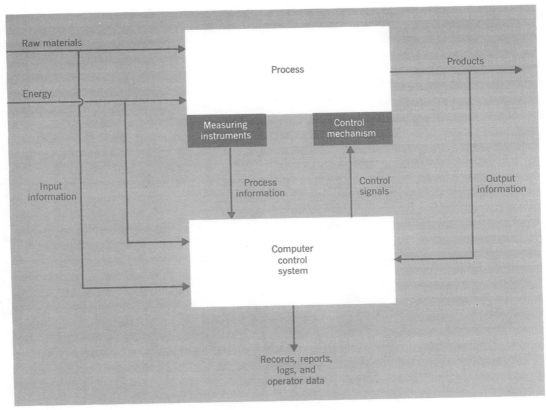

Figure 19-3. *Diagram of a computer process control system.*

possibilities are known. Thus, a computer can be programmed to aid in control of the entire factory through a closed-loop system in which human intervention is required mainly to handle exceptional conditions that the computer indicates. The computer is highly reliable and capable of handling information of a very complex nature. Therefore, industrial engineers can now devise processes so intricate that they are feasible only with the aid of a computer.

Computers used to control industrial processes have certain characteristics that are worthy of note.

1. The central computer in such systems is generally a special purpose computer that is smaller than would be required for problem-solving scientific systems or large-scale data processing systems.
2. There is generally provision for analog input and output because much of the information derived from sensing devices involves measurements. Such information is converted to digital form for processing.

Figure 19-4. *Computer process control system.*

(*Courtesy International Business Machines Corporation.*)

3. Programming requirements are somewhat unique as compared to scientific or business data processing systems. Industrial program preparation demands specialists who are well trained in computer mathematics and in the nature of the process being controlled.

CYBERNATION

Within recent years the term *cybernation* has been coined to describe the application of a computer as a decision-making device in controlling an automatic process. The word is derived from *cybernetics,* a term used by the late Professor Norbert Weiner to mean the processes of communication and control in man and machines. He derived it from the Greek word meaning "steersman." The theory and practice of cybernetics, an interesting study in itself, underlies the systematic design and application of automation and computers.

It should be recognized that it is possible to construct complex control systems based on continuous monitoring and feedback loops without including computers. Not all automated industrial plants have computer systems, and not all computerized plants are equally automatic. However, computers have given a new dimension to automatic control. By linking together machinery, sensing and measuring instruments, control devices, and electronic computers, systems can automatically start, stop, accelerate, decelerate, count, examine, store performance data, and measure and compare the dimensions of space, sound, time, temperature, and other physical characteristics.

Thus, it has become possible to develop integrated, self-regulating systems that can perform extremely complicated operations with little or no human assistance. Further, these cybernated systems perform with a precision and a rapidity that cannot be matched by humans. They also perform in ways that would be impossible or impractical for humans to duplicate.

In short, the advent of electronic control and computation has added one more stage of refinement in meeting the age-old objective of transferring burdensome and repetitious manual and mental tasks to machines.

<hr>

INTEGRATION OF BUSINESS AND PROCESS CONTROL SYSTEMS

The purpose of a business information system is to collect information about the operations of an organization and to disseminate responses to this information. A process control system can be described similarly except that this system relates to a physical process rather than a business process.

In the past these two functions were commonly regarded as essentially separate. Thus, the control computer in the process control system was independent both physically and functionally of the computer or computers used for the organization's information systems. This independence was attributable to several factors: the traditional separation of business and process control systems, the fact that the use of communications systems was a relatively recent development in data processing, and the past distinction between scientific and business computers.

In general there is a close interaction between the information required for control of the manufacturing process and that required for overall management of the business. For example, information about various factors of production, raw materials, process yields, and the status of work-in-process is of common significance. All of the data available to the process control system through measurement of the physical process can, of course, be made available to management by having a human operator record and report instrument readings periodically. Reports printed out by the control computer may also be transmitted for management use. However, as a result of technological advancements, it is now possible to capture data at its sources automatically and communicate it immediately rather than at some later time. First, it is now possible to obtain computers capable of both analyzing operating data for control of the physical process and reporting data for control of the business. Second, modern data communication techniques make it possible to transmit to a remote location the data required for management functions, and this can be accomplished at relatively little additional cost.

Much of the progress in this area is based on the advent of minicomputers and, more recently, microcomputers. It has been predicted that by 1984 microcomputers will control 50 per cent of automated factory equipment and minicomputers will control an additional 26 per cent. In advanced systems these computers are part of an array of small computers that combine computer-aided design with computer control of manufacturing, and the collection and analysis of factory data. In each plant the center of such a system may be a control computer, possibly in communication with the corporate electronic data processing system. The plant computer supervises minicomputers located at strategic points in the factory, and each of these computers in turn supervises its own group of mini or microcomputers that control machines. The result is an integrated system that both controls manufacturing processes and provides information to carry out engineering, financial, marketing, and other management functions.

IMPORTANT WORDS AND PHRASES			
automation	servomechanism	process control
feedback	numerical control	cybernation

REVIEW QUESTIONS

1. What elements of other stages of technological growth are embodied in automation?
2. Explain the principle of feedback.
3. What is the difference between closed-loop controls and open-loop controls?
4. What is numerical control?
5. Describe the primary role of a computer in a numerical control system.
6. Briefly describe the manner in which a computer is used to control production processes.
7. Discuss the value of integrating physical and business systems.

20 SOCIAL AND ECONOMIC EFFECTS OF COMPUTERS

The effects of technological change have been a matter of concern since the days of the Industrial Revolution. In recent decades interest has focused on automation and its immediate and anticipated effects. It is doubtful that any aspect of automation has captured the imagination of the public as has the electronic computer, and no other development is likely to prove as significant.

Over a decade ago Dr. Jerome B. Weisner wrote:

The computer, with its promise of a million-fold increase in man's capacity to handle information, will undoubtedly have the most far-reaching social consequences of any contemporary technical development. The potential for good in the computer, and the danger inherent in its misuse, exceed our ability to imagine. . . . We have actually entered a new era of evolutionary history, one in which rapid change is a dominant conse-

379

quence. Our only hope is to understand the forces at work and to take advantage of the knowledge we find to guide the evolutionary process.*

This statement reflects an attitude toward computers that is widespread today.

History will undoubtedly regard the computer as the ultimate technological achievement of our century. Its applications have been diverse and extensive. There is, in fact, hardly any facet of our lives that has remained unaffected, directly or indirectly, by the rapid development of this device. Nevertheless, a lag exists between the technological capacity and potential uses of the computer and its social acceptance and full utilization. Society finds it difficult to accommodate the computer because, on the one hand, it has proved an indispensable tool in many important applications, and, on the other hand, it has raised basic concerns about individual freedom and well-being.

It is the purpose of this chapter to survey some of these concerns and some of the problems that have prevented the unqualified acceptance of computers and related devices.

EFFECTS OF COMPUTERS ON EMPLOYMENT

A great deal of attention has been given in recent years to automation and its anticipated effects in our society. Views on this subject are widely divergent. One group contends that automation is really nothing very new, but is instead a much more advanced phase of the Industrial Revolution. Thus, it is regarded as a welcome source of many economic and social benefits. These include greater productivity and less waste, lowered cost of production, improved methods of doing things, creation of new industries and occupations, increased employment, and more leisure. While recognizing that various forms of automation will result in some immediate unemployment, this group assumes that the unemployment will be temporary and that in the long run the dislocated workers will be absorbed in new occupations as the result of an expanding economy.

An opposing group maintains that this optimistic outlook is wishful thinking based on economic premises of the nineteenth century that do not necessarily apply to present circumstances. This group believes that the changes taking place as a result of automation cannot be regarded as mere extensions of past technological progress. It is asserted that even though the long-range trend of nationwide employment is upward, the productivity of factories and offices is rising so much faster that the annual additions to the labor force are not being fully absorbed.

The difference in these views makes it evident that the ultimate impact of automation is uncertain. We can be certain, however, about some of the effects of automated data processing because they are already ap-

---

Saturday Review, July 23, 1966, p. 15.

parent. Therefore, let us consider some of the social implications of recent and imminent developments in data processing.

Reduced Clerical Employment

In the long run, it is inevitable that an increasing proportion of clerical work in business firms and government agencies will be taken over by electronic computing systems. As computer systems become more prevalent and as organizations gain experience in using them, more and more routine and repetitive tasks will be shifted to the computer. Also, smaller and less expensive computers are certain to be used in a growing number of smaller establishments. Thus, electronic accounting systems will be used to complete the payroll, billing, and other accounting and reporting functions previously performed manually by bookkeepers and accountants.

In general, office clerks are the workers most affected by these trends. This does not mean that all people in clerical jobs will be displaced. There are certain to be some tasks that can be handled more practically by manual methods. Furthermore, clerks in some jobs may be easily retrained and shifted to work using the new systems. In fact, the displacement to date has been largely offset by the increasing numbers of people needed to handle the input and output information, to plan computer programs, and to undertake the variety of services necessary to use computers effectively.

Occupational Adjustments

Although many displaced workers have been absorbed by new occupations, the gaining momentum of technological progress is already threatening some of these occupations. Punched card machine operators have already become superfluous in most large organizations as a result of conversion to electronic data processing. Many card punch operators have become operators of new data entry devices. However, in the coming decade a significant portion of the work force in this area may be eliminated by character recognition devices and various forms of source data automation.

Already, some of the work associated with computer programming is being eliminated by innovations such as "automatic programming," the use of programs and parts of programs stored in libraries for future use, and other advanced techniques and equipment.

Other forms of office automation promise to affect employment. Included are word processing, facsimile transmission, and microfilm or microfiche as a means of document storage and retrieval. There will, of course, be other advancements. It seems safe to conclude that many existing occupations should be regarded as temporary and subject to modification or termination when new methods are adopted.

Routine clerical jobs are the ones most likely to be reduced by automated data processing and by improvements in other types of office equipment. Typically, many of the jobs eliminated by technological change will be replaced by new jobs requiring greater intelligence and skills. Clerical workers in jobs requiring the use of judgment and the ability to work with other people—secretaries, receptionists, claim and adjustment clerks, for example—will be least affected by automation.

THE INDIVIDUAL AND THE COMPUTER

Human-Machine Interface

A high degree of standardization is required for the efficient use of computers. As a result, many people who have been exposed to automated government and business procedures can cite problems, especially in billing operations, caused by an impersonal, computerized approach.

Examples of depersonalized treatment by a computer have led many individuals to feel that they are being forced to fulfill the computer's needs rather than that the computer is being employed to meet their needs. This attitude was confirmed in a scientific sampling of the U.S. population in 1971 by the American Federation of Information Processing Societies.* Fifty-four per cent of the respondents in this survey believed that computers are dehumanizing people and turning them into numbers. Fifty-five per cent also felt that people are becoming too dependent on computers.

On the positive side, 89 per cent felt that computers will provide information and services for the home, and 65 per cent felt they will help raise the standard of living. Eighty-seven per cent credited computers with doing things that would be impossible without them.

Two significant responses on the survey related to information files. Fifty-eight per cent of the respondents expressed the belief that because of computerized information files, too many people have information about other people. In addition, 53 per cent felt that computerized information files may be used to destroy individual freedom. These statistics reflect widespread apprehension about invasion of privacy, which is discussed in the following section.

Invasion of Privacy

Americans have long been concerned about individual rights, including the right to privacy. These concerns were expressed repeatedly in our Constitution and its various amendments, and the rights provided for individuals have been vigorously defended throughout our history. Concern over invasion of privacy has reached a new peak in the last few years as a result of the growth of computerized data banks.

Compiling data on individuals is not new in this country. Throughout our history files have been developed on individuals for various legal reasons, but their use has generally been restricted to the specific purposes for which they were planned. However, as our society has grown in numbers and complexity, the process of compiling personal data files has multiplied.

*A National Survey of the Public's Attitudes Towards Computers, published by American Federation of Information Processing Societies, Inc., Montvale, New Jersey, 1971.

A great deal of data has been gathered about all of us to meet the needs of government and business. In the public sector, data is collected for census purposes, for social security records, and for military, law enforcement, and tax purposes. According to a government report, 85 federal agencies maintain 6,723 different record systems containing a total of 3.9 billion individual files. This amounts to an average of 18 files for every man, woman, and child in the United States.

In the private sector, a vast amount of data is collected as a basis for granting credit. There are approximately 2,500 credit bureaus in the country that collect and store information in data banks. Most of these bureaus are affiliated and interchange the information they maintain on approximately 130 million persons. The sources of data accumulated by credit bureaus include (a) their own subscribers—the merchants, banks, and finance companies that buy most of their reports; (2) official records of arrests, lawsuits, judgments, mortgages, bankruptcies, tax liens, marriages, and divorces; and (3) news clippings.

The automated storage and retrieval of this data, and consequently its ready availability, have raised basic concerns about individual freedom and the possible misuse of such information. Automated techniques facilitate the storage and dissemination of so much confidential information about individuals that, barring proper safeguards, civil liberties could be jeopardized.

The public controversy over this problem revolves around a number of separate but related issues: privacy, confidentiality, and data security.

Privacy relates to what personal information should be collected in the first place, by whom, and for what purposes. Once information is collected for one purpose, to what extent should it be made available for other purposes? Finally, who should have access to what information, for what purposes, and under what conditions? Privacy, if properly enforced, should protect the individual from unreasonable observation and unauthorized access to highly personal or confidential information.

Confidentiality relates to what is done with personal data, once on file. An individual may wish to treat most facts about his personal life as confidential. However, it may be to his advantage to disclose some personal data to a company or agency to be used for specific purposes he has approved. These purposes might involve employment consideration, bank loans, consumer credit, or insurance. Otherwise, the individual has a right to assume that confidentiality of the data furnished will be maintained and that unauthorized use of the data will not occur.

Data security relates to the safeguarding of information stored within a data bank. It includes protecting information from unauthorized disclosure, modification, or destruction, either accidental or intentional. Data security may encompass the physical protection of files to prevent unauthorized access, technical safeguards in the computer, and various administrative procedures.

The development of technical safeguards to assure data security is an objective of most systems. In systems serving remote terminals, the authorized user may be given a code or password for his exclusive use in gaining access to the system. In some systems special keys or badges may be used to activate terminals.

Confidentiality may also be achieved by restricting the user's access by means of security clearances and restrictions that permit access to only certain files or records, or perhaps only parts of records.

Through programming, the operations of a computer system can be monitored to detect attempted violations. Thus, unauthorized requests may result in immediate preventive action, such as disconnecting the user from the system.

The problem of confidentiality cannot be resolved by technical solutions alone, however. Growing public concern is inducing legislation designed to regulate computerized personal data bases. Passage by Congress of the Fair Credit Reporting Act of 1970 is an example of one step that has been taken. This act is designed to protect the rights of individuals in various ways by regulating the activities of credit bureaus and investigating agencies.

The Privacy Act of 1974 was a piece of milestone legislation passed by Congress in response to concerns regarding the unlimited gathering of information about people by the government. Among other provisions, that act required that federal agencies:

1. Register all their personal data systems
2. Establish a method for people to ascertain what information is on file about them
3. Establish a procedure for individuals to challenge the accuracy of information in federal files, as well as a procedure for resolving conflicts between the individual and the holder of the files
4. Place restrictions on the transfer of information to other agencies without the individual's approval
5. Take action to assure that personal data is kept reasonably accurate
6. Place restrictions on the use of social security numbers by federal, state, and local governments

This act is only one of many destined to be passed in response to concern about information privacy and security. Following the passage of the 1974 legislation, over 100 additional privacy bills were pending before the U.S. Congress and various state legislatures. It seems safe to conclude that every organization that has computerized data about people will be affected by uniform laws imposed by the federal government or by legislative action taken in individual states.

Although there is a great deal of concern about how privacy regulations will affect the field of consumer credit, the legislative impact will be felt by all organizations with data systems containing personal information. Included will be government organizations at all levels, the health and insurance fields, law enforcement agencies, business, and industry.

Overall, the issues of privacy, confidentiality, and data security will be of universal interest, affecting computer manufacturers, private citizens, legislators, all organizations with personal data systems, and government regulatory agencies. All share an obligation to help shape and implement the policies that will be needed to alleviate the growing apprenhension about privacy invasion.

IMPACT ON BUSINESS ORGANIZATIONS

*Overcoming
Credit Losses*

Computers have affected business organizations in many ways, both positive and negative. Earlier chapters contain many examples of how computers have helped increase productivity and reduce overhead in handling ever-growing volumes of paperwork. However, in addition to more efficient data processing techniques, computers have provided other economic benefits.

Reduced credit losses is one example. With over 500 million credit cards outstanding, there is a huge potential for credit card losses from fraud and bad risks. The losses from mislaid or stolen cards alone have been estimated at $350 million to $500 million annually in recent years. Thus, even the smallest of retailers can justify the use of some form of credit authorization.

The most basic and widely used means of checking credit is by a directory listing lost and stolen cards and bad risks. This method is prone to losses, however, because of delays in the issuance, receipt, and posting of updated credit listings. Next in effectiveness and use is the direct telephone call to a credit bureau. This is a cumbersome and time-consuming approach although it does provide access to more up-to-date listings. It also may result in customer resentment over delay and the questioning of his credit standing.

Newer forms of credit authorization employ terminals on-line to computers that maintain active account status files and provide answers to inquiries automatically. The credit authorization process begins with the operator at the sales site establishing communications with the computer. Credit and transaction data is then entered, usually by means of a keyboard. Some terminals use card-reading devices for automatic account number input. Card validation and information about the credit standing of the card holder furnished by the central credit facility may be displayed on a screen, or may take the form of a computer-synthesized voice response from a terminal speaker.

As these sophisticated systems become more widely used, they are certain to have a favorable effect in curtailing credit card losses.

While helping to curtail fraudulent credit transactions, the computer has opened the way to other kinds of fraud that create losses affecting business firms, investors, and ultimately consumers. Cool, calculating white-collar embezzlers are exploiting the computer to steal funds, materials, and trade secrets. Many companies have also become victims of malicious mischief and sabotage through their computer systems.

According to some experts, the problems are attributable to inadequate computer security controls, lack of built-in safeguards, and ineffective auditing practices. This seems to be borne out by one of the biggest frauds in business history, the Equity Funding scandal. In this case over $2 billion in bogus insurance policies were issued to phony customers over a two-year period. The policies were subsequently sold to reinsurance companies, thus raising short-term assets and enabling the company to report impressive increased earnings. Thousands of stockholders and some of the most sophisticated institutional investors on Wall Street were duped by a huge enterprise built on fictitious computer print outs. Although computer technology was not the only factor in this scheme, it is generally acknowledged that the crime would not have reached such magnitude without computers.

An interesting aspect of computer crime is the fact that the computer is an impersonal medium. The challenge to "beat the computer system" seems less offensive than crimes of a direct personal nature. There is an abundance of stories about people whose criminal exploits began with a feeling of gamesmanship and the desire to prove that they could beat the system. Unfortunately, in many of these cases the end result was a serious crime.

Although many computer crimes are relatively petty, the incidence of major crimes is significant. In one study of 12 cases of computer-related embezzlement, the average loss was $1 million. With potential rewards of this magnitude, computer crime seems destined to continue, especially in view of the limited risks.

The low level of risk results to a great extent from the sheer volume of data in a large computer system. Voluminous computer print outs with endless rows and columns of figures can be designed to confuse the auditor. Another factor is that the alteration of electronic records leaves no marks or evidence of erasure. It is done cleanly and quickly.

Because of these circumstances, frauds are generally discovered only accidentally when a system fails or when a change of system requires manual processing or results in close inspection of previous operations.

Computer crimes often originate with company employees who program or operate the computer, or those who submit data for processing and use the output. Crimes have been facilitated in recent years by the influx of data communications systems. Systems with a central computer and remote terminals require the use of telephone lines that are generally outside the physical control of the computer user. These communications lines can be bugged by inserting eavesdropping devices along the circuit, or data can be introduced or retrieved by simulating a legitimate terminal.

As computer users have increasingly recognized the vulnerability of their systems, a number of steps have been taken to reduce fraud. They include better internal controls and the use of safeguards to prevent unauthorized access to systems from remote terminals. More careful methods of hiring computer programmers and operators have been introduced, and their duties have been separated so that the person who writes programs is not the one who controls their use. Other efforts include the frequent rotation of operators, the limitation of access to computers, and improved auditing techniques. Finally, experts point out that if proper management techniques are employed, the computer itself offers the greatest potential for protecting stored data and preventing and detecting unauthorized activity.

The Threat of New Competition

One of the most fascinating aspects of electronic computers and related technologies is the rapid and important impact they have had on business customs and competition. This is especially evident in electronic banking, which is presently the center of controversy in the financial world.

Electronic banking will not soon result in the "cashless-checkless" society that has been discussed so widely, but it will have a radical influence on financial institutions, retailers, and especially consumers. This type of service involves the use of electronic funds-transfer systems (EFTS), which have touched off an unprecedented flurry of competition for the nation's financial business.

By merely inserting a magnetically encoded plastic card into a computer terminal, an individual can now withdraw cash, transfer money among different types of accounts, or complete other transactions without writing a check or entering a conventional financial office (Figure 20–1). The terminal may be located in a retail store, a shopping center mall, or a supermarket. The bank or savings and loan association that owns the computer could be nearby, across town, miles away in another town, or even in another state.

This removal of financial transactions to remote locations and away from the traditional banking environment will dramatically change the banking and savings habits of millions of Americans. It also threatens to upset America's traditional financial network, since electronic terminals are available to institutions other than banks. In fact, savings and loan associations are aggressively moving into this field by setting up terminal operations in chain supermarkets. The threat to banking institutions is further increased by the possibility that institutions not in the business of accepting deposits may be able to do so in the future. It has been suggested that large consumer finance companies and even giant retail chains may eventually get into the business of holding consumer

Figure 20-1. *Consumer transaction facility.*
(Courtesy International Business Machines Corporation.)

cash balances and transferring funds. Some government officials fear that as a result of EFTS several nationwide "superbanks" could evolve from existing credit card organizations, huge bank operations, or large retail chains.

Some bankers believe an unplanned rush into the use of EFTS by large competitors could cause the extinction of small suburban and rural banks and thrift institutions. Others believe that the electronic revolution creates the possibility that a mere handful of institutions could expand across the country and eventually dominate consumer finance.

Competition for financial business has always been lively, with banks and savings and loan institutions competing for both deposits and loan business. Electronic technology has served as a catalyst to accelerate competition, which is now more intense than ever before.

Convenience has traditionally been a major factor in attracting financial business. This explains the numerous branch banks and savings and loan offices in metropolitan and residential shopping centers throughout the states where branch operations are legal. The availability of electronic terminals now makes it cheaper and easier to install a terminal in a supermarket than to open a branch.

In December 1974, Comptroller of the Currency James E. Smith ruled that remote electronic terminals are not branch banks within the meaning of the National Bank Act. This ruling would allow national banks to install remote computer terminals without regard to limitations placed on state-chartered banks. As a result of this challenge, the Independent Bankers Association of America, representing 7,300 commercial banks, filed suit, contending that terminals are branches and must comply with state bank laws.

On March 25, 1976, the U.S. Court of Appeals ruled that unmanned or manned computer terminals outside national bank buildings are branches. Therefore, the court said that national banks must comply with state laws before establishing remote computer hookups in supermarkets or elsewhere.

Legal controversies are as inevitable as the continued growth of EFTS. Eventual decisions by Congress and the courts will determine the future of electronic banking. In the meantime, Congress has chartered the National Commission on Electronic Fund Transfers to guide the evolution of EFT systems and, hopefully, settle disputes by proposing solutions to the complex economic and legal issues arising from this new technology.

SOCIAL RESISTANCE TO TECHNOLOGICAL CHANGES

The introduction to this chapter included a reference to the lag between social acceptance of the computer and its technological capacity and potential uses. Let us consider some examples of this phenomenon, especially in the area of electronic checkout and funds-transfer systems, for which the technology is already available and operating.

Remote Automated Tellers

These systems, identified above as electronic funds-transfer systems, have a far-reaching potential for impersonal efficiency as well as for possible abuse. They have the advantage, through telecommunications, of being able to dispense cash, accept deposits, or transfer funds on a 24-hour basis without regard to distance from the parent financial institution. There are some concerns about their use, however, including the following.

1. The speed with which EFT systems can complete transactions reduces the ability of individuals to benefit from the "float," the time it takes for funds in a conventional check transaction to be transferred from one account to another. The consumer automaticaly loses the grace period he may need if his account balance is low, as once the card is inserted in the terminal and the buttons are pushed, the money is transferred instantly.
2. Cash crime would probably decline, as Americans would not need to carry as much cash. However, home burglaries might increase, and new possibilities would exist for computer fraud.
3. Family spending might be more difficult to control if various members gain access to the system through a family credit card.
4. Large quantities of information on financial transactions would be accumulated in a way that might threaten individual privacy. For example, information about an individual's buying habits and also his whereabouts are available instantly each time he completes a transaction.

Automated Payroll Deposits

Current technology permits salary payments to be electronically recorded on magnetic tape and delivered to the bank or savings institution for deposit directly to the employee's account. Under this system all that employees receive directly is a summary slip indicating how much has been deposited and other pertinent information. The Treasury Department already has plans to route 16 million recurring federal payments, including social security and veterans' benefits, directly to recipients' accounts. By the end of 1976, 4.6 million monthly social security deposits were being handled electronically. The government hopes that by 1980, 40 per cent of all federal payments will be sent as a computer tape message through the Federal Reserve's wire system to financial institutions in all regions of the country.

Bankers are receptive and are encouraging this idea. However, many doubt that efforts to sell the plan can overcome the preference of recipients to receive and cash or deposit their own checks. Direct deposits deprive them of the satisfaction and flexibility that they receive from having a "check in hand."

Preauthorized Bill Payments

Many banks and savings and loan firms are expected to encourage depositors to authorize automatic deductions from accounts to cover fixed bill payments such as mortgages, rent, loans, insurance, and utilities. The typical consumer's fear is that he will lose control of his finances if banking institutions take over the payment of his bills automatically. Another concern that applies to this technique, as well as all of the preceding examples of electronic funds transfers, is how the privacy of individuals will be protected once computers record every bank transaction and purchase they make.

Point-of-Sale Transfers

Retail establishments using this system may be linked directly to bank computers. By inserting the customer's credit card in a terminal, the merchant can obtain instant credit authorization from the bank, or the customer can choose to automatically and instantly transfer the cost of the purchase from his bank account to that of the merchant.

In spite of promotion by the banking industry, this system may not be in full operation for several years for two reasons. First, most Americans are satisfied with using cash or checks for the 250 billion payment transactions that occur each year. Secondly, many persons have some of the same apprehensions about point-of-sale transfers that were discussed above in relation to remote automated tellers.

Nevertheless, it is expected that 70 per cent of the current annual volume of 28 billion check payments will be handled eventually by electronic transfers. This will avert the paperwork crisis that would have been created by an increased volume of checks. In addition, it is anticipated that electronic transfer of funds will result in decreased processing costs, which are presently estimated to be about 30 cents for each check transaction and about 50 cents for each credit card transaction.

Automated Checkout Systems

While the increased use of automated electronic checkout systems in the nation's supermarkets is inevitable, certain aspects of the proposed systems are being challenged by consumer advocates. The major issue is whether or not the marking of prices on each can and package should be discontinued as part of the cost savings plan, leaving the shelf marking as the shopper's sole source of price information. Industry spokesmen consider the elimination of item pricing to be an essential part of the technological advance. They estimate that it could account for as much as one-fourth of the potential savings under the new plan.

A basic element of this system is the use of bar code rather than stamped prices. As the checkout clerk passes each item over a scanning unit, a laser beam reads the bar code imprinted on the label. The scanning unit then sends an impulse to the computer, which looks up the product description and price and transmits the data to the cash register for listing on the tape. Since the clerk does not have to search for a stamped price, the checkout process moves as much as 45 per cent faster, according to tests.

However, while retailers stress savings to buyers, consumer groups such as the Consumer Federation of America, National Consumers League, and the National Consumers Congress are staunch in their insistence that item pricing should not be stopped. They insist that it is an important shopping tool allowing the consumer to compare prices as he moves around the store and later to check prices against the receipt tape. Also of concern is that shelf pricing alone may make it easier and more tempting for stores to raise prices in the computer, which is an easy process, without adjusting shelf prices. The consumer then would have no way to cross-check.

Symbol marking has moved along on schedule, with 75 per cent of all grocery items now bearing the Universal Product Code. However, legislation requiring item pricing may slow down the installation of bar code systems. Several cities, including Chicago, as well as the states of Connecticut, Rhode Island, California, and Massachusetts now have laws specifically requiring item pricing, and more legislative action is likely.

Retailers charge that opposition to the new system is premature and that consumers will benefit from better service and lower prices as a result of its implementation. Even consumer leaders, who admit that the system will be nationwide in a matter of years, believe that automation will ultimately benefit shoppers. In the meantime, the controversy provides another dramatic example of a negative social reaction to technological change.

CONCLUSION

The main purpose of this chapter was to identify some of the continuing problems and typical social and economic conflicts that arise as a result of technological advancements. Many of these problems will be resolved or modified with the passing of time. Their current status will have to be ascertained through classroom discussion or student research in periodicals.

As for the future, we prefer for several reasons not to engage in prolonged speculation about probable new developments. First, we feel that the challenge of comprehending the existing state of technology, applications, and social ramifications is sufficient. Secondly, the rapid rate of technological progress makes even short-range predictions somewhat hazardous. Instead of indulging in flamboyant statements about the future, let it suffice to say that the impressive developments in the field of data processing that have occurred to date will undoubtedly be matched or exceeded by events yet to come. If this is true, the social and economic adjustments to be faced in the next several decades will indeed be awesome.

IMPORTANT WORDS AND PHRASES

privacy
confidentiality
data security

electronic funds-transfer
    system (EFTS)
automated payroll deposits

point-of-sale transfer
preauthorized bill payments
automated checkout system

REVIEW QUESTIONS

1. What types of office employees are most affected by the installation of electronic computing systems?
2. Define data security.
3. List the steps that have been taken to reduce computer fraud.
4. Briefly describe the purposes of an electronic funds-transfer system.
5. In what way do the electronic funds-transfer systems threaten the traditional banking system?
6. What are the main consumer concerns about the use of electronic funds-transfer systems?
7. How are preauthorized bill payments handled?
8. Describe the purposes of a point-of-sale system.
9. Briefly describe the operation of an automatic checkout system.
10. What is the main source of controversy concerning the use of bar code in automatic checkout systems?

APPENDIX **PUNCHED CARD MACHINES**

To facilitate the presentation of punched card machine functions and applications, this appendix is based mainly on equipment manufactured by the International Business Machines Corporation, producers of the majority of the punched card equipment used in the United States. The basic functions performed by UNIVAC and other makes of equipment are comparable, however, even though the machines vary in mechanical detail and methods of performing operations.

Chapter 5 stressed the significance of the basic unit in punched card data processing: the standard card containing numerical and alphabetical data in the form of punched holes. These holes may be read electrically by machines that respond by performing automatically a variety of operations to be explored in this appendix. Before proceeding, however, let us consider the means by which machines are able to read and interpret punched holes.

CONTROLLING PUNCHED CARD MACHINES

Since most punched card machines can perform more than one function, there must be a way to direct each machine so that it will know what function it is to perform and how to handle the information it receives from punched holes. A control panel is provided with most IBM machines so that they may be instructed to produce the desired results. The control panel or board can be removed from, or inserted into, the machine when desired. The panel has many small holes, called *hubs,* into which wires with special tips can be inserted to control the functions of the machine. Each of these hubs has a specific function (Figure A–1).

A control panel is comparable in principle to a telephone switchboard that produces a signal light telling the operator what line an incoming call is on. After answering the call, the operator plugs the cord into a hub on the board that is internally connected to the desired line. In this way the operator completes an electrical circuit to establish a telephone connection. A control panel accomplishes the same thing by enabling electrical circuits to be completed through wires inserted into the panel (Figure A–2). When a control panel is fitted into place on the machine, each inserted wire connected to a jack makes contact with one of the

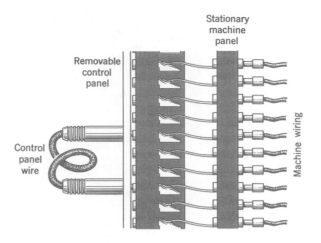

Figure A-1. *Jack contacts on a control panel.*

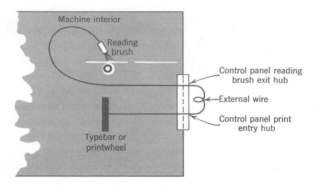

Figure A-2. *Electrical impulse directed to a typebar through a wired control panel.*

metal contacts on the subpanel of the machine itself. In this way the external wiring completes the desired circuits.

CARD PUNCHING AND VERIFYING

Among the most widely used card punches today is the IBM Model 29 (Figure A–3). This machine will be used to describe card-punching equipment.

IBM 29 Card Punch

Two types of keyboards are available on the IBM 29 as well as on other card punch machines. One keyboard, which resembles the keyboard on a ten-key adding machine, records numeric data only. The other, which is similar to the keyboard of a typewriter in appearance and operation, will record alphabetic as well as numeric data (Figure A–4). On the combination keyboard a group of keys controlled by the right hand serves for punching numbers as well as letters (Figure A–5). The shift from numbers to letters is made manually by a shift key or automatically by the program unit, which will be discussed later. Since most card punch-

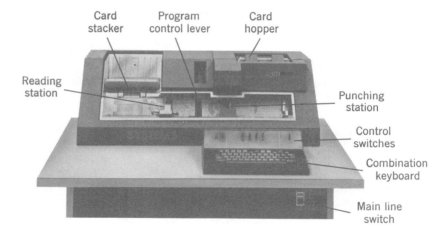

ing is composed of numerical data, the numerical keys on the card punch are conveniently grouped for one-hand, ten-key operation. This eliminates the more difficult two-hand motions that would be required if the numerical keys were arranged as they are on a typewriter.

Cards are fed into the card punch from the card hopper located at the upper right of the machine. The hopper has a capacity of about 500 cards, which are deposited face forward with the 9-edges down. A card is fed from the front of the hopper to the card bed by depressing the

Figure A-5. *IBM 29 Card Punch and 59 Verifier combination keyboard and keyboard chart.*

feed key. The first two cards to be punched must be fed by key depression, but all other cards in the hopper can be fed automatically by setting an automatic feed switch.

Cards are punched at the first of two stations along the card bed. Punching operations are normally started by feeding two cards into the card bed at the right of the punching station. As the second card is fed, column 1 of the first card is automatically positioned at the punching station. While the first card is being punched, the second card remains at its right. When column 80 of the first card passes the punching station, the second card moves into position at the punching station, and the next card in the hopper feeds down to the card bed. It is also possible for a single card to be inserted in the card bed by hand and then positioned at the punching station by depressing the register key.

After the punching of a card has been completed, the card proceeds from the punching station to the reading station, which performs an important function. Some of the information in a group of cards is often repetitive. Duplicating these holes from card to card by manual punching would be time-consuming. Instead, the duplication can be performed automatically by depressing a *duplicate key,* which results in the automatic punching of the holes that are being sensed in the corresponding column of the preceding card at the reading station.

The cards at the punching and the reading stations can be backspaced as far as desired by holding down the backspace key located below the card bed, between the reading and punching stations. The backspace key is also used to release the keyboard when it becomes locked. This may happen if keys 1 to 18 are depressed while the keyboard is in numerical shift.

The operator is able to determine the position of cards passing the punch and read stations by means of a column indicator that identifies the next column to be punched. Column numbers appear on the base of a drum that turns synchronously with the cards being punched and read. The indicator greatly facilitiates the location of a particular column while spacing forward or backward.

Certain repetitive operations can be accomplished automatically by means of a device called the *program unit*. This is a simple and flexible device that permits programs for automatic card-punching operations to be easily prepared and inserted (Figure A–6). The program unit controls automatic skipping over columns not to be punched, automatic duplicating of repetitive information, and the shifting from numerical to alphabetic punching positions and vice versa. These actions are controlled by the *program card* (Figure A–7) and are determined by the manner in which the card is prepared. A separate program card must be prepared for each different series of cards being punched.

After each card passes the reading station, it is fed into the card stacker located at the upper left of the machine. Cards are stacked 12-edges to the rear, face up. Cards are deposited in the stacker, which holds about 500 cards, in the same sequence as they were punched. The main line switch is turned off automatically when the stacker is full.

The printing model of the 29 Card Punch prints data along the top of the card as holes are being punched.

The incorrect punching of cards means that wrong information will be included in reports or that time must be spent in searching for correct

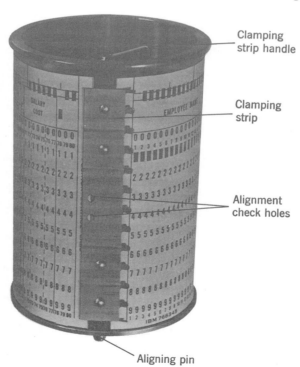

Figure A-6. *Program drum for IBM 29 Card Punch and 59 Verifier.*

(Courtesy International Business Machines Corporation.)

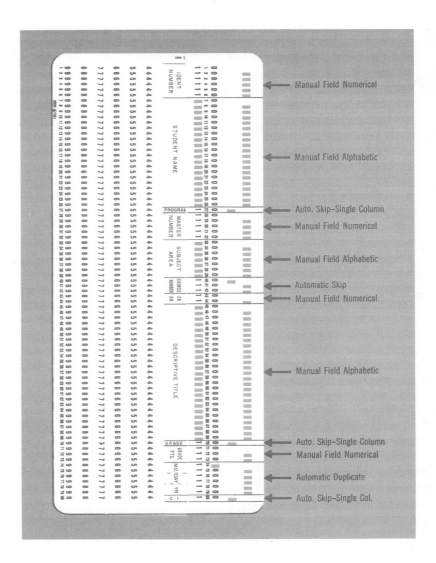

Figure A-7. *Program card showing the use of the 12, 11, 0, and 1 punches.*

IBM 59 Verifier

data on source documents and repunching cards. It is, therefore, important to verify the accuracy of original card punching. Visual verification is possible if cards are punched with a machine that prints. In this case, the printed data at the top of the cards can be visually compared with the data on source documents to assure accuracy. However, the most commonly used method is machine verification.

The features of the IBM 59 Verifier are comparable to those of the IBM 29 Card Punch, and the operating techniques are almost identical.

After a group of cards has been punched by a card punch operator, the cards may be given to a verifier operator to be checked for accuracy.

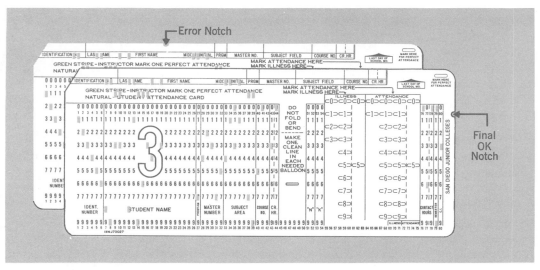

Figure A-8. *Verified cards with error notch on incorrect card (top), and OK notch on right side of correct card (bottom).*

Using the same source documents in the same sequence, the verifier operator duplicates the keystrokes of the card punch operator, but in the verification process no holes are punched. Instead, a sensing mechanism consisting of 12 pins determines the location of the holes that were previously punched. If the verifier operator strikes the same key that the card punch operator used to punch a certain column, the card proceeds to the next column to be checked. If, however, the verifier operator strikes a different key, the machine locks, and a signal light indicates that an error occurred either in the original or in the verifying keystroke. The verifier operator has two more chances to obtain agreement between the verifying and the original keystrokes. If there is no agreement after three attempts, the top edge of the card is notched in the column being checked (Figure A–8). This identifies the column in which the error occurred so that the card punch operator can prepare a new card to replace the one punched in error. All cards that pass the verifier test are notched on the right edge of the card opposite the 1 row and are then ready for the next processing step (Figure A–8).

UNIVAC 1710
Verifying Interpreting
Punch

The UNIVAC 1710 Verifying Interpreting Punch (see Figure 1–3) is designed to punch data into standard 80-column cards using a buffer principle. All keypunching is initiated in the normal manner. However, instead of each keystroke causing the card to be punched, data is entered into core storage. When all information for the card is in storage, the punching operation takes place automatically, as information for the next card is being entered.

The 1710 is a multipurpose machine capable of automatic printing as part of keypunching or verifying. It also provides for separate printing on punched cards. The machine utilizes magnetic core storage permitting instant correction of sensed errors and the storage of programmed instructions used to control the performance of certain automatic operations such as skipping and duplicating.

INTERPRETING

It is possible for humans to determine the contents of a card by analyzing the punched holes. This, however, is a slow and tedious process that may be averted by the use of the *interpreter* (Figure A–9). This machine is designed to read holes punched in a card and print the contents across the face of the same card or another card (Figure A–10). Interpreting makes it possible to use the punched card method for many applications, such as bills or checks, that require visual reference to data included on the cards. Moreover, manual filing of cards is simplified if the cards in the file as well as those to be filed are interpreted. Generally, each card in a file is partially interpreted to facilitate quick reference to the contents.

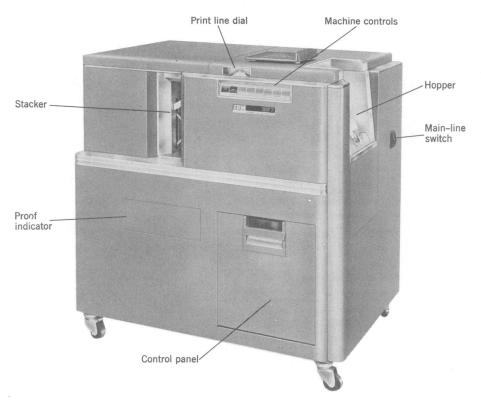

Figure A-9. *IBM 557 Interpreter. (Courtesy International Business Machines Corporation.)*

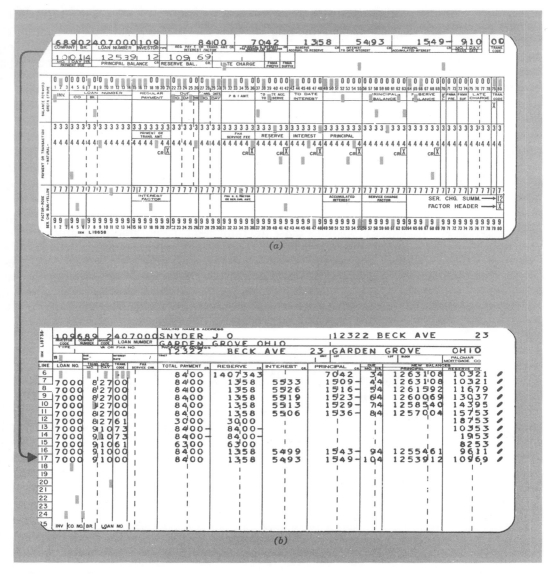

Figure A-10. *Data on payment card (a) posted to installment loan ledger card (b) by punched card*
interpreter.

**AUTOMATIC
PUNCHING**

The need for repetition is a basic characteristic of record keeping. For
example, identical dates are entered repeatedly on data processing records originating on the same date. Records of common origin must contain identical source location data. Information used for one purpose
may need to be duplicated for other purposes. Partial changes may have

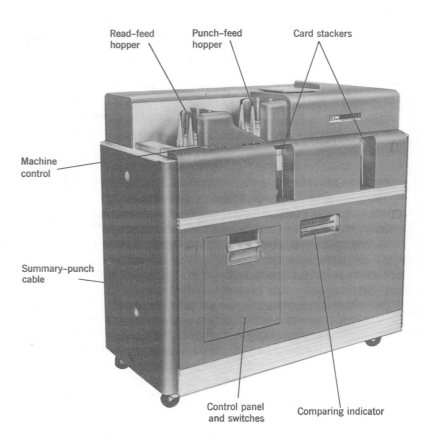

Read–feed hopper
Punch–feed hopper
Card stackers
Machine control
Summary–punch cable
Control panel and switches
Comparing indicator

Figure A-11. *IBM 519 Document-Originating Machine.*
(Courtesy International Business Machines Corporation.)

to be made on entire sets of cards, or original records may have to be partially changed on a continuing basis in order to keep them up to date. When records are maintained in punched card form, these repetitious operations can be performed by *automatic punches* or *reproducers* (Figure A–11).

Automatic Punching Operations

Automatic punches are capable of performing the operations described below.

Reproducing. All or part of the data contained in a card may be automatically punched into another card. The data may be punched into the same location as on the original card, or fields of data may be rearranged into a different sequence. The accuracy of this operation can be simultaneously verified by a comparing feature that proves agreement between originals and reproductions. Differences are automatically detected and cause the machine to stop reproducing.

Gangpunching. Data recorded on a master card can be transferred automatically to each detail card that follows it.

Emitting. By means of a special device the reproducer can be wired to automatically punch into any position of any column without the necessity of reading a comparable punch from another card. This repetitive punching can be performed in conjunction with any other operation.

Summary Punching. When the automatic punch and punched card accounting machine are connected by a cable, totals that have been accumulated in the accounting machine from detail cards can be punched into a total card. These total or summary cards can then be used for various purposes without the need for repeated processing of the detail cards.

Mark Sensing. Data recorded on a card by electrically conductive pencil marks can be detected by the machine and automatically converted into punched holes.

SORTING

After punching and verification, cards must be arranged in an orderly sequence to facilitate further processing. In addition, after initial arrangement, it may be necessary to rearrange cards in various ways for use in preparing special reports. These functions are performed on a machine called a *sorter* (Figure A–12).

One of the greatest advantages of the punched card method is the ease with which cards can be arranged in sequence according to any field on the card. The field selected is called the *control field*. For example, sales data might be sorted according to region, salesperson, commodity, or customer, each of which is recorded in a group of columns called a field.

It is often necessary to arrange cards in a sequence other than that in which they are stored. As an example, cards normally maintained in some numerical sequence may be required in alphabetical sequence for the preparation of a report. Or they may be filed in numerical sequence by one control field but may have to be rearranged into a different numerical sequence as required by another control field. They may have to be arranged in ascending sequence, that is, starting with the lowest control number or letters and proceeding to the highest, or they may have to be arranged in descending sequence. All of these operations are classified as sorting. Although a simple operation in itself, sorting requires a great deal of skill in card handling when performed on a sorter.

Sorting Operations

The various operations that can be performed on a sorter can be classified under four major categories, as follows.

Numeric Sorting. Cards can be arranged in numerical sequence by sorting all columns of the control field one at a time proceeding from

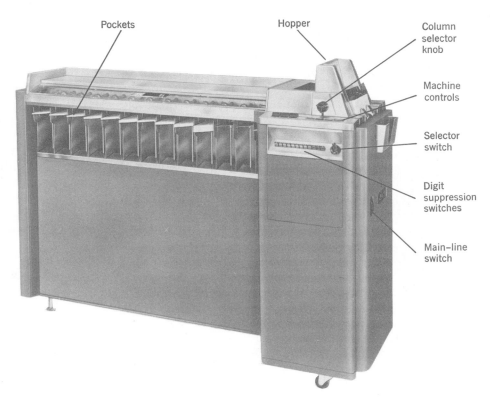

Figure A-12. *IBM 83 Sorter. (Courtesy International Business Machines Corporation.)*

Labels on figure: Pockets, Hopper, Column selector knob, Machine controls, Selector switch, Digit suppression switches, Main–line switch

right to left. A control field can be any field common to all cards used in an operation, such as employee number, invoice number, or loan number.

Upon completion of each pass (the sorting of all cards on a selected card column), the cards are removed from the sorter pockets in ascending sequence 0 through 9. (Pockets 0 to 9 on the sorter are adequate for sorting cards in numerical sequence because the numerals 0 to 9 are represented by only one punch in a column.) As shown in the table below, after the first pass the cards are arranged according to the low-order or units column of the control field. The cards are replaced in the machine, and it is adjusted to sort on the second or tens column. Following the second pass the cards are properly arranged from 00 to 99 according to the first two columns. This process is repeated until all columns have been sorted. Thus, a three-column field requires three passes, a five-column field five passes, and so on.

Alphabetic Sorting. Cards may be arranged in alphabetic sequence by passing them through the sorter twice for each column in the control field. Two sorts are necessary on each column since alphabetic characters are composed of two punches, a zone punch and a digit punch.

Block Sorting.   When the volume of cards is so great that it is inconvenient to finish all sorting in one operation, it is sometimes desirable to separate the cards into blocks. To accomplish this, the cards are first sorted according to the high-order digit of the control field, which separates them into ten blocks. Each block is then sorted separately and can be forwarded to the next processing step before the remainder of the sorting has been completed. For example, if it were necessary to sort ten thousand cards, they could be sorted first into ten groups by the block sorting technique. This would allow the cards in the one thousand series to be sorted completely and forwarded, then the cards in the two thousand series, and so on. It also would allow blocks to be sorted on more than one machine at a time.

| | Sequence of Cards During a Numeric Sort | | |
Random order	End of first pass	End of second pass	End of third pass
579	121	805	024
966	552	121	121
786	344	024	246
478	024	344	344
246	805	345	345
805	345	246	478
552	966	552	552
344	786	966	579
121	246	478	786
024	478	579	805
345	579	786	966

Digit Sorting or Selecting.   In addition to sorting as described above, the sorter can also select specific items from a group of cards. Not all the cards in a file need to be sorted if only cards with a particular digit are needed. Selection switches provide a means of selecting certain items that require special attention without disturbing the sequence of the other cards in the file. Thus, if all credit transactions are needed to prepare a special report, it is possible to remove them from a file containing all types of transactions without affecting the remainder of the file.

COMPARING AND ANALYZING

In the preceding section the importance of arranging cards in an orderly sequence was discussed, and it was indicated that the basic arrangement of cards is performed on the sorter. There are, however, more complex

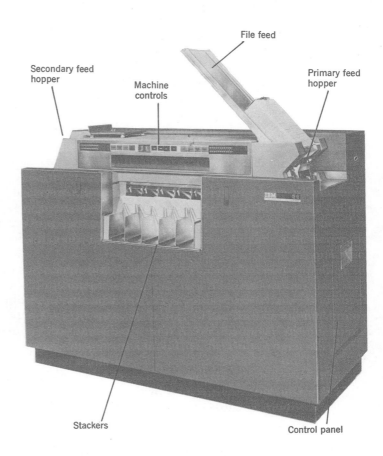

File feed

Secondary feed
hopper

Machine
controls

Primary feed
hopper

Stackers

Control panel

Figure A-13. *IBM 88 Collator.*

(Courtesy International Business Machines Corporation.)

arrangement and handling functions that cannot be done on the sorter. These functions are performed by the *collator* (Figure A–13). Because the collator is capable of more types of operations, it supplements the sorter in many systems.

The basic function of the collator is to feed and compare two files of cards simultaneously in order to match them or combine them into a single file. At the same time the collator will automatically detect and separate cards from each file that do not have a matching card in the other file.

Collating Operations

Collators are used to perform the following types of operations:

Sequence Checking. After the sorter has been used to place a file of cards in a desired sequence, the file can be checked on the collator to determine if the sequence is correct. The collator does this by comparing each card with the one ahead of it. The machine may be directed to stop if an error is detected, or it may be directed to separate all cards that are out of sequence.

Merging.　In this operation two files of cards already in sequence can be combined into one file. As cards from the two files are fed simultaneously, the card at the primary reading station is compared with the card at the secondary reading station and the one with the smaller number is dropped into a designated pocket. As a card advances to replace the one that has dropped, it is compared with the card remaining from the previous operation, and the process is repeated.

Matching.　In this operation instead of merging the two files, cards in either file that do not match the other can be separated, and cards that do match remain in the two original groups. Thus, as cards from the two groups simultaneously pass the primary and secondary reading stations and are compared, those that match are dropped side by side into the two center pockets. The primary cards for which there are no matching secondary cards are dropped into one outside pocket, and the secondary cards for which there are no matching primary cards are dropped into the other outside pocket. (Cards are called primary or secondary according to the feed hopper into which they are placed.) When the operation is completed, there may be four groups of cards: two groups of matched and two groups of unmatched, as illustrated in Figure A–14.

Merging with Selection.　The operation of merging two files into one can be controlled so that if either file contains cards that do not match cards in the other, these cards can be separated. In effect, this operation represents a combination of the procedures described in the two preced-

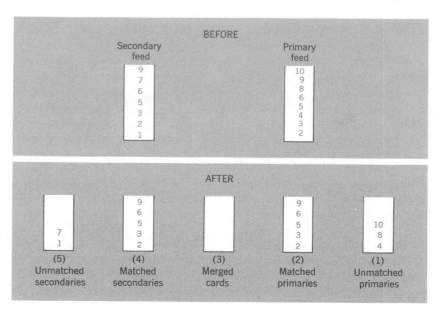

Figure A-14. *Results of a matching operation performed on a collator.*

ing paragraphs. Here, matching cards are merged together rather than being left in their original two groups. As in the case of the matching operation, however, unmatched cards from the primary and secondary groups are deposited in separate pockets. Thus, at the end of the operation, there may be three groups of cards: one group of merged cards and two groups of selected, or unmatched, cards.

Card Selection. The collator also has the ability to select certain types of cards from a file without disturbing the sequence of the others. The selecting task of the collator is similar to that of the sorter, except that the collator can select on more than one card column. Selected cards may be the first card of a group, a single card group, the last card of a group, a card with a particular number, or a card with numbers between two control numbers. Selected cards also may be X or no-X cards. To illustrate, in applications that require a distinction between male and female employees, all female employees might be identified with an X punch (11 punch) in a designated card column. In this case, card selection would consist of separating male from female employees as determined by the presence or absence of an X punch.

Glossary

Absolute address
An address assigned by the machine designer to a particular storage location. A pattern of characters that identifies a unique storage location without additional modification.

Access arm
That part of a disk storage device that is used to hold the reading and writing heads.

Access time
The time interval between the instant at which data is called for from a storage device and the instant delivery is completed, that is, the read time. Also the time interval between the instant at which data is requested to be stored and the instant at which storage is completed, that is, the write time.

Accumulator
A storage device in the arithmetic unit in which the results of arithmetic and logic operations are formed.

Adder
A device whose output represents the sum of the quantities represented by its inputs.

Address
A label, name, or number identifying a register, a storage location, or a device from which information is received or to which it is transmitted. Any part of an instruction that specifies the location of an operand for the instruction.

Address modification
The process of changing the address part of a machine instruction by means of coded instructions.

Address register
A register in which an address is stored.

ADP
Automatic data processing. A system that uses a minimum of manual operations in processing data.

ALGOL
An abbreviation for algorithmic oriented language. An international procedure-oriented language.

Alphabetic string
A character string consisting solely of letters from the same alphabet.

Alphanumeric
Pertaining to a character set that contains letters, digits, or special characters.

Alphanumerical code
A system in which characters may be either letters of the alphabet, numerals, or special symbols.

Analog computer
A calculating device that operates on numbers represented by measurable physical quantities such as the rotaton of a shaft, the amount of voltage, temperature, etc.

AND
A logic operator having the property that if A is a statement, B is a statement, C is a statement . . . , then the AND of A,B,C . . . is true if all statements are true, false if any statement is false.

Annotation
A descriptive comment or explanatory note.

Argument	An independent variable. For example, in looking up a quantity in a table, the number, or any of the numbers, that identifies the location of the desired value.
Arithmetic unit	The part of the computer processing section that does the adding, subtracting, multiplying, dividing, and comparing.
Array	A series of items arranged in a meaningful manner.
ASCII	An acronym for American Standard Code for Information Interchange. The standard code, using a coded character set consisting of bit-coded characters (8 bits including parity check), used for information exchange between data processing systems, communication systems, and associated equipment.
Assembly program	A computer program that takes sequential instructions written by the programmer in a nonmachine language and changes them to codes or language used by the machine on which the program is to be run.
Automatic programming	The process of using a computer to perform some stages of the work involved in preparing a program.
Automation	The implementation of processes by automatic means. The investigation, design, development, and application of methods of making processes or machines self-moving or self-controlling.
Auxiliary operation	An operation performed by equipment not under continuous control of the central processing unit.
Auxiliary storage	A storage that supplements another storage.
Background processing	The automatic execution of lower-priority computer programs when higher-priority programs are not using the system resources.
Bandwidth	The difference, expressed in the number of cycles per second, between the two limiting frequencies of a band.
Bar code	A coding system using bars or stripes of various widths to denote numeric values.
Base address	An address from which an absolute address is created by combination with a relative address.
BASIC	An abbreviation for Beginner's All-purpose Symbolic Instruction Code. A mathematical problem-oriented programming language.
Batch processing	A method by which a number of similar transactions or problems are grouped for processing in sequence during a single continuous machine run.
Baud	A unit of signalling speed equal to the number of discrete conditions or signal events per second. For example, one baud equals one-half dot cycle per second in Morse Code, one bit per second in a train of binary signals, and one 3-bit value per second in a train of signals each of which can assume one of eight different states.
Baudot code	A system of coding data for transmission in which five bits represent one character.
Binary	A characteristic or property involving a selection, choice, or condition in which there are two possibilities, such as the number representation with a radix of two.
Binary coded decimal (BCD)	A decimal notation in which the individual decimal digits are represented by a pattern of ones and zeros; e.g., in the 8-4-2-1 binary coded decimal notation, the number 12 is represented as 0001 0010 for 1 and 2, respectively, whereas in pure binary notation it is represented as 1100.

Binary number system	A number system using the base two, as opposed to the decimal number system, which uses the base ten.
Bit	The smallest unit of information in the binary number system. An abbreviation of "binary digit." Normally, a bit refers to one ("on"), while a no bit means zero (off").
Bit string	A string of binary digits (bits) in which the position of each binary digit is considered as an independent unit.
Block	A group of machine words considered or transported as a unit. In flowcharts, each block represents a logical unit of programming.
Block diagram	A diagram of a system, instrument, computer, or program in which selected portions are represented by annotated boxes and interconnecting lines.
Block sort	A sort of one or more of the most significant characters of a key to serve as a means of making groups of workable size from a large volume of records to be sorted.
Boolean algebra	A process of reasoning or a deductive system of theorems using a symbolic logic, and dealing with classes, propositions, or on-off circuit elements. It employs symbols to represent operators, such as AND, OR, NOT, EXCEPT, IF, THEN, etc., to permit mathematical calculation.
Bootstrap	A technique for loading the first few instructions of a routine into storage, then using these instructions to bring the rest of the routine into the computer from an input device. This usually involves either entering a few instructions manually or using a special key on the console.
Branch instructions	Instructions that cause the computer to switch from one point in a program to another point, thereby controlling the sequence in which operations are performed.
Branching	A computer programming term indicating that a sequence of steps has been completed or is to be broken and that the sequence is to be repeated or changed to a new one.
Broadband	Data transmission facilities capable of handling frequencies greater than those required for high-grade voice communications, i.e., greater than 300 characters per second.
Buffer	A temporary or intermediate storage unit used to hold data being transmitted between internal and external storage units or between input-output devices and internal storage.
Bus	A circuit used to transmit signals or power.
Byte	A sequence of adjacent binary digits operated upon as a unit.
Card code	The combination of punches used to represent alphabetic and numerical data on a punched card.
Card column	One of the vertical areas on a punched card in which a digit, letter, or symbol may be recorded.
Card feed	A mechanism that moves cards serially into a machine.
Card gauge	A metal plate, precisely inscribed with all punches of an 80-column card, used to check the accuracy of punching registration.

Card hopper	A device that holds cards and makes them available to a card feed mechanism. Synonymous with input magazine.
Card jam	A pile-up of cards in a machine.
Card punch	A device or machine that punches holes in cards in specific locations to store data that can be conveyed to other machines or devices by reading or sensing the holes.
Card stacker	An output device that accumulates punched cards in a deck.
Card system	A system that utilizes only punched cards as the medium for bearing data.
Cathode ray tube (CRT)	An electronic vacuum tube containing a screen on which output data may be displayed in graphic form or by character representation.
Central processing unit (CPU)	The unit of a computing system that contains the arithmetic, logical, and control circuits necessary for the interpretation and execution of instructions.
Chad	A portion of tape or card that is removed when a code is punched.
Chadded	The method of punching tape in which chad results.
Chadless	A type of punching of tape in which each chad is left fastened by about a quarter of the circumference of the hole at the leading edge.
Channel	A path over which information is transmitted, generally from some input-output device to storage. With reference to magnetic or punched tape, a channel is one of the parallel tracks in which data is recorded.
Character	A decimal digit, alphabetic letter, or a special symbol.
Character recognition	The identification of characters by automatic means.
Character set	A set of unique representations called characters, such as the 26 letters of the English alphabet or the decimal digits 0 through 9.
Character subset	A selection of characters from a character set, comprising all characters that have a specified common feature. For example, in the definition of character set, digits 0 through 9 constitute a character subset.
Check bit	A binary check digit. (See *Check digit.*)
Check digit	One or more redundant digits in a character or word that depend on the remaining digits in such a fashion that if a change of digits occurs in data transfer operations, the malfunction of equipment can be detected.
Checkpoint	A reference point to which error-free operation of the program has been verified and to which the program may return for restart in the event of subsequent failure.
Circuit	A system of conductors and related electrical elements through which electrical current flows. A communications link between two or more points.
Clear	To remove all information from a storage device of a machine and restore it to a prescribed state, usually that denoting zero or blank.
Clock	A device that generates periodic signals used for synchronization, or a device that measures and indicates time.
Closed shop	The operation of a computer facility in which problem programming is performed by a group of programming specialists rather than the originators of the problem. The use of the computer itself may also be considered as closed shop if trained operators, rather than user or programmers, serve as the operators.

Closed subroutine	A subroutine that can be stored at one place and can be linked to one or more calling routines.
COBOL	Common business oriented language. A coding language by which business data processing procedures may be precisely described in a standard form.
Code	A set of rules used to convert data from one representation to another.
Collate	To take two or more sets of related information already arranged according to the same sequence and to merge them in sequence into a single set.
Collating sequence	An ordering assigned to a set of items, such that any two sets in that assigned order can be collated.
Collator	A device to collate or merge sets of cards or other documents into a sequence.
Column binary	Pertaining to the binary representation of data on punched cards in which adjacent positions in a column correspond to adjacent bits of data, e.g., each column in a 12-row card may be used to represent 12 consecutive bits of a 36-bit word.
Command	A group of signals or pulses initiating one step in the execution of a computer program. Also called instruction.
Common language	A coded structure that is compatible with two or more data processing machines or families of machines, thus allowing them to communicate directly to one another.
Communication control character	A character used to control or facilitate transmission of data over communication networks.
Communication link	The physical means of connecting one location to another for the purpose of transmitting and receiving data.
Compare	To examine the representation of a quantity for the purpose of discovering its relationship to zero, or of two quantities for the purpose of discovering relative magnitude or identity.
Compiler	A programming system that produces a program from a series of source statements. It is capable of replacing single entries with a series of instructions or a subroutine. The compiler produces an expanded and translated version of the original or source program.
Computer network	A system consisting of two or more interconnected computers.
Computer program	A series of instructions, in form acceptable to the computer, prepared so as to achieve a certain result.
Computer word	A sequence of bits or characters treated as a unit and capable of being stored in one computer location.
Conditional jump	A jump that occurs if the criteria specified are met.
Console	The component of a data processing system that provides facilities for manual control and observation of the system's operation.
Constant	Data with a fixed value or meaning that is available for use throughout a program.
Continuous form	Paper or card forms attached for continuous feeding in an accounting machine or computer output device carriage.
Control operation	The action performed by a device; i.e., the starting or stopping of a particular process. Generally, carriage return, rewind, end of transmission, etc., are control operations.

Control panel	The demountable panel containing the external wiring to govern machine operations.
Control unit	The part of a computer system that effects the retrieval of instructions in proper sequence, the interpretation of each instruction, and the application of the proper signals to the arithmetic unit and other parts of the system in accordance with this interpretation.
Converter	A unit that changes the representation of data from one form to another so as to make it available or acceptable to another machine, e.g., from punched cards to magnetic tape.
Corner cut	A diagonal cut at the corner of a card to facilitate identification by sight or by a special rail brush.
Corrective maintenance	Maintenance intended to eliminate an existing fault. It can occur as either emergency maintenance or deferred maintenance.
Counter	A device, register, or storage location for storing integers, permitting these integers to be increased or decreased. A device used to represent the number of occurences of an event.
CPU	An abbreviation of central processing unit.
Crosstalk	The unwanted energy transferred from one circuit, called the "disturbing" circuit, to another circuit, called the "disturbed" circuit.
CRT display	Cathode ray tube display.
Cybernetics	The comparative study of the control and communication of information-handling machines and the human nervous system in order to understand and improve communication.
Cycle	An interval during which one set of events or phenomena is completed. A set of operations repeated regularly in the same sequence.
Data	A general term used to denote any facts, numbers, letters, and symbols, or facts that refer to or describe an object, idea, condition, situation, or other factors.
Data bank	A collection of libraries of data. Specifically, one line of an invoice may form an item; a complete invoice may form a record; a complete set of such records may form a file; the collection of inventory control files may form a library; and the libraries used by a business organization are known as its data bank.
Data base	A minimally redundant shared collection of data.
Data base management system	A combination of hardware and software that controls and processes all requests for data in data bases.
Data communications	The transmission of data between two or more points.
Data element	The smallest unit of data stored on some medium to which a reference or name may be assigned.
Data hierarchy	A data structure consisting of sets and subsets so that the data of every subset of a set is of lower rank than the data of the set.
Data management system	A series of computer programs used primarily in the manipulation of computer files and extraction of data from the files for report preparation.
Data name	A name given to a unit of data for the purpose of uniquely identifying that unit of data.

Data processing	Any operation or combination of operations on data to achieve a desired result.
Data reduction	The transformation of raw data into more useful form.
Data security	The protection of data from loss by unauthorized disclosure, destruction, or modification.
Debug	To detect, locate, and remove all malfunctions from a computer or all mistakes from a routine.
Decimal	The characteristic or property involving a selection, choice, or condition in which there are ten possibilities.
Decision table	A table that combines contingencies to be considered in the description of a problem, along with the actions to be taken. Decision tables are sometimes used instead of flowcharts to describe and document problems.
Deck	A collection of punched cards, commonly a complete set of cards that has been punched for a specific purpose.
Decode	To apply a code so as to reverse some previous encoding.
Decoder	A device that decodes. A matrix of switching elements that selects one or more output channels according to the combination of input signals present.
Detail printing	Printing information from each punched card passing through the machine.
Diagnostic check	A specific routine designed to locate a malfunction in the computer or a mistake in coding.
Digital computer	A calculating device utilizing numbers to express all the variables and quantities of a problem.
Direct access	An addressing scheme or random access storage medium that permits direct addressing of data locations.
Direct address	An address that specifies the location of an operand.
Display	A visual presentation of data or information.
Display station	A device that provides a visual representation of data on the face of a cathode ray tube.
Display tube	A tube, usually a cathode ray tube, used to display data or information.
Distributed processing	A system that assigns tasks in a large organization to smaller computers on the basis of location or type of task. These smaller computers may augment or replace a large, centralized computer.
Documentation	The collecting, organizing, and disseminating of documents or the information recorded in documents.
Dump	A copying or print out of all or part of the contents of a particular storage device. Synonymous with memory dump.
Duplicating	The automatic punching of information from a card or tape into succeeding cards or tape.
EBCDIC	An abbreviation of Extended Binary Coded Decimal Interchange Code.
Edge-notched card	A card in which holes have been punched around the edges. Notches made in the holes are used in coding information for a simple mechanical-search technique.

Edge-punched card	A card of fixed size into which information may be recorded or stored by punching holes along one edge in a pattern similar to that used for punched tape.
Edit	To rearrange information. Editing may involve the deletion of unwanted data, the selection of pertinent data, and the insertion of symbols.
EDP	Electronic data processing.
Electronic data processing system	The general term used to define a system for data processing by means of machines utilizing electronic circuitry at electronic speed, as opposed to electro-mechanical equipment.
Emulate	To imitate one system with another so that the imitating system accepts the same data, executes the same programs, and achieves the same results as the imitated system.
Encode	To apply a set of rules specifying the manner in which data may be represented such that a subsequent decoding is possible.
Erase	To replace all the binary digits in a storage device by binary zeros. To remove data from a magnetic surface or other memory unit.
Error message	An indication that an error has been detected.
Execution cycle	That part of a machine cycle during which an instruction is carred out.
Expression	A statement of one or more arithmetic operations to be performed on variables or constants.
External storage	The storage of data on a device such as magnetic tape that is not an integral part of a computer, but is in a form prescribed for use by a computer.
Facsimile	Transmission of pictures, maps, diagrams, etc., by wire.
Feedback	The process of returning portions of the output of a machine, process, or system for use as input in a further operation.
Ferromagnetics	In computer technology, the science that deals with the storage of information and the logical control of pulse sequences through the utilization of the magnetic polarization properties of materials.
Field	A group of related characters treated as a unit in computer operations. A set of one or more columns of a punched card consistently used to record similar information.
File	A collection of related records treated as a unit.
Fixed point	An arithmetic system in which all numerical quantities are expressed in a specified number of places with the radix point implicitly located at some predetermined position.
Fixed word length	Pertaining to a storage device in which the capacity for digits or characters in each unit of data is a fixed length as opposed to a variable length.
Flip-flop	A circuit or device containing active elements capable of assuming either one of two stable states at a given time.
Floating point	A system of representing numerical quantities with a variable number of places in which the location of the point does not remain fixed.
Flowchart	A graphical representation of the definition, analysis, or solution of a problem using symbols to represent operations, data flow, and equipment.

Flowchart symbol	A symbol used to represent data flow, operations, or equipment on a flowchart.
Format	The arrangement of data on a form or in storage.
FORTRAN	Formula translator. A programming language designed for problems that can be expressed in algebraic notation, allowing for exponentiation and up to three subscripts. The FORTRAN compiler is a routine for a given machine that accepts a program written in FORTRAN source language and produces a machine-language object program.
Gangpunching	The automatic punching of data read from a master card into the following detail cards.
General purpose computer	A computer that may be used to solve a wide variety of problems.
Generator	A program for a computer that generates the coding of a problem.
Group indication	Printed information identifying a group of data.
Group printing	Printing group totals and group indication as cards pass through an accounting machine.
Hardware	A colloquialism applied to the mechanical, electrical, and electronic features of a data processing system.
Hash total	A sum of numbers in a specified field of a record or batch of records used for checking or control purposes. The total may be insignificant except for audit purposes, as in the case of part numbers or customer numbers.
Head	A device that reads, records, or erases data on a storage medium, e.g., an electromagnet used to read, write, or erase data on a magnetic drum or tape, or the set of perforating, reading, or marking devices used to punch, read, or print on paper tape.
Header card	A prepunched record of the basic information pertaining to a specific individual or firm used to automatically create the upper portion of a document.
Heuristic	Exploratory method of problem solving in which solutions are discovered by evaluation of the progress made toward the final result.
Hexadecimal numbering system	A numbering system using the equivalent of the decimal number 16 as a base.
High-order position	The leftmost position of a number or word.
HIPO	An abbreviation for Hierarchy plus Input-Process-Output. A design and documentation technique to describe systems functions.
Hollerith code	A standard 12-channel punched card code in which each decimal digit, letter, or special character is represented by one or more rectangular holes punched in a vertical column.
Housekeeping routine	That part of a program, usually performed only at the beginning of machine operations, that establishes the initial conditions for instruction addresses, accumulator setting, switch setting, etc.
Hybrid computer	A computer system that combines analog and digital capabilities.

Identifier	A symbol whose purpose is to identify or name data in a programming language.
Idle time	That part of available time during which the computer is not being used.
IDP	Integrated data processing.
Illegal character	A character or combination of bits that is not valid according to the criteria used in the representation.
Index register	A register whose content may be added to or subtracted from the operand address prior to or during the execution of an instruction.
Index word	A storage position or register, the contents of which may be used to modify automatically the effective address of any given instruction.
Indexed sequential file	A file in which records are organized sequentially with indexes that permit quick access to individual records as well as rapid sequential processing.
Indexing	A method of address modification performed automatically by the data processing system.
Indirect address	An address that specifies a storage location containing either a direct address or another indirect address.
Information	The meaning derived from data. The subject, about which data is recorded, together with its associations with other subjects.
Information retrieval	The methods and procedures for recovering specific information from stored data.
Initialize	To set program variables, such as addresses, counters, program switches, etc., to zero or other starting values at the beginning of, or at prescribed points in, a computer routine.
In-line processing	The processing of data in random order without preliminary editing or sorting.
Input	Information transferred into the internal storage of a data processing system, including data to be processed or information to help control the process.
Input area	An area of storage reserved for input.
Input-output control system (IOCS)	A standard set of subroutines provided with an operating system to initiate and control the reading of input data and the writing of output data.
Inquiry station	Data terminal station used for inquiry into a data processing system.
Instruction	A set of characters that, when interpreted by the control unit, causes a data processing system to perform one of its operations.
Instruction cycle	That part of a machine cycle during which a computer instruction is transferred from a specified primary storage location to the instruction register in the control unit, where it is decoded before being executed.
Instruction register	The register that stores the current instruction governing a computer operation.
Integrated data processing	A system that treats all data processing requirements as a whole to reduce or eliminate duplicate recording or processing while accomplishing a sequence of data processing steps or a number of related data processing sequences.
Intelligent terminal	A communications station containing storage and some of the components of a small computer, thus allowing batched data to be organized and edited before being transmitted to a central computer.
Item	A collection of related characters, treated as a unit.

Interface	A common boundary between two systems or devices.
Internal storage	Storage facilities integrated as a physical part of the computer and directly controlled by the computer. Also called memory, main storage, primary storage, real storage, and central storage.
Interpret	To translate into or restate in human language. To print at the top of a punched card the information punched in it, using a machine called an interpreter.
Inter-record gap	An area on a data medium that signals the end of a block or record.
Interrupt	A break in the normal flow of a system or routine. Usually the normal operation can be resumed from that point at a later time. An interrupt is usually caused by a signal from an external source.
Job control statement	A statement in a program used to identify the job or describe its requirements
JCL	to the operating system.
Joggle	To align a deck of cards by jostling them against a plane surface.
Key punch	A keyboard-operated device that punches holes in a card to represent data.
Label	One or more characters used to identify or describe an item of data, record, message, or file. Occasionally it may be the same as the address in storage.
Language	A set of representations, conventions, and rules used to convey data or information.
Language translator	A general term for any assembler, compiler, or other routine that accepts statements in one language and produces equivalent machine-language instructions.
Library	A collection of standard proven computer routines, usually kept on a library tape or random access file, by which problems or portions of problems may be solved.
Library routine	A tested and usable routine maintained in a program library.
Line printing	The printing of an entire line of characters as a unit.
Literal	A symbol that names and defines itself.
Load	To put data into a register or into internal storage. To put a magnetic tape onto a tape drive, or to put cards into a card reader.
Load-and-go	An operating technique in which there are no stops between the loading and execution phases of a program, and which may include assembling or compiling.
Logarithm	The exponent of a number, indicating how many times the number must be multiplied by itself to produce another given number.
Logical operations	Nonarithmetical operations such as selecting, sorting, matching, comparing, etc.
Logical record	A record whose scope, direction, or length is governed by the specific nature of the information or data that it contains rather than by some feature or limitation of the storage device that holds it. Such records differ in size from the physical records in which they are contained.

Loop	The repetition of a group of instructions in a routine until certain conditions are reached.
Low-order position	The rightmost position of a number or word.
Machine instruction	An instruction that a machine can recognize and execute.
Machine language	The instructions written in a form intelligible to the internal circuitry of the computer; not ordinarily comprehensible to persons without special training. Sometimes called "actual" or "absolute."
Machine-sensible	Term denoting information in a form that can be read by one or more machines.
Macro instruction	A symbolic instruction in a source language that produces a number of machine-language instructions. It is made available for use by the programmer through an automatic programming system.
Magnetic card	A card with a magnetic surface on which data can be stored by selective magnetization of portions of the flat surface.
Magnetic core	A small doughnut-shaped piece of ferromagnetic material, about the size of a pin head, capable of storing one binary digit represented by the polarity of its magnetic field. Thousands of these cores strung on wire grids form an internal memory device. Cores can be individually charged to hold data and sensed to issue data.
Magnetic disk	A storage device by which information is recorded on the magnetizable surface of a rotating disk. A magnetic disk storage system is an array of such devices, with associated reading and writing heads mounted on movable arms.
Magnetic drum	A rotating cylinder, the surface of which is coated with a material on which information may be recorded as small magnetic spots representing binary information.
Magnetic ink	An ink that contains particles of a magnetic substance whose presence can be detected by magnetic sensors.
Magnetic ink character reader	A device capable of interpreting data typed, written, or printed in magnetic ink.
Magnetic ink character recognition	Machine recognition of characters printed with magnetic ink.
Magnetic tape	A tape or ribbon of material impregnated or coated with magnetic material on which information may be placed in the form of magnetically polarized spots.
Magnetic thin-film	A layer of magnetic material, usually less than one micron thick, often used for logic or storage elements.
Main storage	See *Internal storage*.
Management information system	Usually regarded as an on-line computer and communication system designed to furnish management personnel with data for decision-making. Generally, the data provided is in response to on-line interrogation.
Mass storage	An auxiliary storage device that provides on-line access to a very large collection of data.
Master file	A file of records containing a cumulative history or the results of accumulation; updated in each file-processing cycle, and carried forward to the next cycle.

Matching	Checking two files to see that there is a corresponding card or group of cards in each file.
Mathematical model	A mathematical representation of the behavior of a process, device, or concept.
Matrix	In mathematics, a two-dimensional rectangular array of quantities. Matrices are manipulated in accordance with the rules of matrix algebra. In computers, a logic network in the form of an array of input leads and output leads with logic elements connected at some of their intersections.
Memory	The part of a computer that stores the program, holds intermediate results and various constant data. Same as storage.
Memory dump	To copy the contents of all or part of a storage, usually from an internal storage into an external storage.
Merge	To combine items from two or more similarly sequenced files into one sequenced file without changing the order of the items.
Message switching	The technique of receiving complete messages and forwarding the messages at a switching center.
MICR	Magnetic ink character recognition. Machine recognition of characters printed with magnetic ink.
Microcomputer	A system based on the use of a microprocessor, a single chip that performs the basic arithmetic and logical as well as control functions equivalent to the central processing unit of a conventional computer.
Microprocessor	A programmable large-scale integrated chip containing all of the elements required to process binarily encoded data. Contains tens of thousands of components on a silicon chip measuring only a few millimeters in size and requiring only milliwatt power.
Microsecond	One-millionth of a second.
Microwave	Very short electromagnetic waves used in high-capacity communication networks for transmitting voice or data messages at ultra-high speeds.
Millisecond	One-thousandth of a second.
Minicomputer	A smaller version of a standard computer, applying large-computer technology to a scaled-down unit. Performs most of the operations executed by a larger computer, but circuitry, storage, and other features are reduced in scale and capacity to make them appropriate and economical for simpler or specialized applications.
Mnemonic	Assisting, or intended to assist, memory.
Modem	A contraction of MOdulator DEModulator. Its function is to interface with data processing devices and convert data to a form compatible for sending and receiving on transmission facilities.
Modifier	A quantity used to alter the address of an operand.
Modify	To alter in an instruction the address of the operand; to alter a subroutine according to a defined parameter.
Multiprocessing	A computer configuration consisting of multiple arithmetic and logical units for simultaneous use.
Multiprogramming	A technique whereby more than one program may reside in primary storage at the same time and be executed concurrently by means of an interweaving process.

Nanosecond	One-billionth of a second.
Network	The interconnection of a number of points by communication facilities.
Nondestructive read	A read process that does not erase the data in the source.
Normalize	In programming, to adjust the exponent and fraction of a floating point quantity so that the fraction lies in the prescribed normal standard range.
Numerical analysis	The study of methods of obtaining useful quantitative solutions to problems that have been stated mathematically, and the study of the errors and bounds on errors in obtaining such solutions.
Numerical control	Pertaining to the automatic control of processes by the proper interpretation of numerical data.
Object program	A program in machine language; generally, one that has been converted from a program written in symbolic language.
OCR	Optical character recognition. Machine recognition of printed characters.
Octal	Pertaining to the number base of eight. In octal notation, octal 214 is 2 times 64, plus 1 times 8, plus 4 times 1, and equals decimal 140.
Off-line	Equipment or devices not under the direct control of the central processing unit.
Off-line storage	A storage device not under control of the central processing unit.
OMR	An abbreviation of optical mark recognition.
On-line	Peripheral equipment or devices in direct communication with the central processing unit, and from which information reflecting current activity is introduced into the data processing system as soon as it occurs.
On-line storage	A storage device under direct control of the central processing unit.
Open subroutine	A tested subroutine that is inserted into a program at each place it is used.
Operand	That which is operated on. An operand is usually identified by an address part of an instruction.
Operating system	An organized collection of techniques and procedures for operating a computer.
Operating time	That part of available time during which the computer is operating and yielding correct results.
Operation	A defined action; one step in a procedure. The action specified by a single computer instruction. That which occurs when something is created, changed, or added to, such as writing, calculating, posting, or computing.
Operation code	The part of the command code of an instruction that designates the operation to be performed.
Operations research	The use of analytic methods adopted from mathematics for solving operational problems. The objective is to provide management with a more logical basis for making sound predictions and decisions.
Operator	In the description of a process or arithmetic statement, that which indicates the action to be performed on operands.
Optical character recognition	Machine recognition of printed characters through use of light-sensitive devices.
Optical mark recognition (OMR)	Machine recognition of marks on paper in the form of dots, check marks, or other recognizable symbols.

Optical scanner	A device that optically scans printed or written data and generates its digital representations.
Output	Information transferred from the internal storage of a data processing system to any device external to the system. Also, the results of operations performed on the data in data processing.
Overflow	In an arithmetic operation, the generation of a quantity beyond the capacity of the register or location that is to receive the result.
Parallel	To handle simultaneously in separate facilities. To operate on two or more parts of a word or item simultaneously.
Parameter	A quantity to which an arbitrary value may be assigned but which remains fixed for each program. In a program generator, parameters are used to specify certain machine hardware and data limits to be observed in the program being generated.
Parity bit	A binary digit appended to an array of bits as required to make the sum of all the bits always odd or always even.
Parity check	A check that tests whether the number of ones (or zeros) in an array of binary digits meets the established odd or even standard.
Patch	A section of coding inserted in a program in order to rectify an error in the original coding or to change the sequence of operation.
Peripheral equipment	Units that work in conjunction with the computer but are not part of the computer itself, e.g., tape reader, card reader, magnetic tape feed, high-speed printer, typewriter, etc.
Physical record	Two or more records that are written, read, or stored as a single block.
Plugboard	A removable panel containing an array of terminals that can be interconnected by short electrical leads in prescribed patterns to control various machine operations. Synonymous with control panel.
Powers code	A system of representing data by round holes punched in a 90-column card, invented by James Powers and now used with equipment produced by the UNIVAC Division of Sperry Rand Corporation.
Problem-oriented language	A programming language that reflects the type of problem being solved rather than the computer on which the program is to be run.
Procedure	A precise step-by-step method for effecting a solution to a problem.
Process control	A system in which computers, usually analog computers, are used for automatic regulation of operations or processes.
Processor	A machine-language program that accepts a source program written in a symbolic form and translates it into an object program acceptable to the machine for which the source program was written.
Program	The complete plan for the solution of a problem; more specifically, the complete sequence of machine instructions and routines necessary to solve a problem.
Program card	A punched card, punched with specific coding, placed around a program drum to control automatic operations in a card punch and verifier.
Program loop	See *Loop*.

Programmer	A person who prepares the planned sequence of events the computer must follow to solve a problem.
Programming flowchart	A flowchart depicting the sequence of operations in a computer program.
Programming language	A language used to write computer programs.
Programming Language I (PL/I)	A high-level problem-oriented programming language.
Punched card	A heavy stiff paper of uniform size and shape suitable for being punched with a pattern of holes to represent data and for being handled mechanically.
Punched tape	A tape, usually paper, on which a pattern of holes or cuts is used to represent data.
Query language	A language, for the terminal user, to retrieve and update data in a managed data base.
Radix	The fundamental number in a number system, e.g., 10 in the decimal system, 8 in the octal system, and 2 in the binary system. Synonymous with base.
Random access storage	A storage device, such as magnetic core, magnetic disk, and magnetic drum, in which each record has a specific, predetermined address that may be reached directly. Access time in this type of storage is effectively independent of the location of the data.
Random file	Data records stored in a file without regard to the sequence of the key or control field.
Raw data	Data that has not been processed. Such data may or may not be in a form acceptable by machines.
Read in	To sense information contained in some source and to transfer this information by means of an input device to internal storage.
Read out	To transfer data from internal storage to an external storage device, or to display processed data by means of a printer, automatic typewriter, etc.
Real time	The processing of data derived from a particular operation in a sufficiently rapid manner that the results of the processing are available in time to influence the continuing operation.
Record	A collection of related items of data treated as a unit.
Record block	A collection of contiguous records recorded as a unit.
Register	A device capable of temporarily storing a specified amount of data, usually one word, while or until it is used in an operation.
Registration	The accuracy of the positioning of punched holes in a card.
Remote access	Pertaining to communication with a data processing facility by one or more stations that are at a distant point from that facility.
Remote batch processor	A terminal device, located some distance from the central computer, used to process data by batches of records.
Remote processing	A method of using a computer system from remote locations. This direct access connection can be accomplished using conventional voice grade telephone lines to exchange information between the computer and terminals.

Remote station	The terminal equipment for communicating with a data processing system from a distant location.
Report generator	A programming system for producing a complete report given only a description of the desired content and format of the output reports, and certain information about the input file and hardware available.
Reproducing (punched card)	Copying punched information from one deck of cards into another.
Routine	A set of coded instructions arranged in a logical sequence and used to direct a computer to perform a desired operation or series of operations.
Row binary	A method of representing binary numbers on a card where successive bits are represented by the presence or absence of punches in a successive position in a row as opposed to a series of columns. Row binary is especially convenient in 40-bit word, or less, computers wherein the card frequently is used to store 12 binary words on each half of an 80-column card.
Run	A single, continuous performance of a computer routine.
Search	The process of examining a set of items for one or more items having a desired property.
Selecting	Removing cards from a file, or processing cards according to predetermined conditions.
Sequence	An arrangement of items of data according to a specified set of rules.
Sequence checking	Checking items in a file to assure that they are all in ascending (or descending) order.
Sequential file	See *Sequential storage*.
Sequential processing	The procedure of processing data records in the same order that they occur.
Sequential storage	Storing of data in sequential order.
Serial	The handling of data in a sequential fashion, such as to transfer or store data in a digit-by-digit time sequence, or to process a sequence of instructions one at a time.
Serial operation	The flow of information through a computer in time sequence, using one digit, word, line, or channel at a time, as opposed to parallel operation.
Servomechanism	A device to monitor an operaton as it proceeds, and make necessary adjustments to keep the operation under control.
Shared control	A facility that allows multiple concurrent interactions with a particular unit of data in a data base.
Shift	To move the characters of a unit of data to the right or left.
Short card	A punched card of less than 80 columns.
Simulator	A computer program that represents certain features of the behavior of another program or system.
Snapshot dump	A selective dump performed at various points in a computer machine run.
Software	The programs and routines used to extend the capabilities of computers, such as compilers, assemblers, routines, and subroutines. Also, all documents associated with a computer, e.g., manuals, circuit diagrams. Cf. hardware.
Solid state	Refers to electronic components that convey or control electron flow within solid materials such as transistors, crystal diodes, and ferrite cores.

Sort	To arrange items of information according to rules dependent on a key or field contained in the items, e.g., the arranging of items according to date, code number, etc.
Source document	The original paper on which are recorded the details of a transaction.
Source program	A program usually written in some form of symbolic language and intended for translation into a machine-language program.
Special character	A character that is neither a numeral nor a letter, for example, $ / & #.
Special purpose computer	A computer designed principally to solve a restricted class of problems.
Storage	A device into which data can be entered, in which it can be held, and from which it can be retrieved at a later time.
Storage protection	An arrangement for preventing one program from interfering with another program during reading or writing operations.
Stored program computer	A computer that has the ability to store, to refer to, and to modify instructions to direct its step-by-step operations.
String	A set of records in ascending or descending sequence according to a key contained in the records.
Subroutine	A subset of a routine, usually a short sequence of instructions designed to solve a specified part of a problem.
Supervisor	The general reference to the programs of a system that are responsible for scheduling, allocating, and controlling the system resources and application programs.
Switch	A point in a programming routine at which two courses of action are possible, the correct one being determined by conditions specified by the programmer; a branch point.
Symbolic address	An address expressed in symbols that are convenient to the programmer.
Symbolic program	A program written in a language that makes use of mnemonic codes and in which names, characteristics of instructions, or other symbols convenient to the programmer are used instead of the numeric codes of the machine.
Systems analysis	The study of an activity, procedure, method, technique, or a business to determine what must be accomplished and how the necessary operations may best be accomplished.
Table	Data arranged into rows or columns in such a way that each element of a row or column has a common format.
Table look up	To obtain a function value corresponding to an argument, stated or implied, from a table of function values stored in the computer. Also, the operation of obtaining a value from a table.
Telecommunication	Any transmission or reception of signals, writing, sounds, or intelligence of any nature by wire, radio, visual, or any other electromagnetic means.
Terminal	A device in a system or communication network at which point data can either enter or leave the system.
Test routine	A procedure that shows whether or not a computer is functioning properly.
Time-sharing	A computing system that permits many users to operate or use the system simultaneously or apparently simultaneously in such a way that each is unaware of the fact that the system is being used by others.

Total systems concept	The complete integration of all major operating systems within a business organization into one functional organized system operating under the discipline of a data processing facility.
Transaction file	A file containing transient data to be processed in combination with a master file.
Transistor	A tiny solid electronic device that performs the same function as a vacuum tube. In a vacuum tube, current flows through the gas and space within the tube. In a transistor, the current travels through solid materials only, which explains the familiar term "solid state."
Turn-around document	A document or form prepared as output at one stage of the data processing cycle, and sent to a customer or other user with the intention of having it returned and used as input at a later stage.
Unit record	A record in which all data concerning each item in a transaction is punched into one card.
Update	To put into a master file changes required by current information or transactions.
Utility program	Standard programs prepared and generally used to assist in the operation of a data processing system.
Variable	A quantity that, when identified by a symbolic name, can assume any of a given set of values.
Verify	To determine whether a transcription of data or other operation has been accomplished accurately. To check the results of key punching.
Virtual storage	A concept by which primary storage capacity is increased beyond that available in the computer by storing segments of programs and data in auxiliary devices. The program segments and data are brought into primary storage under control of the virtual operating system as they are needed for execution by the computer.
Word	A set of characters that occupies one storage location and is treated by the computer circuits as a unit and transported as such.
X-punch	A punch in the second row, one row above the zero row, on a Hollerith punched card.
Y-punch	A punch in the top row, two rows above the zero row, on a Hollerith punched card.
Zero suppression	The elimination of nonsignificant zeros to the left of the integral part of a quantity before printing operations are initiated.
Zone punches	Punches in the Y, X, and O position on a Hollerith punched card used in combination with digit punches 1 to 9 to code alphabetic and special characters.

INDEX

429